RAG from First Principles

Engineering retrieval-augmented generation systems with Python, LangChain, and LlamaIndex

Jia Huang

<packt>

RAG from First Principles

This book was written by Jia Huang. Generative AI tools were used only to assist with ideation, phrasing, and diagram drafts, and all technical content and code were created, verified, and tested by the author and Packt's editorial team. Packt does not accept AI-generated content that replaces expert authorship.

Portfolio Director: Gebin George

Relationship Lead: Akash Sharma

Project Manager: Prajakta Naik

Content Engineer: Afzal Shaikh

Technical Editors: Sumant Jadhav/Rahul Limbachiya

Indexer: Rekha Nair

Production Designers: Prashant Ghare/Shankar Kalbhor

Growth Lead: Akash Sharma

First published: May 2026

Production reference: 2290726

Published by Packt Publishing Ltd.

Grosvenor House

11 St Paul's Square

Birmingham

B3 1RB, UK

ISBN 978-1-83588-866-7

www.packtpub.com

Contributors

About the author

Jia Huang is a Lead Research Engineer at A*STAR (Agency for Science, Technology and Research), Singapore, where his work focuses on NLP, large language models, and applied AI engineering. With over twenty years of experience leading large-scale AI and data projects across government, finance, healthcare, and e-commerce, he brings an unusually practical lens to technically rigorous subjects. In recent years, his research has primarily focused on NLP pre-trained large models and FinTech applications.

He is the author of six bestselling technical books, including *Hands-on AI Agent Development for Large Model Applications*, selected as one of JD Best Books of 2024, and *GPT: How Large Models Are Built*, named CSDN's Most Influential IT Book of 2023. His online RAG engineering course has been completed by over 10,000 students.

About the reviewer

Naresh Dulam is a visionary technology leader with deep expertise in data analytics, cloud computing, and artificial intelligence. With a career spanning influential roles across Healthcare, Telecom, and financial sectors, he has led transformative analytical platforms that deliver sustainable and impactful solutions to address evolving industry needs. As a forward-thinking innovator, Naresh combines technical expertise with a passion for knowledge-sharing, mentoring aspiring professionals, and fostering ethical practices. His commitment to driving innovation and creating meaningful impact is matched by his vision of inspiring the next generation of technologists. Beyond his professional achievements, Naresh enjoys exploring nature on adventurous expeditions and empowering others to achieve their full potential.

Subscribe for a free ebook

New frameworks, evolving architectures, research drops, production breakdowns – *AI_Distilled* filters the noise into a weekly briefing for engineers and researchers working hands-on with LLMs and generative AI systems. Subscribe now and receive a free eBook, along with weekly insights that help you stay focused and informed.

Subscribe at `https://packt.link/8Oz6Y` or scan the QR code below.

Table of Contents

Chapter 4: Vector Storage 141

Chapter 6: Index Optimization 281

Chapter 7: Retrieval Post-Processing 321

Chapter 8: Response Generation 373

Chapter 9: System Evaluation 399

Preface

Retrieval-augmented generation (**RAG**) has rapidly become one of the most important approaches for building reliable and intelligent AI systems. By combining large language models with external knowledge retrieval, RAG enables applications to generate responses that are more accurate, contextual, and grounded in enterprise data. In this book, you will explore the complete RAG pipeline from first principles, beginning with the foundations of embeddings, vector storage, and vector databases, before moving into advanced retrieval optimization and response generation strategies. The book explains not only how RAG systems work conceptually, but also how they are implemented in practical, production-ready environments.

You will first learn how vector representations are created and managed, including how embeddings are stored, indexed, and retrieved efficiently using vector databases such as Milvus and frameworks like LlamaIndex. The book explains the architecture of vector storage systems, indexing methods such as FLAT and IVF, and the trade-offs involved in similarity search and large-scale retrieval. From there, you will discover pre-retrieval processing techniques, including query construction, query translation, Text-to-SQL workflows, metadata filtering, and query routing, enabling natural language questions to interact seamlessly with structured and unstructured data sources.

Once the retrieval foundations are established, the book focuses on improving retrieval quality through index optimization strategies. You will learn how to design more accurate retrieval pipelines using sentence-window retrieval, parent-child chunking, hierarchical indexing, and context-expansion techniques with both LlamaIndex and LangChain. These chapters emphasize practical engineering decisions that improve retrieval precision while preserving sufficient context for generation. Through detailed code examples and architectural explanations, you will understand how to balance chunk granularity, contextual recall, and scalability when building high-quality RAG applications.

Finally, the book explores the response generation stage of RAG systems, covering prompt engineering, structured output parsing, factuality improvement, and generation control techniques. You will learn how to guide large language models using templates, examples, fact-checking strategies, and structured parsers in LangChain and LlamaIndex. The book also discusses the selection of generation models, the use of APIs and locally deployed models, and advanced optimization strategies such as Self-RAG and iterative refinement approaches. By the end of this book, you will be able to design, optimize, and deploy end-to-end RAG systems that integrate retrieval, reasoning, and generation into scalable AI applications suitable for real-world enterprise use cases.

Who this book is for

This book is for AI engineers, ML practitioners, and software developers building LLM-powered applications who want a deeper understanding of how retrieval actually works, not just how to call a framework. It is ideal for readers who have built a basic RAG pipeline and now want architectural clarity and optimization strategies. Technical leads and architects designing production AI systems will find the systematic treatment of indexing, hybrid search, reranking, and evaluation particularly valuable. Familiarity with Python and foundational LLM concepts is assumed.

What this book covers

Chapter 1, Data Import, introduces the foundational process of importing and parsing data for RAG systems. It covers techniques for loading and processing multiple file types using tools such as LangChain, LlamaIndex, Unstructured, and Marker, including handling text, PDFs, images, Markdown, CSV files, databases, and web content. The chapter also explores document structuring, metadata management, OCR, multimodal parsing, and PDF-to-Markdown conversion strategies for building effective knowledge bases.

Chapter 2, Text Chunking, focuses on one of the most important preprocessing stages in RAG systems: dividing documents into optimized text chunks for embedding, indexing, retrieval, and generation. The chapter explains why chunking is necessary, emphasizing retrieval precision, semantic coherence, context-window constraints, and avoiding topic dilution. It discusses how embedding models compress text into fixed-dimensional vectors and why overly large chunks can reduce retrieval quality.

Chapter 3, Information Embedding, introduces embedding technology as the process of encoding external information into vector representations for RAG systems. It covers the evolution of embedding models, multilingual and multimodal embeddings, sparse and dense embeddings, model evaluation, and fine-tuning practices.

Chapter 4, Vector Storage, explains how vector embeddings are stored, indexed, and retrieved using vector databases. It discusses vector database components, indexing methods, similarity metrics, mainstream vector databases, and practical Milvus-based vector search examples.

Chapter 5, Pre-Retrieval Processing, explores techniques used before retrieval to improve query quality and routing. It covers query construction, Text-to-SQL, Text-to-Cypher, metadata filtering, query translation, and routing strategies for selecting the most appropriate retrieval path.

Chapter 6, Index Optimization, focuses on improving retrieval accuracy by optimizing how text chunks are indexed and retrieved. It covers small-to-large retrieval strategies, sentence-window retrieval, parent-child chunk retrieval, metadata optimization, and other indexing techniques for better RAG performance.

Chapter 7, Retrieval Post-Processing, explores sophisticated retrieval strategies that improve the accuracy, relevance, and contextual quality of RAG systems beyond basic vector similarity search. It covers methods such as hybrid retrieval, reranking, query transformation, HyDE, parent-child retrieval, metadata filtering, and graph-based retrieval to handle complex enterprise-scale knowledge systems more effectively.

Chapter 8, Response Generation, examines the generation stage of RAG systems and how to improve the quality of LLM outputs. It covers prompt refinement, response formatting, output parsing, fact-checking, and advanced generation strategies such as Self-RAG and corrective retrieval-generation approaches.

Chapter 9, System Evaluation, explains how RAG systems are evaluated by separately assessing retrieval quality and response generation quality using metrics such as Precision, Recall, F1, MRR, MAP, BLEU, ROUGE, METEOR, faithfulness, and answer relevancy. It introduces the RAG TRIAD and emphasizes that effective RAG evaluation requires both quantitative metrics and human judgment.

Chapter 10, Complex RAG Paradigms, introduces emerging paradigms such as GraphRAG, contextual retrieval, Modular RAG, Agentic RAG, and Multimodal RAG, highlighting how they improve multi-hop reasoning, contextual understanding, flexibility, and cross-modal intelligence in modern AI systems. The chapter also examines evolving approaches such as iterative retrieval, adaptive retrieval, PlanRAG, AutoRAG, and **Retrieval-Augmented Fine-Tuning** (**RAFT**), emphasizing the shift toward more autonomous, scalable, and intelligent retrieval-generation frameworks for enterprise and real-world applications.

Download the example code files

The code bundle for the book is hosted on GitHub at `https://github.com/PacktPublishing/RAG-from-First-Principles`. We also have other code bundles from our rich catalog of books and videos available at `https://github.com/PacktPublishing`. Check them out!

Download the color images

We also provide a PDF file that has color images of the screenshots/diagrams used in this book. You can download it here: `https://packt.link/gbp/9781835888667`.

Conventions used

There are a number of text conventions used throughout this book.

`CodeInText`: Indicates code words in text, database table names, folder names, filenames, file extensions, pathnames, dummy URLs, user input, and Twitter handles. For example: "The `from_language` method of `RecursiveCharacterTextSplitter` provides text splitting capabilities optimized for different programming languages."

A block of code is set as follows:

```
from langchain_text_splitters import CharacterTextSplitter
text = """
    ......
"""
text_splitter = CharacterTextSplitter(
    chunk_size=50,
    chunk_overlap=0,
    separator="\n"
)
### Use the create_documents Method to Split the Text
chunks = text_splitter.create_documents([text])
print(chunks)
```

Any command-line input or output is written as follows:

```
Number of chunks generated by the semantic splitter: 4
Number of chunks generated by the basic sentence splitter: 29
```

Bold: Indicates a new term, an important word, or words that you see on the screen. For instance, words in menus or dialog boxes appear in the text like this. For example: "In practical applications, you also need to reserve space for other content, such as **detailed instructions**, **role definitions**, or a few in-context examples."

Warnings or important notes appear like this.

Tips and tricks appear like this.

Get in touch

Feedback from our readers is always welcome.

General feedback: If you have questions about any aspect of this book or have any general feedback, please email us at `customercare@packt.com` and mention the book's title in the subject of your message.

Errata: Although we have taken every care to ensure the accuracy of our content, mistakes do happen. If you have found a mistake in this book, we would be grateful if you reported this to us. Please visit `http://www.packt.com/submit-errata`, click **Submit Errata**, and fill in the form.

Piracy: If you come across any illegal copies of our works in any form on the internet, we would be grateful if you would provide us with the location address or website name. Please contact us at `copyright@packt.com` with a link to the material.

If you are interested in becoming an author: If there is a topic that you have expertise in and you are interested in either writing or contributing to a book, please visit `http://authors.packt.com/`.

Free benefits with your book

This book comes with free benefits to support your learning. Activate them now for instant access (see the *"How to Unlock"* section for instructions).

Here's a quick overview of what you can instantly unlock with your purchase:

DRM-Free PDF Version

Download DRM-free PDF and ePub copies of this book.

7-Day Packt Library Access

Get 7-day unlimited access to 8,000+ books and videos. No credit card required.

Available for first-time Packt+ trial users only.

Next-Gen Reader Access

Read this book on Packt Reader with progress sync, dark mode and note-taking.

How to unlock

Scan the QR code (or go to `packtpub.com/unlock`). Search for this book by name, confirm the edition, and then follow the steps on the page.

UNLOCK NOW

Note: Keep your invoice handy. Purchases made directly from Packt don't require one

Share your thoughts

Once you've read *RAG from First Principles*, we'd love to hear your thoughts! Scan the QR code below to go straight to the Amazon review page for this book and share your feedback.

`https://packt.link/r/1835888674`

Your review is important to us and the tech community and will help us make sure we're delivering excellent quality content.

Join our Discord and Reddit Space

You're not the only one navigating fragmented tools, constant updates, and unclear best practices. Join a growing community of professionals exchanging insights that don't make it into the documentation.

Join our Discord at `https://packt.link/z8ivB` or scan the QR code below:	Follow us on Reddit at `https://packt.link/0rExL` or scan the QR code below:

1

Data Import

Whether you are building a **RAG system** with low-code tools like **Coze** or **Dify**, or coding with open-source frameworks such as **LangChain** or **LlamaIndex**, parsing files and reading their content is the crucial first step in the entire **embedding, retrieval, and generation (RAG)** process. If the system cannot accurately recognize and parse files, it will not be able to construct a **knowledge base** for the corresponding domain, and subsequent RAG tasks will not be possible.

Figure 1.1: Lewis and Anna sit at a desk discussing RAG systems

Does the parsing process depend on file type?

In enterprise environments, file types are often diverse. Not only are there common formats such as **PDF**, `.doc`/`.docx`, etc., but there may also be uncommon or proprietary formats. To handle this complexity, it is necessary to establish clear parsing strategies for each file type and select suitable tools. Priority should be given to using universal parsing libraries or tools to cover common file formats. For example, the **Unstructured** tool can handle multiple file formats in the same directory in a unified manner.

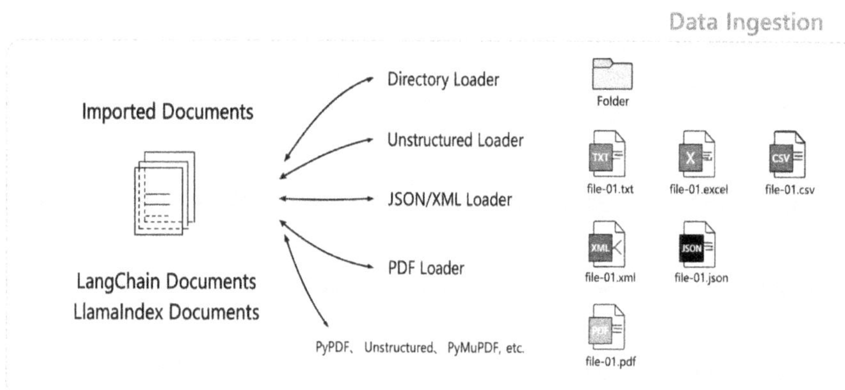

Figure 1.2: The document import process using LangChain and LlamaIndex with various file types

For common and important file types (such as **PDF**), you can choose specialized tools (such as **PyPDF2**, **PyMuPDF**, **Marker**, **MinerU**, and **PDFPlumber**) to parse and extract the required content. The specific choice depends on the application scenario (such as structured data extraction, text content search, **OCR**, or image extraction, etc.).

For less common file types, you need to find out the tool that generated the file, its data structure, and its purpose. For example, if a directory contains a `product_sales.jsonl` file, you might infer from the name that it is a **product sales log** in **JSON Lines** format, which is a text file format where each line contains a single independent JSON object without commas or other delimiters between lines. This must be considered during parsing.

For complex documents, you can first convert them to an intermediate format that is easier to parse. For instance, you can convert **PPT** files to **PDF** format before extracting information (since PDF extraction tools are more plentiful and offer more options). Similarly, sometimes it is best to first convert PDF files uniformly into **Markdown** documents and then process them, because the **Markdown** format is more standardized and thus makes it easier to extract headings, paragraphs, and lists as pure text. Moreover, since large models are trained on web resources, they are naturally more familiar with Markdown format, which is more conducive to their understanding.

In addition, large models can also be used to assist in parsing **structured**, **semi-structured**, and **unstructured data**, especially in certain complex scenarios (such as **multimodal situations**), where they can achieve very good results.

In the next section, let's delve into how to parse various types of documents into plain text and import them into the RAG system.

Reading simple text with a DataLoader

Let's start by explaining how to read documents with the simplest and most intuitive TXT file format.

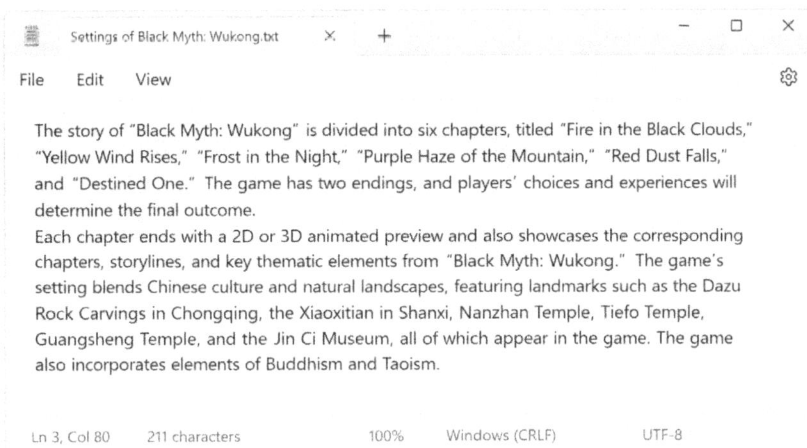

Figure 1.3: A text file in Notepad describes game story chapters and cultural elements in detail

Frameworks such as **LangChain** and **LlamaIndex** offer various **data loaders** to parse documents into data objects of specific formats. If you do not wish to use these frameworks, you can choose standalone document parsing tools like **Unstructured**.

Using LangChain to read TXT files and generate document objects

LangChain's `TextLoader` class can be used to read TXT files and parse them into LangChain `Document` data objects. First, ensure that the `langchain`, `langchain-core`, and `langchain_community` packages are installed. The following code can then be used to read a TXT file using LangChain (refer to `https://github.com/PacktPublishing/RAG-from-First-Principles` for the complete code):

```
from langchain_community.document_loaders import TextLoader
loader = TextLoader("data/black myth/ The setting of Black Myth Wukong.
```

```
txt")
documents = loader.load()
print(documents)
```

```
[Document(metadata={'source': 'data/black myth/The setting of Black
Myth Wukong.txt'}, page_content='The story of "Black Myth: Wukong" can
be divided into 6 sections, namely "Fire Illuminates Black Clouds",
"Wind Rises at Dusk", "Night Gives Birth to White Dew", "Curved Purple
Mandarin Ducks", "Sunset in the Mortal World", and "Unfinished", and
features two endings. The player's choices and experiences will affect the
final outcome.\nAt the end of each section, two-dimensional and three-
dimensional animated cutscenes are attached, showcasing and exploring
the narrative and thematic elements in "Black Myth: Wukong".\nThe game's
setting blends Chinese culture and natural landmarks. For example, the
Dazu Rock Carvings in Chongqing, Xiaoxitian, Nanchan Temple, Tiebusi
Temple, Guangsheng Temple, and the Stork Tower in Shanxi Province, etc.,
all appear in the game. The game also incorporates philosophical elements
of Buddhism and Taoism.')]
```

In LangChain, the `Document` object is a core data structure that represents text content loaded from external files or other data sources. As you can see in the preceding code, the `Document` object primarily contains the following two attributes:

- `metadata`: Stores metadata related to the document, such as the document's source path, author, date, etc.
- `page_content`: Stores the actual text content, which is the main data part of the document

> The chapters in this book are presented as an ongoing conversation between a teacher and his two students. You'll learn alongside Anna and Alex, two curious students who aren't afraid to ask the questions many readers may already have. Guiding them is Lewis, an experienced engineer who helps them navigate the world of Retrieval-Augmented Generation (RAG) through practical insights and real-world experience. As their conversations unfold, complex concepts are explored step by step, misconceptions are clarified, and theory is connected to practical applications. Think of it as joining an interactive learning journey where questions lead the way and understanding develops naturally through dialogue.

Alex: Why do we need to use this `Document object`?

Lewis: First of all, the `metadata` recorded in the `Document object` is very important. Although this `metadata` is not the actual content of the document, it contains rich information and plays an important role in RAG systems. The data of a document may come from various formats, such as TXT, PDF, HTML, or database records. Relying on the raw string alone makes it impossible to track its source or obtain related additional information (such as date, category, etc.). In many **natural language processing** or **information retrieval** tasks, combining metadata for filtering, sorting, or analysis is an essential step. In some advanced indexing techniques, `metadata` can also be used to store summaries of the text content, associated parent document IDs, etc.

Moreover, since different **data sources** have their own characteristics (such as **chunking strategies, paragraph breaks**, etc.), it is necessary to perform abstraction and standardization through a unified data structure (like the `Document` object). The `Document` object can abstract diverse data sources into a unified and structured form, making it convenient for seamless processing within LangChain, ensuring that documents can be smoothly delivered to **embedding models**, **classifiers**, or **Q&A systems**.

The following code example demonstrates how to directly create a LangChain `Document` object:

```
from langchain_core.documents import Document
documents = [ Document( page_content="Black clouds lit by fire",
metadata={"source": "scene_list.txt"}, ),
Document( page_content="Wind rises at dusk", metadata={"source": "scene_
list.txt "}, ), ]
```

Data loaders in LangChain

LangChain's data import tools are not limited to just `TextLoader`. For example, `CSVLoader` can load data in CSV table format, `JSONLoader` can import JSON files, while `PyPDFLoader` or `PyMuPDFLoader` can be used to parse PDF files.

It is worth noting that for the same document format, LangChain may provide several different loaders. Take PDF files as an example; LangChain offers more than 10 different loaders, which can sometimes be overwhelming and make it hard to determine which one is the most suitable.

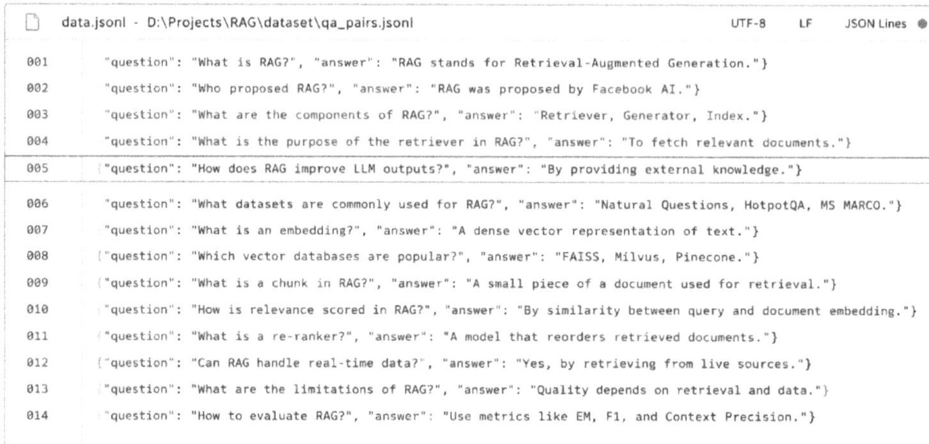

Figure 1.4: A code editor shows a Python dictionary mapping loader names to module paths for document loaders

Although LangChain's vast ecosystem adds to its complexity, which is a point it is often criticized for, it also gives LangChain powerful document processing capability, enabling it to easily handle a wide range of data sources and support complex natural language processing workflows.

In LangChain's official documentation, we can find detailed explanations of loaders for common file types.

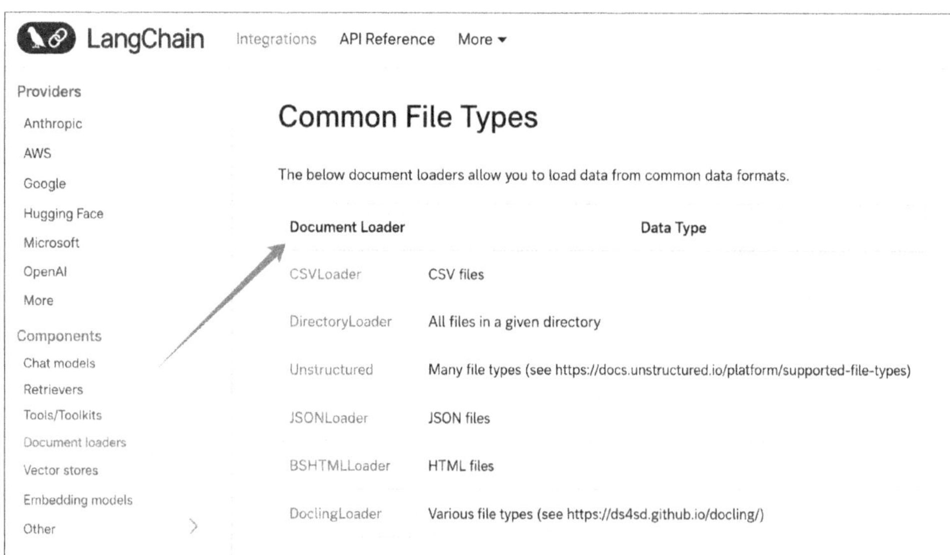

Figure 1.5: A LangChain web page shows a table listing document loaders and their supported file types

Using LangChain to read all files in a directory

Usually, you may want to read all different types of files in a directory at once and convert them into `Document` objects for unified management. In LangChain, this can be achieved using the `DirectoryLoader` (directory file loader).

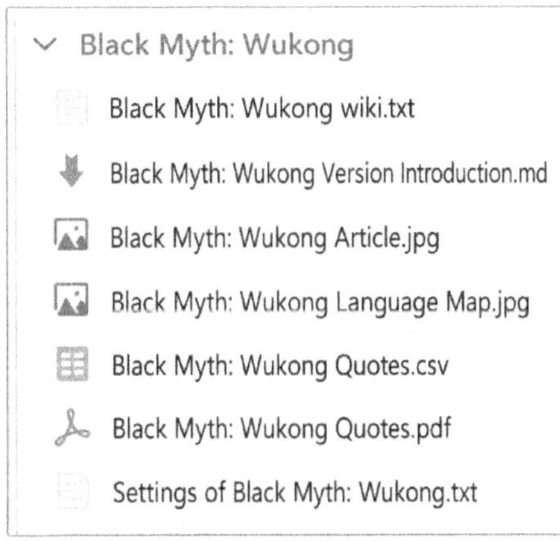

Figure 1.6: A folder named contains files in formats like txt, md, jpg, csv, pdf, and settings.txt

To use `DirectoryLoader`, you can follow these steps:

1. Install the `unstructured` package using the following commands:

```
pip install unstructured
pip install 'unstructured[image]'
pip install 'unstructured[md]'
sudo apt-get install tesseract-ocr # Here we take Ubuntu as an
example
pip install pytesseract
```

2. The following code shows how to use `DirectoryLoader` to load various types of files from a specified directory and generate an object for each document (refer to `https://github.com/PacktPublishing/RAG-from-First-Principles` for the complete code):

```
from langchain_community.document_loaders import DirectoryLoader
loader = DirectoryLoader('./data/black myth')
docs = loader.load()
print(f'Number of documents: {len(docs)}') # Print the total number
of documents
```

```
Number of documents: 7
```

3. Specific file types in a particular directory can be loaded by specifying the `file path` and file matching pattern (such as wildcards)

```
loader = DirectoryLoader('./', glob='**/*.md') # Load only Markdown
files in the directory
```

4. If you want to see a progress bar during the loading process, you can install the **tqdm** library and enable the `show_progress` parameter

```
loader = DirectoryLoader('./', show_progress=True) # Display a
progress bar during loading
```

5. By default, `DirectoryLoader` uses a single thread to load files. To increase loading speed, you can enable multithreading:

```
loader = DirectoryLoader('./', use_multithreading=True) # Enable
multithreading for document loading
```

6. Under the hood, `DirectoryLoader` uses `UnstructuredLoader` by default (this is LangChain's integration of the document parsing tool `unstructured`) to load and parse files. However, we can also specify other loaders through the `loader_cls` parameter. For example, in the following code we use `TextLoader` to load TXT files (including Markdown and similar files):

```
from langchain_community.document_loaders import DirectoryLoader
from langchain_community.document_loaders import TextLoader
loader = DirectoryLoader('data/Black Myth',
glob='**/*.md',
loader_cls=TextLoader # Specify a particular loader
)
docs = loader.load()
print(docs[0].page_content[:100]) # Print the first 100 characters
of the first document's content
```

`TextLoader` preserves the formatting of headings when processing Markdown files, whereas `UnstructuredLoader` does not retain this formatting when processing. The following figure illustrates this difference:

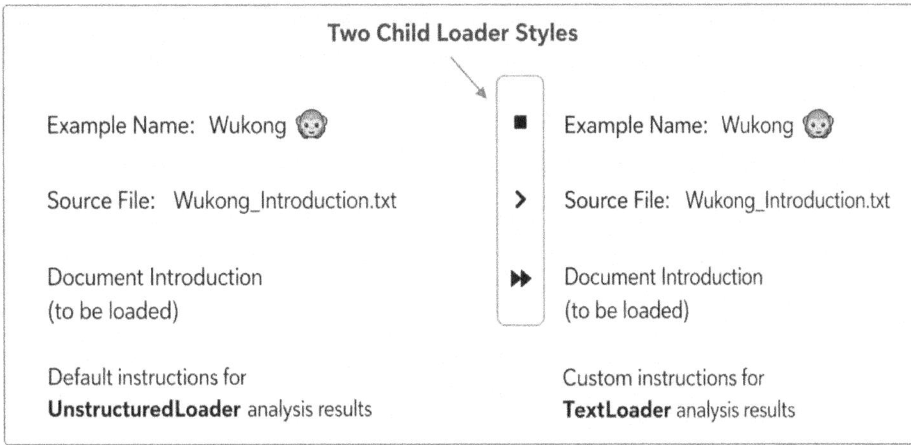

Figure 1.7: Image compares UnstructuredLoader and TextLoader results for text formatting with emojis

The difference shown here is mainly to illustrate that different loaders may produce different results when parsing the same type of file. This does not mean that `TextLoader` is superior to `UnstructuredLoader`, or vice versa. In fact, each loader has its own appropriate scenarios: `TextLoader` is more suitable for loading pure text files with simple structure, including but not limited to Markdown files; while `UnstructuredLoader` has broader applicability, is suitable for more types of file formats, and is able to extract richer structured information during processing.

7. If you attempt to use `TextLoader` to import all types of files without specifying the file type, **it** will throw an error when it encounters a file type it does not support

```
UnicodeDecodeError: 'utf-8' codec can't decode byte 0xb5 in position
11: invalid start byte
```

To prevent the program from being interrupted by these errors, you can set the parameter `silent_errors=True` to allow the loader to skip files that cannot be loaded and continue processing the remaining files:

```
loader = DirectoryLoader(''data/black myth'',
silent_errors=True, # Skip files that cannot be Loaded
loader_cls=TextLoader
)
Error loading file data/black myth/black myth wukong.pdf
Error loading file /data/black myth/Black Myth in English.jpg
```

With this configuration, when `TextLoader` attempts to load all files in the directory, it will skip unsupported file types such as PDFs or images and log the error message instead of raising an exception that interrupts program execution.

Using LlamaIndex to read all documents in a directory

Similar to LangChain, **LlamaIndex** provides powerful tools to load documents from a directory and parse these documents into LlamaIndex's `Document` objects. In LlamaIndex, these kinds of tools are known as **data connectors** or **readers**.

One simple and easy-to-use **Reader** is `SimpleDirectoryReader`. It can load various types of files from a specified directory, including Markdown, PDF, PPT, Word, and audio/video files.

The following code gives the number of documents in the directory:

```
from llama_index.core import SimpleDirectoryReader
dir_reader = SimpleDirectoryReader('data/black myth')
documents = dir_reader.load_data()
print(f'Number of documents: {len(documents)}')
```

```
Number of documents: 11
```

Next, let's print one of the `Document` objects to see its overall structure:

```
print(documents[1])
```

```
Document (id_='d48c275b-c62b-450b-a575-a6ff45ca9a91', embedding=None,
metadata={'file_path': '/home/huangjia/Documents/08_RAG/Book2411/
rag_240917/data/black myth/
Black Myth Version Introduction.md', 'file_name': 'Black Myth Version
Introduction.md', 'file_type': 'text/markdown', 'file_size': 1418,
'creation_date': '2024-11-26', 'last_modified_date': '2024-11-26'},
excluded_embed_metadata_keys=['file_name', 'file_type', 'file_size',
'creation_date', 'last_modified_date', 'last_accessed_date'], excluded_
llm_metadata_keys=['file_name', 'file_type', 'file_size', 'creation_date',
'last_modified_date', 'last_accessed_date'], relationships={}, text='\n\
nBlack Myth: Wukong \n\n> Black Myth: Wukong is a highly anticipated
action-adventure game developed by a Chinese game development team. Based
on Journey to the West, it reinterprets the classic story and delivers
an impactful visual and gameplay experience.\n', mimetype='text/plain',
start_char_idx=None, end_char_idx=None, text_template='{metadata_str}\n\
n{content}', metadata_template='{key}: {value}', metadata_seperator='\n')
```

You can see that the metadata generated in the Document object by LlamaIndex is richer than that generated by LangChain, including **file path, file type, file size, creation date, modification date**, etc. This metadata provides more contextual support for document management and subsequent analysis. In addition, LlamaIndex also offers the `excluded_embed_metadata_keys` and `excluded_llm_metadata_keys` options, which can be used to specify which metadata should not be included in information embedding or large model processing. This is particularly useful when you need to streamline the context or improve retrieval efficiency.

Overall, LlamaIndex excels in the structuring and granular management of Document objects, meeting the needs of enterprises for handling diverse and complex data.

Alex: I also noticed that when importing the same directory using LlamaIndex, the number of generated Document objects is higher than that generated by LangChain.

Lewis: Yes. By default, LangChain generates one Document object for each original file when importing, without performing chunking. LlamaIndex, in principle, also works this way. However, for certain specific file types, such as CSV files, LlamaIndex will automatically split them into multiple parts, with each part treated as an independent Document object. This means that during the import process, LlamaIndex performs chunking for CSV files, resulting in a higher number of Document objects.

You can read specific files in a directory using the following code (refer to `https://github.com/PacktPublishing/RAG-from-First-Principles` for the complete code):

```
file_reader = SimpleDirectoryReader(input_files=['data/black myth/The
setting of Black Myth Wukong.txt'])
documents = file_reader.load_data()
```

The following code demonstrates how to generate a LlamaIndex Document object directly and manually add metadata:

```
from llama_index.core import Document
documents = [
Document(
text='An underground cave filled with flames and the scent of sulfur,
where fire jets continuously erupt from below, illuminating the whole
abyss. Wukong must use his jumping ability and golden staff to make his
way through the lava.',
metadata={
'filename': 'Blazing Abyss.md',
'category': 'Game Scene',
```

```
'author': 'Ka Ge AI',
'creation_date': '2024-11-20',
},
), ... ]
```

Now that you know how to load various types of files from a specific directory, the next step is to read the data from the files.

Connect learner with LlamaHub and read database entries

For file types that cannot be processed by `SimpleDirectoryReader`, LlamaIndex supports downloading and installing more advanced Readers through **LlamaHub**.

Next, we introduce the **MySQL database Reader** as an example. Before usage, you should first install the **Database Reader connector**.

First, execute the following commands to perform the necessary installation:

```
pip install llama-index-readers-database
sudo apt-get install libmysqlclient-dev
sudo apt-get install python3-dev
pip install mysqlclient
```

Then use the following code to load data from a MySQL database:

```
from llama_index.readers.database import DatabaseReader
reader = DatabaseReader(
scheme='mysql',
host='localhost',
port=3306,
user='username',
password='password',
dbname='example_db'
)
query = 'SELECT * FROM game_scenes' # Select all game scenes
documents = reader.load_data(query=query)
print(f'Number of documents loaded from the database: {len(documents)}')
print(documents)
```

```
[Document(id_='43594ec8-2751-496f-b0eb-dbfa183d20a4', embedding=None,
metadata={}, excluded_embed_metadata_keys=[], excluded_llm_metadata_
keys=[], relationships={}, metadata_template='{key}: {value}', metadata_
```

```
separator='\n', text_resource=MediaResource(embeddings=None, data=None, 
text='id: 1, scene_name: Zhu Jia Village, description: The first village 
where the game starts, full of strong ancient Chinese rural flavor, 
region: Eastern Plains, environment_type: village, main_enemies: 
Bandits, monster minions, special_features: Important NPC blacksmith 
shop, weapons can be upgraded', path=None, url=None, mimetype=None), 
image_resource=None, audio_resource=None, video_resource=None, text_
template='{metadata_str}\n\n{content}'),  ... ]
```

This approach can directly convert the database query results into `Document` objects, while defining the `{key}: {value}` data structure pattern in the `metadata_template` field.

Alex, you can spend some time reading the official documentation on LlamaHub at `https://developers.llamaindex.ai/python/framework/module_guides/loading/connector/`.

Reading various types of documents with the unstructured tool

If you prefer not to use any framework and want to build your own **RAG** system from scratch, using the **Unstructured** tool to read various types of documents is a good choice. Unstructured is an open-source document processing tool specifically designed to support parsing multiple types of documents, and it can effectively preserve the original structural information of documents during processing.

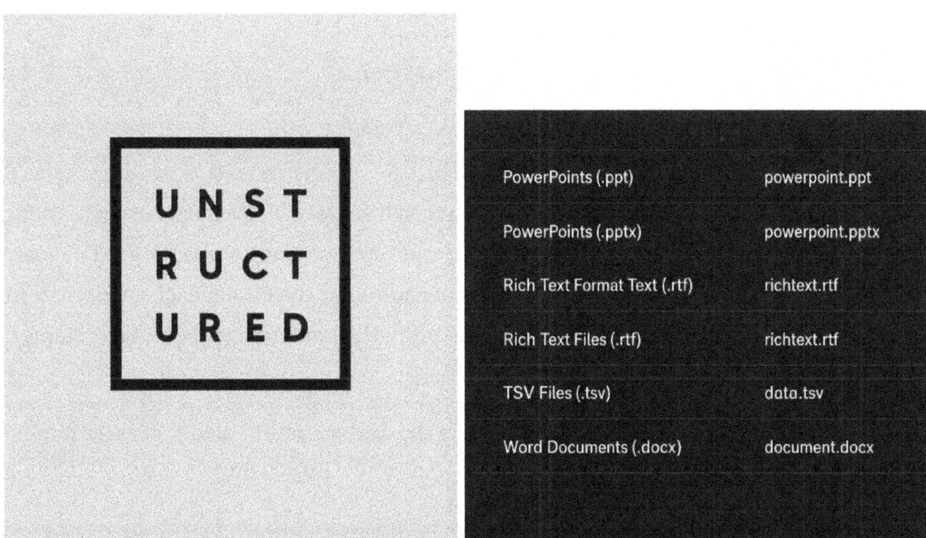

Figure 1.8: The Unstructured tool

Similar to LangChain and LlamaIndex, after importing documents using the Unstructured tool, it generates a unique type of data object called `Element`.

First, use the `partition_text` function to examine the process of reading a text file:

```
from unstructured.partition.text import partition_text
text = 'data/black myth/The setting of Black Myth Wukong.txt'
elements = partition_text(text)
for element in elements:
    print(element)
```

In fact, the `partition_text` function is part of the underlying logic of the **LangChain directory loader**.

Next, let's see what details are contained in the generated `elements` data objects:

```
for i, element in enumerate(elements):
    print(f"\n--- Element {i+1} ---")
    print(f"Element type: {element.__class__.__name__}")
    print(f"Text content: {element.text}")
    if hasattr(element, 'metadata'):
        print('Metadata:')
        metadata = vars(element.metadata)
        valid_metadata = {k: v for k, v in metadata.items()
                          if not k.startswith('_') and v is not None}
        for key, value in valid_metadata.items():
            print(f"  {key}: {value}")
```

The story of "Black Myth: Wukong" can be divided into 6 sections, named "Fire Illuminates Black Clouds", "Wind Rises at Dusk", "Night Gives Birth to White Dew", "Twisted Purple Mandarins", "Sunset in the Mortal World", and "Unfinished", and has two possible endings. The learner's choices and experiences will influence the ultimate ending. At the end of each section, there are 2D and 3D animated cutscenes that present and explore the narrative and thematic elements of "Black Myth: Wukong".

In this way, the Unstructured tool not only imports the document but also processes it in blocks according to specific rules.

By using the partition function, you can automatically read files of any type:

```
from unstructured.partition.auto import partition
filename = 'data/black myth/black myth wukong.pdf'
elements = partition(
filename=filename,
content_type='application/pdf'
)
print('\n\n'.join([str(el) for el in elements][:10]))
```

Although the partition function is generic and applicable to a variety of file types, its functionality is relatively simple when processing specific files. In contrast, specialized functions like partition_html and partition_pdf can showcase more distinctive features and advantages when dealing with their respective document types.

Although the Unstructured tool is powerful, it is not the only choice. In actual projects, we often need to choose different tools based on specific requirements. For example, to process PDF files, PyMuPDF is also a common choice (of course, there are many other options as well). Before using PyMuPDF, please install it first by using the following command:

```
pip install pymupdf
```

The following code example demonstrates how to carry out the operation:

```
import pymupdf
doc = pymupdf.open(''data/black myth/black myth wukong.pdf'')
text = [page.get_text() for page in doc]
```

You can compare the differences in the text formats parsed by different tools.

This concludes the introduction to simple text reading. Although the content introduced in these sections is basic, it covers a variety of technical aspects. The key point is that each tool will generate its own structured data objects, which contain a set of metadata. Hopefully, you can practice these hands-on to deepen your understanding of the various tools.

Parsing specific elements with the JSON loader

Choosing the appropriate **loader** for specific file types can improve the efficiency of data processing. In this section, we will explore the usage and characteristics of the **JSON loader** in LangChain.

First, let's look at a JSON file containing rich data result information:

```
{ } Journey to the West – Characters.json > ···
{
   "gameTitle": "Journey to the West",
   "basicInfo": {
      "engine":  "Unreal Engine 5", "releaseDate": "2024-08-20", "genre": "Action RPG"
      "mainCharacter": {  "name":  "Sun Wukong", "backstory": "At the time of the great chaos,
        the heavens and the earth were opened, and an extraordinary stone was born from
        the essence of heaven and earth..." },
      "supportCharacters": [
         {  "name":  "White Dragon Horse", "identity":  "The Third Prince of the West Sea",
            "background":  "The son of the Dragon King of the West Sea." },
         {  "name":  "Zhu Bajie", "identity":  "Tian Pengyuan Marshal",
            "background":  "A celestial general who was demoted to the mortal realm
                            and became a disciple." },
         {  "name":  "Sha Wujing", "identity":  "The Sand Monk",
            "background":  "Originally a celestial general who was banished to Earth
                            for causing a flood." }
   ],
   "gameFeatures": {  "worldSetting":  "Based on the background of Journey to the West,
      it combines traditional mythology with a fantastical world." }
}
```

Figure 1.9: A JSON file for a Journey to the West game showing main and support character details

If we use `TextLoader` to load a JSON file, the input and output will be as follows:

```
from langchain_community.document_loaders import TextLoader
text_loader = TextLoader("data/Journey_to_the_West_Characters.json")
text_documents = text_loader.load()
print(text_documents)
```

```
[Document(metadata={'source': 'data/Journey_to_the_West_Characters.json'},
page_content='{
  "gameTitle": "Journey to the West",
  "basicInfo": {
    "engine": "Unreal Engine 5",
    "releaseDate": "2024-08-20",
    "genre": "Action Role-Playing",
    "platforms": ["PC", "PS5", "Xbox Series X/S"],
    "supportedLanguages": ["Simplified Chinese", "Traditional Chinese"]
  },
  "mainCharacter": {
    "name": "Sun Wukong",
```

```
    "backstory": "At the dawn of chaos... Sun Wukong.",
    "abilities": ["Seventy-Two Transformations", "Golden Hoop Staff",
"Cloud Somersault", "Fire Eyes Golden Gaze"],
    "supportCharacters": [
      {
        "name": "White Dragon Horse",
        "identity": "One of the Eight Heavenly Dragons",
        "background": "Originally the Third Prince of the West Sea Dragon
King...",
        "abilities": ["Water Escape", "Riding Clouds and Mist",
"Transformation"]
      },
      {
        "name": "Red Boy",
        "identity": "Holy Infant King",
        "background": "Son of Bull Demon King and Princess Iron Fan...",
        "abilities": ["Samadhi True Fire", "Fire Eyes", "Combat Form"]
      },
      {
        "name": "Six-Eared Macaque",
        "identity": "Clone of Sun Wukong",
        "background": "A mysterious figure matching the Monkey King's
abilities.",
        "abilities": ["Imitation", "Stealth", "Speed"]
      }
    ]
  }
}')]
```

From the above code, you can see that `TextLoader` reads the JSON file as plain text. This means the entire JSON content is stored as a string in the `page_content` field. If you want to use specific field values from `page_content`, you still need to further parse this string.

If you use `JSONLoader`, you can directly extract specific elements from the JSON file through **jq query syntax**.

First, we need to install the necessary library **jq**, which is a lightweight JSON processing tool suitable for parsing, manipulating, and formatting JSON data:

```
pip install jq
```

The following code example demonstrates how to use `JSONLoader` to parse a JSON file (refer to `https://github.com/PacktPublishing/RAG-from-First-Principles` for the complete code):

```
from langchain_community.document_loaders import JSONLoader
## Extract and Print Main Character Information
print("Main character information:")
main_loader = JSONLoader(
file_path="data/black myth/black mythpersona.json",
jq_schema='.mainCharacter | "Name:" + .name + ",Backstory:" + .backstory',
text_content=True
)
main_char = main_loader.load()
print(main_char)
## Extract and Print Supporting Character Information
print("\nSupporting character information:")
support_loader = JSONLoader(
file_path="data/black myth/black mythpersona.json",
jq_schema='.supportCharacters[] | "Name:" + .name + ",Background:" +
.background',
text_content=True
)
support_chars = support_loader.load()
print(support_chars)
```

Now let's look at an example where we split characters into document objects:

```
Main character information:
[Document(metadata={'source': '/journey_to_the_west_persona.json', 'seq_
num': 1}, page_content='Name: Sun Wukong......')]
Supporting character information:
[Document(metadata={'source': ' journey_to_the_west_persona.json', 'seq_
num': 1}, page_content='Name: White Dragon Horse......')
Document(metadata={'source': ' journey_to_the_west_persona.json', 'seq_
num': 2}, page_content='Name: Red Boy......', ......)]
```

As you can see, `JSONLoader` can split each character into multiple `Document` objects and assign them numbers using `seq_num`. Each `Document` object not only contains the original document's metadata (such as source file name), but also parses the internal data structure of the document, i.e., the specific field information.

Reading text from images

Lewis: In many real-world AI applications, valuable information is embedded not only in plain text files but also in images, scanned documents, presentations, and PDFs. Let's explore how modern technologies can be used to read, parse, and process image-based information in practical AI workflows.

Reading text using UnstructuredLoader

Alex: Lewis, the Unstructured tool can read files in various formats. You also mentioned earlier that LangChain's directory loader uses `UnstructuredLoader` by default to load documents. Could you explain this tool in detail?

Lewis: Unstructured is a text extraction toolkit provided by Unstructured.IO. It can run locally or be used via the Unstructured API, and it supports parsing multiple types of documents.

If you wish to run the Unstructured tool with minimal installation, you can execute the following command and install the dependencies for different document types as needed:

```
pip install unstructured
```

If you want to call the Unstructured API, you need to execute the following command:

```
pip install unstructured-client
```

You will then need to apply for and configure the corresponding API Key.

If you want to use this tool in LangChain, you can run the following command to install the related package:

```
pip install langchain-unstructured
```

Besides the general `UnstructuredLoader`, LangChain has also integrated various other Unstructured document loaders for specific file formats, such as `UnstructuredExcelLoader`, `UnstructuredMarkdownLoader`, and `UnstructuredImageLoader`. For a complete list of loaders, you can visit the official LangChain website for more information.

Reading text using UnstructuredImageLoader

In this section, we'll choose to use `UnstructuredImageLoader` to attempt reading an image containing English text.

Figure 1.10: A warrior monkey in ornate armor stands holding a staff with Black Myth Wukong text above

Let's load the image and read the pixels:

```
from langchain_community.document_loaders import UnstructuredImageLoader
image_path = "data/black myth/Black Myth in English.jpg"
loader = UnstructuredImageLoader(image_path)
data = loader.load()
print(data)
```

This code yields the following output:

```
yolox_l0.05.onnx: 100%|██████████| 217M/217M [00:01<00:00, 116MB/s]
[Document(metadata={'source': 'data/black myth/Black Myth in English.
jpg'}, page_content=',\n\nPons\n\n= ens eens WUKONGY\n\n4')]
```

From the preceding output, you can see that this process invoked deep learning models (such as **YOLO**) to analyze the image pixel information in order to recognize and extract the text content, which is one way **OCR technology** works. Additionally, you can specify other OCR methods such as **Tesseract** by setting parameters. The extracted text is also encapsulated in a `Document` object.

However, in this example, "Black Myth WUKONG" was incorrectly recognized as "ens eens WUKONGY," which indicates the **OCR result** is not ideal. In such cases, it may be due to the characteristics of the image itself that make accurate recognition difficult.

Reading text from a PPT

Alex: This is just text extraction. What about analyzing image content?

Lewis: The Unstructured tool specializes in extracting and parsing textual content from files, rather than analyzing or processing images themselves. This means it cannot directly read the content of images, nor can it tell us there's a majestic monkey in a picture. If you want to understand the specific content of images (or files such as PPTs or PDFs), you need to call the API of a **large model** or use a local **multimodal model** capable of analyzing images (such as **BLIP**).

Alex: LangChain's loader integrates the capabilities of external tools like Unstructured and generates `Document` objects. If we directly use these external tools for file parsing, that's also totally fine, right?

Lewis: That's right.

The following code example demonstrates how to directly use the `partition_ppt` function of the Unstructured tool to read text from a PPT (refer to `https://github.com/PacktPublishing/RAG-from-First-Principles` for the complete code):

```
from unstructured.partition.ppt import partition_ppt
ppt_elements = partition_ppt(filename="data/black myth wukongPPT.pptx")
for element in ppt_elements:
    print(element.text)
```

```
Facing Destiny
Prologue
"Black Myth: Wukong" is a Chinese mythological action RPG adapted from
"Journey to the West". Players take on the role of the "Chosen One" and
pursue the secrets behind the legend during a perilous Westward adventure.
Adapted from the Chinese fantasy novel "Journey to the West"......
After obtaining the parsed raw text, the next step is to manually convert
the contents of pdf_elements into LangChain's Document object.
```

```
from langchain_core.documents import Document
documents = [
    Document(page_content=element.text,
             metadata={"source": "data/black myth wukongPPT.pptx"})
    for element in ppt_elements
]
print(documents[0:3])
```

This is equivalent to manually implementing a `UnstructuredPPTLoader` required by LangChain.

Using large models for holistic image-text parsing

In **Q&A systems**, we hope to directly upload PDF or PPT files to the knowledge base and answer questions based on the image content within them. To achieve **holistic parsing** of images, certain tools (such as Unstructured) cannot accomplish this yet. However, modern **multimodal large models** can easily complete this task.

For example, when we upload a **PDF file** containing both text and images, the model first parses the image content and generates a description such as "A majestic monkey stands on the mountaintop, surrounded by drifting clouds," then builds a contextual knowledge base by combining the textual information. This approach makes the integration of text and images more intuitive and complete, enabling **cross-modal reasoning**. That is, it can provide more complex answers by leveraging both the implicit semantics in the image and the information in the text. For example, it can answer questions like **What background environment might be related to the monkey's ability to ride the clouds?**.

Figure 1.11: A PDF page shows a Chinese fantasy game scene with a warrior character and text overlay

To read both images and texts from a PDF file, the implementation steps begin with invoking a **large model** to generate a caption for each page, and then converting these captions into LangChain's required `Document` objects. (Running this program requires setting an OpenAI API Key in the environment variable.) Let's look at the code for doing this:

1. Use `pdf2image` to extract each page from the PDF file as an image:

```
from pdf2image import convert_from_path
import base64
import os
output_dir = "temp_images"
if not os.path.exists(output_dir):
    os.makedirs(output_dir)
## Convert the PDF File to Images and Save to the Specified
Directory
images = convert_from_path("data/black myth/black myth wukong.pdf")
image_paths = []
for i, image in enumerate(images):
    image_path = os.path.join(output_dir, f'page_{i+1}.jpg')
    image.save(image_path, 'JPEG')
    image_paths.append(image_path)
print(f"Successfully converted {len(image_paths)} pages")
```

2. Next, use a **multimodal large model** to analyze the extracted images and generate descriptive text:

```
from openai import OpenAI
client = OpenAI()
print("\nStarting image analysis......")
results = []
for image_path in image_paths:
    with open(image_path, "rb") as image_file:
        base64_image = base64.b64encode(image_file.read()).
decode('utf-8')
    response = client.chat.completions.create(
        model="gpt-4o-mini",
        messages=[
            {
                "role": "user",
```

```
                    "content": [
                        {"type": "text", "text": "Please describe
this slide in detail, including its title, main text, and image
content."},
                        {
                            "type": "image_url",
                            "image_url": {
                                "url": f"data:image/jpeg;base64,{base64_
image}"
                            }
                        }
                    ]
                }
            ],
            max_tokens=300
        )
        results.append(response.choices[0].message.content)
```

3. Finally, convert the generated descriptive text and related metadata into LangChain `Document` objects:

```
from langchain_core.documents import Document
documents = [
    Document(
        page_content=result,
        metadata={'source': 'data/BlackMyth/BlackMythWukong.pdf',
'page_number': i+1}
    )
    for i, result in enumerate(results)
]
print('\nAnalysis results:')
for doc in documents:
    print(f'Content: {doc.page_content}\nMetadata: {doc.
metadata}\n')
```

Now, before we proceed further, let's first convert the images and their contained text content from each page of the PDF file into structured text descriptions.

Wukong title

The main title is "Wukong," accompanied by a red seal-style graphic.

Body

The central text is "BLACK MYTH WUKONG," indicating this slide may be related to a game or project called "Black Myth: Wukong."

The date below shows "08.20," possibly hinting at an important release or event date.

There is also a phrase "Face Your Destiny," which may convey the game's theme or challenge.

Image content

The background of the slide features a mysterious black patterned design.

In the center is a close-up of a character's face, featuring dense fur and intense eyes, giving a strong sense of power and aura.

The character's expression is stern, highlighting its characteristics and creating a striking atmosphere.

Overall, this slide appears to showcase game information related to "Wukong," delivering a fusion of ancient mythology and modern gaming.

Prologue title

Section ("Prologue")

Body

The body describes a game called Black Myth: Wukong, a Chinese mythology action role-playing game adapted from Journey to the West. It highlights the player's role as an adventurer in the game environment and explores background stories related to the Destined One.

Image content

The image shows a circle of blazing halo, seemingly glowing on a rock, creating a mysterious and fantastical atmosphere. The background is dark-toned, adorned with intricate patterns, adding visual appeal to the image.

Overall, the slide aims to introduce the game's theme and background, using visual elements to enhance the feeling of exploring mythological stories.

Adaptations from Journey to the West

Adapted from the Chinese mythological novel "Journey to the West."

Body

The slide contains no other text except the title.

Image content

The background is dark-toned, seemingly with a blurred human figure, possibly relevant to the plot or characters of Journey to the West, depicting a mysterious and classical atmosphere.

Overall, the design style of this slide likely aims to create a sense of history and mystery, focusing on the classic work *Journey to the West*.

Through the above steps, we have successfully converted the images and their contained text content from each page of the PDF file into structured text descriptions. Next, by combining frameworks such as **LangChain** and **LlamaIndex**, we can convert this textual information and corresponding image descriptions into **Document objects**. After saving these **Document objects** to the knowledge base, they can become part of the RAG system, enabling the question-answering engine in subsequent processes to utilize this text information to answer user queries.

Importing table data in CSV format

When processing and parsing data, importing **CSV files** is a common requirement. The `CSVLoader` tool provided by LangChain can fulfill this need.

Importing data using CSVLoader

When loading CSV files, `CSVLoader` automatically generates `page_content` and `metadata` for each row of data. Among these, `metadata` includes the data source (`source`) and row number (`row`), which is very useful for subsequent data processing and querying.

	A	B	C	D
1	Category	Name	Description	Power Level
2	Equipment	Ruyi Jingu Bang	A staff made of refined iron, capable of growing or shrinking at will; it can make a powerful sound when swung, ideal for close-range combat.	85
3	Equipment	Armor of Hundred Battle	Exquisite armor that provides strong defense and resistance to various spells and toxins.	90
4	Skill	Heaven-Splitting Strike	Summons almighty heavenly power to strike enemies, causing massive area electric damage.	95
5	Skill	Fire Cloud Dance	Creates and manipulates fire clouds to attack enemies and form a wall of fire for defense.	92
6	Character	Sun Wukong	The protagonist, possessing the seventy-two transformations, cloud somersault, and a sharp sense of justice.	100
7	Character	Bull Demon King	One of the powerful demon kings, skilled in various magical treasures and techniques, with extremely high combat strength.	88

Figure 1.12: Spreadsheet table with category names, descriptions, and power levels in numbers

The following code example demonstrates a simple operation process (refer to `https://github.com/PacktPublishing/RAG-from-First-Principles` for the complete code):

```
from langchain.document_loaders import CSVLoader
file_path = 'data/BlackMyth/BlackMythWukong.csv'
loader = CSVLoader(file_path=file_path)
data = loader.load()
for record in data[:2]:
    print(record)
```

```
page_content='Category: Equipment Name: Bronze Cloud Staff Description:
A sturdy bronze staff that emits a sharp sound when swung, suitable for
melee attacks. PowerLevel: 85'
metadata={'source': 'data/BlackMyth/BlackMythWukong.csv', 'row': 0}
page_content='Category: Equipment Name: Hundred Tricks Undergarment Armor
Description: A finely crafted battle armor that provides strong defense
and resists potent poison damage. PowerLevel: 90'
metadata={'source': 'data/BlackMyth/BlackMythWukong.csv', 'row': 1}
```

In this example, page_content contains the detailed contents of each row, while `metadata` provides the file path and row number of the data source, which is helpful for subsequent data querying and processing. It is important to note that the first row of the CSV file is considered the header row, and its contents are used as the field names by default, i.e., column names.

In the code example below, we specify some parameters of the CSV file through csv_args and use custom column names:

```
loader = CSVLoader(
file_path=file_path,
csv_args={
'delimiter': ',',
'quotechar': '\'',
'fieldnames': ['Category', 'Name', 'Description', 'PowerLevel'],
},
)
data = loader.load()
for record in data[:2]:
    print(record)
```

```
page_content='Category: Category Name: Name Description: Description
PowerLevel: PowerLevel'
metadata={'source': 'data/black myth/black myth wukong.csv', 'row': 0}
page_content='Category: Equipment Name: Bronze Cloud Staff Description:
A sturdy bronze staff that can produce a swooshing sound when swung,
suitable for melee attacks. PowerLevel: 85'
metadata={'source': 'data/black myth/black myth wukong.csv', 'row': 1}
```

After this processing, new column names such as Category, Name, etc., will replace the original field names in page_content. Since additional field names are specified, this import method will treat the first line inside the file directly as a data row rather than a header row.

You can use a specific column from the CSV file to set the value for the metadata source. The content from this column will replace the default CSV filename and become the source identifier for each document entry. This is demonstrated in the following code example:

```
loader = CSVLoader(file_path=file_path, source_column='Name')
data = loader.load()
for record in data[:2]:
    print(record)
```

```
page_content='Category: Equipment Name: Bronze Cloud Rod Description: A
sturdy bronze rod that produces a whistling sound when swung, suitable for
close combat attacks. PowerLevel: 85'
metadata={'source': 'Bronze Cloud Rod', 'row': 0}
```

```
page_content='Category: Equipment Name: Hundred Tricks Coin Armor
Description: A finely crafted combat armor that provides strong defense
and resists powerful poison damage. PowerLevel: 90'
metadata={'source': 'Hundred Tricks Coin Armor', 'row': 1}
```

In this example, the `source_column` parameter specifies the Name column as the data source. Therefore, the `source` field in metadata takes the value of the corresponding `Name` column for each row. For example, for the first record, the `source` value is "Bronze Cloud Rod"; for the second record, it is "Hundred Tricks Coin Armor".

This newly generated metadata information is very useful when querying specific items. For example, in a Q&A chain, if you want to query only records related to Hundred Tricks Coin Armor, you can filter by the `source` field.

Comparing CSVLoader and UnstructuredCSVLoader

Alex: Lewis, you mentioned earlier that the Unstructured tool can load almost all types of files. Can we compare the results of `CSVLoader` and `UnstructuredCSVLoader`?

Lewis: Of course. The following code example shows how to use `UnstructuredCSVLoader` to load data from a specified `path` and print it out:

```
from langchain_community.document_loaders import UnstructuredCSVLoader
loader = UnstructuredCSVLoader(file_path=file_path)
data = loader.load()
print(data)
```

```
[Document(metadata={'source': 'data/black myth/black myth wukong.csv'},
page_content='\n\nCategory\nName\nDescription\nPowerLevel\n\nEquipment\
nBronze Cloud Staff\nA sturdy bronze staff that makes a whistling sound
when swung, suitable for close combat.\n85\n\nEquipment\nHundred Show
Lining Armor\nAn exquisite battle armor that provides strong defense and
resists poisonous damage.\n90\n\nSkill\nHeavenly Thunder Strike\nSummon
heavenly thunder to attack enemies, causing a wide range of lightning
damage.\n95\n\nSkill\nFlame Dance\nPerform a fiery dance, surrounding
enemies in searing flames.\n92\n\nCharacter\nWukong\nThe protagonist,
possesses the abilities of seventy-two transformations and riding clouds
and mist, upholding justice.\n100\n\nCharacter\nSilver Horn King\nOne of
the powerful demon kings, skilled at wielding various magical artifacts,
with extremely high combat power.\n88\n\n')]
```

Alex: For CSV files, LangChain's `CSVLoader` is more practical than `UnstructuredCSVLoader` because the document structure is preserved better. Each row is processed as an independent `Document` object, and the metadata retains the important `row id` field, which can be used as a "data source index" in the retrieval process. Of course, if your task requires treating the entire CSV file as a single text block, that's a different story.

Lewis: Yes, preserving the structural information of the original document as much as possible is an eternal goal in data ingestion for RAG systems, and it is also a challenge. For example, row numbers in CSV files, headings and hierarchy in Markdown files, and the placement of images on PDF pages with both text and images—all these are factors that need to be considered during the data ingest process.

Alex: So, Lewis, if I use `DirectoryLoader` to load multiple types of documents at once, and I want to use the default loader for files like PDFs, but use `CSVLoader` for CSV files, how should I do it?

Lewis: That's also very simple. You can refer to the following code to do it (refer to `https://github.com/PacktPublishing/RAG-from-First-Principles` for the complete code):

```
loader = DirectoryLoader(
path= 'data/Black Myth',
glob='**/*.csv',    # Pattern to match all CSV files
loader_cls=CSVLoader  # Specify using CSVLoader for matched files
)
```

After this setup, `DirectoryLoader` will use `CSVLoader` to load all CSV files located in the specified directory instead of using the default `UnstructuredCSVLoader`.

Crawling and parsing web documents

In this section, we will explore how to crawl web pages and convert them into LangChain's `Document` objects. Web content not only includes textual information but also images and other multimedia elements, which are usually encoded in HTML format and may contain links to other pages or resources.

LangChain provides various web document loaders to accommodate different application scenarios. These loaders are described in *Table 1.1*:

Document Loader	Description	Package/API	Features
WebBaseLoader	Loads and parses web pages using urllib and BeautifulSoup	Package	Easy to operate, suitable for basic web content crawling
UnstructuredLoader	Loads and parses web pages using the Unstructured tool	Package	Supports complex web structures, suitable for handling heterogeneous content
RecursiveURLLoader	Recursively crawls all sub-links starting from a root URL	Package	Automates the link-crawling process; suitable for large-scale website data collection
SitemapLoader	Crawls all web pages based on the provided sitemap	Package	Efficiently parses website structure and quickly obtains all web content
Firecrawl	Provides a locally deployed API service; hosted version offers a free quota	API	Flexible and scalable, suitable for applications requiring real-time crawling and conversion

Table 1.1: Various document loaders and their descriptions

In the following subsections, we will focus on the specific implementations of `WebBaseLoader` and `UnstructuredLoader`.

Parse web pages with WebBaseLoader

You can use `WebBaseLoader` to quickly load web page files and generate a `Document` object for each page containing "flattened" string content.

First, you need to install the `beautifulsoup4` library:

```
pip install beautifulsoup4
```

The following code example demonstrates how to load the Wikipedia page for *Black Myth: Wukong* into a `Document` object:

```
import bs4
from langchain_community.document_loaders import WebBaseLoader
page_url = 'https://zh.wikipedia.org/wiki/black myth,Wukong'
loader = WebBaseLoader(web_paths=[page_url])
```

```
docs = loader.load()
print(f"{docs[0].metadata}\n")
print(docs[0].page_content.strip())
```

The preceding code will extract the text and produce the following output:

```
{'source': 'https://zh.wikipedia.org/wiki/black myth,Wukong', 'title':
'black myth,Wukong - Wikipedia, the free encyclopedia', 'language': 'zh'}
Black Myth: Wukong - Wikipedia, the free encyclopedia Skip to content
Main menu Main menu Move to sidebar Hide navigation Home Category Index
Featured Content News......Table of Contents Move to sidebar Hide Preface
1 Gameplay 2 Plot 2.1 Setting 2.2 Story 2.2.1 Prologue 2.2.2 Seeking
Root......
```

The preceding method extracts the complete text of the page but may include unnecessary information, such as titles or navigation bars. If you are familiar with the HTML structure of the web page, you can use BeautifulSoup to specify the required `<div>` class names to filter out unwanted content.

The following code example demonstrates how to parse and extract only the main body of the web page content:

```
loader = WebBaseLoader(
web_paths=[page_url],
bs_kwargs={ 'parse_only': bs4.SoupStrainer(id='bodyContent'), }, # Only
parse the main part of the webpage content
bs_get_text_kwargs={'separator': ' | ', 'strip': True},
)
```

Here's how the extracted web page content looks in the output:

```
{'source': 'https://zh.wikipedia.org/wiki/black myth,Wukong'}
Wikipedia, The Free Encyclopedia | Black Myth: Wukong | Genre | Role-
playing | | Platform | Microsoft Windows | PlayStation 5 | Xbox Series X/S
| Developer | Game Science | ...
```

Here, `parse_only: bs4.SoupStrainer(id="bodyContent")` refers to the HTML element in the webpage with `id="bodyContent"`. This usually represents the main content section of the webpage, mainly comprising the core information of the article or page, and does not include navigation bars, footers, or other auxiliary elements.

This produces a cleaner result, filtering out meaningless link text such as Jump to content, Main menu, Move to sidebar, Hide navigation, Home Page, Category, Index, Featured Content, and directly focusing on the knowledge main body.

Granular webpage parsing with UnstructuredLoader

If you need more granular control over the content, a more advanced parsing method can be chosen, such as parsing using the Unstructured Loader. This method is suitable for scenarios where precise indexing of specific webpage content is required. After processing, multiple `Document` objects will be generated for each webpage, each representing different structures on the page, such as titles, main text, lists, or tables.

First, ensure that the `langchain-unstructured` interface package is installed. Here, we use the Unstructured package via local invocation (later content will also show how to call the Unstructured tool via API):

```
pip install 'langchain-unstructured[local]'
```

The following code example demonstrates how to use the Unstructured tool to load the same webpage:

```
from langchain_unstructured import UnstructuredLoader
page_url = 'https://zh.wikipedia.org/wiki/black myth,Wukong'
loader = UnstructuredLoader(web_url=page_url)
docs = loader.load()
for doc in docs[:5]:
    print(f'{doc.metadata['category']}: {doc.page_content}')
```

```
Title: Black Myth: Wukong
ListItem:
![Arabic word in bold black script on a white background with distinct
looping and dots above](../images/9787115671851_01_14.png)
ListItem:
![Arabic calligraphy in black on a white background spelling out the word]
(../images/9787115671851_01_15.png)
ListItem: Azerbaijani
ListItem: Belarusian (Taraškievica)
...
```

Each `Document` object output here represents one element of the page. The `metadata` includes the element's category, such as title or main text.

Tips from Lewis

In this section, we learned that the Unstructured tool is capable of analyzing various unstructured elements in files and parsing them into Element data objects.

With the help of LangChain's Unstructured-Loader, we can further convert these Element data objects into Document objects.

The parsed page elements may have parent-child relationships. For example, a paragraph might belong to a specific heading or table (where the category is **Title** or **Table**). You can extract and combine these page elements using the following code:

```
from langchain_unstructured import UnstructuredLoader
from typing import List
from langchain_core.documents import Document
page_url = 'https://zh.wikipedia.org/wiki/black myth,Wukong'
def _get_setup_docs_from_url(url: str) -> List[Document]:
    loader = UnstructuredLoader(web_url=url)
    setup_docs = []
    for doc in loader.load():
        if doc.metadata['category'] == 'Title' or doc.metadata['category']
== 'Table':
            parent_id = doc.metadata['element_id']
            current_parent = doc  # Update the current parent element
            setup_docs.append(doc)
        elif doc.metadata.get('parent_id') == parent_id:
            setup_docs.append((current_parent, doc))  # Store the parent
and child elements together
    return setup_docs
docs = _get_setup_docs_from_url(page_url)
for item in docs:
    if isinstance(item, tuple):
        parent, child = item
        print(f'Parent element - {parent.metadata['category']}: {parent.
page_content}')
        print(f'Child element - {c
hild.metadata['category']}: {child.page_content}')
```

```
    else:
        print(f'{item.metadata['category']}: {item.page_content}')
```

In the preceding code, the current_parent variable is used to store the current parent element. When a child element is encountered, it will be stored together with the current parent element as a tuple. During output, it checks whether the element is a tuple; if so, it prints the parent and child elements separately. This ensures that each child element and its corresponding parent element can be clearly displayed.

Understanding the cultural and story background of Black Myth: Wukong

Black Myth: Wukong is an **action role-playing game** developed and published by **Game Science**, hailed by the media as China's first **AAA game**.

The game's content is adapted from one of China's Four Great Classical Novels, *Journey to the West*. Before its official release, the game already received widespread praise from industry media and critics, lauding its **combat system**, **visual design**, and **worldbuilding**. After launch, the game quickly topped sales charts on multiple platforms, and sold over 20 million copies worldwide within a month of release, making it one of the fastest-selling games of all time.

Tips from Lewis

In the Element data objects parsed by the Unstructured tool, parent_id is an important metadata field. It indicates the parent element of the current element. This field helps build and maintain the hierarchical structure of documents, clearly defining the relationship between the current element and upper-level structures, which is especially important when parsing complex documents.

For example, a table item may contain a parent_id pointing to the title or section it belongs to. This makes it possible to accurately restore the position and hierarchical relationship of each content block when reconstructing the tree structure of a document.

When displaying or analyzing the document structure, content can be reorganized according to parent_id. For instance, table items can be correctly assigned under their corresponding headings.

Markdown file titles and structure

Alex, by now you may have noticed that we emphasize the importance of preserving the *original information* after loading a document. Indeed, the inherent format of these documents (such as line IDs in CSV files or the element hierarchy in HTML files) contains structural or relational information that could play an important role in the indexing, retrieval, and generation processes of a RAG system.

Why Markdown?

The Markdown documents we are about to discuss are an extremely important file type when building a RAG system. There are several reasons behind the approach of unifying source data into Markdown format:

- Markdown is a lightweight markup language, easy to read and parse. Compared with more complex markup languages like HTML or XML, Markdown syntax is much simpler and clearer, making it easier to parse both manually and automatically. This is beneficial for preprocessing, splitting, and summarizing documents, and the subsequent steps of feature extraction and index building.
- Its style is close to the training data used by large models: Most large models (such as ChatGPT and DeepSeek) have already been exposed to a large amount of Markdown-formatted text (including GitHub READMEs, technical documents, blog articles, etc.) during training. This means that when facing Markdown content, these large models can extract useful information more effectively and generate more natural and appropriate responses.
- Retains the hierarchical structure and basic formatting information of the text: Markdown can preserve titles, paragraphs, lists, tables, code blocks, and other structural information in a relatively simple way. This capability helps large models in RAG systems understand the logical hierarchy and semantic partitioning of the text, thereby enabling better referencing and organization of information when answering questions.
- Unifies and simplifies data formats: Since different data sources (such as HTML, PDF, CSV tables, database texts) have significant differences in format and structure and may include complex HTML tags or different encoding methods, converting all data to Markdown can, to a certain extent, achieve format unification and simplify subsequent processing steps.
- Convenient for subsequent presentation: In the final output, the RAG system can directly produce text in Markdown format, allowing answers on the front-end interface (such as chat windows) to have both good readability and visual effect, without the need for additional format conversion.

Therefore, Markdown format is not only beneficial for data preprocessing and large models' understanding and parsing of data, but also convenient for clearly presenting information. It is worth noting that Markdown files also contain hierarchical structure information. Each heading has corresponding content underneath it, which should not be separated. This means that during the parsing process, ensuring the hierarchical structure of "heading - the text under it" is very important.

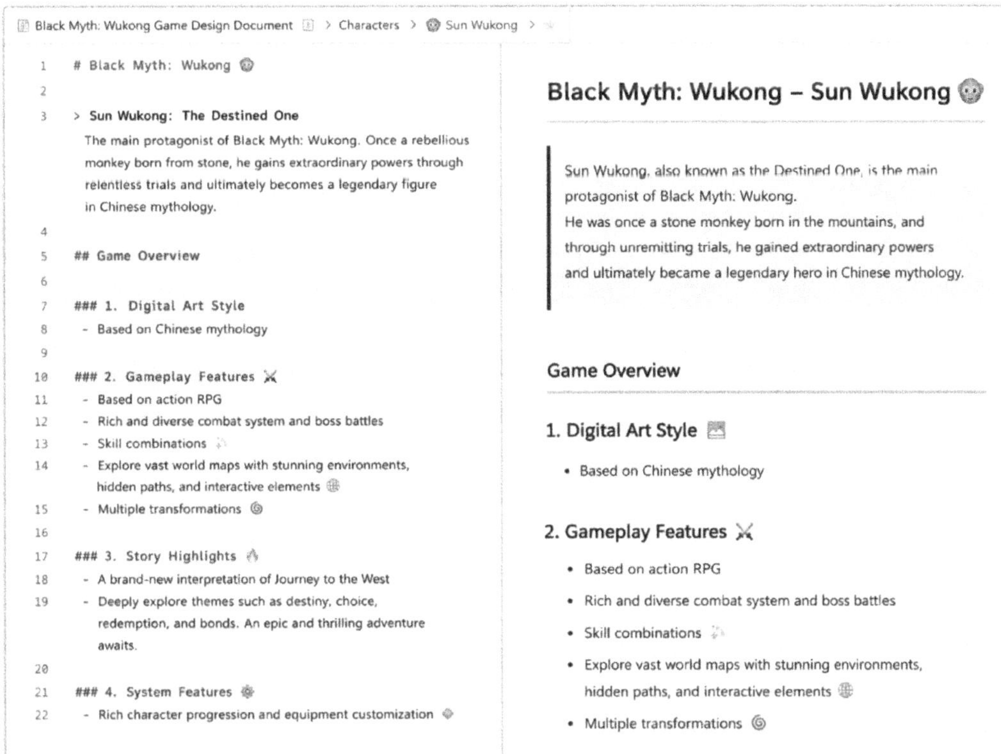

Figure 1.13: A screenshot shows a Markdown editor with game introduction notes and their preview

Implementing UnstructuredMarkdownLoader

Next, let's look at the application details of `UnstructuredMarkdownLoader`. In its default mode, `UnstructuredMarkdownLoader` loads the entire Markdown file as a single `Document` object. This means that the parsed content is stored together in a data list, and that list contains only one `Document` object whose `page_content` attribute will contain the full text content of the file. This approach is especially suitable for handling documents that are short in content or do not need further subdivision, as it is convenient for overall reading and processing. Here's how you use this function (refer to `https://github.com/PacktPublishing/RAG-from-First-Principles` for the complete code):

```
from langchain_community.document_loaders import
UnstructuredMarkdownLoader
from langchain_core.documents import Document
markdown_path = "data/black myth/Black Myth Version Introduction.md"
loader = UnstructuredMarkdownLoader(markdown_path)
data = loader.load()
print(data[0].page_content)
```

Here are the application details from the output:

```
Game Version Introduction
Digital Standard Edition
Includes the base game
Digital Deluxe Edition
```

When `mode="elements"` is enabled, `UnstructuredMarkdownLoader` will parse the Markdown file into multiple elements. As shown in the following code, each element will be treated as an independent `Document` object, representing a separate content block, such as headings, paragraphs, list items, and so on. This approach allows for finer granularity in handling course content, making it easier for indexing and retrieval.

```
loader = UnstructuredMarkdownLoader(markdown_path, mode="elements")
data = loader.load()
print(f"Number of documents: {len(data)}\n")
for document in data:
    print(f"{document}\n")
```

The following output shows the result after the parsing operation:

```
Number of documents: 22
page_content='Black Myth: Wukong ' metadata={'source': 'data/black myth/
Black Myth Version Introduction.md', 'category_depth': 0, 'languages':
['zho'], 'file_directory': 'data/black myth', 'filename': 'Black
Myth Version Introduction.md', 'filetype': 'text/markdown', 'last_
modified': '2024-11-26T12:15:59', 'category': 'Title', 'element_id':
'b89add9386b58a1638e0b96d19f08d0d'}
page_content='Black Myth: Wukong is a highly anticipated action-
```

```
adventure game developed by a Chinese game development team. Inspired
by Journey to the West, it reinterprets the classic story, delivering
an impactful visual and gaming experience.' metadata={'source': 'data/
black myth/Black Myth Version Introduction.md', 'languages': ['zho'],
'file_directory': 'data/black myth', 'filename': 'Black Myth Version
Introduction.md', 'filetype': 'text/markdown', 'last_modified': '2024-11-
26T12:15:59', 'parent_id': 'b89add9386b58a1638e0b96d19f08d0d', 'category':
'UncategorizedText', 'element_id': '4d1fd58a257960aafb046fc47605c217'}
```

When parsing complex documents, the `category` field in the metadata (such as `Title`) helps to understand the document structure and provides meaningful context. For example, a title usually indicates the topic or classification of the following content. Therefore, treating the title as a separate `Document` object helps to locate and organize content for subsequent retrieval or analysis. For instance, in a RAG system, content from specific sections can be filtered according to the title, enabling more precise answers to learners' questions. In addition, through the `parent_id` field in the metadata, it's possible to further determine which elements belong to a particular title, thus organizing relevant content as a unified text block.

Text formats, layout recognition, and table parsing in PDF files

For most RAG systems, parsing PDF files is a key step in building the system. PDF files not only contain textual information but may also include elements such as tables and images, making their parsing more challenging compared to other types of documents.

Currently, common parsing methods for handling PDF files can be roughly divided into three categories: **rule-based parsing**, **deep learning-based parsing**, and **multimodal large model-based parsing**.

PDF parsers that use these methods may perform the following operations:

- Recombine separated text boxes into logical units, such as lines or paragraphs, through heuristic methods or machine learning techniques
- Apply **OCR** technology to images in the file to recognize and extract the text within them
- Classify textual content to determine whether it belongs to paragraphs, lists, tables, or other structures
- Organize the extracted text into table formats, or present data in key-value pairs

Tips from Lewis

Many modern large models now support multimodal input and can directly process multimedia files such as images and PDFs. We already provided an example earlier.

In some application scenarios, especially those requiring question answering and analysis of PDF documents with complex layouts, charts, or illustrations, the PDF documents can be passed directly to the large model for understanding, without first converting them into a simpler format.

Using loading tools for PDF files

LangChain can integrate with a variety of PDF parsers. Among these parsers, some are designed to be simple and relatively basic, suitable for lightweight text parsing scenarios, while others support **OCR functions, mathematical formula processing** and **image analysis**, or can perform **advanced document layout analysis**.

Parser	Description	Package/API	Features
PyPDF	Loads and parses PDF files using `pypdf`	Package	Efficient and lightweight, suitable for handling simple PDF files
Unstructured	Loads PDF files using the open-source Unstructured tool library	Package/API	Supports multiple document formats, has content extraction and analysis capabilities
Amazon Textract	Loads PDF files via AWS API	API	Provides cloud service support, suitable for large-scale document OCR processing
Mathpix	Loads and parses PDF files using MathPix	API	Specially designed for mathematical formulas, can accurately parse complex content
PDFPlumber	Loads PDF files using PDFPlumber	Package	Provides rich PDF content control and processing functions
PyPDFDirectory	Loads PDF files in directories	Package	Supports batch loading, convenient for processing multiple PDF files

Parser	Description	Package/API	Features
PyPDFium2	Loads PDF files using PyPDFium2	Package	Efficient parsing, supports rendering and conversion of PDF pages
PyMuPDF	Loads PDF files using PyMuPDF	Package	Speed-optimized, supports fine-grained processing of complex PDF files
PDFMiner	Loads PDF files using PDFMiner	Package	Suitable for text extraction, especially adept at handling PDFs containing embedded text

Table 1.2: Parser functions and their features

The difficulty of deploying and using these tools can be analyzed from several perspectives, such as the following:

- **Local deployment type**: Tools such as PyPDF, PDFPlumber, and PDFMiner are all Python libraries, so their installation and use are relatively simple. Such tools usually only require installation via `pip` or other package managers to get started quickly, making them suitable for users who want to avoid complicated configuration processes.
- **API service type**: Amazon Textract and MathPix belong to this category and require applying for an API Key, often involving paid usage. Although these services offer powerful functions, such as batch document processing and mathematical formula parsing, their usage threshold is relatively high.
- **Hybrid type**: Unstructured, as an open-source library, can be used directly for its basic functions, but fully utilizing all its features may require additional service support.

From the perspective of functional characteristics, **PyPDF** is a lightweight tool that provides basic PDF text extraction; **PDFPlumber** excels at processing table data and shows strong capability in layout analysis; **PyMuPDF** offers comprehensive functions, supporting PDF rendering, editing, and fine-grained processing of complex documents; **Amazon Textract** has **OCR** capabilities and is especially suitable for scanned documents; **MathPix** is designed for mathematical formula recognition; **PDFMiner** has very powerful underlying parsing capabilities, being able to precisely locate text positions.

From the performance perspective, **PyPDF** is known for its fast processing speed but performs only moderately in terms of accuracy; **PyMuPDF** excels in both performance and accuracy; **Unstructured** performs well in handling complex layouts, and thus has been chosen as the default loader for **LangChain's DirectoryLoader**. Its **API version** also provides high-accuracy parsing services, though network conditions may affect processing speed.

From the perspective of application scenarios, for simple document text parsing, **PyPDF** is sufficient; if you need to process table data in PDF files, **PDFPlumber** is recommended; when faced with complexly formatted PDF files, **PyMuPDF** or **Unstructured** are better choices; for dealing with scanned documents, **Amazon Textract** is an ideal choice; for math PDF documents with many formulas, **MathPix** is recommended.

Overall, if you need to process PDF files in bulk at scale, **PyMuPDF** stands out as particularly well balanced due to its comprehensive features and high efficiency.

PDF parsing is a broad topic. Next, we can further explore some basic approaches. By learning and practicing the specific implementation details of each tool, mastering them will no longer be difficult.

Simple text extraction with PyPDFLoader

If you only need to extract the embedded text as simple string representations from a PDF file, you can use the `PyPDFLoader` method. This method returns a list of `Document` objects, with each page corresponding to a `Document` object. The extracted text will be stored in the `page_content` attribute of the `Document` object.

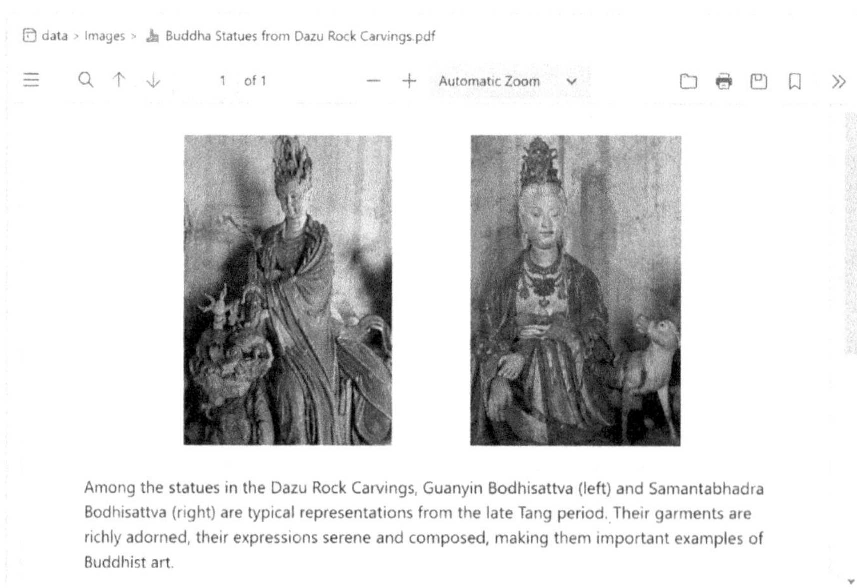

Figure 1.14: Two traditional statues are displayed side by side each depicting a robed figure with unique features

The following code example demonstrates how to install the PyPDF tool:

```
pip install pypdf
```

This method does not parse images or scanned PDF pages (i.e., it does not support **OCR** functionality), as shown in the following code:

```
from langchain_community.document_loaders import PyPDFLoader
file_path = "data/black myth/ Kang Jinlong and Lou Jingou.pdf"
loader = PyPDFLoader(file_path)
pages = loader.load()
print(f"Loaded {len(pages)} page(s) of PDF document")
for page in pages:
    print(page.page_content)
```

The preceding code returns standard text content:

```
Loaded 1 page(s) of PDF document
Some characters in the game, such as Kang Jinlong (left) and Lou Jingou
(right), draw their inspiration from the painted sculptures at the Jade
Emperor Temple in Jincheng, Shanxi. The character Kang Jinlong appears in
both human and dragon form, serving as a boss enemy.
```

In the next section, we will see how to convert PDF documents to Markdown format.

Using the Marker tool to convert PDF documents to Markdown format

When dealing with PDF documents containing structured content, such as hierarchical headings used to organize and logically structure the content, the ideal approach is to preserve this hierarchy while parsing the PDF document. For such needs, converting PDF documents to Markdown format is a good choice. Standardizing all types of text to Markdown format helps simplify subsequent processing and analysis steps.

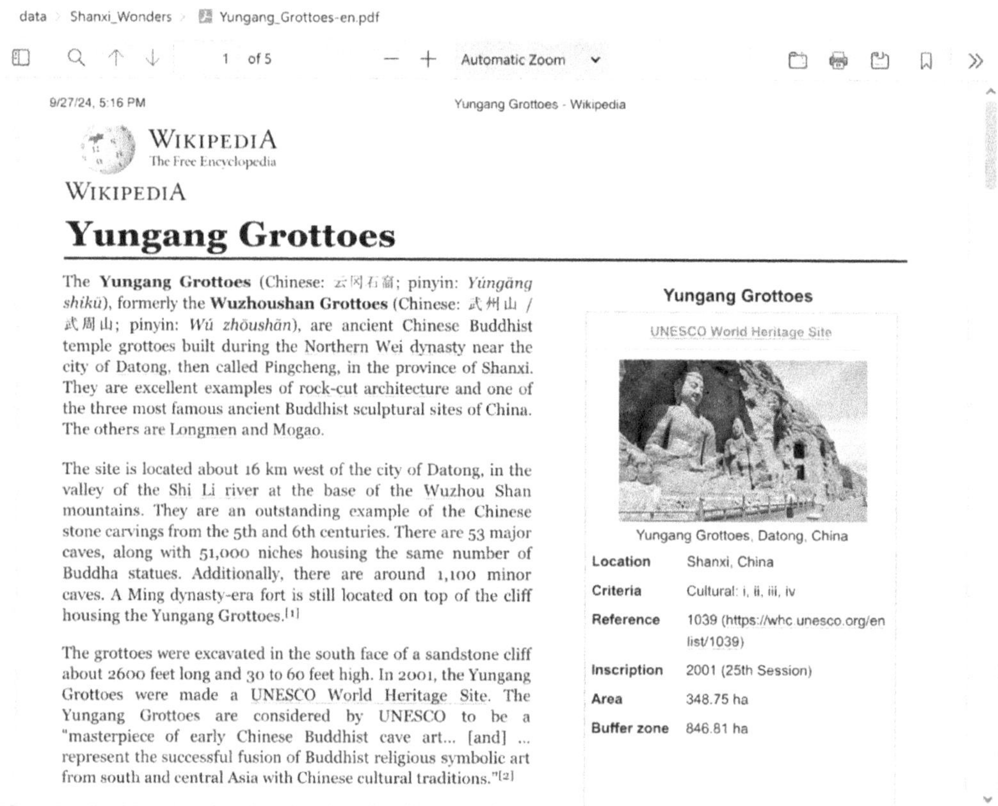

data > Shanxi_Wonders > Yungang_Grottoes-en.pdf

1 of 5 — + Automatic Zoom

9/27/24, 5:16 PM Yungang Grottoes - Wikipedia

WIKIPEDIA
The Free Encyclopedia

WIKIPEDIA

Yungang Grottoes

The **Yungang Grottoes** (Chinese: 云冈石窟; pinyin: *Yúngāng shíkū*), formerly the **Wuzhoushan Grottoes** (Chinese: 武州山 / 武周山; pinyin: *Wǔ zhōushān*), are ancient Chinese Buddhist temple grottoes built during the Northern Wei dynasty near the city of Datong, then called Pingcheng, in the province of Shanxi. They are excellent examples of rock-cut architecture and one of the three most famous ancient Buddhist sculptural sites of China. The others are Longmen and Mogao.

The site is located about 16 km west of the city of Datong, in the valley of the Shi Li river at the base of the Wuzhou Shan mountains. They are an outstanding example of the Chinese stone carvings from the 5th and 6th centuries. There are 53 major caves, along with 51,000 niches housing the same number of Buddha statues. Additionally, there are around 1,100 minor caves. A Ming dynasty-era fort is still located on top of the cliff housing the Yungang Grottoes.[1]

The grottoes were excavated in the south face of a sandstone cliff about 2600 feet long and 30 to 60 feet high. In 2001, the Yungang Grottoes were made a UNESCO World Heritage Site. The Yungang Grottoes are considered by UNESCO to be a "masterpiece of early Chinese Buddhist cave art... [and] ... represent the successful fusion of Buddhist religious symbolic art from south and central Asia with Chinese cultural traditions."[2]

Yungang Grottoes

UNESCO World Heritage Site

Yungang Grottoes, Datong, China

Location	Shanxi, China
Criteria	Cultural: i, ii, iii, iv
Reference	1039 (https://whc.unesco.org/en/list/1039)
Inscription	2001 (25th Session)
Area	348.75 ha
Buffer zone	846.81 ha

Figure 1.15: Wikipedia page about Yungang Grottoes with a photo of large Buddha statues carved in rock

In the process of converting PDF documents to Markdown format, at a minimum, the following key elements should be preserved:

- **Markdown heading hierarchy**: In the document, headings are used to organize the content of different sections. This hierarchy not only helps learners navigate quickly, but also enhances the comprehensibility, overall readability, and organization of the document.
- **Image and text structure**: Given that many PDF documents contain charts or multi-column layouts to further explain textual content, it is necessary to parse images during the conversion process and save them in a dedicated image directory, then embed them in the Markdown file. Meanwhile, appropriate formatting should be used to retain the presentation of tabular data, ensuring the accuracy and completeness of information delivery.

The following figure shows a document about Yungang Grottoes listing UNESCO site details in a table:

```
## History

After  the decline of the Western Jin dynasty, the northern parts of China came under the
control of the Tuoba-ruled Northern Wei. They made the city of

#### Yungang Grottoes

UNESCO World Heritage Site

![@_image_1.png](@_image_1.png)

| Location                           | Shanxi, China                |
|------------------------------------|------------------------------|
| Criteria                           | Cultural: i, ii, iii, iv     |
| Reference                          | 1039 (https://whc.unesco.org/e |
|                                    | n/list/1039)                 |
| Inscription                        | 2001 (25th Session)          |
| Area                               | 348.75 ha                    |
| Buffer zone                        | 846.81 ha                    |
| Coordinates 40°06'38"N 113°07'33"E |                              |

![@_image_2.png](@_image_2.png)

Yungang Grottoes

![1_image_1.png](_image_1.png)
```

Figure 1.16: Screenshot of a document about Yungang Grottoes listing UNESCO site details in a table

Lewis: Although there are many open-source or commercial tools for converting PDF to Markdown, I personally recommend a tool with a very good user experience—**Marker** (another highly regarded tool is **Docking**). Marker can effectively remove headers, footers, and other irrelevant content, support formatting of tables and code blocks, and convert most formulas into LaTeX format, which is especially useful for scientific papers. In addition, it can accurately extract images. The core of Marker comprises a series of deep learning models, specifically designed for text extraction, OCR, page layout detection, and formatting cleaning. Marker intelligently selects the most suitable model according to the specific format of the PDF file to be parsed, ensuring the optimal balance between parsing speed and accuracy.

Alex: Lewis, this is the second type of PDF parsing method you mentioned at the beginning of this section – **Deep Learning-based parsing**.

The following code example demonstrates how to use **Marker** to parse PDF documents.

First, install Marker with the following command:

```
pip install marker-pdf
```

Next, you can directly use the command line to parse PDF files:

```
marker_single ''data/Shanxi Cultural Tourism/Yungang Grottoes-en.pdf''
```

In addition, you can also use the following code example to parse PDF files (refer to `https://github.com/PacktPublishing/RAG-from-First-Principles` for the complete code):

```
import os # Import os library
import subprocess # Import subprocess library
def convert_pdf_to_markdown(input_pdf_path, output_folder, batch_
multiplier=2, max_pages=12):
    if not os.path.exists(output_folder):
        os.makedirs(output_folder)
    command = [
        'marker_single',
        input_pdf_path,
        output_folder,
        f'--batch_multiplier={batch_multiplier}',
        f'--max_pages={max_pages}'
    ]
    try:
        subprocess.run(command, check=True)
        print(f"PDF document successfully converted to Markdown format,
files saved to {output_folder}")
    except subprocess.CalledProcessError as e:
        print(f"PDF document conversion failed: {e}")
if __name__ == "__main__":
    input_pdf_path = "data/Shanxi Cultural Tourism/Yungang Grottoes-en.
pdf"
    output_folder = "data/marker/output/Yungang Grottoes-en"
    convert_pdf_to_markdown(input_pdf_path, output_folder)
```

The parsing operation returns the following output:

```
Loaded detection model **vikp/surya_det3** on device **cuda** with dtype
**torch.float16**
Loaded detection model **vikp/surya_layout3** on device **cuda** with
```

```
dtype **torch.float16**
Loaded reading order model **vikp/surya_order** on device **cuda** with
dtype **torch.float16**
Loaded recognition model **vikp/surya_rec2** on device **cuda** with dtype
**torch.float16**
Loaded texify model to **cuda** with **torch.float16** dtype
Loaded recognition model **vikp/surya_tablerec** on device **cuda** with
dtype **torch.float16**
Detecting bboxes: 100%|██████████| 1/1 [00:01<00:00,  1.10s/it]
Recognizing Text: 100%|██████████| 4/4 [03:18<00:00, 49.75s/it]
Detecting bboxes: 100%|██████████| 1/1 [00:02<00:00,  2.16s/it]
Finding reading order: 100%|██████████| 1/1 [00:00<00:00,  2.05it/s]
Recognizing tables: 100%|██████████| 1/1 [00:07<00:00,  7.89s/it]
Saved markdown to the `data/marker/output/Yungang-Grottoes-en` folder
Total time: 238.9289002418518
PDF document was successfully converted to Markdown format, file has been
saved to `data/marker/output`
```

After running the program, a Markdown file will be generated, along with a series of parsed PNG image files and a JSON file containing metadata information.

Figure 1.17: A file explorer shows two folders with images and documents, mainly PNGs and a JSON file

Open the **Yungang Grottoes-en.md** file, and you can see the expected content.

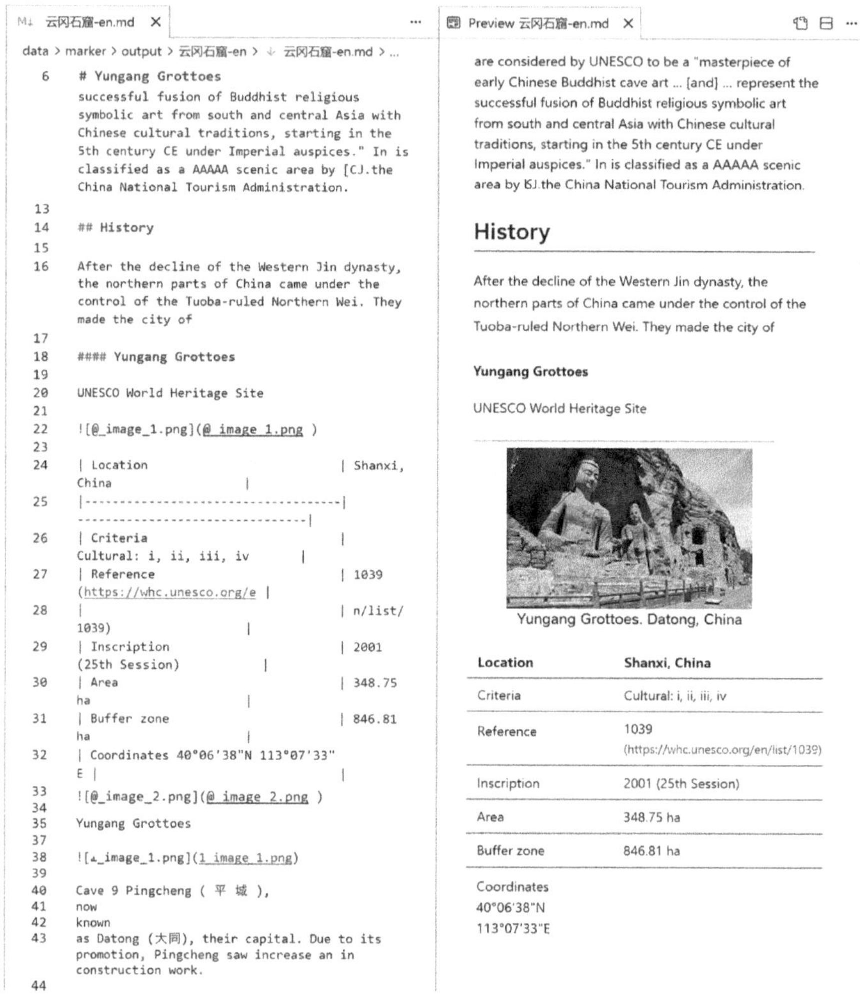

Figure 1.18: A comparison of Markdown code (left-side) with its formatted preview of the Yungang Grottoes (right-side)

Marker has achieved automatic conversion from PDF documents to Markdown format, accurately preserving the formatting information from the original PDF document. Additionally, it provides flexible configuration options, including batch processing and page number limits, allowing users to adjust performance and resource usage according to their needs.

This Markdown-format document can not only be read as a Document object by frameworks such as LangChain or LlamaIndex, but also serve as the original material for RAG-based knowledge bases.

Structured parsing with UnstructuredLoader

In the previous section, we explored how to use Marker to parse PDF documents into Markdown format. However, in some cases, simply relying on this conversion method may not meet all requirements. For example, when it's necessary to segment the text at a finer granularity (such as dividing by paragraphs, headings, or table structures), or to extract text from images containing text, more detailed approaches are required.

As we know, the `UnstructuredLoader` provided by LangChain returns a list composed of `Document` objects. Each `Document` object represents an independent structure or element on the page and contains rich metadata, which greatly facilitates subsequent document analysis and processing.

The following figure shows a JSON file containing the description of the Yungang Grottoes' coordinates and layout info:


```json
{
  "page_number": 1,
  "category": "NarrativeText",
  "content": "The Yungang Grottoes (Chinese: = X/ f1 i ; pinyin: Yíngang shikū),
  formerly the Huzhoushan Grottoes (Chinese: = /M 1 / # N I ; pinyin: hú zhōushān),
  are ancient Chinese Buddhist temple grottoes built during the Northern Wei dynasty
  near the city of Datong, then called Pingcheng, in the province of Shanxi. They
  are excellent examples of rock-cut architecture and one of the three most famous
  ancient Buddhist sculptural sites of China. The others are Longmen and Mogao.",
  "coordinates": {
    "points": [
      [
        95.88139343261719,
        390.1837158203125
      ],
      [
        95.88139343261719,
        831.3316040039062
      ],
      [
        931.9985961914062,
        831.3316040039062
      ],
      [
        931.9985961914062,
        390.1837158203125
      ]
    ],
    "system": "PixelSpace",
    "layout_width": 1700,
    "layout_height": 2200
  },
  "element_id": "b2283b64ecaec23700a3cca86df6dc55",
  "parent_id": "83492be26a7187c173f75f4a3686bbdc6"
},
```


Figure 1.19: JSON data describing the Yungang Grottoes coordinates and layout info

In such a data structure, not only is basic metadata (such as page number and text content) preserved, but also detailed layout information (such as the coordinates and types of elements):

- **Basic metadata**: Includes `page_number` (page number information), `category` (used to distinguish different types of content, such as "NarrativeText" for narrative text), `content` (text content, for example, basic information describing the Yungang Grottoes), `element_id` (the unique identifier of the element), and `parent_id` (the identifier of the parent element, which helps to understand the hierarchical structure of the document and facilitates the structured processing of document content).
- **Layout information (coordinates)**: Includes the coordinates of the top-left, bottom-left, top-right, and bottom-right corners, the coordinate system type, and page width and height information. With these coordinates, precise layout analysis can be performed to determine the exact position of the content, extract content from specific areas, or reconstruct the visual layout of the document. This supports location-based content filtering, sorting, and layout reconstruction and rearrangement.

Large models with powerful capabilities may be able to automatically achieve perfect PDF layout restoration based on the above information, thereby greatly improving the efficiency and accuracy of document processing.

Alex: Lewis, I don't understand this part. Since we have to restore it sooner or later, why are we putting so much effort into breaking down the PDF document?

Lewis: This means you haven't truly understood the RAG system. The purpose of breaking it down is to make the subsequent **vectorization process** more refined; only by splitting the document into independent elements can we accurately retrieve information in the RAG system according to the user's query. For example, when a user asks what year the Yungang Grottoes were built, we need to quickly locate the relevant document fragment, rather than passing the entire PDF document to the large language model. That way, it would not only be less accurate but also waste token resources. The **restoration** during the generation process is for ultimately presenting a complete, visually rich answer to the user.

In addition to the previously installed `langchain-unstructured` interface package, since we are going to demonstrate how to call the Unstructured tool through an API here, we also need to obtain an Unstructured API Key and set the `UNSTRUCTURED_API_KEY` environment variable. The following code example shows how to use `UnstructuredLoader` to parse a PDF document:

```
file_path = ("data/Shanxi Cultural Tourism/Yungang Grottoes-en.pdf")
from langchain_unstructured import UnstructuredLoader
```

```
loader = UnstructuredLoader(
file_path=file_path,
strategy="hi_res",
partition_via_api=True, # If you are calling the local Unstructured tool,
comment out this line and the next line
coordinates=True, # Call the Unstructured tool via API and return element
coordinates
)
docs = []
for doc in loader.lazy_load():
docs.append(doc)
```

The generated doc files contain not only the text content but also structural information.

Tips from Lewis

`strategy="hi_res"` means "high-resolution mode." It attempts to capture more details in the document, especially complex layouts, tables, coordinates, and similar content.

When using this strategy to process documents, it is suitable for PDF files with very complex formats, such as files containing images, tables, graphics, and multiple columns of text. This mode leverages more advanced technologies, such as OCR analysis and high-resolution image parsing.

If the fast mode is used instead (setting strategy="fast", which is the default mode), processing is faster and consumes fewer resources. It can complete basic parsing tasks, but its support for complex layouts is less detailed, making it more suitable for PDF documents with relatively simple formats.

Next, extract the **document structure** of each page using the following function:

```
def extract_basic_structure(docs):
    """Basic structure extraction: organize content by document type"""
    # Define category mapping
    category_map = {
        'Title': 'title',
        'NarrativeText': 'text',
        'Image': 'image',
        'Table': 'table',
```

```
        'Footer': 'footer',
        'Header': 'header'
    }
    # Initialize structure dictionary
    structure = {cat: [] for cat in category_map.values()}
    structure['metadata'] = []  # Add metadata category
    # Iterate over documents and classify
    for doc in docs:
        category = doc.metadata.get('category', 'Unknown')
        content = {
            'content': doc.page_content,
            'page': doc.metadata.get('page_number'),
            'coordinates': doc.metadata.get('coordinates')
        }
        target_category = category_map.get(category)
        if target_category:
            structure[target_category].append(content)
    return structure
## Call the Function to Extract the Document Structure
structure = extract_basic_structure(docs)
Output the content with metadata as Title on page 2.
print('Title on page 2:')
for title in [t for t in structure['title'] if t['page'] == 2]:
    print(f'- {title["content"]}')
```

If you observe this page of the PDF document, you can see the title **"Deterioration and Conservation"**. The document's parsing of title-type elements is accurate in this instance. Of course, sometimes the Unstructured tool may also misclassify elements, categorizing items that do not appear to be titles as titles.

The following code example can be used to display the layout of all elements on a page:

```
def analyze_layout(docs):
    '''''Analyze the document's layout structure'''''
    layout_analysis = {}
    for doc in docs:
        page = doc.metadata.get('page_number')
        coords = doc.metadata.get('coordinates', {})
        # Initialize page information
```

```
        if page not in layout_analysis:
            layout_analysis[page] = {
                'elements': [],
                'dimensions': {
                    'width': coords.get('layout_width', 0),
                    'height': coords.get('layout_height', 0)
                }
            }
        # Get element position information
        points = coords.get('points', [])
        if points:
            # Only need the top-left and bottom right coordinate points
            (x1, y1), (_, _), (x2, y2), _ = points
            # Construct element information
            element = {
                'type': doc.metadata.get('category'),
                'content': (doc.page_content[:50] + '...') if len(doc.
page_content) > 50 else doc.page_content,
                'position': {
                    'x1': x1, 'y1': y1,
                    'x2': x2, 'y2': y2,
                    'width': x2 - x1,
                    'height': y2 - y1
                }
            }
            layout_analysis[page]['elements'].append(element)
    return layout_analysis
## Call the Function to Analyze the Document Layout
layout = analyze_layout(docs)
```

Next, output the content of the page layout on page 1:

```
print("Page 1 layout analysis:")
if 1 in layout:
    page = layout[1]
    print(f"Page size: {page['dimensions']['width']} x {page['dimensions']
['height']}")
    print("\nElement distribution:")
```

```
    ## Sort and display elements by vertical position
    for elem in sorted(page['elements'], key=lambda x: x['position']
['y1']):
        print(f"\nType: {elem['type']}")
        print(f"Position: ({elem['position']['x1']:.0f}, {elem['position']
['y1']:.0f})")
        print(f"Size: {elem['position']['width']:.0f} x {elem['position']
['height']:.0f}")
        print(f"Content: {elem['content']}")
```

The preceding code sorts and displays elements by vertical position:

```
Page 1 layout analysis:
Page size: 1700 x 2200
Element distribution:
Type: Header
Position: (827, 41)
Size: 304 x 30
Content: Yungang Grottoes - Wikipedia
Type: Image
Position: (98, 104)
Size: 427 x 142
Content: 4y WIKIPEDIA [ 1 The Free Encyclopedia WIKIPEDIA
Type: Title
Position: (1120, 411)
Size: 326 x 43
Content: Yungang Grottoes......
```

Document elements may have parent-child relationships (for example, a paragraph may belong to a section with a heading), and you can determine whether it belongs to the target section by checking each element's category and content. For instance, to extract content under a specific heading (such as the introduction about "Cave 6" on page 3, as shown in the following figure), you can use the code example that follows.

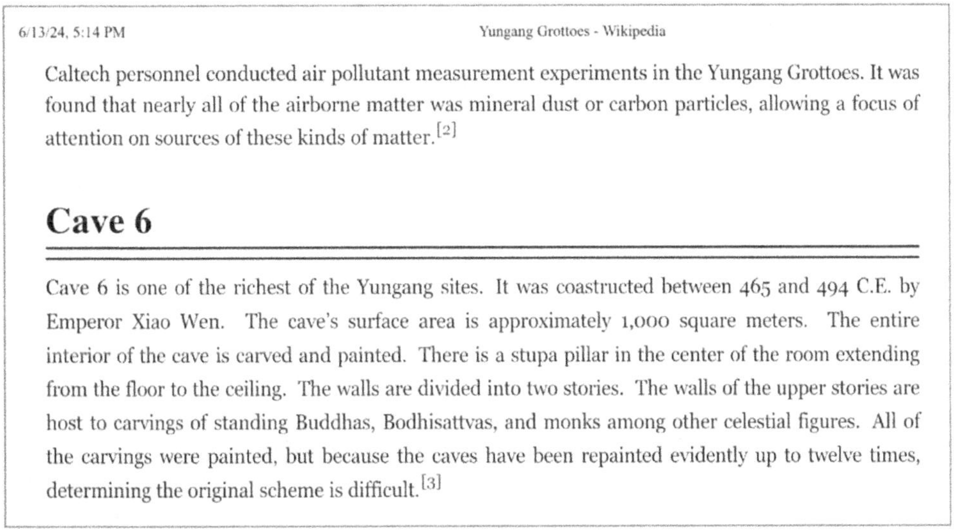

6/13/24, 5:14 PM Yungang Grottoes - Wikipedia

Caltech personnel conducted air pollutant measurement experiments in the Yungang Grottoes. It was found that nearly all of the airborne matter was mineral dust or carbon particles, allowing a focus of attention on sources of these kinds of matter.[2]

Cave 6

Cave 6 is one of the richest of the Yungang sites. It was coastructed between 465 and 494 C.E. by Emperor Xiao Wen. The cave's surface area is approximately 1,000 square meters. The entire interior of the cave is carved and painted. There is a stupa pillar in the center of the room extending from the floor to the ceiling. The walls are divided into two stories. The walls of the upper stories are host to carvings of standing Buddhas, Bodhisattvas, and monks among other celestial figures. All of the carvings were painted, but because the caves have been repainted evidently up to twelve times, determining the original scheme is difficult.[3]

Figure 1.20: Air pollutant studies at Yungang Grottoes and Cave 6's art

To extract content under a specific heading, you can use the code example that follows:

```
cave6_docs = []
parent_id = -1
for doc in docs:
    if doc.metadata["category"] == "Title" and "Cave 6" in doc.page_
content:
        parent_id = doc.metadata["element_id"]
    if doc.metadata.get("parent_id") == parent_id:
        cave6_docs.append(doc)
for doc in cave6_docs:
    print(doc.page_content)
```

Here's how the site description would appear in the output:

```
Cave 6 is one of the richest of the Yungang sites. It was constructed
between 465 and 494 C.E. by The entire Emperor Xiao Wen. The cave's
surface area is approximately 1,000 square meters. interior of the cave
is carved and painted. There is a stupa pillar in the center of the room
extending from the floor to the ceiling. The walls are divided into two
stories. The walls of the upper stories are host to carvings of standing
Buddhas, Bodhisattvas, and monks among other celestial figures. All of the
carvings were painted, but because the caves have been repainted evidently
up to twelve times, determining the original scheme is difficult.
```

Visualizing layout with PyMuPDF and coordinate information

So far, we have obtained detailed element information with **coordinates**. Next, we can use this data to perform **fine-grained layout analysis** and visualization.

In this section, we will combine the PyMuPDF library and the coordinate information parsed by UnstructuredLoader to visualize PDF pages and label content regions (such as titles, images, and tables) for easier understanding of the PDF page's layout structure or for processing information about specific sections.

Tips from Lewis

PyMuPDF is a library widely used for PDF document operations, supporting efficient reading, modification, and rendering of PDF files. PyMuPDF can open and read PDF documents, extract text and images from pages, and access page layout details (such as paragraph coordinates and image positions). At the same time, it also supports converting PDF pages into bitmap formats and allows operations such as scaling and rotation. In addition, PyMuPDF supports modifying PDF documents. You can add text, images, or graphical elements to a PDF and annotate existing documents, such as highlighting text or adding comments, so that PDF layout analysis results can be displayed in other applications.

The following code demonstrates how to use PyMuPDF to read a PDF page and convert it to an image, then use `matplotlib` to draw the PDF page and add rectangular boxes to mark section regions. Different box colors are set according to the section category (such as "Title", "Image", "Table"):

```
import fitz  # PyMuPDF library, used for processing PDF files
import matplotlib.patches as patches  # Used to draw polygons on images
import matplotlib.pyplot as plt  # Matplotlib library, for plotting
from PIL import Image  # For image processing
def render_pdf_page(file_path, doc_list, page_number):
    # Open the PDF document and load the specified page
    pdf_doc = fitz.open(file_path)
    pdf_page = pdf_doc.load_page(page_number - 1)
    segments = [doc.metadata for doc in doc_list if doc.metadata.
get('page_number') == page_number]
    # Convert the PDF page to bitmap format
    pix = pdf_page.get_pixmap()
```

```
    pil_image = Image.frombytes('RGB', [pix.width, pix.height], pix.
samples)
    # Create a plotting environment
    fig, ax = plt.subplots(figsize=(10, 10))
    ax.imshow(pil_image)
    # Define category-to-color mapping
    category_to_color = {'Title': 'orchid', 'Image': 'forestgreen',
'Table': 'tomato'}
    categories = set()
    # Draw section annotation boxes
    for segment in segments:
        points = segment['coordinates']['points']
        layout_width = segment['coordinates']['layout_width']
        layout_height = segment['coordinates']['layout_height']
        category = segment.get('category', 'Other')
        color = category_to_color.get(category, 'gold')
        # Unpack coordinates to box
        x0, y0 = points[0]
        x1, y1 = points[2]
        width = x1 - x0
        height = y1 - y0
        rect = patches.Rectangle((x0, y0), width, height, linewidth=2,
edgecolor=color, facecolor='none')
        ax.add_patch(rect)
        # Annotate category
        ax.text(x0, y0 - 5, category, fontsize=10, color=color,
weight='bold', backgroundcolor='white')
        categories.add(category)
    plt.axis('off')
    plt.show()
```

In the preceding code, the function `render_pdf_page` will open the given PDF file, render the specified page using PyMuPDF, and draw rectangles on regions specified by your element metadata. Each type of region (title, image, table, etc.) receives a different color for visual clarity. Make sure the coordinate information in your `doc_list` matches the coordinate system of the PDF rendering for accurate annotation.

Here's a nice code example for scaling layout coordinates, and generating a matching visualization legend:

```
layout_height = segment['coordinates']['layout_height']
scaled_points = [(x * pix.width / layout_width, y * pix.height / layout_
height) for x, y in points]
box_color = category_to_color.get(segment['category'], 'deepskyblue')
categories.add(segment['category'])
rect = patches.Polygon(scaled_points, linewidth=1, edgecolor=box_color,
facecolor='none')
ax.add_patch(rect)
## Add Legend
legend_handles = [patches.Patch(color='deepskyblue', label='Text')]
for category, color in category_to_color.items():
    if category in categories:
        legend_handles.append(patches.Patch(color=color, label=category))
ax.axis('off')
ax.legend(handles=legend_handles, loc='upper right')
plt.tight_layout()
```

Since the original paragraph coordinates are based on the layout ratio of the PDF page, they need to be scaled according to the actual pixel width and height of the page. After specifying the page number, the program will filter out the paragraphs that belong to that page from the document list and draw the **annotation boxes** for those paragraphs on the page.

You can call the preceding function for displaying the layout using the following code:

```
render_pdf_page(file_path,docs, 1)
```

The PDF is generated:

Figure 1.21: A textbook page with photos, diagram, and text discussing the Yungang Grottoes in China

Alex: Oh, I see. According to the layout, we can organize similar types of information together. For example, we can pass all the elements in the green image layout group in the figure to the large model as a whole, in order to generate question and answer content related to the image (Yungang Grottoes). Without precise layout analysis, this would be quite difficult.

Lewis: Really smart.

Using UnstructuredLoader to parse tables in PDF pages

Next, let's look at reading table information from PDF pages. The PDF document discussed previously did not contain any tables, so we will switch to a PDF document that includes tables. The 12th page of this file contains data about major cities in Shanxi Province (data sourced from Wikipedia).

First, we will use the same method as before to parse the layout elements of page 12 of the PDF document, shown in the following figure, by calling the statement `render_pdf_page(file_path,docs, 12)` and visualizing them.

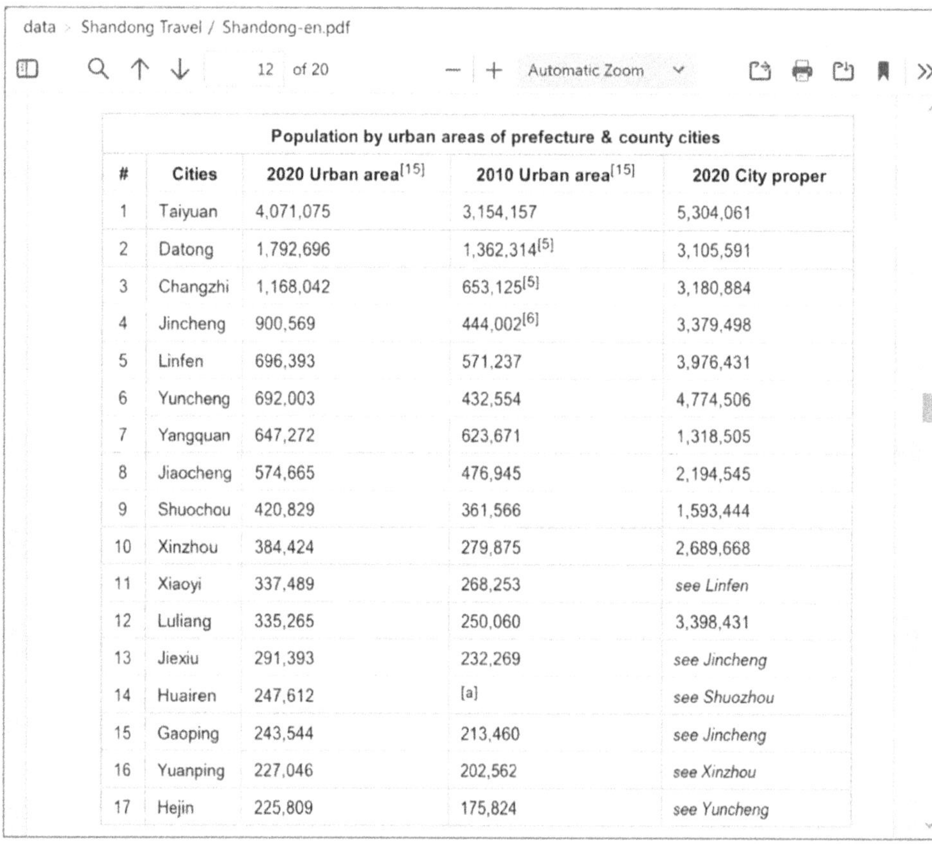

Population by urban areas of prefecture & county cities				
#	Cities	2020 Urban area[15]	2010 Urban area[15]	2020 City proper
1	Taiyuan	4,071,075	3,154,157	5,304,061
2	Datong	1,792,696	1,362,314[5]	3,105,591
3	Changzhi	1,168,042	653,125[5]	3,180,884
4	Jincheng	900,569	444,002[6]	3,379,498
5	Linfen	696,393	571,237	3,976,431
6	Yuncheng	692,003	432,554	4,774,506
7	Yangquan	647,272	623,671	1,318,505
8	Jiaocheng	574,665	476,945	2,194,545
9	Shuochou	420,829	361,566	1,593,444
10	Xinzhou	384,424	279,875	2,689,668
11	Xiaoyi	337,489	268,253	*see Linfen*
12	Luliang	335,265	250,060	3,398,431
13	Jiexiu	291,393	232,269	*see Jincheng*
14	Huairen	247,612	[a]	*see Shuozhou*
15	Gaoping	243,544	213,460	*see Jincheng*
16	Yuanping	227,046	202,562	*see Xinzhou*
17	Hejin	225,809	175,824	*see Yuncheng*

Figure 1.22: A table displays urban populations of cities in Shanxi, China, for 2020 and 2010 plus city proper

The highlighted element in the table indicates that the entire table has been successfully parsed and that the element type is `Table`:

Header (Text)

Section Title (Title)

Text

Title

Table

The 11 prefecture-level cities of Shanxi are subdivided into 118 county-level divisions (23 distri- county-level cities, and 86 counties). Those are in turn divided into 1938 township-level divisions (towns, 694 townships, and 193 subdistricts). At the end of 2017, the total population of Shanxi is 37.02 million. [a]

Urban areas

Population by urban areas of prefecture & county cities

#	Cities	2020 Urban area[b]	2010 Urban area[b]	2020 City proper
1	Taiyuan	4,071,075	3,154,157	5,304,061
2	Datong	1,792,686	1.362,349[b]	3,105,591
3	Changzhi	1,168,042	663,129[b]	3.180,884
4	Jincheng	900,569	444,002[b]	3,379,498
5	Linfen	696,369	571,237	3,376,431
6	Yuncheng	662,003	432,554	4.774,506
7	Yangquan	647,272	632,671	1,318,505
8	Jiaocheng	574,666	476,945	2,194,545
9	Shuochou	420,829	361,566	1,593,444
10	Xinzhou	384,434	279,875	2,686,666
11	Xiaoyi	337,489	268,253	see *Linfen*
12	Luliang	335,265	250,060	3.398,431
13	Jiexiu	291,393	232,269	see *Jincheng*
14	Huazhou	247,612	–	see *Shuozhou*
15	Gaoping	243,544	213,460	see *Jincheng*
16	Yuanyang	237,046	202,562	see *Xinzhou*
17	Hejin	225,800	175,824	see *Yuncheng*
18	Fenyang	207,473	149,222	see *Luliang*
19	Pingding	183,575	156,803	see *Linfen*
20	Yongji	162,248	179,028	see *Yuncheng*
21	Houma	175,373	137,020	see *Linfen*
22	Qixian	159,503	146,161	see *Taiyuan*
–	**11 Cities**	19.02 million	16.07 million	36.47 million

a. Area 157K Chinese: formerly romanized as **Shanxl**.

b. New district established after 2010 census, Yuncheng (Daliang County). The new district not included in the urban area count of the pre-expanded city.

Footer (Page number)

P12

Figure 1.23: Table listing urban populations for cities in Shanxi, China, with 2020 and 2010 data

Next, we display the metadata of all the elements on page 12:

```
page_number = 12
page_docs = [doc for doc in docs if doc.metadata.get('page_number') ==
page_number]
for doc in page_docs:
    print('Metadata:')
    for key, value in doc.metadata.items():
        print(f'  {key}: {value}')
```

A portion of the output is shown here:

```
-----------------------------------------------
Metadata:
  source: /home/huangjia/Documents/08_RAG/Book2411/rag_240917/data/山东文旅/山东-en.pdf
  detection_class_prob: 0.7882586886927214
  coordinates: ('points': ((98.26784515338886, 329.00006103515625), (98.26784515338886, 368.65481038855074),
 4990234375, 329.00006103515625)), 'system': 'PixelSpace', 'layout_width': 1700, 'layout_height': 2200)
  last_modified: 2024-12-13T17:45:36
  filetype: application/pdf
  languages: ['eng']
  page_number: 12
  parent_id: c573572a18629abc8960b04a3628d4324
  file_directory: /home/huangjia/Documents/08_RAG/Book2411/rag_240917/data/山东文旅
  filename: 山东-en.pdf
  category: Title
  element_id: 7bab58c932e489ed5ebde44f9bcaf6fc
-----------------------------------------------
Metadata:
  source: /home/huangjia/Documents/08_RAG/Book2411/rag_240917/data/山东文旅/山东-en.pdf
  detection_class_prob: 0.38452645819120086
  coordinates: ('points': ((390.90316772246094, 417.7234191894531), (390.90316772246094, 452.1907361154569),
 9.5964084921875, 417.7234191894531)), 'system': 'PixelSpace', 'layout_width': 1700, 'layout_height': 2200)
  last_modified: 2024-12-13T17:45:36
  filetype: application/pdf
  languages: ['eng']
  page_number: 12
  parent_id:  7bab58c932e489ed5ebde44f9bcaf6fc
  file_directory: /home/huangjia/Documents/08_RAG/Book2411/rag_240917/data/山东文旅
  filename: 山东-en.pdf
  category: FigureCaption
  element_id: f97e03f0ebb05bc262760232b37e390b
-----------------------------------------------
Metadata:
  source: /home/huangjia/Documents/08_RAG/Book2411/rag_240917/data/山东文旅/山东-en.pdf
  detection_class_prob: 0.9293269014353532
  coordinates: ('points': ((101.37579345703125, 451.8600158691406), (101.37579345703125, 1892.4716796875),
 244140625, 451.8600158691406)), 'system': 'PixelSpace', 'layout_width': 1700, 'layout_height': 2200)
  last_modified: 2024-12-13T17:45:36
  filetype: application/pdf
  languages: ['eng']
  page_number: 12
  parent_id:  7bab58c932e489ed5ebde44f9bcaf6fc
  file_directory: /home/huangjia/Documents/08_RAG/Book2411/rag_240917/data/山东文旅
  filename: 山东-en.pdf
  category: Table
  element_id: 52ac373811962249418c45857db17178
-----------------------------------------------
```

Figure 1.24: Screenshot of metadata for three PDF elements showing file path IDs and categories

Although a lot of metadata information is output here, the key point is that we can see the category in the metadata contains Table, and this Table element has a `parent_id`. The `parent_id` links to the table's title. This is very important because a table cannot exist independently from its associated title. The table element may contain only numbers, while the table title might indicate the meaning of these numbers.

For example, when comparing the GDP of two groups of cities in Shanxi Province, if one table is titled "2024 GDP of Each City" and another table is titled "2025 GDP of Each City", you must link the elements within the table to those of their corresponding titles. This process is a necessary step in your RAG system. Otherwise, simply possessing the figures without knowing their corresponding years will lead to retrieval results that lack accuracy.

Integrating content under the same title using ParentID

If you need to integrate a table with the title text above it, you can achieve this by following these steps:

1. Filter by page_number: Filter out all elements on a specific page (such as page 12)
2. Classify by category: Identify elements of types Table and Title, and determine whether the Title is above the Table (by comparing their y coordinate values)
3. Integrate tables and titles: Combine the table with its nearest title into one structure and output the integrated information

Alex: However, this logic seems a bit complicated to implement.

Lewis: Indeed. Since the Unstructured tool automatically saves parent-child relationships, a more direct approach is to locate elements with the category "Table". For each table, find its parent element corresponding to the `parent_id`, and then output the combined content of the table and its parent element.

Next, use the following function to automatically locate the sub-elements of a table and its parent element and output them as a whole:

```
def find_tables_and_titles(docs):
    results = []
    for doc in docs:
        ## Check if the document is of table type
        if doc.metadata.get('category') == 'Table':
            table = doc
            parent_id = doc.metadata.get('parent_id')
            ## Find the title document corresponding to the table (parent_
id matches element_id)
            title = next((doc for doc in docs if doc.metadata.
get('element_id') == parent_id), None)
            if title:
                results.append({'table': table.page_content, 'title':
```

```
title.page_content})
    return results
results = find_tables_and_titles(page_docs)
if results:
    for result in results:
        print('Found table and title:')
        print(f'Title: {result['title']}')
        print(f'Table: {result['table']}')
else:
    print('No tables and titles found')
```

The output gives a list of urban areas:

	Cities	2020 Urban area	2010 Urban area	2020 City proper
1	Taiyuan	4,071,075	3,154,157	5,304,061
2	Datong	1,792,696	1,362,314	3,105,591
3	Changzhi	1,168,042	653,125	3,180,884
4	Jinzhong	900,569	444,002	3,379,498
5	Linfen	696,393	571,237	3,976,481
6	Yuncheng	692,003	432,554	4,774,508
7	Yangquan	647,272	623,671	1,318,505
8	Jincheng	574,665	476,945	2,194,545
9	Shuozhou	420,829	381,566	1,593,444
10	Xinzhou	384,424	279,875	2,689,668
11	Xiaoyi	337,489	268,253	see Lüliang
12	Lüliang	335,285	250,080	3,398,431
13	Jiexiu	291,393	232,269	see Jinzhong
14	Huairen	247,612		see Shuozhou
15	Gaoping	243,544	213,460	see Jincheng
16	Yuanping	227,046	202,562	see Xinzhou
17	Hejin	225,809	175,824	see Yuncheng
18	Fenyang	207,473	149,222	see Lüliang
19	Huozhou	183,575	156,853	see Linfen

20	Yongji	182,248	179,028	see Yuncheng
21	Houma	175,373	137,020	see Linfen
22	Gujiao	159,593	146,161	see Taiyuan

This way, we have successfully associated the data in the table with its header information. With the header information, we can retrieve relevant tables based on the user's question.

Let's look at another example of a parent-child relationship combination. In the following screenshot, you can see that there are a total of four child elements under the Title element **External links**. If you need to combine these four child elements with their parent element (i.e., the title) and output them as an integrated chunk, you can do so through the parent-child relationship.

The following code example demonstrates how to integrate these related pieces of information:

```
external_docs = [] # Create a list to store child documents of external links
parent_id = -1 # Initialize parent_id as -1
for doc in docs:
    # Check if the document is of type Title and its content contains 'External links'
    if doc.metadata['category'] == 'Title' and 'External links' in doc.page_content:
        parent_id = doc.metadata['element_id']
        external_docs.append(doc)
    # Check if the document's parent_id matches the ID of the title we found
    if doc.metadata.get('parent_id') == parent_id:
        external_docs.append(doc) # Add all child documents belonging to this title to the result list
for doc in external_docs:
    print(doc.page_content)
```

With that we complete our discussion on parsing, loading, and generating PDF files.

Summary

At this point, **Lewis** believes that the most commonly used and important, as well as the most inspiring **data import scenarios**, have been covered. The tools **Lewis** selected are far from comprehensive, but are instead focused on solving specific scenarios and problems. As for more **file types, tools**, and **scenarios**, further exploration is up to everyone.

Other scenarios that may arise in project practice are as follows:

- Importing code blocks (refer to the **LangChain documentation** on loading code, which is also covered in Section 2)
- Cleaning redundant information from PDF documents, such as headers, footers, etc. (refer to the **Unstructured documentation** for file cleaning instructions)
- Connecting various databases and cloud service data platforms (refer to the **integration interface** sections of **LangChain** and **LlamaIndex**).
- Importing audio and video data (refer to related **multimodal large models**)

Alex: There's still so much to learn!

Lewis: Of course. You have seen only a part of the bigger picture. We've only worked on a small part among the many file types, scenarios, and tools, and we've only explained a little. There is still much knowledge about **data import and parsing** for you all to discover.

Alex: What we've learned is just a drop in the ocean.

Anna: Everyone should learn to see the bigger picture from the small details.

Lewis: You have indeed understood what I wanted to say.

In the next chapter, we will see how to divide long texts into appropriately sized fragments to facilitate embedding, indexing, and storage, and to improve retrieval accuracy. You will learn to perform text chunking, also known as text splitting.

2

Text Chunking

After importing unstructured data, we need to perform **text chunking**, also known as **text splitting**. This process involves dividing long texts into appropriately sized fragments to facilitate **embedding**, **indexing**, and **storage**, and to improve retrieval accuracy.

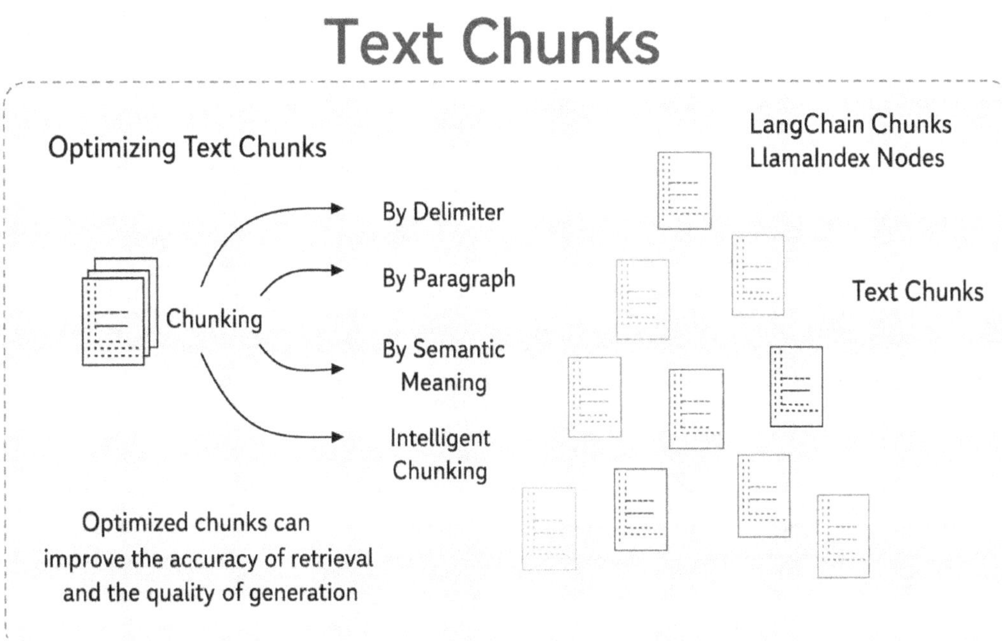

Figure 2.1: Text chunking optimization methods with flowcharts

Lewis: Why do we need to do this step? It's not hard to understand, right?

Alex: Exactly. The results of retrieval are composed of individual units, which we call **chunks**. The size of these units is very important. Take *Journey to the West* as an example; this work is nearly a million words long. If a user asks what the last of the Eighty-One Tribulations is, and we simply pass the entire course to the large model as a reference, although this isn't necessarily a retrieval failure, the information provided is too broad and not precise enough.

Why chunking is very important

Lewis: I really like the definition of **chunking** on Wikipedia, because it not only applies to **RAG** but is also used in cognitive psychology. Wikipedia mentions that "**chunking** is the process of binding together small fragments of information into a group. The purpose of these **chunks** is to improve the short-term retention of material, thus bypassing the limited capacity of working memory and making working memory more efficient."

Dividing large datasets into smaller, meaningful pieces of information serves to utilize the non-parametric memory of large models more effectively. First, this can improve retrieval accuracy, as the system can more precisely match keywords and semantics, thus optimizing search results. Second, it can also optimize model performance, because large models may encounter bottlenecks when processing excessively long texts, and **chunking** helps with the model's comprehension and response efficiency, making its answers more accurate.

One of the most important things I didn't understand about the world when I was a child is the degree to which the returns for performance are superlinear.

Teachers and coaches implicitly told us the returns were linear. "You get out," I heard a thousand times, "what you put in." They meant well, but this is rarely true. If your product is only half as good as your competitor's, you don't get half as many customers. You get no customers, and you go out of business.

It's obviously true that the returns for performance are superlinear in business. Some think this is a flaw of capitalism, and that if we changed the rules it would stop being true. But superlinear returns for performance are a feature of the world, not an artifact of rules we've invented. We see the same pattern in fame, power, military victories, knowledge, and even benefit to humanity. In all of these, the rich get richer. [1]

You can't understand the world without understanding the concept of superlinear returns. And if you're ambitious you definitely should, because this will be the wave you surf on.

It may seem as if there are a lot of different situations with superlinear returns, but as far as I can tell they reduce to two fundamental causes: exponential growth and thresholds.

The most obvious case of superlinear returns is when you're working on something that grows exponentially. For example, growing bacterial cultures, when they grow at all, they grow exponentially. But they're tricky to grow, which means the difference in outcome between someone who's adept at it and someone who's not is very great.

Startups can also grow exponentially, and we see the same pattern there. Some manage to achieve high growth rates. Most don't. And as a result you get qualitatively different outcomes: the companies with high growth rates tend to become immensely valuable, while the ones with lower growth rates may not even survive.

Y Combinator encourages founders to focus on growth rate rather than absolute numbers. It prevents them from being discouraged early on, when the absolute numbers are still low. It also helps them decide what to focus on: you can use growth rate as a compass to tell you how to evolve the company. But the main advantage is that by focusing on growth rate you tend to get something that grows exponentially.

YC doesn't explicitly tell founders that with growth rate "you get out what you put in," but it's not far from the truth. And if growth rate were proportional to performance, then the reward for performance p over time t would be proportional to p^t.

Even after decades of thinking about this, I find that sentence startling.

Figure 2.2: Superlinear returns for performance growth and ambition

Therefore, the main reason for **chunking** is to ensure that the content we embed is as noise-free as possible while maintaining semantic relevance. This is an indispensable preprocessing step when preparing data for **RAG** systems.

In addition, another reason **chunking** is necessary is that large models have context window limitations.

Context window limits the maximum chunk length

RAG systems rely on two types of models during operation: **embedding models** and **generation models**. Both types of models have their own context window limitations.

Each text segment must be processed by the **embedding model** to generate embedding vectors, so it's necessary to consider the context window limitation of the embedding model. This limitation varies depending on the specific model. For commercial models, related information is typically provided in the official documentation; for open-source models, this information is often found in the model card on platforms such as **Hugging Face Hub**.

The following figure shows the Hugging Face page for the BGEM3 model and displays an overview of its features and description:

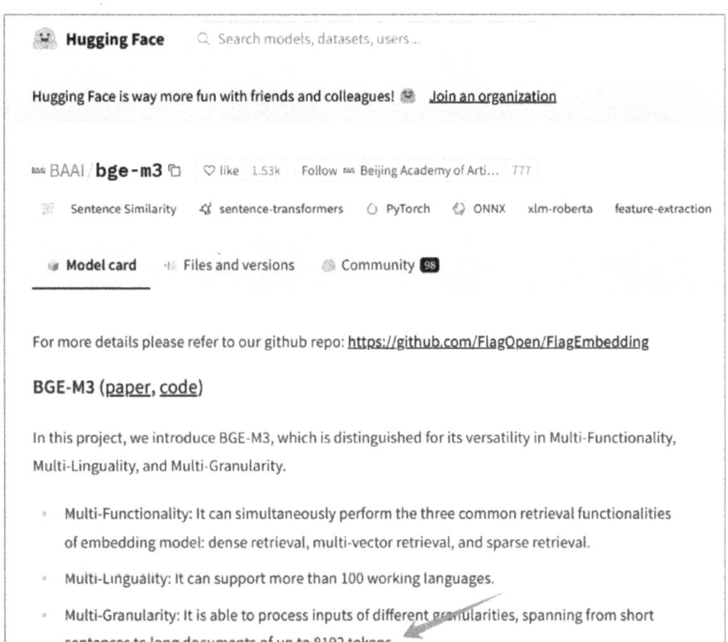

Figure 2.3: Hugging Face page for BGEM3 model

If the model card does not include this information, you can select the **Files and versions** tab, then locate relevant fields in files such as `tokenizer_config.json` or `config.json`. In these files, the `model_max_length` field in the BERT model specifies the maximum number of input tokens the model can accommodate.

Here's where you can find the tokenizer_config.json field on the Hugging Face page:

Figure 2.4: Hugging Face page for bert-base-uncased

Once the **embedding model** for generating embeddings has been determined, you can identify the maximum chunk length (measured in tokens, not characters or words). Typically, the context window limit of embedding models is less than 8,000 tokens.

The retrieved chunks are fed as context into the prompt of the **generation model** to generate responses. This means the total length of all retrieved chunks cannot exceed the context window limitation of the generation model. Small models may only be able to process a small amount of information. In practical applications, you also need to reserve space for other content, such as **detailed instructions**, **role definitions**, or a few in-context examples. Therefore, the retrieved knowledge context should be as concise as possible. Sometimes, to fit within the constraint, we need to compress prompts (methods for compressing prompts will be introduced later in this course).

Although this problem is becoming less prominent with the development of large models, many modern large models offer huge context windows—for example, **GPT-4o** can accept a context of up to 128,000 tokens. However, even when chunk capacity is no longer an issue, you still need to be careful when using very large chunks, as excessive redundant information may negatively impact the relevance of the conversation outcome.

Impact of chunk size on retrieval accuracy

Although **embedding models** specify a maximum number of tokens per chunk, this does not mean your chunks need to reach this maximum length. In fact, to improve **retrieval accuracy**, we often prefer to divide the text into smaller chunks.

Chunking and embedding processes

Let's "give a spoiler" about what happens when generating the **embedding vector** for a piece of text. Most embedding models are based on the **encoder-only Transformer architecture**, mapping input text into a fixed-dimensional vector (e.g., 768 dimensions) through a **pooling layer**.

Here's an example showing how short and long texts are tokenized and averaged to get a 768-dim vector:

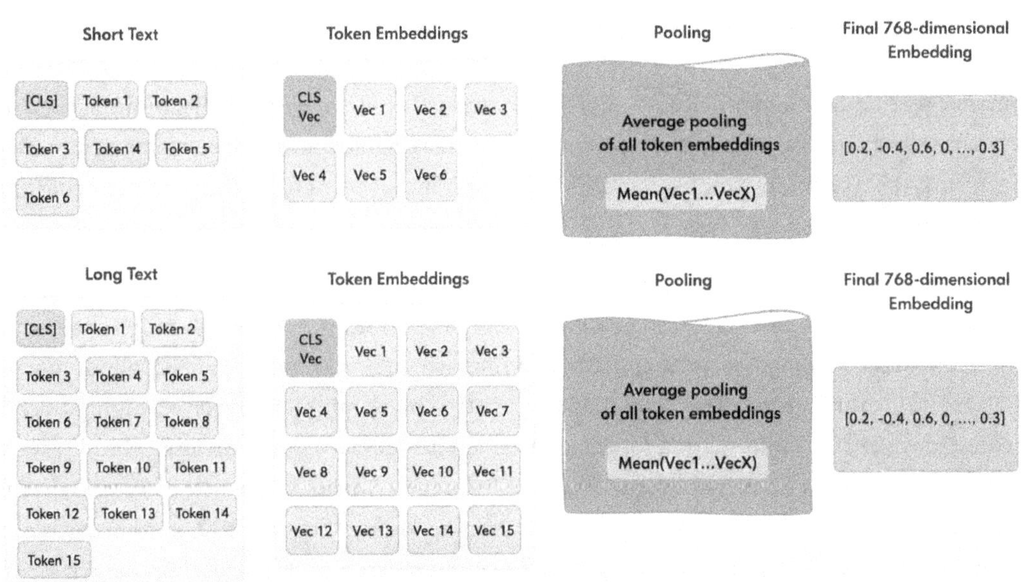

Figure 2.5: A comparison of short and long texts

First, the input text is **tokenized**, and a special [CLS] token is added at the beginning. Then, the **Transformer** generates a corresponding vector representation for each token. Next, all token vectors are compressed into a single vector through one of the following **pooling methods** (which can be seen as a form of compression), resulting in a final **text embedding vector** of a specific dimension:

- **CLS pooling**: Uses the vector of the special [CLS] token to represent the meaning of the entire sequence
- **Mean pooling**: Averages the vector representations of all tokens
- **Max pooling**: Selects the largest value from the token vectors as the representation of the entire sequence

Therefore, whether the input is a sentence of 10 words or a paragraph of 1,000 words, the dimension of the generated **embedding vector** is the same.

This process is inherently **lossy**. For larger chunks, the vector representation may be too general, causing some key details to become blurred. This is why you should not select the maximum number of tokens supported by the embedding model as the chunk size.

Chunking and topic dilution

A larger **text chunk** may cover multiple topics, some of which are relevant to your query while others are not. In such cases, a single vector attempting to represent multiple topics may lead to **topic dilution**, thereby affecting retrieval accuracy.

Smaller **text chunks** can maintain a more concentrated context, which helps in more precise matching and retrieval of relevant information. By breaking documents into meaningful small segments, the retriever can more accurately locate specific pieces or facts, thereby enhancing the performance of the **RAG system**.

For example, suppose *Shanxi Cultural Tourism* establishes a knowledge base containing tourist attractions and activities across Shanxi Province. If a **text chunk** contains descriptions about "Mount Wutai, Yungang Grottoes, and Taiyuan Amusement Park," when you ask about **attractions suitable for children**, this combined information block might not receive a high retrieval score. However, if the information for each attraction is separated into individual chunks, such as "Mount Wutai: Famous Buddhist Mountain," "Yungang Grottoes: Pinnacle of Tang Dynasty Stone Carving," and "Taiyuan Amusement Park: Summer Guide," then the **RAG system** can more accurately locate the relevant information and avoid unrelated content diluting the similarity retrieval process.

However, **text chunks** should not be too small either. For instance, if you ask **What time does Taiyuan Amusement Park open** and the introduction of Taiyuan Amusement Park and its opening hours are split into different chunks, the retrieved result may contain the opening hours of other attractions. This is because, in the absence of other metadata, the connection between time information and the attraction information has been severed.

Impact of chunk size on generation quality

From a generation perspective, although many modern large models offer very large **context windows**, completely filling this window can still lead to the **needle in a haystack problem**, where it becomes difficult to find key parts among a large amount of information. This phenomenon is referred to as **lost in the middle** in the **RAG field**, meaning that as the amount of information increases, extracting key information becomes more difficult.

In medical question-answering systems, if **chunks** are too large, when a learner asks, `What antihypertensive drugs can be taken by patients with hypertension?`, the system might return a vast amount of information related to hypertension mixed with irrelevant content, including diagnostic information, treatment plans, drug contraindications, etc. This not only increases your reading burden but may also obscure key information.

By applying a reasonable **chunking strategy**, the content in the knowledge base can be split into small, thematically clear pieces, such as **Hypertension: Common Medications**, **Hypertension: Medication Contraindications**, and **Hypertension: Lifestyle Recommendations**, with each chunk kept to around 500 characters. This allows the retrieval process to capture the core information for each topic more accurately and pass this information to the generation model, thereby producing precise answers; for example, **Common antihypertensive drugs include Drug A and Drug B, which should be taken under a doctor's guidance.**

How small can the chunk size be while still retaining enough context?

Alex: So, how small can the chunk size be while still retaining enough context?

Lewis: That depends on the nature of the course and the requirements of the project. How to perform **chunking**, as well as the logic and size of text segmentation, should be based on the specific application scenario and usually requires some experimentation to optimize. If the retrieval goal is relatively broad, such as simply locating which course is relevant, **chunks** can be larger or even not segmented at all; but if the goal is to find a specific sentence or paragraph, more fine-grained **chunking** is needed. Usually, a **chunk size** of about 500 tokens is a reasonable starting point.

Different chunking strategies

When processing text data, choosing an appropriate **chunking strategy** is crucial for maintaining the integrity of information and improving the quality of retrieval and generation. Below are several common chunking methods:

- **Chunking by fixed character count**: This is the most straightforward method, where a large document is split into smaller chunks by setting a fixed character count. Although simple, this approach can lead to **semantic discontinuity**, such as splitting a complete sentence or code block apart. To address this issue, **separators** are usually set to avoid forcibly splitting sentences or paragraphs, and a certain `chunk_overlap` is retained between chunks to ensure continuity of semantic context. This helps prevent the issue where the connection between "Taiyuan Amusement Park" and "opening hours" is broken. (Alex interjects: Why use character count instead of the **token count** that large models understand for chunking? Lewis answers: Because during text chunking, **embedding** hasn't been performed yet, so the token count can't be determined—one can only estimate based on character or word count, and therefore cannot choose to chunk by token count.)
- **Recursive chunking**: By specifying a set of **separators**, the text is gradually split into smaller parts to better preserve the integrity of individual sentences or paragraphs. For example, first split using double line breaks (`\n\n`) as paragraph separators, then further split using punctuation such as periods (`.`), spaces, and so on. If a paragraph exceeds the preset length, continue using the next level of separator for splitting, ensuring each part is of an appropriate length and semantically complete.
- **Format-based chunking**: To recognize complex document structures (such as paragraphs, titles, footnotes, lists, or tables), chunking tools based on specific formats (such as **Markdown**, **LaTeX**, **HTML**, or code) can be used. These tools can split content according to the document's **structural elements** (such as headings or sections), ensuring the completeness of content structure. For example, Markdown files can be split using the # tag, while code files can be split by the `class` or `def` keywords.
- **Layout-based chunking**: For documents containing **layout information** (such as **PDFs** or **PPTs**), layout-based chunking strategies provided by **Unstructured** tools are very useful. This strategy can split content based on logical units (such as paragraphs, tables, images, code, etc.) while allowing flexible adjustment of chunk sizes and merging strategies to meet different needs.

- **Semantic chunking**: This is an advanced chunking strategy that first splits the text by sentences, then uses embedding techniques to analyze the semantics of the sentences, and groups similar sentences together to form chunks. This approach ensures semantic consistency within each section and is suitable for scenarios requiring deep semantic understanding. **LlamaIndex's SemanticSplitterNodeParser** and **LangChain's SemanticChunker** both provide tools for implementing this feature.
- **Proposition chunking**: **Proposition chunking** based on language models breaks down long text into multiple propositions, each expressing a complete idea. Each proposition serves as a small semantic unit, facilitating retrieval and storage, and is suitable for scenarios that require efficient search and reference.

Visualize chunking with the ChunkViz tool

The **ChunkViz** tool can help you visualize different **chunking methods** and allows you to optimize the chunking results according to different parameters. Here's an example of the ChunkViz v01 interface showing text chunking options sliders for chunk size and overlap stats:

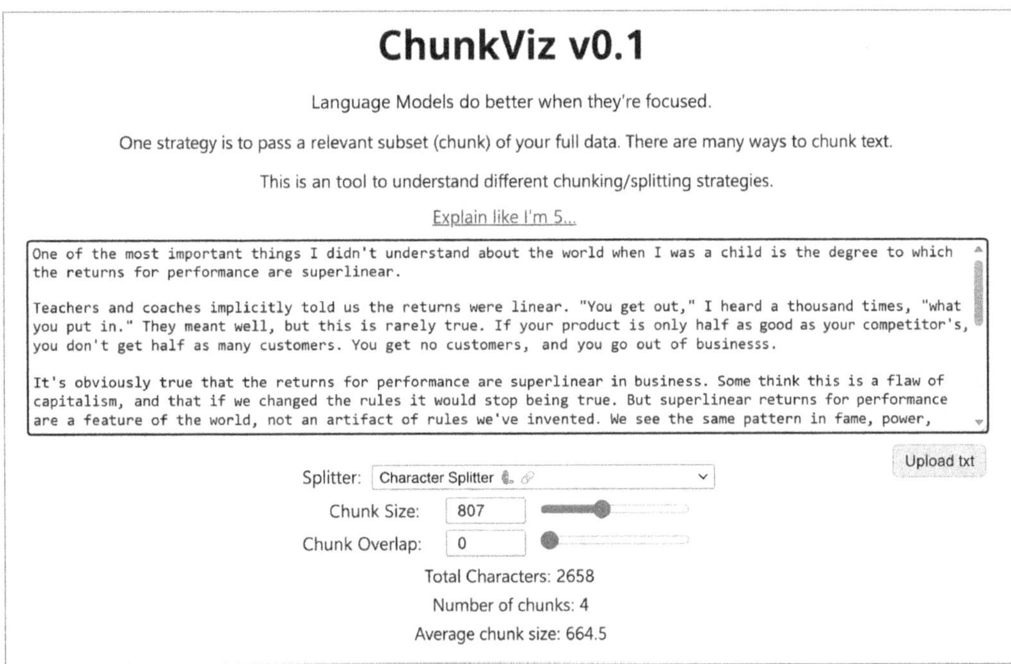

Figure 2.6: Text chunking options

After pasting a segment of text into the input box, you can select different **chunkers** (**Splitters**, which are various chunking strategies) to set the **chunk size**, and then observe the chunking results under different settings. Under the dropdown menu labeled **Splitter,** you can select options for various character and recursive text splitters:

Figure 2.7: Options for various character and recursive text splitters

Chunking by a fixed number of characters

Next, we will explore how to implement different **chunking strategies**. First, let's introduce the simplest method: splitting courses by a fixed number of characters. This method is simple and efficient, and it is a common approach.

The CharacterTextSplitter tool in LangChain

LangChain uses **CharacterTextSplitter** to split text by a fixed number of characters, words, or tokens. Let's visualize the steps for splitting and merging text blocks by size with the following flowchart:

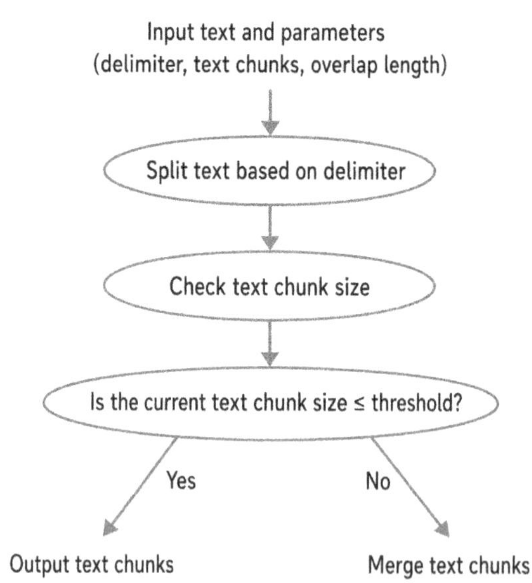

Figure 2.8: Checking and merging text blocks by size

CharacterTextSplitter first splits the text according to a specified character separator (the default is "\n\n", which means two line breaks, a line break plus a blank line), then keeps accumulating the fragmented segments and checks whether the currently accumulated text exceeds the preset size limit. If it does, a new chunk will be started. In addition, **CharacterTextSplitter** allows you to set the number of overlapping characters between chunks to better capture the connections between pieces of information.

The following code example demonstrates how to use the `split_documents` method of **CharacterTextSplitter** to perform text chunking:

```
from langchain_community.document_loaders import TextLoader
from langchain_text_splitters import CharacterTextSplitter
loader = TextLoader("data/ Shanxi Cultural Tourism/Yungang Grottoes.txt")
documents = loader.load()
### Set Up the Splitter, Specify Chunk Size as 50 Characters, No Overlap
text_splitter = CharacterTextSplitter(
chunk_size=50,
chunk_overlap=0,
)
chunks = text_splitter.split_documents(documents)
print(chunks)
```

Anna: The `split_documents` method reads **Document objects** from **LangChain**. If you want to split plain text, how should you handle it?

Lewis: You can use the `create_documents` method to take a list of texts (not **LangChain Document objects**) and split them into new **Document objects**, as shown in the following code snippet:

```
from langchain_text_splitters import CharacterTextSplitter
text = """
The Yungang Grottoes are located at the southern foot of Wuzhou Mountain,
17 kilometers west of Datong City in northern Shanxi Province, China. The
grottoes are carved into the mountain and extend one kilometer from east
to west. There are 45 main caves preserved,...... """
text_splitter = CharacterTextSplitter(
    chunk_size=50,
    chunk_overlap=0,
    separator="\n"
)
### Use the create_documents Method to Split the Text
```

```
chunks = text_splitter.create_documents([text])
print(chunks)
```

Anna: What if I only want to perform **chunking operations** and keep the document in plain string format, without creating **LangChain's Document** objects? How should I do that?

Lewis: You should use the `split_text` method to segment the text string. This method will only return the split plain text fragments and will not generate **Document objects**. Of course, this also means that you won't be able to retain any metadata. See the following code block:

```
from langchain_text_splitters import CharacterTextSplitter
text = """
The Yungang Grottoes are located at the southern foot of Wuzhou Mountain,
17 kilometers west of Datong City, Shanxi Province, northern China. The
grottoes are carved into the mountain, stretching one kilometer from east
to west. There are 45 main caves preserved... """
text_splitter = CharacterTextSplitter(
chunk_size=50,
chunk_overlap=0,
separator="\n"
)
### Use the SplitText Method to Split the Text
chunks = text_splitter.split_text(text)
print(chunks)
```

```
The Yungang Grottoes are located at the southern foot of Wuzhou Mountain,
17 kilometers west of Datong City, Shanxi Province, northern China.
The grottoes are carved into the mountain, stretching one kilometer from
east to west. There are 45 main caves preserved,
```

It should be noted that if you set the **chunk size** to 1000 characters, with the default separator `"\n\n"`, and a particular paragraph actually exceeds this limit (for example, 1200 characters), then this splitting method will not break up that paragraph, but will directly produce a chunk of 1200 characters and issue a warning: "Created a chunk of size 1200, which is longer than the specified 1000." To solve this, it is recommended to use the `RecursiveCharacterTextSplitter` method, which can handle such situations more intelligently and ensure that no chunk exceeds the specified maximum length.

Setting chunk size parameters in LlamaIndex

In **LlamaIndex**, the **SimpleDirectoryReader** can perform **chunking** directly while loading documents; you only need to set the global parameters related to chunking in advance. Below is a code example showing how to configure these parameters in **LlamaIndex** and use them to process and query text data (refer to `https://github.com/PacktPublishing/RAG-from-First-Principles` for the complete code):

```
from llama_index.core import SimpleDirectoryReader, VectorStoreIndex
from llama_index.core import Settings
documents = SimpleDirectoryReader(input_files=["data/ShanxiCulture/
CloudCave.txt"]).load_data()
## Set Chunking Parameters
Settings.chunk_size = 512  # Set the size of text chunks to 512 characters
Settings.chunk_overlap = 50  # Set the overlap between text chunks to 50
characters
index = VectorStoreIndex.from_documents(documents)
query_engine = index.as_query_engine(similarity_top_k=4)
response = query_engine.query("Where is the Yungang Grottoes located?")
print(response)
```

```
The Yungang Grottoes are located at the southern foot of Mount Wuzhou, 17
kilometers west of Datong City, Shanxi Province, northern China.
```

Recursive chunking

Lewis: In LangChain, the **RecursiveCharacterTextSplitter** (the default chunking method in LangChain) optimizes fixed-length character chunking through **recursion**. Recursion here refers to using a set of **separators** to progressively split the text. If the initially split text chunks are too large, the splitting process is further refined until each chunk reaches the desired size.

The following figure shows the logical flow for the text segmentation process using a labeled decision path:

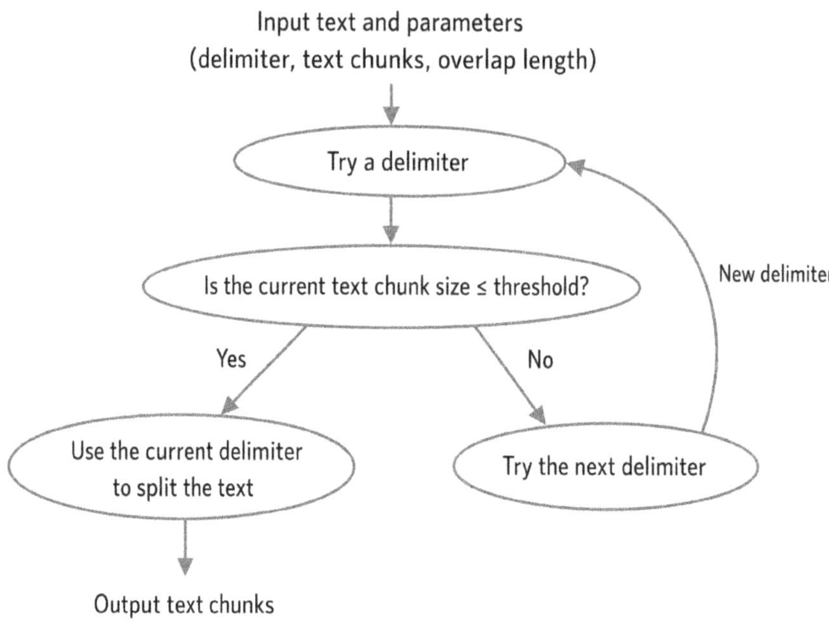

Figure 2.9: Text segmentation process with labeled decision paths

Alex: Compared with **CharacterTextSplitter**, what are the main optimizations?

Lewis: In **CharacterTextSplitter**, only a single separator is specified for splitting, whereas **RecursiveCharacterTextSplitter** tries to split using a list of characters (the default is `["\n\n", "\n", " ", ""]`) as separators, and it prioritizes keeping paragraphs, sentences, and words intact until the chunks are small enough. For example, if each chunk is required to contain 500 characters, and each paragraph is about 400 characters, then **paragraph separators** are used; if paragraphs are too large, reaching several thousand characters, new separators are recursively introduced to further split at the **sentence level**.

The following code example demonstrates how to perform recursive chunking:

```
from langchain_text_splitters import RecursiveCharacterTextSplitter
text = """
The Yungang Grottoes are located at the southern foot of Wuzhou Mountain,
17 kilometers west of Datong City, Shanxi Province, northern China. The
grottoes are dug into the mountain and stretch 1 kilometer from east to
west. There are 45 main caves remaining... """
## Define a List of Separators Used in Order of Priority
separators = ["\n\n", ".", ",", " "]
## Create a Recursive Chunker and Pass in the Separator List
```

```
text_splitter = RecursiveCharacterTextSplitter(
chunk_size=100,
chunk_overlap=10,
separators=separators
)
split_texts = text_splitter.split_text(text)
print(split_texts)
```

Chunking based on specific formats

When dealing with **programming language code**, it is very important to use appropriate tools to correctly segment the code. The `from_language` method of `RecursiveCharacterTextSplitter` provides text splitting capabilities optimized for different programming languages.

Alex: In what business scenarios do we need to split code blocks?

Lewis: There are many. For example, when different teams collaborate and develop in parallel, **code review** and **version control systems** are needed, or when analyzing **performance bottlenecks** and **memory usage optimization** by functional modules; in debugging and testing for **unit test granularity control**, **bug localization and fixing**, **behavior debugging**, etc. All of these can use the **RAG system** to extract the needed code blocks from massive code libraries.

`RecursiveCharacterTextSplitter` contains a pre-built list of separators for splitting text by specific programming languages. The supported languages are stored in the enumeration data object `langchain_text_splitters.Language`.

By passing a language value to the `RecursiveCharacterTextSplitter.get_separators_for_language` method, you can view the list of separators for the given programming language. See the following code snippet:

```
from langchain_text_splitters import RecursiveCharacterTextSplitter
from langchain_text_splitters import Language
separators = RecursiveCharacterTextSplitter.get_separators_for_
language(Language.PYTHON)
print(separators)
```

```
['\nclass ', '\ndef ', '\n\tdef ', '\n\n', '\n', ' ', '']
```

The following code example demonstrates how to split a segment of **Python code**:

```
from langchain_text_splitters import (
Language,
RecursiveCharacterTextSplitter,
)
GAME_CODE = """
class CombatSystem:
def __init__(self):
self.health = 100
self.stamina = 100
self.state = "IDLE"
self.attack_patterns = {
"NORMAL": 10,
"SPECIAL": 30,
"ULTIMATE": 50
}
def update(self, delta_time):
self._update_stats(delta_time)
self._handle_combat()
def _update_stats(self, delta_time):
self.stamina = min(100, self.stamina + 5 * delta_time)
def _handle_combat(self):
if self.state == "ATTACKING":
self._execute_attack()
def _execute_attack(self):
if self.stamina > self.attack_patterns["SPECIAL"]:
damage = 50
self.stamina -= self.attack_patterns["SPECIAL"]
return damage
return self.attack_patterns["NORMAL"]
"""
python_splitter = RecursiveCharacterTextSplitter.from_language(
language=Language.PYTHON,  # Specify the programming language as Python
chunk_size=100,
chunk_overlap=0
)
python_docs = python_splitter.create_documents([GAME_CODE])
print(python_docs)
```

This splitting tool separates **classes** and **functions** using language-specific keywords, thus maintaining the integrity and semantics of code blocks. There are many similar format-based splitting tools in **LangChain**. You can check the official website when you need them.

Chunking based on document structure or semantics

In certain document processing scenarios, splitting text only by line breaks or blank lines may not accurately capture the document's logical structure. For example, in documents such as papers, reports, or manuals, paragraphs, headings, tables, and list items all have specific semantics. Therefore, we hope to perform more intelligent **document splitting**, not only based on line breaks, but also according to the document's layout structure (such as **headings**, **body text**, **tables**, **pagination**, etc.), to generate text chunks with richer semantics.

Using the unstructured tool for document structure-based chunking

As mentioned earlier, **LangChain** provides the **Unstructured-Loader** by integrating with the **Unstructured tool**. This allows for the automatic extraction and splitting of text into **document elements** when loading a variety of documents, such as PDF, Word, HTML, etc. Then, based on the specified **chunking strategy** and maximum character limit, these document elements are combined or further split to generate text chunks that better meet specific requirements.

There are two main **chunking strategies** in the **Unstructured tool**: **Basic** and **By Title**. Both of these strategies are based on recognizing the document's **semantic structure**, rather than simply splitting text by blank lines or newline characters.

- The **Basic strategy** sequentially merges text elements into the same chunk until reaching the maximum character count (`max_characters`) or a soft limit (`new_after_n_chars`). If a single element (such as a particularly long body paragraph or a large table) exceeds the maximum character count by itself, it will be further split. **Table elements** are treated as independent chunks; if a table is too large, it will also be split into multiple **TableChunks**. Chunk overlap can be configured using the `overlap` and `overlap_all` parameters.
- The **By Title strategy**, while retaining the base behavior of the Basic strategy, immediately closes the current chunk and starts a new one when a new **title (Title element)** is detected. Additional behavior, such as merging or splitting cross-page fragments and short segments, can be further controlled using the `multipage_sections` and `combine_text_under_n_chars` parameters.

In addition, when calling the **Unstructured tool** via API, there are two extra smart chunking strategies available:

- **By page**: Ensures that the content of each page is chunked independently
- **By similarity**: Uses embedding models to group thematically similar elements into chunks

Next, we will apply the two main chunking strategies above to the same file:

```
from langchain_unstructured import UnstructuredLoader
loader = UnstructuredLoader(
"data/black myth/The setting of Black Myth Wukong.txt",
chunking_strategy="basic",  # Specify chunking strategy as Basic
max_characters=1000,
include_orig_elements=False # Do not retain original element information; only keep merged text chunks
)
docs = loader.load()
print("Number of Documents after chunking in LangChain:", len(docs))
print("Text length of the first chunk:", len(docs[0].page_content))
```

```
Number of LangChain Documents after chunking: 9
Text length of the first chunk: 815
```

If we change the strategy, we will get different results:

```
loader = UnstructuredLoader(
"data/BlackMyth/BlackMythWukongSettings.txt",
chunking_strategy="by_title",  # Specify the chunking strategy as By Title, chunking by title
)
```

```
Number of LangChain Documents after chunking: 9
Text length of the first chunk: 627
```

You can compare the results of the two **chunking strategies** yourself. In theory, the **By Title** strategy is a more intelligent way of chunking, no longer relying on traditional line breaks and blank lines. Instead, it is based on precise recognition of the document's logical structure (such as **titles, paragraphs, tables**, etc.), which improves the accuracy and usability of text splitting.

Using LlamaIndex SemanticSplitterNodeParser for semantic chunking

Semantic chunking is an advanced and complex text processing technique, different from chunking methods based on a fixed number of characters. A **semantic chunker** adaptively selects breakpoints between sentences using **embedding similarity** to ensure that each chunk is semantically coherent. In **LlamaIndex**, text chunks are referred to as **Nodes**, and the chunking tool is called a **NodeParser**. **SemanticSplitterNodeParser** is a tool for semantic chunking implementation.

The following code example demonstrates how to use **SemanticSplitterNodeParser** for semantic chunking (refer to `https://github.com/PacktPublishing/RAG-from-First-Principles` for the complete code):

```
from llama_index.core import SimpleDirectoryReader
from llama_index.core.node_parser import (
SentenceSplitter,
SemanticSplitterNodeParser,
)
from llama_index.embeddings.huggingface import HuggingFaceEmbedding
embed_model = HuggingFaceEmbedding(model_name="BAAI/bge-small-zh")
documents = SimpleDirectoryReader(input_files=["data/black myth/The
setting of Black Myth Wukong.txt"]).load_data()
### Create a Semantic Chunker
splitter = SemanticSplitterNodeParser(
buffer_size=1,  # Buffer size
breakpoint_percentile_threshold=95, # Breakpoint percentile threshold
embed_model=embed_model # Embedding model to use
)
### Create a Basic Sentence Chunker for Comparison
base_splitter = SentenceSplitter(chunk_size=512)
### Use the Semantic Chunker to Split the Document
semantic_nodes = splitter.get_nodes_from_documents(documents)
print("Number of chunks generated by the semantic splitter:",
len(semantic_nodes))
### Chunking Documents Using the Basic Sentence Splitter
base_nodes = base_splitter.get_nodes_from_documents(documents)
```

```
print("Number of chunks generated by the basic sentence splitter:",
len(base_nodes))
```

```
Number of chunks generated by the semantic splitter: 4
Number of chunks generated by the basic sentence splitter: 29
```

Due to space limitations, the specific content inside each **Node** is not shown here. After running the above program, you will notice that the **semantic splitter** organizes the content as much as possible, while the **basic sentence splitter** simply splits based on the preset length.

LlamaIndex provides more advanced **semantic chunking** tools, such as the following two:

- **SemanticDoubleMergingSplitterNodeParser** (Double Semantic Merging Splitter) segments text into semantically consistent segments through multiple merging strategies. It considers multiple thresholds to ensure that chunking both captures topic changes and merges nearby semantic units whenever appropriate.
- **TopicNodeParser** (Topic Node Chunker) splits documents into semantically consistent text blocks based on topic similarity. It can use large models or embedding models for topic similarity calculation, thereby maintaining semantic consistency between text blocks.

For the same set of documents, you can try different tools and compare their chunking results, performance, and efficiency. Because of their complex design, **semantic chunking** tools take longer to process the same batch of documents. In general RAG system design, **recursive chunking** is usually sufficient and does not necessarily require semantic chunking methods. According to Occam's Razor, choosing simple and effective tools is the wiser choice.

Advanced indexing techniques related to chunking

In RAG systems, **index construction** broadly refers to establishing a data storage mechanism for **text chunks**, in which the "data" includes both the **embedding vectors** and the **metadata** of the text chunks. This mechanism is designed to optimize **retrieval effectiveness** as much as possible, enabling the system to quickly locate the content most relevant to a query from vast amounts of data, thereby generating contextually relevant responses.

Alex: Are there techniques in the RAG system index construction process that are very closely related to chunking technology?

Lewis: Of course there are. The following examples will give you great inspiration for hands-on project work.

Sentence splitting with sliding window

LlamaIndex provides a chunking tool called **SentenceWindowNodeParser**, which can parse courses into single-sentence nodes while creating a **window** in the metadata for each node that contains the sentences on either side of the node. During retrieval, a single sentence is first matched with the query, then the surrounding sentences are found based on the window, and finally the overall content is passed to the large model.

Here's an example showing document segmentation with sentences grouped and highlighted in columns:

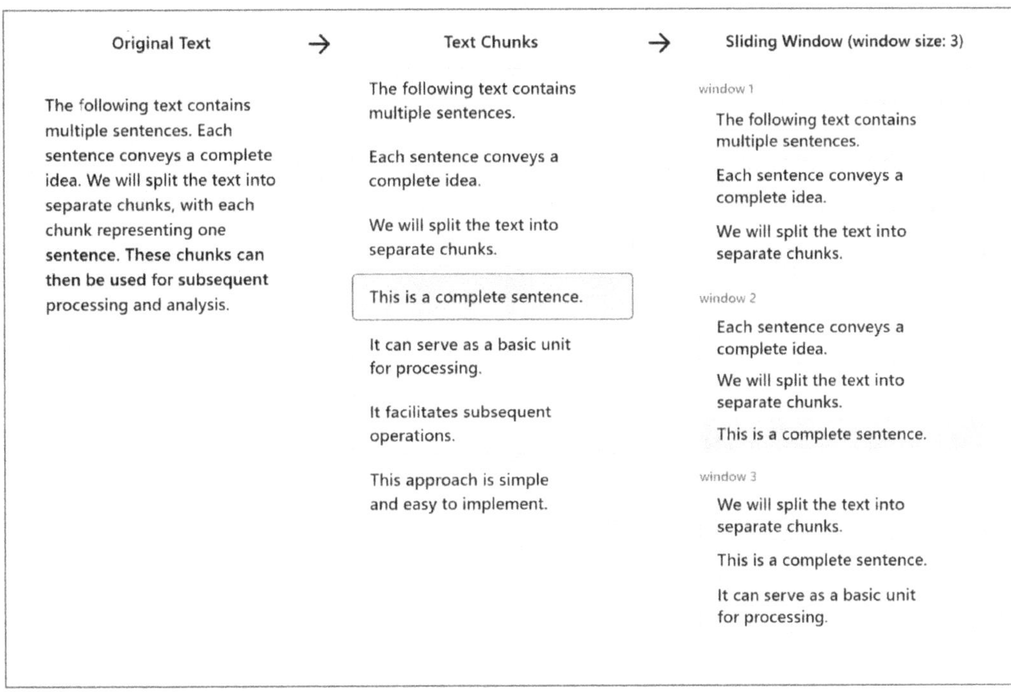

Figure 2.10: Document segmentation

The following code example demonstrates how to use **SentenceWindowNodeParser** to chunk sentences:

```
from llama_index.core.node_parser import SentenceWindowNodeParser
from llama_index.core.node_parser import SentenceSplitter
node_parser = SentenceWindowNodeParser.from_defaults(
window_size=3,  # Set the window size to 3 sentences
window_metadata_key="window",  # Set the window metadata key to "window"
original_text_metadata_key="original_text",  # Set the original text
```

```
    metadata key to "original_text"
)
nodes = node_parser.get_nodes_from_documents(documents)
sentence_index = VectorStoreIndex(nodes)
```

This technique is useful for indexing large courses, as it not only helps retrieve finer-grained details but also preserves a large amount of **context**.

Mixed generation of parent and child text blocks during chunking

In the process of course chunking, balancing the **accuracy of small data chunks** and the **completeness of the larger context** is a key challenge. **LangChain** provides a retriever called **ParentDocumentRetriever** specifically to solve this problem.

When chunking courses, **ParentDocumentRetriever** first divides the original course into larger **parent text blocks**, and then further subdivides these parent text blocks into smaller **child text blocks**. Each child block retains an **ID** referencing its parent block, thereby ensuring coherence and traceability of information.

Here's how parent and child chunks are treated and grouped:

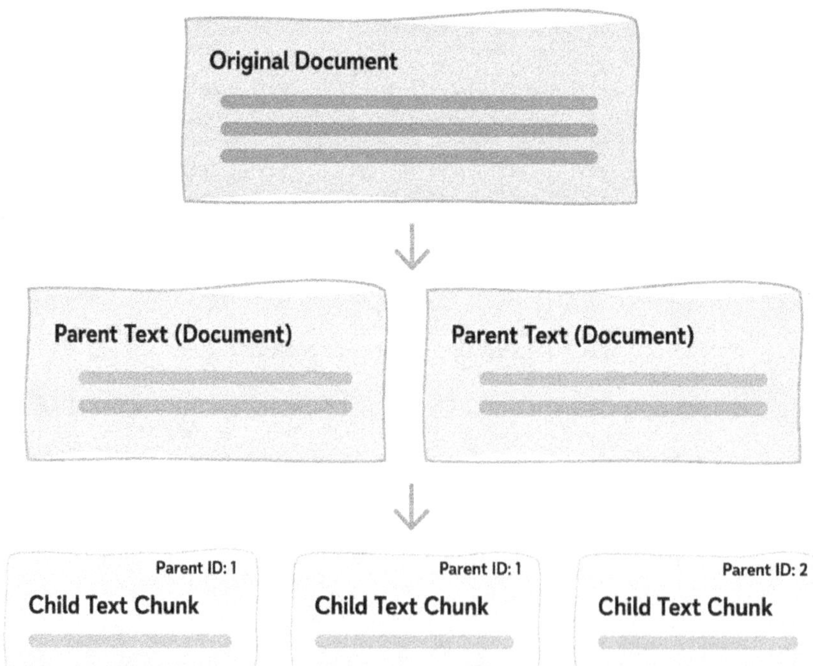

Figure 2.11: The hierarchy from an original document to parent and child text blocks

During the storage phase, **embedding vectors** are generated for the child text blocks and stored in a **vector database**, while the parent text blocks are stored separately. These two storages are linked by the **parent text block 's ID**.

The following figure shows a parent document and child chunk stored with vector embedding data:

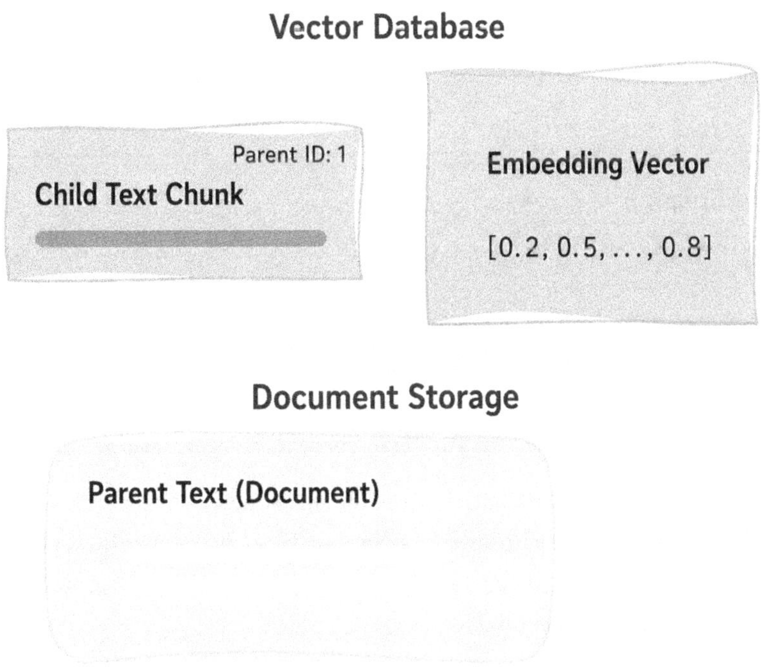

Figure 2.12: A parent document and child chunk stored with vector embedding data

During the retrieval phase, the system finds the **child text blocks** most relevant to the query. In the generation phase, the corresponding **parent text blocks** are located using their IDs, and both are combined and passed to the **large model**, thereby providing richer and more accurate responses.

Here's an example showing how a query leading to a child text block is linked to a parent text block:

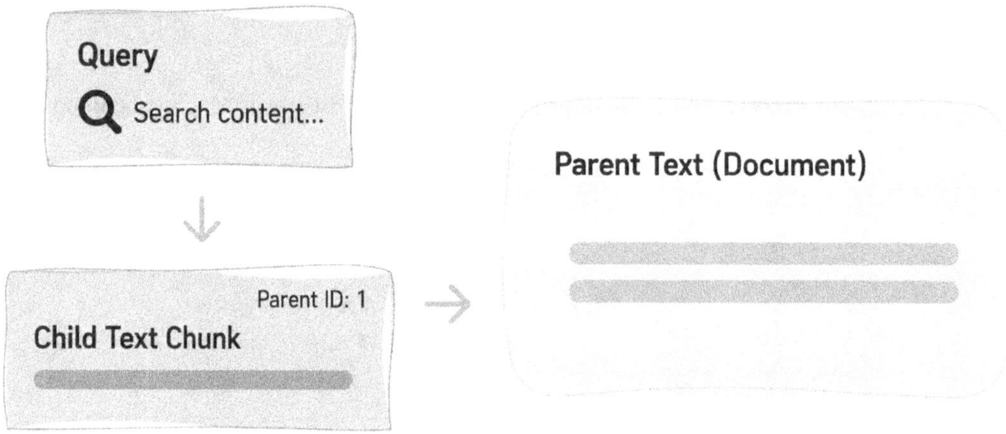

Figure 2.13: A query invoking the parent text block via the child text block

This approach finds a balance between course splitting, embedding, and retrieval, which both improves retrieval accuracy and retains sufficient contextual information.

Alex: Lewis, when introducing the **Unstructured** tool in Section 1, the metadata parsed from **Elements** also contains similar information on **parent text blocks (parent elements)**. This method can also be applied to extend the current element, which is equivalent to automatically expanding the context during the generation phase.

Lewis: Absolutely! That's a great example of drawing inferences from one instance.

Creating metadata for text chunks during chunking

Another effective strategy to improve indexing accuracy is to add **metadata** that can serve as filtering criteria to text chunks during the chunking process. This **metadata** can then be leveraged to enhance retrieval efficiency, enabling more precise identification of the information you need.

For example, common types of **metadata** include examples, page numbers, timestamps, type, and course title, which can be used to mark and describe the fundamental attributes of a course.

The following figure shows metadata fields such as `file name`, `page` and `year` for 2024 financial report data:

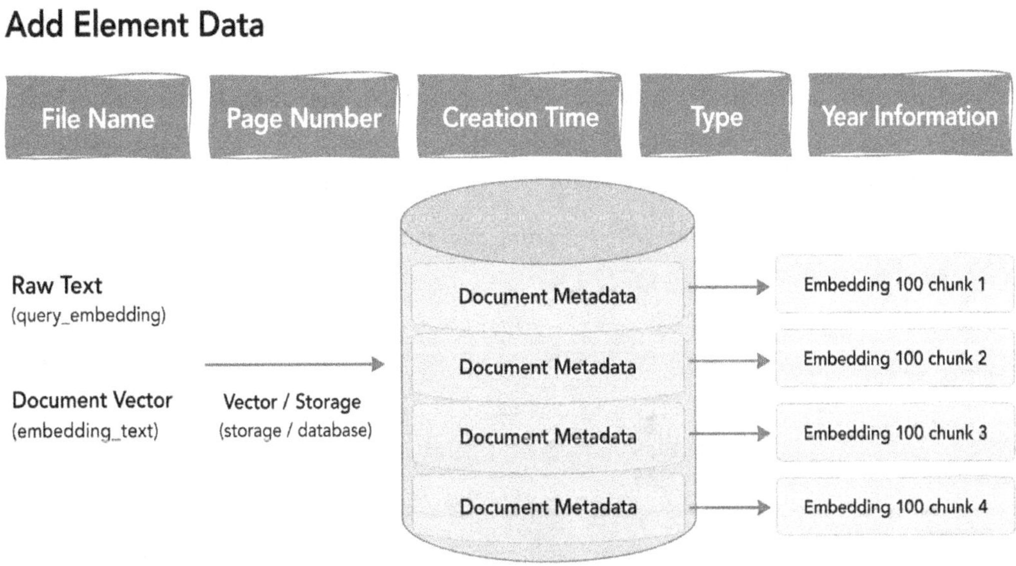

Figure 2.14: Metadata fields

During retrieval, in addition to semantic-based retrieval, these **metadata** can also serve as extra filtering conditions to further enhance the relevance of generated results. For example, content within a specific time frame can be filtered by **timestamp**, or the retrieval scope can be limited to text of a certain **category**.

The following code example demonstrates how to use the **Milvus** vector database to implement conditional filtering:

```
filter_expr = 'type == "BOSS battle" and difficulty == "Hard"'
results = collection.search(
    data=[search_embedding],
    anns_field="embedding",
    param=search_params,
    limit=5,
    expr=filter_expr, # Only return results that meet the metadata
filtering conditions
    output_fields=["yokai", "battle_scene", "difficulty"]
)
```

In addition to explicit filtering using metadata, you can also utilize **Hypothetical Document Embeddings (HyDE)** technology to enhance retrieval effectiveness (Gao et al., 2022). The core idea behind **HyDE** is to first use a large model (such as **GPT**) to generate a hypothetical document based on the user's query, then convert that document into a vector for retrieval in order to find the real document with the closest semantics.

The following architecture shows GPT generating passages in English and Korean matched with real document info:

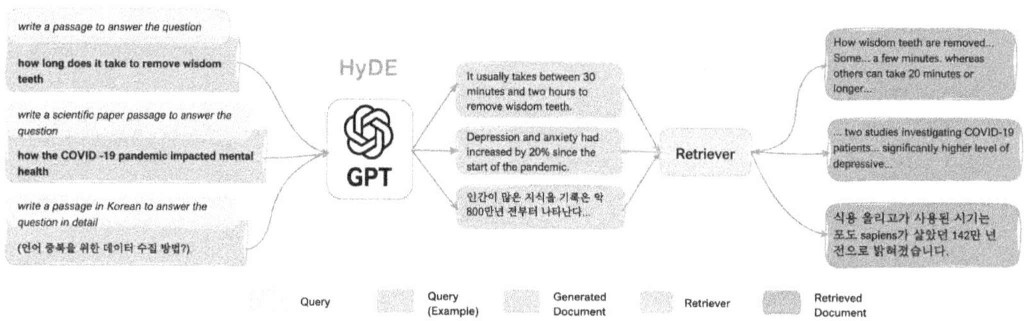

Figure 2.15: GPT generating text in English and Korean

Workflow of HyDE technology

This approach is usually more effective than directly querying the original vectors because the documents generated by **HyDE technology** can better capture the underlying intent of the query and provide more relevant results.

Forming hierarchical indices during chunking

Following the idea of **metadata construction** in section 2.6.3, the next strategy to introduce is manually constructing **metadata** during chunking and forming **hierarchical indexes.** The core idea of this strategy is to enhance retrieval and generation effectiveness through hierarchical organization of the corpus.

In fact, this approach is similar to the **sliding window technique** and the **parent-child text block technique**, all aiming to optimize **RAG systems** by forming a document hierarchy. This section will introduce the **Summary→Document technique** as well as the **Document→Embedded Objects technique**.

Traditional **full-text search** may yield too many irrelevant documents. The essence of the **Summary→Document technique** is to create a summary and associated nodes for each text chunk during chunking; during retrieval, document summaries are retrieved first instead of the full document, and then expanded to the associated documents. This more accurately captures user intent, improves retrieval efficiency, and enhances result relevance.

Here's an example of a search query leading to document summaries and node details:

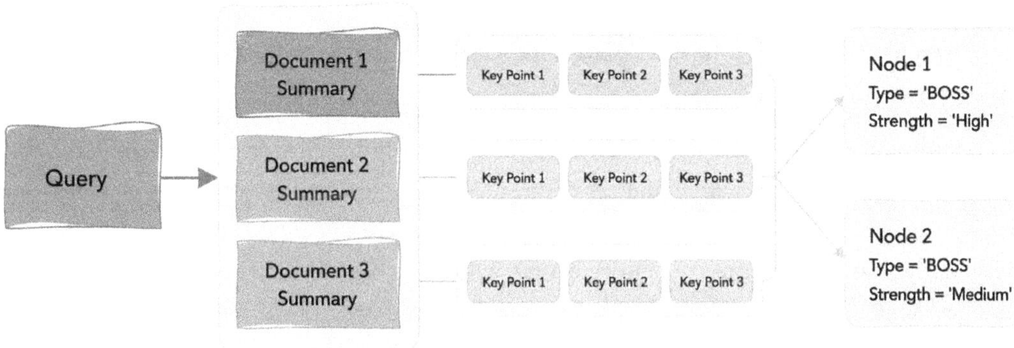

Figure 2.16: A search query

For example, when a user queries **"latest sports news"**, the system will first locate the **summaries** of relevant documents, then further retrieve the full documents containing those summaries and their associated nodes, ensuring not only that core content is retrieved but also that additional background information is provided. This method is especially effective in managing long documents and multi-level documents.

The following code example demonstrates the specific implementation of the **Summary→Document technique**:

```
from langchain_unstructured import UnstructuredLoader
from langchain_core.documents import Document
from langchain_deepseek import ChatDeepSeek
from langchain.chains import StuffDocumentsChain
loader = UnstructuredLoader("data/black myth/q1 The settings of Wukong.
txt.pdf")
documents = loader.load()
llm = ChatDeepSeek(model="deepseek-chat")
for doc in documents[:5]:
    response = llm.invoke(f"Please briefly summarize the following content
in Chinese:\n\n{doc.page_content}")
    doc.metadata['summary'] = response.content # Add the summary to the
metadata
print(documents)
```

In this example, the first paragraph of text is summarized through a large language model and saved in the **metadata**. In frameworks such as **LangChain** and **LlamaIndex**, there are also tools that can automatically generate summaries for text blocks, such as the **DocumentSummaryIndex** in LlamaIndex.

Document embedded object technology for complex data structures

The **Document→Embedded Object technology** is specifically designed to perform special chunking for courses containing complex data structures. When a course contains not only plain text but also structured content such as **tables, images, database references**, etc., traditional chunking methods typically only return the entire course while ignoring these critical data. In contrast, the Document→Embedded Object technology preserves the structure of complex objects during the chunking process. This method first matches the course itself and then further retrieves the embedded objects.

During retrieval, the Document→Embedded Object technology first identifies and retrieves the entity-referenced objects (main text blocks) in the course, and then queries other related content of these objects as needed, such as **tables, image information**, and other **sub-nodes**. This approach can better handle the diverse content in complex courses, making the retrieval results more precise and comprehensive.

Here's an example showing how knowledge base documents are split into nodes, text blocks, and a database:

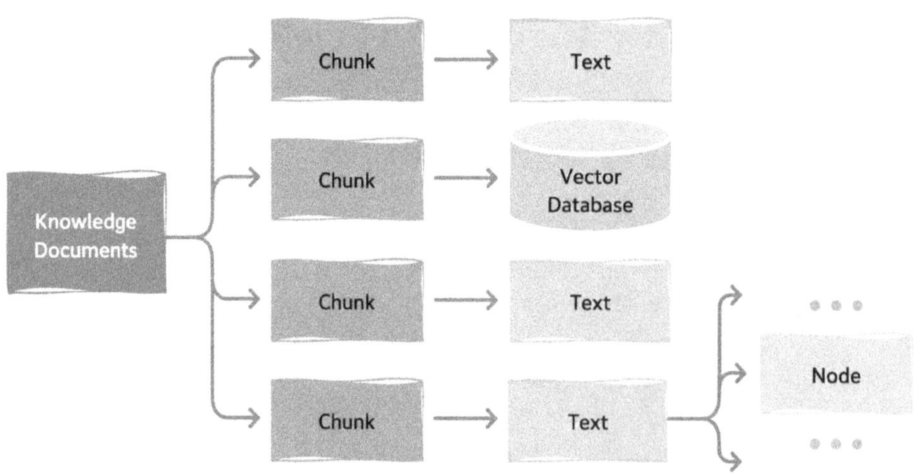

Figure 2.17: Split operation on knowledge base documents

For example, when querying **What BOSSes are there in 'Black Myth: Wukong'**, the system will not only find the relevant game documentation, but will also further analyze the tables, SQL data tables, etc., within it to ensure the returned information is more accurate and better meets the query requirements. This approach is especially important for **multimodal information retrieval scenarios** such as technical documentation, game databases, and enterprise knowledge bases, making information extraction more comprehensive and accurate.

In **LlamaIndex**, you can establish a hierarchical index for table objects under the main course via the `IndexNode` object. For more advanced examples of LlamaIndex, please refer to the official documentation.

The above-mentioned techniques essentially optimize the retrieval process by establishing hierarchical relationships within document content. They enable **RAG systems** to more intelligently understand and leverage structured information in documents, thereby providing more accurate and comprehensive retrieval results.

Summary

Text chunking plays a crucial role in the RAG workflow. It not only addresses the limitation of **context windows** but can also significantly enhance model performance in tasks like generation and retrieval. Different chunking strategies and tools have their own characteristics when processing text. For example, chunking by number of characters or tokens is suitable for quickly handling well-structured text, while **semantic chunking** can more accurately capture semantic consistency within the text.

Additionally, selecting the appropriate chunking tool for specific scenarios, along with techniques such as **sliding window methods** and **metadata construction** (such as extracting summaries and labels for each text chunk), can further improve the effectiveness and applicability of chunking.

As the context window size of large models continues to expand, the importance of chunking techniques may not be as prominent as before. However, flexibly choosing **chunking strategies** and optimizing them according to actual needs remains an important means to improve efficiency and quality in text processing.

By adopting various approaches during the chunking process—such as **semantic chunking, hierarchical chunking, metadata generation**, and **summary construction** for text chunks—we can gain new perspectives on optimizing RAG systems.

In the next chapter, we will cover various aspects of embedding technology from its origins to the latest developments. We'll also provide many concrete practical examples to help learners understand and practice.

Subscribe for a free eBook

New frameworks, evolving architectures, research drops, production breakdowns – *AI_Distilled* filters the noise into a weekly briefing for engineers and researchers working hands-on with LLMs and generative AI systems. Subscribe now and receive a free eBook, along with weekly insights that help you stay focused and informed.

Subscribe at `https://packt.link/8Oz6Y` or scan the QR code below.

3

Information Embedding

Alex: Lewis, after text chunking, the next step should be **Embedding**, also known as **embedding technology**. I know that **vector embeddings** are the knowledge core of modern AI systems, and of course, also the core of **RAG systems**. Their importance goes without saying.

Lewis: Of course. Today, large models can absorb world-class knowledge perhaps more efficiently and faster than we humans do. You can think of a well-trained large model as an unimaginably huge library, or a crystal ball of knowledge, filled with all the books, blogs, audio, and video information it could possibly collect from humanity. Every book, every web page, every video segment is magically transformed into a string of numbers, all thanks to embedding technology.

Embedding: Encoding external information

Before delving into technical details, let's use the human brain as an analogy: how do we perceive external information, encode it, and store it? This is a complex, multi-layered biological and neural process. First, external information enters the brain through the senses (such as **vision**, **hearing**, **touch**, **smell**, and **taste**). Each sense has specialized receptors responsible for converting physical or chemical stimuli (like light, sound waves, pressure, chemical molecules) into neural signals. These neural signals are transmitted via the peripheral nervous system, passing through the spinal cord or other relay stations (like the thalamus) to the corresponding areas of the brain.

Once neural signals reach the brain, they are processed by cortical regions. This step is known as **information encoding**, which mainly includes the following two coding methods.

- **Spatial encoding**: The brain represents different stimuli by activating neurons in different locations. For example, different parts of the visual cortex correspond to different regions in the visual field.

- **Temporal encoding**: The frequency and temporal pattern of neuronal firing also carry information. Neurons emit electrical impulses at specific rates and sequences to represent different sensory features (such as pitch, intensity, etc.).

After processing and encoding by the cerebral cortex, information is stored short-term, and then consolidated in long-term memory. The brain can retrieve information from long-term memory and reactivate it in **working memory** through memory recall. Each time a memory is retrieved, the brain reprocesses the information, which may also result in the information being re-encoded and updated.

As external information continuously flows in, the neural networks in the brain change. This change is called **neural plasticity**, meaning the brain's structure and function can constantly adjust based on experience and learning. During this process, synaptic connections between neurons may be strengthened or weakened, and new synaptic connections can even be formed. The entire process involves complex connections and **synaptic plasticity** between neurons, enabling us to perceive, understand, and remember information from the external world.

Similarly, **embedding** is the process by which AI systems based on large models "perceive" and internalize information from the external world. It is the core part of the **RAG system** responsible for perceiving, understanding, and expressing external data, and is a key tool for understanding and processing high-dimensional data.

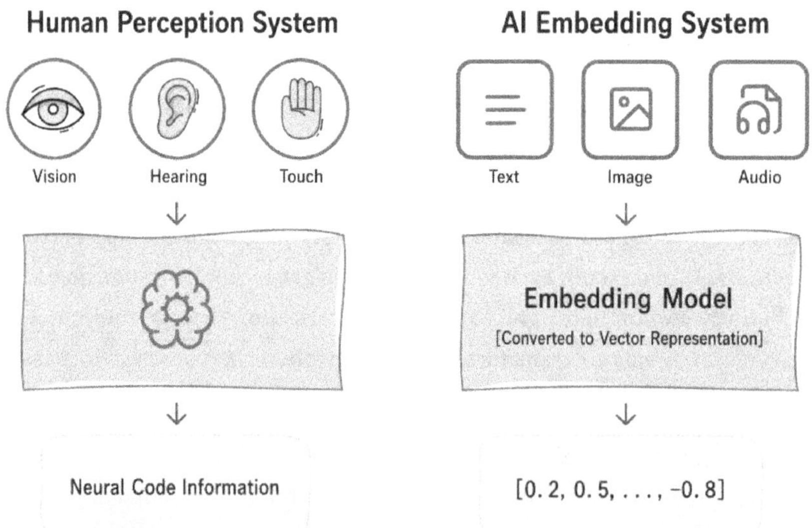

Figure 3.1: Comparison between human sensory system and AI embedding system showing parallel information flows

Just as the brain perceives external information through vision, hearing, touch, and so on, **embedding models** allow the system to "perceive" the semantic content of data by converting text, images, audio, and other data from natural language into vector representations.

The perceptual system not only possesses **sensory functions** but can also integrate different types of sensory inputs—the things seen by the eyes and heard by the ears are comprehensively processed by the brain. Similarly, **embedding models** are capable of handling not just text, but also images, audio, and other multimodal data, converting these different modalities into the same vector space, so information from various sources can be processed consistently.

Perceptual information and memory (and even the **subconscious** formed by the internalization of this information and memory) influence a person's actions. In the same way, the quality of the **embedding model** directly affects subsequent retrieval and generation processes. An excellent embedding model can help **vector databases** find the most relevant information, thereby guiding the system to generate more accurate answers; conversely, a poor embedding model may cause the system's "perception" of a query to be biased, affecting the accuracy of the generated results.

A person's perceptual system becomes more sensitive and precise with accumulated experience. Similarly, **embedding models** can also continuously improve their performance through training and **fine-tuning**, enabling AI embedding systems to capture semantic meaning more accurately, thereby enhancing the performance of **RAG systems**.

> The choice of an embedding model may be one of the most important and decisive steps in the development process of a RAG system. Without a strong embedding model, it is almost impossible for the subsequent retrieval and generation stages to produce satisfactory results. However, this does not mean that simply choosing the top-ranked embedding model will guarantee superior performance in a RAG system, because factors such as indexing methods and retrieval strategies must also be considered.
>
> In practical applications, the choice of embedding model is often constrained by factors such as cost, speed, and privacy. For example, although OpenAI's embedding models perform very well, if the data cannot be sent externally due to privacy concerns, an open-source model deployed locally may be required. In such cases, the key is no longer to find the "best" model, but to balance the available options and choose the most suitable local model.

From a technical perspective, by mapping discrete data (such as words, sentences, or images) into a continuous **vector space**, embedding models are able to capture the semantic and syntactic relationships between data.

These numbers are not simply 0s and 1s, but complex **high-dimensional vectors** containing rich semantic information as well as world-class knowledge.

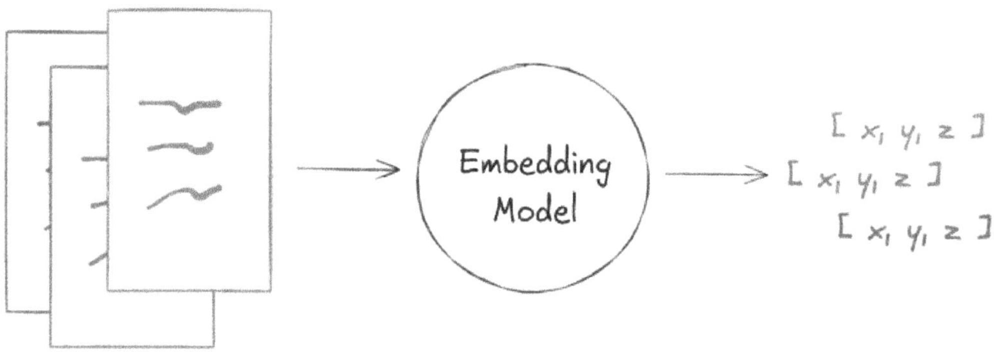

Figure 3.2: Three layered inputs enter embedding model producing different vectors as output

> The dimension of an embedding, which may be any value such as 512, 768, or 1024, is like assigning each word a position in a multidimensional space. Each dimension can be viewed as a feature that helps describe meaning, such as topic, sentiment, entity type, or other semantic characteristics. Every word defines itself through these features.
>
> The higher the number of dimensions, the richer the details that can be represented, but the computational complexity also increases. Choosing an appropriate embedding dimension is key to enabling a large model to understand word meanings accurately without causing performance degradation.

Each embedding dimension is essentially a set of **coordinates** (vector, also known as a vector), usually situated in a **high-dimensional space**. In this space, the position of each point (embedding) reflects the meaning of its corresponding text. Just as similar words in a thesaurus are likely to be close to each other, similar concepts will also end up close to each other in this embedding space. This allows us to intuitively compare different texts.

By simplifying text to these numerical representations, we can use simple mathematical operations to rapidly measure the similarity between two pieces of text, without regard for their original length or structure. In this way, we turn the comparison of two texts, two images, or two pieces of video into an operation on numerical differences—this is the fundamental principle that enables retrieval in **RAG systems**. This also echoes Pythagoras's famous saying: Everything is a number.

Measuring similarity between vectors

Some common **metrics** are as follows:

- **Euclidean distance**: Measures the straight-line distance between two points.
- **Manhattan distance**: Measures the distance between two points along the axes (not the straight-line distance); this metric is less commonly used to compare vector similarity.
- **Cosine similarity**: Measures the cosine value of the angle between two vectors.
- **Dot product** or **inner product (IP)**: Measures the projection of one vector onto another. In Euclidean space, the inner product and dot product are equivalent.

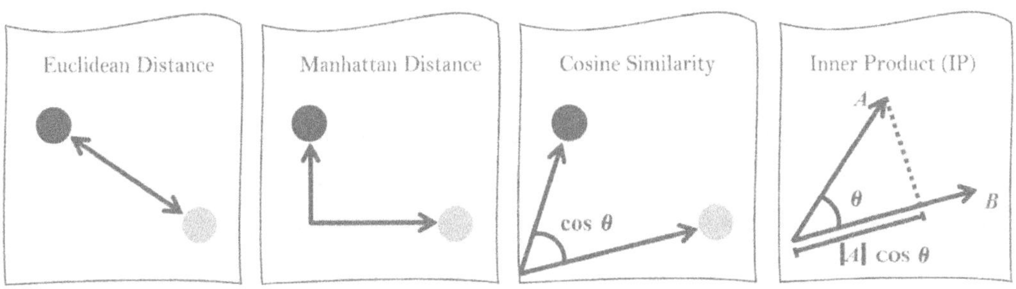

Figure 3.3: Four panels explaining Euclidean distance, Manhattan distance, cosine similarity, and inner product

The choice of **similarity metric** should be based on the specific application scenario. For example, **OpenAI** recommends using **cosine similarity** to measure its embeddings. A code example is as follows:

```
import numpy as np
def cosine_similarity(vec1, vec2):
    dot_product = np.dot(vec1, vec2)
    norm_vec1 = np.linalg.norm(vec1)
    norm_vec2 = np.linalg.norm(vec2)
    return dot_product / (norm_vec1 * norm_vec2)
similarity = cosine_similarity(query_result, document_result)
print("Cosine Similarity:", similarity)
```

That covers the basics of **embeddings**. Welcome to the world of **data vectors**, where the pulsating information forms the core component of **RAG systems**.

From early word embedding models to large model embeddings

Over the years, the landscape of **embedding models** has undergone significant changes. From the earliest word vector models such as *Word2Vec* and *GloVe*, to dynamic embedding methods based on deep learning, embedding technology has developed and evolved rapidly. Early models mainly focused on **word-level embeddings**, but as demands became more complex, the focus gradually shifted to models capable of handling sentences and paragraphs. In 2018, there was a key turning point—Google introduced **BERT** (Bidirectional Encoder Representations from Transformers). By leveraging the **Transformer model**, BERT transformed text into concise vector representations, achieving unprecedented performance improvements across various natural language processing tasks.

However, BERT was not optimized for efficiently generating **sentence-level embeddings**. This limitation led to the creation of **Sentence-BERT**, which later evolved into the well-known *SentenceTransformers* framework. This framework now supports training and deploying a variety of open-source embedding models. Sentence-BERT modified the original BERT architecture to generate semantically rich sentence embeddings, greatly reducing the computational cost of tasks such as finding similar sentences.

Today, the **embedding model ecosystem** is characterized by diversity, with numerous service providers offering their own embedding solutions. To address this diversity, researchers and practitioners often rely on evaluation standards such as **large-scale text embedding benchmarks** to objectively compare various embedding models.

Early word embedding models

Word2Vec is a **word embedding model** proposed by Google, which includes two architectures: **Continuous Bag-of-Words (CBOW)** and **Skip-Gram**. This model learns low-dimensional vector representations of words by predicting the relationship between target words and context words. Despite its relatively simple mechanism, **Word2Vec** can effectively capture the semantic similarity between words, and after training, generates word vectors containing semantic information. This marked an important step into the fascinating world of word vectors and laid a foundation for the era of large-scale models.

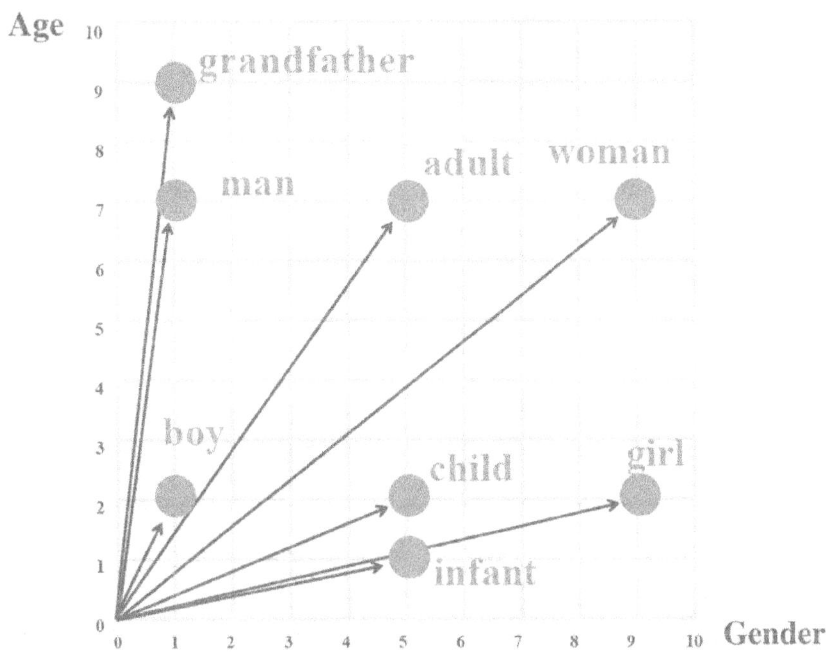

Figure 3.4: Scatter plot with arrows illustrating stages of life, labeled as grandfather, man, adult, woman, boy, girl, child, and infant

GloVe (*Global Vectors for Word Representation*) is another word embedding method proposed by Stanford University. Unlike **Word2Vec**, **GloVe** leverages a global co-occurrence matrix and trains the model by constructing a loss function based on word co-occurrence probabilities. This approach performs excellently in handling sparse data and capturing global semantic information.

FastText is a word embedding model proposed by the **Facebook AI Research** team. Its uniqueness lies in considering subword information by decomposing words into character n-grams. This strategy makes **FastText** more effective when handling out-of-vocabulary words and word morphological variations, thereby enhancing the model's generalization ability.

Contextual word embedding models

Although traditional **word embedding models** (such as **Word2Vec**, **GloVe**, **FastText**) have achieved significant success in capturing semantic similarity between words, the embeddings they generate are **static**. This means that each word is assigned the same vector representation no matter its context, leading to poor performance when dealing with polysemous words and complex contexts. To address this limitation, researchers developed **contextual word embedding**

models, which allow word representations to dynamically change depending on their specific context, thereby more accurately reflecting word meanings.

ELMo (Embeddings from Language Models), proposed by the AllenNLP team, is a **language model** based on **bidirectional LSTM**. It can dynamically generate word embeddings according to a word's context, allowing the same word to have different vector representations in different contexts. This provides a better way to capture word polysemy.

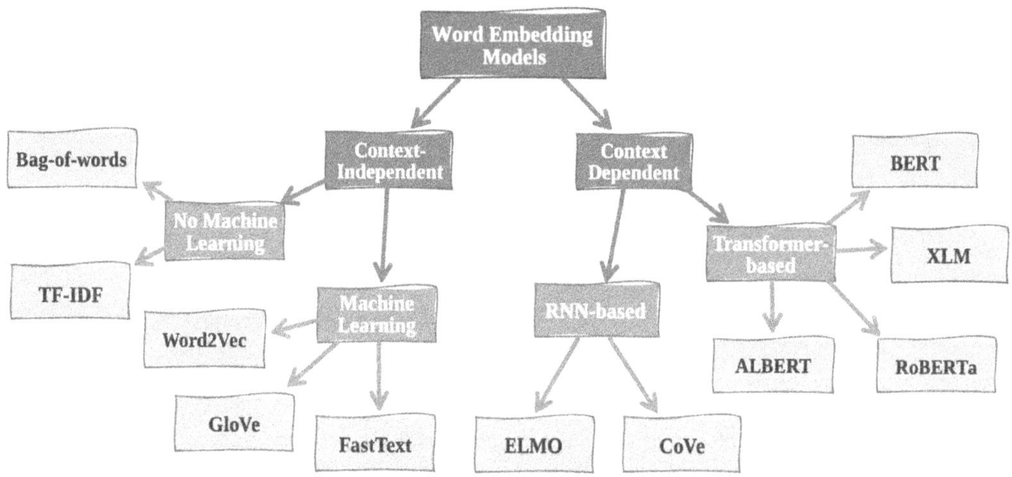

Figure 3.5: A flowchart of word embedding models branching into context-independent and context-dependent methods

If you are interested in the foundational architecture of large models such as the **Transformer**, or the technical details of various word embedding models, you can refer to the relevant papers for each model to learn more. Additionally, you can read the course *GPT Illustrated: How Large Models Are Built* by Lewis. This course provides an approachable yet in-depth explanation of various core technologies in natural language processing.

Sentence embedding models and the SentenceTransformers framework

Sentence-BERT (SBERT) is an extension of **BERT** designed to generate fixed-length vector representations for sentences. By adding a **twin-tower architecture** and **contrastive learning** training methods to BERT, SBERT can efficiently compute semantic similarity between sentences, making it suitable for scenarios such as **information retrieval** and **question answering systems**.

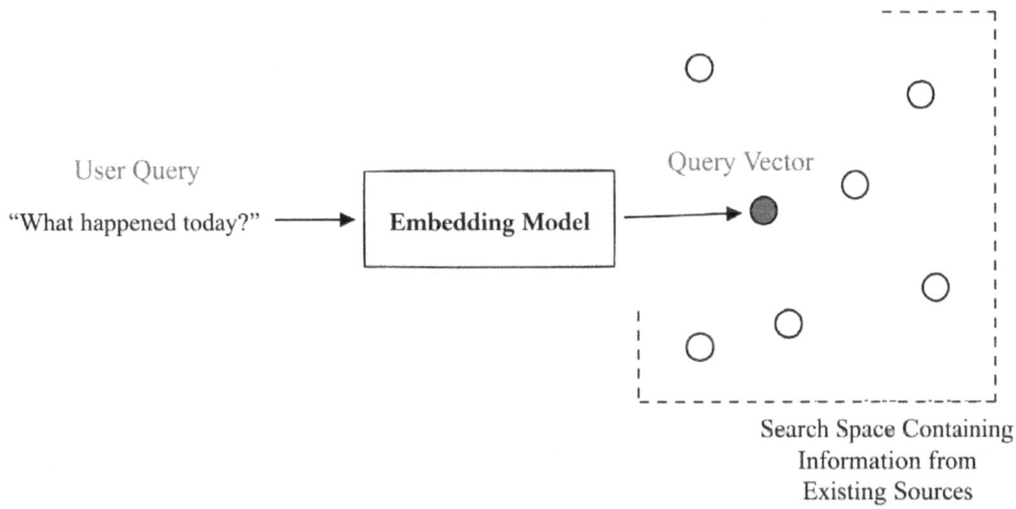

Figure 3.6: A flowchart showing a user query processed by an embedding model and plotted as a vector

To date, SBERT is still widely used in the industry, though it has since been renamed as the **SentenceTransformers** framework. This framework is the most commonly used foundational Python library for downloading, fine-tuning, and training text and image embedding models.

> The SentenceTransformers framework was created by UKPLab and is maintained by Hugging Face. Hugging Face provides more than 5,000 pre-trained SentenceTransformers models, including many advanced models that appear on the MTEB leaderboard. Using the SentenceTransformers framework, models can also be easily trained or fine-tuned to meet the requirements of specific use cases.

In the **SentenceTransformers** framework, commonly used open-source embedding models include `all-MiniLM-L6-v2` and `all-mpnet-base-v2`. These two models are based on the **MiniLM architecture** (a lightweight Transformer model) and the **MPNet architecture** (which combines the strengths of BERT and XLNet), respectively, and both are optimized using Hugging Face's `transformers` library. They are often used as baseline models in **RAG systems**, where their performance serves as a foundation for evaluating the advantages or improvements of other models. Among them, the `all-mpnet-base-v2` model provides higher embedding quality, while the `all-MiniLM-L6-v2` model is known for being about 5 times faster than the former.

Model name	Parameters	Embedding dimension	Features/ strengths	Weaknesses/ limitations	Application scenarios
paraphrase-MiniLM-L6-v2	33M	384	Specially optimized for text similarity and semantic retrieval; efficient and suitable for low-resource environments.	Lower embedding dimension may limit performance in more complex semantic tasks.	Comparing sentence or paragraph similarity; suitable for common natural language processing tasks.
all-MiniLM-L6-v2	33M	384	Broadly trained for different use cases; fast inference speed and good overall performance.	Weaker multilingual support compared with larger or multilingual models.	Search engine optimization, semantic search, sentence similarity, and lightweight retrieval tasks.
all-mpnet-base-v2	110M	768	Larger MPNet-based model with stronger semantic representation and higher accuracy.	Requires more computing resources than MiniLM-based models.	High-precision semantic retrieval, ranking, clustering, and applications requiring greater accuracy.

Table 3.1: Comparison of selected **SentenceTransformer** *embedding models, including model size, embedding dimension, strengths, limitations, and application scenarios*

Computing semantic similarity between two sentences

We will now use models from the **sentence-transformers** library to compare similarity between two sentences.

First, install the **sentence-transformers** library.

```
pip install sentence-transformers
```

Next, compute the **semantic similarity** between two sentences using the following code:

```
from sentence_transformers import SentenceTransformer, util
model = SentenceTransformer('paraphrase-MiniLM-L6-v2')
sentence1 = "How is the gameplay of this game?"
sentence2 = "I want to learn about the combat system of this one."
embedding1 = model.encode(sentence1, convert_to_tensor=True)
embedding2 = model.encode(sentence2, convert_to_tensor=True)
cosine_similarity = util.pytorch_cos_sim(embedding1, embedding2)
print(f"The similarity between the two sentences is: {cosine_similarity.
item():.4f}")
```

When running the program for the first time, the **SentenceTransformers** framework will download the configuration and parameters of the specified pre-trained model to the local cache. Make sure there is sufficient storage space for the downloaded model files.

The **sentence-transformers** library relies on **Hugging Face's**'s model storage mechanism, and by default uses Hugging Face's cache folder `path`.

- **Cache folder path on Windows operating systems:** `C:\Users\<username>\.cache\huggingface\transformers`
- **Cache folder path on macOS or Linux operating systems:** `/home/<username>/.cache/huggingface/transformers`

When loading a model (such as *paraphrase-MiniLM-L6-v2*) for the first time, the model files are downloaded and stored in the above directory. If the same model has been previously downloaded using Hugging Face, it will not be downloaded again. You can customize the cache path by setting the **TRANSFORMERS_CACHE** environment variable.

```
export TRANSFORMERS_CACHE="your custom cache path"
```

Multilingual embedding models

Although early **word embeddings** and **sentence embedding models** performed well in monolingual settings, they faced challenges in cross-lingual tasks and were difficult to apply directly. To address this issue, some embedding models specifically designed for multilingual environments (such as **MUSE** and **XLM-R**) emerged.

MUSE (**Multilingual Unsupervised or Supervised Embeddings**) is a multilingual word embedding tool developed by Facebook (now Meta). It supports both unsupervised and supervised modes, allowing word embeddings from different languages to be mapped into the same vector space, thus enabling cross-lingual semantic comparison.

XLM-R (**XLM-RoBERTa**) is a cross-lingual model developed by the Facebook AI Research team. It is built on the **RoBERTa architecture** and is trained on a large-scale dataset covering 100 languages. This large-scale and diverse training enables XLM-R to perform excellently in multilingual understanding and translation tasks.

The **Universal Sentence Encoder** (**USE**) proposed by Google is another sentence embedding model based on **Transformer**, designed to generate universal vector representations for sentences and paragraphs. USE also performs well in multilingual environments and is suitable for tasks such as text classification, clustering, and semantic similarity computation.

Modern **large models** are typically equipped with strong multilingual capabilities. For example, OpenAI's `text-embedding-3-small` and `text-embedding-3-large`, BGE's `M3-Embedding`, as well as Cohere's multilingual embedding models, all support close to or more than 100 languages.

Embedding models for different data types

Embedding models are not limited to text. They can also be used to represent images, audio, videos, graphs, and knowledge graphs as vectors. This allows different types of data to be searched, compared, and retrieved using similar mathematical operations.

Image, audio, and video embedding models

Reverse search of **image data** is a core function in many applications. For example, if a user wants to find more images related to Wukong, *a well-known character from Chinese mythology*, they can upload a reference image and ask the search engine to identify visually similar images. Traditionally, such tasks rely on **convolutional neural network (CNN)** models such as **ResNet50**, which was trained by Microsoft in 2015 based on the **ImageNet** dataset. This model is capable of efficient **image feature extraction** and **similarity matching**.

Similarly, in reverse video search, **ResNet50** can also be used for **video embeddings**. By converting video frames into **feature vectors** and conducting **similarity retrieval** in a video frame database, it is possible to locate other video clips most similar to the input video.

For audio data, processing can be done via **PANN (Pretrained Audio Neural Network)**. **PANN** is pretrained on large-scale **audio datasets**. It allows learners to perform **reverse audio search** by inputting an audio clip and is widely used in **audio retrieval tasks** and **sound classification systems**.

Joint image and text embedding models

The emergence of **joint image and text embedding models** has opened new directions for embedding technologies. These **multimodal embedding models** can simultaneously capture semantic representations of text as well as various forms of unstructured data such as images, audio, and even video. Such models not only allow users to search images using **text**, but can also generate **image descriptions** and perform **reverse image search**, among other functions.

In 2021, OpenAI's *CLIP (Contrastive Language-Image Pretraining)* model became the standard architecture for such joint embedding models. OpenAI collected a dataset containing over 400 million image-text pairs and used **contrastive learning** on these pairs to map images and text into the same vector space, thereby establishing connections between text and images. This kind of **cross-modal embedding** enables machines to understand and associate information from different modalities more effectively when processing image and text data, bringing breakthroughs to **multimodal learning**.

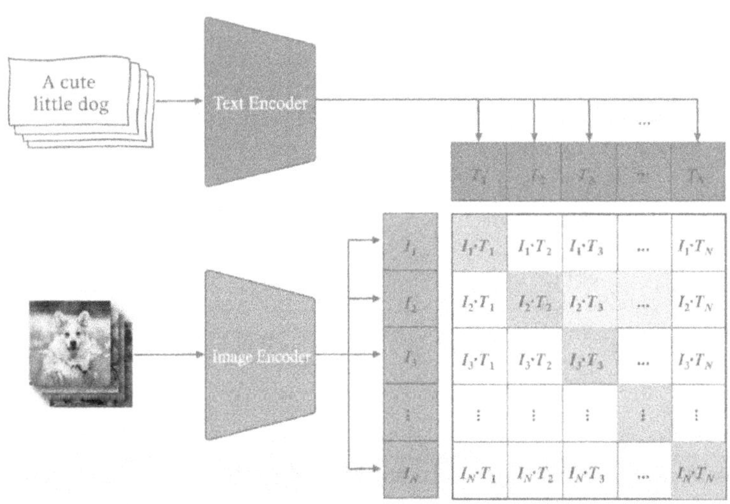

Figure 3.7: A photo of dog and text processed by encoders and combined in a matrix

In 2024, Google released the *SigLIP (sigmoidal-CLIP)* model, an improved version of the *CLIP* model that performs excellently in **zero-shot tasks** and is even easier to use. With advancements in hardware technology and improvements in model optimization, **small-sized models** have become increasingly popular. For example, **Unum** provides small-scale multimodal embedding models. Due to their **low memory usage**, such small models can run smoothly on devices like laptops, achieving low latency and faster processing speeds. This not only broadens the application scope of **multimodal technologies** but also makes their application more convenient and widespread.

Graph and knowledge graph embedding models

Graph Embedding and **Knowledge Graph Embedding** are of significant value when handling data involving complex relationships and structures. **Graph embedding** mainly focuses on the structural relationships between nodes, while **knowledge graph embedding** emphasizes semantic relationships between entities.

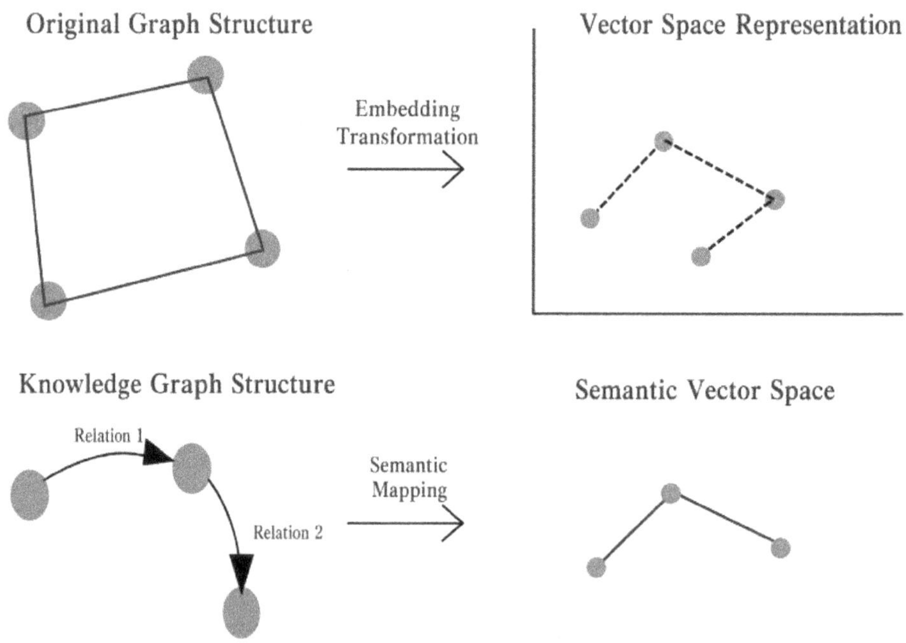

Figure 3.8: The transformation of graph and knowledge graph structures into vector spaces with arrows

Graph embedding maps nodes, edges, and their relationships in a graph into a low-dimensional vector space, while preserving the structural information of the graph. For example, models like **Node2Vec** and **GraphSAGE** encode the local and global structure of a graph into vector representations by means such as random walks or aggregating neighbor information. These vectors can be directly used in downstream tasks such as **node classification**, **clustering**, or **relation prediction** on graphs.

Graph embedding is widely used in fields such as **social network analysis, recommendation systems, financial networks, medical networks**, etc., and can effectively handle complex relational structures and network features found in these data. Through graph embedding, systems can learn the semantic and structural information of nodes, making similar nodes closer in the vector space, thereby improving performance in tasks such as node classification and link prediction.

Knowledge graph embedding (such as **TransE**, **TransR**, **DistMult**, etc.) maps entities and relationships into the same vector space, effectively capturing semantic relationships between entities. These models are widely used in **knowledge graph completion** and **link prediction** tasks, helping to discover potential relationships within knowledge graphs. For example, the **TransE** model uses a simple translation operation to capture relationships between entities, while models like **TransR** and **DistMult** further enhance the modeling capacity for complex and multi-dimensional relationships.

Knowledge graph embedding plays an important role in scenarios such as **intelligent question answering, recommendation systems, semantic search**, etc. For instance, in QA systems, embeddings can help identify complex relationships between questions and entities in the knowledge base, thereby providing more accurate answers.

Embedding models in the era of large language models

With the advent of the era of large models, models represented by **BERT** and **GPT** have revolutionized and reshaped the traditional **embedding architectures**, resulting in a unified landscape. These large models not only excel in **text generation** tasks, but their hidden layer outputs also serve as powerful text embedding tools, effectively capturing deep semantic information within text. This capability has greatly improved the performance of tasks such as similarity calculation, classification, and search.

In addition to "trimming" **BERT** and **GPT** for use as embedding models, OpenAI and other AI providers or open-source organizations have also offered a wealth of **embedding models** specifically designed for this purpose, available to developers through **APIs** or open-source code. These models demonstrate excellent adaptability in various natural language processing applications, providing rich semantic representations for text, suitable for similarity calculation, classification, search, and other tasks.

Therefore, like other **AI technologies**, **embedding technology** has experienced significant breakthroughs and development over the past few years. Machines' understanding of language and images has been enhanced, providing a solid foundation for various downstream tasks and thus promoting the development of the **Scaling Law**.

> OpenAI co-founder and former Chief Scientist Ilya Sutskever pointed out that high-quality human-generated text data has largely been exhausted, and the further development of scaling laws requires exploring new directions. In terms of text data, we may have already used most of the existing resources, but there is still a large amount of video and multimodal information waiting to be analyzed and understood by large models.
>
> In addition, the future development of scaling laws will also involve several areas, including hardware expansion, resource and performance optimization, and AI systems actively creating high-quality training data. These perspectives provide valuable directions for future exploration.

Next, we will further focus on the **modern embedding models** used in **RAG systems**.

Modern embedding models: OpenAI, Jina, Cohere, Voyage

In the field of modern **embedding models**, many companies offer commercial embedding models. These commercial embedding models are usually not fully open source, but are provided to users via **API calls**. Although sometimes there is a charge, overall, the cost of these services is not high, and with technological advancement and increased service competition, prices are gradually decreasing, which is similar to the pricing trend for large models.

Nevertheless, from a usage habit perspective, Lewis's most frequently used models are still OpenAI's `text-embedding-3-small` and `text-embedding-3-large` models. However, in this highly competitive market, OpenAI's advantage in embedding models is not significant. For example, Google has already launched the `text-embedding-005` model in its Gemini series, and some startups such as **Jina**, **Cohere**, and **Voyage** also provide the latest commercial embedding models. These companies' models perform excellently in scenarios such as **semantic similarity computation**, **search**, and **recommendations**, offering developers a diverse range of options.

Using OpenAI's text-embedding-3-small for product recommendations

OpenAI offers a variety of powerful commercial **embedding models**, including the earlier **text-embedding-ada-002**, as well as the current flagship models **text-embedding-3-small** and **text-embedding-3-large**. The **text-embedding-3-large** model has a higher dimension (3072 dimensions), allowing it to capture finer semantic information, but it also means higher computational cost.

Model Name	Dimension	MTEB Performance	Price/1M tokens	Features
text-embedding-3-small	1536	62.3%	$0.02	High cost performance
text-embedding-3-large	3072	64.6%	$0.13	Strong performance
text-embedding-ada-002	1536	61.0%	$0.08	Early model

Table 3.2: Comparison of OpenAI embedding models by vector dimension, MTEB performance, pricing, and key features

Prices and benchmark scores are subject to change. Check the provider's official documentation before using these figures in production.

Example product recommendation scenario using embeddings

Next, let's build a simulated scenario using **embedding technology**. Suppose there is a group of players who have provided short evaluations and ratings for various action-type games. First, use OpenAI's **text-embedding-3-small** model to generate **embedding vectors** for user reviews as well as for each game's description. Then, calculate the **cosine similarity** between the user's review embedding vector and the embedding vector of the game *Myth of the Vanquished Gods: Monkey King*. In this way, the obtained similarity score becomes the recommended rating of this game for the user, thereby identifying the user group who may enjoy playing *Myth of the Vanquished Gods: Monkey King*.

```
import os
import openai
import pandas as pd
import numpy as np
import json
from sklearn.metrics.pairwise import cosine_similarity
```

```
### Read User Reviews Dataset
df = pd.read_csv("data/Chronicles of Godslaying/user_reviews.csv")
### Read Game Description File
with open("data/Chronicles of Godslaying/game_description.json", "r") as
f:
    game_descriptions = json.load(f)
### Define Function to Get Embedding Vector
def get_embedding(text, model="text-embedding-3-small"):
    response = openai.embeddings.create(
input=[text],
model=model
)
return response.data[0].embedding
## Get Embedding Vectors for All Games
unique_games = df['game_title'].unique().tolist()
target_game = "Killing God: Hu Sun"  # Change target game name
if target_game not in unique_games:
    unique_games.append(target_game)  # Ensure the target game is in the
list
game_embeddings = {}
for game in unique_games:
    description = game_descriptions[game]
    game_embeddings[game] = np.array(get_embedding(description))
Compute embedding vector for user reviews (average of embedded vectors for
all games reviewed by user)
user_vectors = {}
for user_id, group in df.groupby("user_id"):
    user_game_vecs = []
    for idx, row in group.iterrows():
        g_title = row['game_title']
        g_vec = game_embeddings[g_title]
        user_game_vecs.append(g_vec)
    user_vectors[user_id] = np.mean(np.array(user_game_vecs), axis=0)
## Get the Embedding Vector for "Killing God: Hu Sun"
target_vector = game_embeddings[target_game]
## Calculate Cosine Similarity Between Each User's Review Embedding and
the Target Game's Embedding
results = []
for user_id, u_vec in user_vectors.items():
```

```
    u_vec_reshaped = u_vec.reshape(1, -1)
    t_vec = target_vector.reshape(1, -1)
    similarity = cosine_similarity(u_vec_reshaped, t_vec)[0,0]
    results.append((user_id, similarity))
## Sort and Find Users Most Likely to Like Killing God: Hu Sun
result_df = pd.DataFrame(results, columns=["user_id", f"similarity_to_
{target_game}"])
result_df = result_df.sort_values(by=f"similarity_to_{target_game}",
ascending=False)
print(f"\nTop 5 users most likely to like {target_game}:")
print(result_df.head())
```

```
Top 5 users most likely to like Killing God: Hu Sun:
user_id  similarity_to_Killing God: Hu Sun
U001                             0.923190
U004                             0.922800
U005                             0.917884
U002                             0.910476
U003                             0.909157
```

If a user's past favorite games (such as **Souls-like**, **action RPGs**) have a style similar to *Killing God: Hu Sun*, their similarity score should be higher.

Using Jina embeddings for cross-lingual clustering

jina-embeddings-v3 is a cutting-edge multilingual text embedding model based on **XLM-RoBERTa**, with multiple improvements enabling efficient encoding of longer text sequences. The model boasts 570 million parameters and supports 89 languages, including Arabic, Chinese, French, German, and Japanese, performing excellently across a variety of multilingual tasks. In addition to its robust support for multiple languages, the **jina-embeddings-v3** model is especially enhanced for processing long contexts, supporting inputs up to 8192 tokens, making it highly suitable for tasks such as **long document retrieval** and **long text embeddings**.

The **jina-embeddings-v3** model adopts task-specific **low-rank adaptation** techniques to generate high-quality embeddings for tasks such as **retrieval**, **clustering**, **classification**, and **text matching**. This flexibility allows the model to generate optimal embeddings tailored to different task requirements. To further enhance efficiency and reduce resource consumption, the model leverages **FlashAttention2** and the **DeepSpeed** framework, significantly improving distributed training efficiency and reducing memory usage.

Additionally, the **jina-embeddings-v3** model integrates the **Matryoshka representation learning** method, enabling learners to flexibly adjust embedding dimensions, with a minimum of 32 dimensions, without negatively impacting overall performance. This offers significant advantages for applications requiring large-scale vector storage in production environments or on edge devices.

The **jina-embeddings-v3** model provides three main API parameters for learner customization:

- task: Used to adjust the information embedding strategy according to downstream tasks (such as retrieval, classification, or text matching) to optimize performance for specific tasks
- dimensions: Learners can flexibly adjust the embedding dimensionality according to their needs, optimizing storage costs while ensuring performance
- late_chunking: Applies chunking to the text after embedding, particularly optimizing representations of long documents and helping to improve retrieval performance

Next, we will use the **jina-embeddings-v3** model to demonstrate semantic retrieval and clustering of multilingual game descriptions, showing how to find game descriptions similar in style to 'Legend of Deicide: Monkey King' across multiple languages and perform simple text clustering.

First, install the related library **einops**, which is a Python library for simplifying and enhancing **vector** (multi-dimensional array) operations.

```
pip install einops
```

Then, configure the **Jina API** (which you need to obtain from the official Jina website) and read the game data.

```
import pandas as pd
import numpy as np
import requests
from sklearn.cluster import KMeans
### Configure Jina API
url = 'https://api.jina.ai/v1/embeddings'
headers = {
'Content-Type': 'application/json',
'Authorization': 'Bearer your Jina API'
}
### Read Game Description Data
df = pd.read_csv("data/Chronicles of Godslaying/game_descriptions.csv")
texts = df['description'].tolist()
```

```
### Get Text Embeddings
data = {
"model": "jina-embeddings-v3",
"task": "text-matching",
"dimensions": 1024,
"normalized": True,
"input": texts
}
response = requests.post(url, headers=headers, json=data)
if response.status_code != 200:
    raise RuntimeError(f"API call failed: {response.status_code} - 
{response.text}")
embeddings = [item['embedding'] for item in response.json().get('data', 
[])]
if not embeddings:
    raise RuntimeError("API did not return embedding vectors")
embeddings = np.array(embeddings)
### Clustering Analysis
kmeans = KMeans(n_clusters=3, random_state=42)
labels = kmeans.fit_predict(embeddings)
print("\nClustering results:")
for i, lbl in enumerate(labels):
    print(f"Cluster {lbl}: {texts[i]}")
```

```
Cluster 2: "Killing God: Hu Sun" is an action RPG game adapted from the
classic *Journey to the West*, known for its high-quality graphics and
hardcore combat style.
Cluster 2: Killing God: Hu Sun is an action RPG game inspired by the
classic *Journey to the West*, known for its stunning visuals and
challenging combat.
Cluster 2: Ein actiongeladenes RPG, Killing God: Hu Sun, inspiriert von
der klassischen chinesischen Literatur, kombiniert mythische Kreaturen und
intensiven Nahkampf.
Cluster 2: *Sekiro: Shadows Die Twice* is a challenging action-adventure
game set in a reimagined Sengoku-era Japan, focusing on precise sword
combat and stealth.
Cluster 2: The player explores a vast open world full of mysteries,
terrifying enemies, and hidden treasures in *Elden Ring*.
Cluster 0: *Elden Ring* is an open-world action RPG developed by
```

```
FromSoftware and George R.R. Martin, known for its vast world and diverse
builds.
Cluster 0: *Bloodborne* is an action RPG set in a Victorian-style horror
world, known for its fast-paced offensive and defensive combat and eerie
atmosphere.
Cluster 0: *Dark Souls III* is a dark fantasy action RPG game, renowned for
its extreme difficulty and deep world-building.
Cluster 1: **Organic skin care**: A segment unrelated to gaming, used to
test clustering with an irrelevant topic.
Cluster 1: This text is unrelated to games and is only used to test the
effect of text clustering.
```

Next, the **t-SNE algorithm** is used to reduce the high-dimensional **embedding vectors** (1024 dimensions) to 2 dimensions, and then the clustering results are visualized. Due to space limitations in the *Chapter*, the specific code is not shown here. For the complete code, you can visit Lewis's **GitHub repository** (Refer to `GitHub - PacktPublishing/RAG-from-First-Principles: RAG from First Principles Published by Packt Pub` for the complete code).

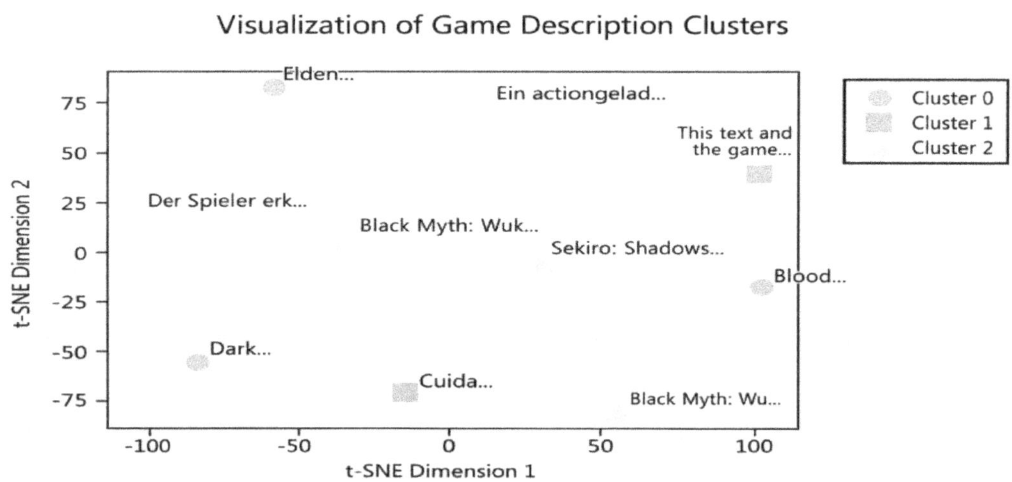

Figure 3.9: Scatter plot showing three game description clusters

It can be seen that, regardless of whether it is Chinese, English, or another language, as long as the game is similar to "Legend of Destroying Gods: Monkey King," it will be assigned the same class label. Modern embedding models' support for multiple languages is very practical.

Models such as `jina-embeddings-v3`, OpenAI's commercial embedding models, and Cohere's `embed-english-v3.0` have all been integrated into cloud platforms such as **AWS SageMaker** and

Azure Marketplace. Vector databases like **Pinecone**, **Qdrant**, and **Milvus**, as well as open-source frameworks like **LangChain** and **LlamaIndex**, are also seamlessly integrated with these models to enable users to efficiently perform **similarity retrieval** and **search tasks**.

Evaluating embedding models with MTEB

Alex: Many open-source and commercial **embedding models** perform differently in various scenarios. Which embedding model is the best, and who decides?

Lewis: MTEB (*Massive Text Embedding Benchmark*) was jointly proposed by **Hugging Face** and the large-scale text retrieval community. It is a **benchmark framework** specifically designed to evaluate the performance of **text embedding models**. It covers multiple languages and tasks, providing a unified, large-scale benchmark that can systematically assess the performance of embedding models in different application scenarios.

The **MTEB** page on the Hugging Face community website provides a ranking table of the best text embedding models for various tasks, offering a reference for model users.

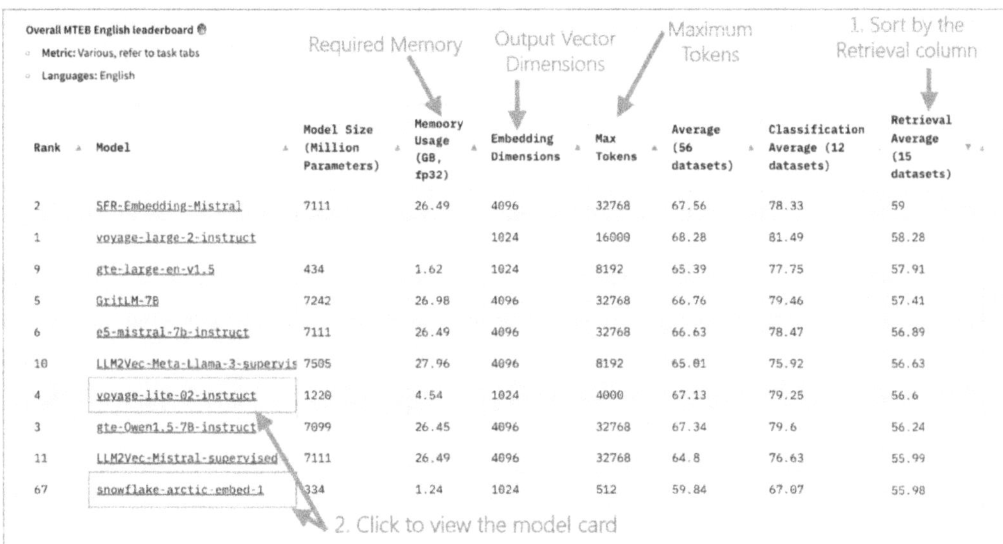

Rank	Model	Model Size (Million Parameters)	Memory Usage (GB, fp32)	Embedding Dimensions	Max Tokens	Average (56 datasets)	Classification Average (12 datasets)	Retrieval Average (15 datasets)
2	SFR-Embedding-Mistral	7111	26.49	4096	32768	67.56	78.33	59
1	voyage-large-2-instruct			1024	16000	68.28	81.49	58.28
9	gte-large-en-v1.5	434	1.62	1024	8192	65.39	77.75	57.91
5	GritLM-7B	7242	26.98	4096	32768	66.76	79.46	57.41
6	e5-mistral-7b-instruct	7111	26.49	4096	32768	66.63	78.47	56.89
10	LLM2Vec-Meta-Llama-3-supervis	7505	27.96	4096	8192	65.01	75.92	56.63
4	voyage-lite-02-instruct	1220	4.54	1024	4000	67.13	79.25	56.6
3	gte-Qwen1.5-7B-instruct	7099	26.45	4096	32768	67.34	79.6	56.24
11	LLM2Vec-Mistral-supervised	7111	26.49	4096	32768	64.8	76.63	55.99
67	snowflake-arctic-embed-l	334	1.24	1024	512	59.84	67.07	55.98

Figure 3.10: Leaderboard table of English AI models with rankings scores and annotated column labels

A major feature of **MTEB** is the diversity of its tasks. Given that the real-world applications of embedding models are varied and require validation on tasks such as **retrieval, clustering**, and **classification**, **MTEB** covers eight major categories of tasks.

Task category	Task example	Description
Retrieval	Information Retrieval (BEIR)	Retrieve documents semantically matching the query
Text Matching	Semantic Similarity (STS-B)	Determine the semantic similarity between two sentences
Classification	Sentence Classification (Amazon Reviews)	Predict sentence categories, such as sentiment analysis
Clustering	Topic Clustering (TREC)	Group similar texts together
Ranking	Semantic Ranking (MS MARCO)	Rank documents by query and semantic similarity
Summary Evaluation	Summary Quality Evaluation (SummEval)	Assess the degree of match between machine-generated summaries and reference summaries
Regression	Sentence Regression (STS-B)	Perform regression analysis on sentences, outputting similarity scores
Generation Task Assistance	Evaluate input and output quality	Assist in evaluating the embedding quality of inputs and generated outputs for generative models

Table 3.3: Overview of MTEB task categories, representative benchmark examples, and the embedding capabilities evaluated by each task

Whenever an **embedding model** finishes training, the responsible organization, institution, or company usually evaluates their model using the various datasets and tasks provided by **MTEB**. Afterwards, they submit the model's scores and code to the **MTEB leaderboard** via **GitHub Repo**.

Of course, as mentioned earlier, although the **MTEB evaluation tasks** have wide coverage and are quite challenging, since the datasets it uses are mostly public, if an organization specifically optimizes its model for these tasks and datasets to improve its ranking, its performance on the **MTEB leaderboard** will naturally stand out. However, whether such models can achieve the same results on other tasks that have not been specially optimized remains uncertain.

The best way to choose an embedding model is to evaluate it on your own use case. To find the **embedding model** that best fits specific needs, it is necessary to build an evaluation dataset tailored to your own application scenarios, and repeatedly test and compare different embedding models—including various commercial embedding models, as well as open-source models provided by Hugging Face and SentenceTransformers. This process is not easy, but it is an effective way to ensure the best model is selected. Next, we will introduce an excellent example of **embedding model evaluation** conducted independently by an individual for learners to learn from and reference.

Comparing and selecting embedding models

Jonathan Ellis conducted an evaluation and comparison of commonly used **embedding models** in his article "*Best Embedding Models for Information Retrieval in 2025.*"

The test data comes from the ViDoRe image search benchmark dataset, which was converted to text using the **Gemini Flash 1.5 OCR tool**. The reason Jonathan Ellis chose these datasets is that most classic text search datasets have already been repeatedly used for model training by developers, making them unsuitable for evaluation. By applying OCR processing to image search datasets, he believes these models are exposed to data they have never seen before. Given that many large models are trained on known public datasets, his initiative to create his own test data is an excellent innovative practice.

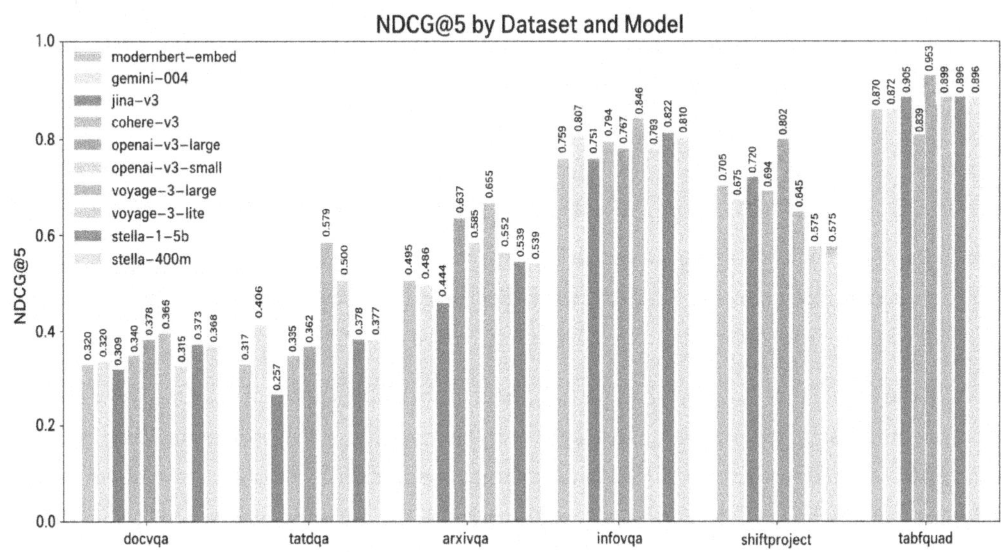

Figure 3.11: Comparison of NDCG@5 scores across datasets and models

The evaluation results reveal some interesting findings. For example, **ModernBERT** and **Gemini's text-embedding-004** models only support **English**, while most other models support multiple languages. In terms of performance, the **voyage-3-large** model stands out as the top performer, whereas the **voyage-3-lite** model excels in the low-cost domain.

Among open source models, the **Stella** model delivers an impressive performance. However, despite `stella-1.5b` being four times the size of `stella-400m`, its accuracy does not improve significantly.

Gemini's text-embedding-004 model is recognized as the best value model, offering medium-level performance for free, with a reasonable limit of **1,500 requests per minute**. The only drawback is that it is not possible to increase throughput via payment.

In contrast, `jina-embeddings-v3` and **Cohere's embed-v3** models performed relatively ordinarily in this test and were surpassed by models with better performance and lower costs.

Of course, a single independent test result does not represent everything. The embedding model landscape changes quickly.. Choosing the most suitable embedding model, whether it is a commercial or open-source one, requires a deep understanding of each model and should be based on the specific application scenario, usage volume, performance requirements, and budget constraints.

These results reflect one independent evaluation at a specific point in time. Model performance, pricing, limits, and availability may change, so readers should verify current details before selecting a model.

Sparse embedding, dense embedding, and BM25

Alex: Lewis, I've been organizing the battle logs in *Chronicles of Godslaying: The Monkey*, and I often hear friends talk about concepts like **sparse embedding** and **dense embedding**, but I always get them mixed up. Could you explain the differences between them?

Lewis: In the era of large models, when we talk about **embeddings**, most of the time we're referring to **dense embeddings** (also known as **dense vectors**). Sometimes, we also use **sparse embeddings** (also known as **sparse vectors**). If you hear technical people discussing **sparse embedding** in a project, it usually means they're doing **hybrid retrieval**. We'll go deeper into this topic later on.

Next, let's use a simple analogy to explain the difference between these two embedding methods. Imagine you're describing a person. **Sparse embedding** is like using tags to describe this person, `[tall=1, glasses=1, long hair=0, round face=0, ...]`; while **dense embedding** is like using a set of abstract features to describe the person, `[0.8, -0.2, 0.5, 0.3, ...]`. For example, **sparse embedding** lists Wukong's feature checklist directly, while **dense embedding** compresses these features into an abstract numerical representation.

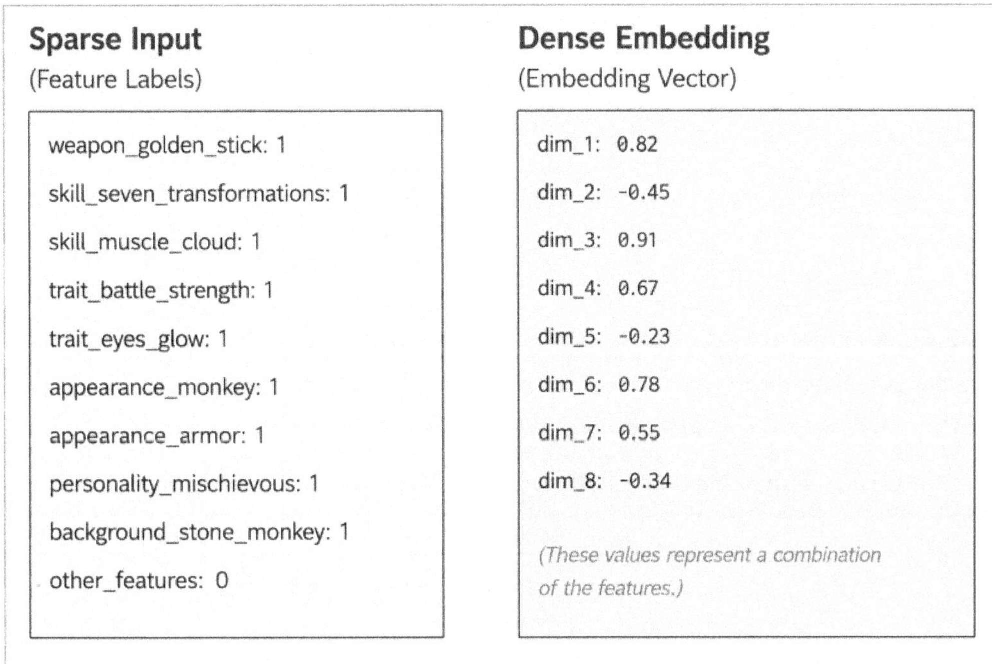

Figure 3.12: Comparison of sparse and dense features

Understanding sparse and dense embeddings

Alex: Oh? That analogy is vivid! What are their respective characteristics?

Lewis: Let's take a look at their characteristics. **Sparse embeddings** typically have a very high dimension (possibly up to tens of thousands), but most of the values are 0. Each dimension has a clear meaning, such as corresponding to a specific word. Because most values in sparse embeddings are 0, their storage and computation are very efficient, since only non-zero values need to be handled. In contrast, **dense embeddings** have relatively smaller dimensions (usually several hundred to several thousand), and every dimension has a value. However, the meaning of these dimensions is more abstract, representing features learned by the model. Unlike **sparse embeddings**, **dense embeddings** require storage and computation for all dimensions, which means they demand more computational resources.

Implementing sparse embeddings with BM25

BM25 can be viewed as a **sparse lexical representation method** used in information retrieval and search engines. Its core idea is to match documents and queries based on the importance of words. The following explains in detail how BM25 implements sparse embedding.

First, build a **vocabulary** containing all the words in the corpus. Each word in the vocabulary corresponds to one dimension of the vector. Suppose we have compiled the battle logs of Sun Wukong in the game *Chronicle of Godslaying: Sun Wukong*. The vocabulary is equivalent to the "set of battle terms" that appear in the logs.

- Divine weapon
- Monster
- Flame Fist

All the words will form a large vocabulary, and each term will be assigned a unique index, that is, a one-dimensional vector. For instance, if the vocabulary size is 10,000 and "Wukong" is at index 103 in the vocabulary, then it corresponds to the 103rd dimension of the sparse vector.

For each word w, BM25 calculates its weight based on the following formula:

$$\text{Score}(w,d) = \text{IDF}(w) \cdot \frac{\text{TF}(w,d) \cdot (k_1 + 1)}{\text{TF}(w,d) + k_1 \cdot (1 - b + b \cdot \frac{|d|}{\text{avgdl}})}$$

Where TF (Term Frequency) refers to the number of times the word w appears in the document; for example, "Flame Fist" appears three times.

IDF (Inverse Document Frequency) is used to measure the global importance of word w; rare words have higher weights. For example, **Diamond Body** may appear in most logs, so its weight is lower, while **Destructive Roar** may appear less often, so its weight is higher. The calculation for IDF is as follows.

$$\text{IDF}(w) = \log\left(\frac{N - n(w) + 0.5}{n(w) + 0.5} + 1\right)$$

k and b are **hyperparameters** that control the impact of term frequency on the weight and the degree of document length normalization, respectively.

A sparse vector is generated based on the vocabulary, with its dimensionality equal to the vocabulary size. For a document or query, only the weights for the words that appear are assigned, while the dimensions for words that do not appear are 0.

The following Python code example demonstrates how to use BM25 to analyze and retrieve Sun Wukong's battle logs.

```
from collections import Counter
import math
```

```
## Sun Wukong's Battle Logs
battle_logs = [
    "Sun Wukong uses Flame Fist to repel the monster; then activates
Diamond Body to block attacks from divine weapons.",
    "The monster uses an Ice Arrow to attack Sun Wukong, but is countered
and defeated by the Flame Fist.",
    "Sun Wukong summons Flame Fist and Destructive Roar to defeat the
monster and then collects the monster's essence."
]
## Hyperparameters
k1 = 1.5
b = 0.75
## Build Vocabulary
vocabulary = set(word for log in battle_logs for word in log.split(","))
vocab_to_idx = {word: idx for idx, word in enumerate(vocabulary)}
## Calculate IDF
N = len(battle_logs)
df = Counter(word for log in battle_logs for word in set(log.split(",")))
idf = {word: math.log((N - df[word] + 0.5) / (df[word] + 0.5) + 1) for
word in vocabulary}
## Log Length Information
avg_log_len = sum(len(log.split(",")) for log in battle_logs) / N
## BM25 Sparse Information Embedding
def bm25_sparse_embedding(log):
    tf = Counter(log.split(","))
    log_len = len(log.split(","))
    embedding = {}
    for word, freq in tf.items():
        if word in vocabulary:
            idx = vocab_to_idx[word]
            score = idf[word] * (freq * (k1 + 1)) / (freq + k1 * (1 - b +
b * log_len / avg_log_len))
            embedding[idx] = score
    return embedding
## Generate Sparse Vectors
for log in battle_logs:
    sparse_embedding = bm25_sparse_embedding(log)
    print(f"Sparse embedding: {sparse_embedding}")
```

```
Sparse Embedding: {0: 0.9285957424963089, 2: 0.9285957424963089, 5:
0.9285957424963089}
```

The highlight of **BM25** lies in its efficient storage method. When storing the combat logs of the **Monkey King**, there's no need to save the weights for all dimensions. If only 5 terms have nonzero weight values, then only this information is stored. Each nonzero dimension clearly corresponds to a specific combat term; for example, the score for **Blazing Fist** is calculated based on its frequency and importance. When you need to retrieve all logs where **Diamond Body** was used to block an attack, it's enough to compute the dot product between the query and the sparse vector of the log. This approach not only delivers speed but also ensures accurate results.

By efficiently representing and retrieving key battle information through **sparse embeddings**, **BM25** combines the local frequency and global rarity of combat terms. This ensures both storage efficiency and the ability to capture keyword importance based on local frequency and global rarity.

Hybrid retrieval with BGE-M3

After understanding the concepts of **sparse** and **dense embeddings**, let's introduce the **BGE-M3 model**. This is an open-source text embedding model developed by **Beijing Academy of Artificial Intelligence (BAAI)**. BGE-M3 is available through HuggingFace and the FlagEmbedding package. The **BGE-M3 model** enhances performance through **self-knowledge distillation**, enabling it to excel in a variety of retrieval tasks. In addition, the model employs optimized **batching strategies** and **caching mechanisms** to efficiently handle long texts, meeting the needs of long-document retrieval. The **BGE-M3 model** aims to support **multilingual**, **multifunctional**, and **multi-granularity** text retrieval and representation tasks.

Why is it called M3? Because the **BGE-M3 model** primarily has 3 features:

- Multi-functionality: The BGE-M3 model integrates three retrieval capabilities: dense retrieval, sparse retrieval, and multi-vector retrieval, and can flexibly meet different retrieval requirements
- Multi-linguality: The BGE-M3 model supports over 100 languages, providing strong multilingual and cross-lingual retrieval capabilities
- Multi-granularity: The BGE-M3 model can handle text from short phrases up to long documents of 8192 tokens, meeting processing needs for texts of different lengths

How BGE-M3 generates sparse and dense embeddings

The unique feature of the **BGE-M3 model** is that its output interface can return both **sparse vectors** and **dense vectors** at the same time. **Sparse embeddings** are mainly used to capture keyword features, while **dense embeddings** capture semantic features. Additionally, the **BGE-M3 model** provides the functionality of **hybrid re-ranking** using both sparse and dense embeddings, which can further improve the accuracy and relevance of retrieval results.

To use the **BGE-M3 model**, you should first install the **FlagEmbedding** package from **BAAI**.

```
pip install flagembedding
```

Next, initialize the model and input your text.

```
from FlagEmbedding import BGEM3FlagModel
model = BGEM3FlagModel("BAAI/bge-m3", use_fp16=False)
passage = ["The monkey uses the Blazing Flame Fist to drive away the
monster; then activates the Vajra Body to resist attacks from divine
weapons."]
```

By setting parameters such as **return_sparse**, **return_dense**, and **return_colbert_vecs**, you can obtain different types of vector representations from the model. For more details on **ColBERT's multi-vector re-ranking mechanism**, see *Chapter 7*.

```
### Encode Text and Obtain Sparse and Dense Embeddings
passage_embeddings = model.encode(
passage,
return_sparse=True,      # Return sparse embeddings
return_dense=True,       # Return dense embeddings
return_colbert_vecs=True  # Return multi-vector embeddings
)
### Extract Sparse Embeddings, Dense Embeddings, and Multi-Vector
Embeddings Separately
dense_vecs = passage_embeddings["dense_vecs"]
sparse_vecs = passage_embeddings["lexical_weights"]
colbert_vecs = passage_embeddings["colbert_vecs"]
### Show Examples of Sparse and Dense Embeddings
print(dense_vecs[0][:10])  # Display only the first 10 dimensions
print(list(sparse_vecs[0].items())[:10])  # Display only the first 10 non-
zero values
print(colbert_vecs[0][:2])  # Display only the first two multi-vector
embeddings
```

Now, we have obtained multiple types of **vector representations** (we will no longer describe the related computation process or display these vectors). In Section 4.6, we will demonstrate how to build a **hybrid retrieval system** using mixed embedding models, which can both match keywords accurately and understand the semantic intent of queries.

Multimodal embedding model visualized_BGE

Anna: Lewis, **embedding models** for a single modality (such as text or image) are already relatively mature. However, in our actual application scenarios, we often need to process **multi-modal data** such as text, images, and even audio and video at the same time to achieve richer and more flexible functions.

Lewis: **Multimodal embedding models** have emerged to address such needs. They can map data from different modalities into the same vector space, thereby supporting **cross-modal retrieval, cross-modal generation**, and **multimodal analysis.**

A representative work is the **Visualized_BGE** model from BAAI, which is a visualized version launched based on the **BGE model** to meet the needs of multimodal processing. The Visualized_BGE model mainly focuses on the joint processing of image and text modalities. By measuring the similarity between image and text vectors in the same embedding space, the model enables cross-modal retrieval and image-text search. For example, learners can retrieve the most relevant images based on a text description or find the best matching text description based on an image.

The technical architecture of the Visualized_BGE model mainly includes the following modules:

- **Vision encoder**: Usually based on **ViT** or other deep convolutional networks, used to extract image features. By dividing the input image into patches or using convolution operations, the model can extract multi-level visual information and finally generate a global vector representation of the image.
- **Text encoder**: Based on large model architectures such as **BERT** or **RoBERTa**, used to extract text semantics. For the input text sequence, the model outputs a vector representing the overall semantics.
- **Contrastive learning**: The model is trained using contrastive learning methods, so that related (matched) image-text pairs are closer together in the vector space, while unrelated (unmatched) image-text pairs are farther apart, thereby enabling cross-modal alignment and retrieval capabilities.

The **Visualized_BGE** model is currently in the research stage. It is recommended to visit the official Github repository of **FlagEmbedding** for the latest installation instructions. Currently, installation is done as follows:

```
git clone https://github.com/FlagOpen/FlagEmbedding.git
cd FlagEmbedding/research/visual_bge
pip install -e .
```

The following code example demonstrates how to use **FlagEmbedding** to import and visualize a multimodal embedding:

```
from visual_bge.modeling import Visualized_BGE
model = Visualized_BGE(
model_name_bge="BAAI/bge-base-en-v1.5",
model_weight="path/to/weights"
)
### Joint Image-Text Encoding
embedding = model.encode(image="image.jpg", text="description")
### Image-Only Encoding
img_embedding = model.encode(image="image.jpg")
### Text-Only Encoding
text_embedding = model.encode(text="description")
```

Here, we have only performed joint **image and text encoding**, vector extraction, and representation. To achieve complete image similarity retrieval or **cross-modal retrieval** functionality, it is usually necessary to combine with a vector database (such as **Milvus**) or other efficient similarity retrieval tools.

Using embedding models with frameworks like LangChain and LlamaIndex

In the previous examples, we either called commercial **embedding model** APIs directly or downloaded open-source **embedding models** via the Hugging Face platform. This section will demonstrate how to load and use **embedding models** with mainstream application frameworks such as **LangChain** and **LlamaIndex**. A significant advantage of this approach is that it allows developers to seamlessly switch between different embedding models within a unified development framework. Developers do not need to rewrite adaptation code for various embedding models and can focus more on implementing business logic. In addition, caching mechanisms provided by these frameworks can avoid redundant embedding computations, greatly improving retrieval and query efficiency.

Embedding interfaces in LangChain

LangChain offers a variety of components and tools to conveniently integrate large language models into applications. It also provides a well-designed abstraction for **embeddings**, making it easy to switch between different **embedding models** (including **OpenAI Embeddings**, **Hugging Face Embeddings**, and local models).

The common embedding classes in LangChain are as follows:

- OpenAIEmbeddings: Used to call the text embedding API provided by OpenAI
- HuggingFaceEmbeddings: Used to call Hugging Face models either locally or remotely
- SelfHostedPipelineEmbeddings: Used to call custom deployed Pipelines
- CacheBackedEmbeddings: Can "wrap" any embedding model into a cache-backed version to avoid redundant computation of embeddings

The following code example demonstrates how to use `OpenAIEmbeddings` to encode text and view the dimension or values of the returned vector (Refer to `https://github.com/PacktPublishing/RAG-from-First-Principles` for the complete code).

```
from langchain.embeddings import OpenAIEmbeddings
embeddings = OpenAIEmbeddings(
    model="text-embedding-3-small",  # Other OpenAI models can be
specified
)
text = "This is a sample sentence for embedding."
text_vector = embeddings.embed_query(text)
print(len(text_vector))
print(text_vector[:10])  # View the first 10 elements of the vector
```

After passing in a segment of text, `OpenAIEmbeddings` will return a list of floating-point numbers as the encoded vector (e.g., 1536 dimensions). These vectors can be stored in vector databases (such as Faiss, Milvus, etc.) for similarity search.

If you want to switch to another **embedding model**, simply make the following adjustments.

```
from langchain.embeddings import HuggingFaceEmbeddings
embed_model = HuggingFaceEmbeddings(
    model_name="sentence-transformers/all-MiniLM-L6-v2"  # Any Hugging
Face model can be specified
)
text = "This is a sample sentence for embedding."
```

```
text_vector = embed_model.embed_query(text)
print(len(text_vector))
print(text_vector[:10])  # View the first 10 elements of the vector
```

Embedding interfaces in LlamaIndex

Similar to **LangChain**, **LlamaIndex** also provides a unified **embedding interface**, allowing developers to easily switch between different embedding models as needed. The use of embedding models like **OpenAI** has already been described earlier and will not be repeated here. Below is a code example for setting a global embedding model via **Settings**.

```
from llama_index.core import SimpleDirectoryReader, VectorStoreIndex,
Settings
from llama_index.embeddings.huggingface import HuggingFaceEmbedding
## Set the Global Embedding Model
Settings.embed_model = HuggingFaceEmbedding(model_name="BAAI/bge-small-
zh")
## Load Documents
documents = SimpleDirectoryReader("data/Chronicles of Godslaying").load_
data()
## Create Index, Which Will Automatically Use the Embedding Model Set in
Settings
index = VectorStoreIndex.from_documents(documents)
## Create Query Engine
query_engine = index.as_query_engine()
response = query_engine.query("Please briefly summarize the content of the
file")
print(response)
```

Similarly, you can also set a global embedding model using `Settings.llm`.

Embedding caching via LangChain cache

When dealing with large amounts of text or frequent repeated queries on the same batch of text, recalculating **embeddings** each time consumes a significant amount of computing power and time. To address this issue, **LangChain** provides the **CacheBackedEmbeddings** feature, which allows embedding results to be persistently stored in the local file system or other key-value databases. When encoding the same text again, the framework will fetch the cached result directly instead of recomputing it.

LangChain uses the hash of the input text as the key, and the corresponding embedding as the value, storing them in the specified `ByteStore`. The next time the embedding for the same text is calculated, it first checks if the cache exists; if so, it returns the cached result directly. If not, it calls the underlying embedding model to generate it.

The following code example demonstrates how to use **LocalFileStore** as a file system cache and combine it with **Faiss** for embedding retrieval.

```
from langchain.storage import LocalFileStore
from langchain_community.document_loaders import TextLoader
from langchain_community.vectorstores import FAISS
from langchain_huggingface import HuggingFaceEmbeddings
from langchain_text_splitters import CharacterTextSplitter
### Initialize the Embedding Model
embed_model = HuggingFaceEmbeddings(model_name="BAAI/bge-small-zh")
### Initialize the Local Cache Storage Path
store = LocalFileStore("./cache/")
### Create a Wrapper Using CacheBackedEmbeddings.from_bytes_store
from langchain.embeddings import CacheBackedEmbeddings
cached_embedder = CacheBackedEmbeddings.from_bytes_store(
underlying_embeddings=embed_model,
document_embedding_cache=store,    # Used to cache document vectors
namespace=embed_model.model_name  # Prevents conflicts between different
models
)
### Prepare Test Text and Split It
raw_documents = TextLoader("state_of_the_union.txt").load()
text_splitter = CharacterTextSplitter(chunk_size=1000, chunk_overlap=0)
documents = text_splitter.split_documents(raw_documents)
### Build a Faiss Embedding Retrieval Library; the First Run Requires
Actual Embedding Computation
db = FAISS.from_documents(documents, cached_embedder)
### The Next Run Uses Cached Results and the Processing Speed Improves
Significantly
db2 = FAISS.from_documents(documents, cached_embedder)
```

The first time you build an **embedding retrieval database** may take a long time because it actually needs to call OpenAI's **embedding model** to compute embeddings for all text chunks. However, when you perform the same operation a second time, embeddings can be read from the local cache, significantly reducing the runtime.

Of course, you can also choose other cache storage mechanisms such as **InMemory**, **Redis**, etc. If your application only needs to cache data during program execution (and will not be used across processes or across machines), you can use in-memory caching.

```
from langchain.storage import InMemoryByteStore
store = InMemoryByteStore()
cached_embedder = CacheBackedEmbeddings.from_bytes_store(
underlying_embeddings,
store,
namespace=underlying_embeddings.model
)
```

For more robust persistent storage such as **Redis**, **SQLite**, cloud storage, etc., you only need to implement or use the corresponding `ByteStore` interface, and you can cache the embeddings to your chosen storage medium. In this way, you can meet the needs of large-scale distributed deployment or cross-team sharing.

Fine-tuning embedding models

In this section, we will discuss **fine-tuning embedding models.**

Fine-tuning refers to the process of adjusting a **pre-trained model** to suit a specific task. Its core lies in ensuring a close connection between the task and existing data. Importantly, before starting fine-tuning, it is necessary to clarify whether fine-tuning is truly needed. If the task objectives are unclear or do not match the characteristics of the available data, fine-tuning may waste resources or even lead to negative effects. For example, if the goal is to answer several specialized questions with a large model, and existing open-source models already provide satisfactory answers, then there is no need for fine-tuning.

Scenarios where fine-tuning may be considered include the following:

- Highly specialized tasks: such as generating medical reports in a specific subfield
- Requirements for specific formats: such as generating answers that conform to internal documentation standards
- Localization needs: such as generating content for a particular language or cultural context

In summary, **fine-tuning** should revolve around actual tasks and existing data, avoiding "fine-tuning for the sake of fine-tuning."

Next, we will use the open-source embedding model **Stella** as an example to introduce how to fine-tune. First, install the following tools and libraries: **Hugging Face's transformers library**, **PyTorch** (GPU version is preferred), and **Datasets library** for data loading.

```
pip install transformers datasets torch
```

The **Stella model** has several versions as follows:

- stella-400m: Moderate parameter count (about 400 million parameters), suitable for resource-constrained environments
- **stella-1.5b**: High-performance version (about 1.5 billion parameters), requires more computing resources, at least a GPU with 16GB VRAM

The following sample code uses a pre-prepared dataset, inputs two segments of text in batches, generates **embedding vectors** respectively, and calculates **cosine similarity**. Then, it compares the calculated results with the actual similarity labels and fits the model parameters using gradient descent. Through such training, the model can make the distance between similar text pairs in the dataset closer in the embedding space.

First, import the necessary libraries.

```
from transformers import AutoModel, AutoTokenizer, TrainingArguments,
Trainer
import torch
import torch.nn as nn
from datasets import Dataset, DatasetDict
```

The sample data is stored in the form of text pairs, each pair representing two sentences that require similarity computation. The **similarity** represents the human-annotated similarity score between the two texts (ranging from 0 to 1), which is used for supervised training. (Note: The actual data required for fine-tuning will be much larger than what is shown here.)

```
## Sample Data Is in the Form of Text Pairs
train_data = [
{
"text1": "How is the gameplay of 'Chronicles of the God Slayer: Monkey'?",
"text2": "I want to know about the combat system of 'Chronicles of the God
Slayer: Monkey'.",
"similarity": 0.8  # Similarity score
},
{
```

```
"text1": "Are the visual details of 'Chronicles of the God Slayer: Monkey' 
good?",
"text2": "How is the open world design of this game?",
"similarity": 0.3  # Not very similar
}
]
val_data = [
{
"text1": "How is the combat experience of 'Chronicles of the God Slayer: 
Monkey'?",
"text2": "How is the game's fighting system?",
"similarity": 0.9
}
]
```

The `SentenceEmbeddingModel` class encapsulates a basic pre-trained model (such as `stella-400m-v5`) to generate **sentence embeddings.** Both texts are input into the base model, and the **CLS token embedding** is extracted as the sentence's vector representation. At the same time, `nn.CosineSimilarity` is used to calculate the cosine similarity of the two texts, and the mean squared error (**MSE**) loss is calculated against the similarity label for supervised training.

```
## Custom Model Class
class SentenceEmbeddingModel(nn.Module):
    def __init__(self, base_model):
        super().__init__()
        self.model = base_model
    def forward(self, input_ids1, attention_mask1, input_ids2, attention_
mask2, similarity=None):
        # Get embeddings of the two texts
        outputs1 = self.model(input_ids=input_ids1, attention_
mask=attention_mask1)
        outputs2 = self.model(input_ids=input_ids2, attention_
mask=attention_mask2)
### Use the Embedding of the CLS Token as the Sentence Vector 
Representation
embeddings1 = outputs1.last_hidden_state[:, 0]
embeddings2 = outputs2.last_hidden_state[:, 0]
### Calculate Cosine Similarity
cos = nn.CosineSimilarity(dim=1)
```

```
pred_similarity = cos(embeddings1, embeddings2)
### If Similarity Labels Are Provided, Compute MSE Loss
loss = None
if similarity is not None:
    loss_fn = nn.MSELoss()
    loss = loss_fn(pred_similarity, similarity)
return {"loss": loss, "predictions": pred_similarity} if loss is not None
else pred_similarity
```

The data preprocessing function performs **tokenization**, **truncation**, and **padding** separately on the two text segments (`text1` and `text2`) to make their lengths consistent. Then it returns the tokenized results, including `input_ids` and `attention_mask`, for model usage.

```
### Data Preprocessing Function
def preprocess_function(examples):
    ## Encode the two texts separately
    text1_encodings = tokenizer(
        examples["text1"],
        truncation=True,
        padding="max_length",
        max_length=128
    )
    text2_encodings = tokenizer(
        examples["text2"],
        truncation=True,
        padding="max_length",
        max_length=128
    )
    ## Merge the encoding results
    return {
        "input_ids1": text1_encodings["input_ids"],
        "attention_mask1": text1_encodings["attention_mask"],
        "input_ids2": text2_encodings["input_ids"],
        "attention_mask2": text2_encodings["attention_mask"],
        "similarity": examples["similarity"]
    }
### Convert Data to Dataset
train_dataset = Dataset.from_list(train_data)
```

```
val_dataset = Dataset.from_list(val_data)
raw_datasets = DatasetDict({
    "train": train_dataset,
    "validation": val_dataset
})
```

Next, load the Hugging Face pretrained model **stella_en_400M_v5** and its **tokenizer**, and initialize the custom **SentenceEmbeddingModel** with the pretrained model.

```
## Load Pretrained Model and Tokenizer
model_name = "NovaSearch/stella_en_400M_v5"  # This can be replaced with
the stella-400m-v5 model
tokenizer = AutoTokenizer.from_pretrained(model_name)
base_model = AutoModel.from_pretrained(model_name, trust_remote_code=True)
model = SentenceEmbeddingModel(base_model)
```

Apply the `preprocess_function` to the original dataset (`raw_datasets`) for preprocessing. The processed dataset contains tokenized **input IDs** and **attention masks**, as well as similarity labels.

```
## Data Preprocessing
tokenized_datasets = raw_datasets.map(preprocess_function, batched=True)
```

Training parameters are configured through **TrainingArguments**. See the comments in the code for descriptions of the main parameters.

```
## Set Training Parameters
training_args = TrainingArguments(
output_dir="./results",  # Output directory
evaluation_strategy="epoch",  # Evaluate at the end of each epoch
learning_rate=2e-5,  # Learning rate
per_device_train_batch_size=8,  # Training batch size
per_device_eval_batch_size=8,  # Evaluation batch size
num_train_epochs=3,  # Number of training epochs
weight_decay=0.01,  # Weight decay
save_steps=10,  # Save model every 10 steps
logging_dir='./logs',  # Logging directory
logging_steps=10,  # Log every 10 steps
save_total_limit=2,  # Save at most two checkpoints
)
```

Next, start training the model. Use the **Trainer** class to encapsulate the training logic. The model is the custom **SentenceEmbeddingModel**, and `train_dataset` and `eval_dataset` are the preprocessed training and validation datasets. `training_args` are the training parameters defined earlier.

```
## Define the Trainer Class and Start Training
trainer = Trainer(
model=model,
args=training_args,
train_dataset=tokenized_datasets["train"],
eval_dataset=tokenized_datasets["validation"],
)
## Start Training
trainer.train()
```

```
100%|██████████| 3/3 [00:02<00:00,  1.49it/s].
{'eval_runtime': 0.0412, 'eval_samples_per_second': 24.288, 'eval_steps_per_second': 24.288, 'epoch': 3.0}
{'train_runtime': 7.4859, 'train_samples_per_second': 0.802, 'train_steps_per_second': 0.401, 'train_loss': 0.04166938861211141, 'epoch': 3.0}
```

After fine-tuning the model, you can save the model parameters and tokenizer.

```
model.save_pretrained("./my_stella_model")
tokenizer.save_pretrained("./my_stella_model")
```

You can use this model to generate fine-tuned **embedding vectors** just like you would with HuggingFace open source models; you can also operate through the custom embedding model interface provided by frameworks such as **LangChain** or **LlamaIndex** (please refer to the respective framework documentation).

By fine-tuning the **Stella model**, higher-quality text **embeddings** can be generated, making semantically similar texts closer together in the embedding space. To further improve model performance, it is recommended to provide more high-quality training data to enhance the model's generalization ability.

It should be emphasized that modern **large models** are already very powerful in all aspects. Fine-tuning should be considered only when existing models do not meet the task requirements.

Summary

Embedding is one of the core technologies of **large models**. Embedding refers to the process of encoding external information. Without embedding technology, a large model would have no way to perceive the world, understand, or process knowledge. In order to manage the complexity of unstructured data, we apply embedding technology to convert data into numerical vectors so as to capture its fundamental features.

This section covered various aspects of **embedding technology**, from its origins to the latest developments, and provided many concrete practical examples to help learners understand and practice.

Currently, **text embedding technology** is already very mature. However, multi-modal unstructured data (such as images, audio, and video) come in various formats and carry rich underlying semantics.

In the future, the focus of **embedding technology** will be on the coordinated development of **multi-modality** (such as text, image, and audio/video, etc.). Through **cross-modal embedding technology**, it will be possible to more effectively capture the associations and commonalities between different data types, thereby enhancing the model's performance in understanding complex real-world scenarios.

4

Vector Storage

If **embedding technology** is regarded as **text representation learning**, then **vector storage technology** involves processes such as indexing, saving, and querying vectors. **Embeddings** are responsible for forming and transmitting the "neural medium" by encoding external information, converting input information into understandable and processable vector representations. The **vector database**, on the other hand, is like the hippocampus, storing and organizing vectorized information in a complex semantic space and enabling efficient memory retrieval when needed.

By using **embedding technology**, an article is converted into a series of numbers; by using **vector storage technology**, we can quickly find the most relevant one from billions of vectors. This technology focuses on optimizing this process to achieve faster, more accurate, and more resource-efficient results.

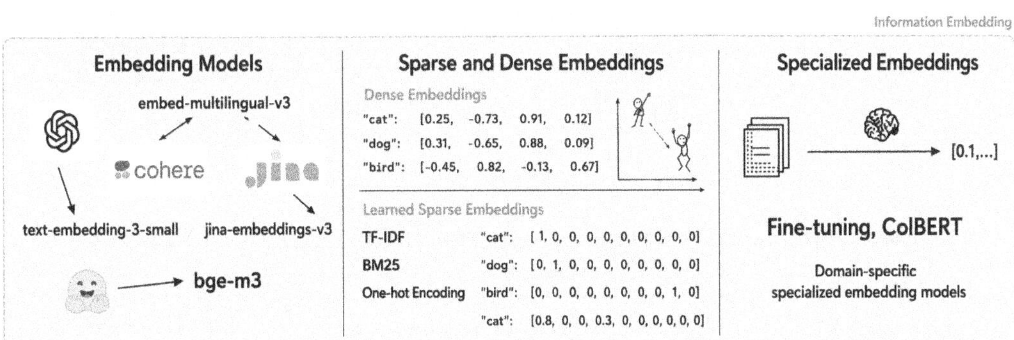

Figure 4.1: Overview of embedding approaches, including common embedding models, sparse and dense embedding representations, and specialized embedding methods such as fine-tuning and ColBERT for domain-specific retrieval.

A **vector database** is a typical application of **vector storage technology**. Traditional databases store data in the form of tables and establish data indices by assigning values to data points. When a query request is received, a traditional database returns results that exactly match the query. In contrast, a **vector database** stores vectors in the form of **embeddings** and supports vector search functions based on similarity metrics (rather than exact matches). Although both are called **databases**, they are suitable for different scenarios, and neither is inherently superior.

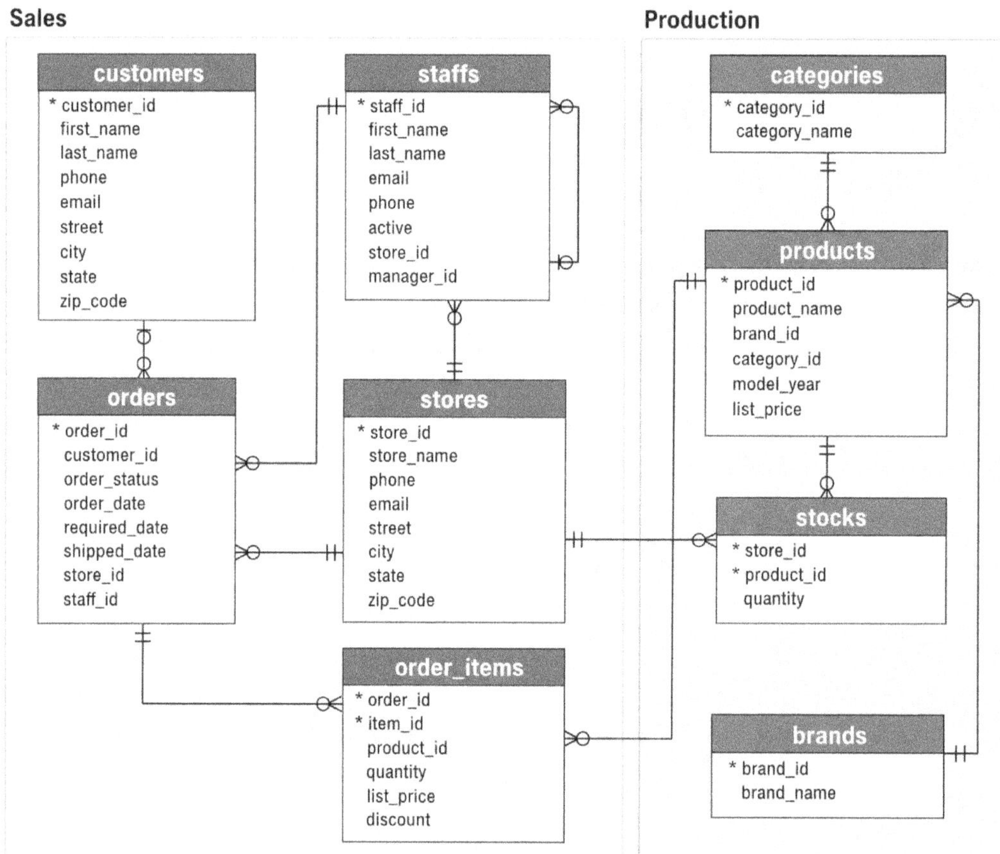

Figure 4.2: Database schema diagram showing sales and production tables with relationships and key fields

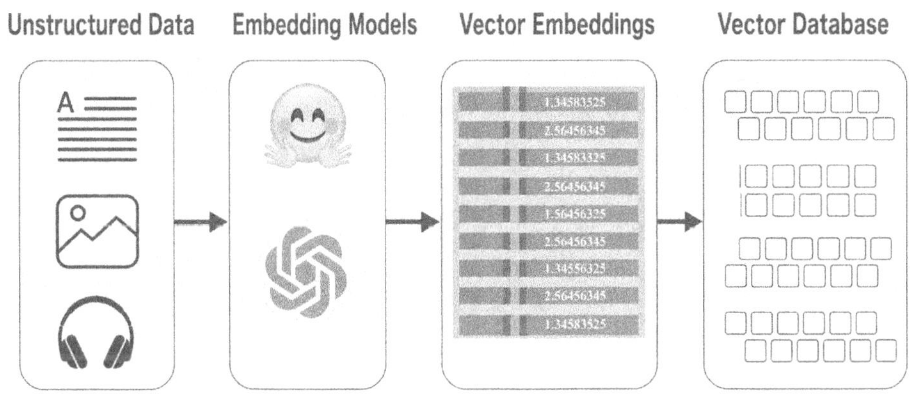

Figure 4.3: A flowchart showing unstructured data processed by embedding models into a vector database

With the development of **AI technology**, **vector databases** are becoming increasingly important in modern applications. Their technology stack is not only limited to "storing vectors" but also optimizing mechanisms for vector indexing and searching. Next, we will discuss these topics in detail.

How are vectors stored

Even without installing a commercial **vector database**, by simply using **LlamaIndex**, you can quickly establish a **vector storage mechanism** based on memory or local disk.

A simple vector index from the perspective of LlamaIndex's design

Although small, it is fully equipped—using **LlamaIndex** to implement the vector storage mechanism. Lewis refers to this as a **simple vector index**. Let's look at a simple example next.

First, read all the documents in the directory. Then, generate the index, that is, store the vectors (Refer to `GitHub - PacktPublishing/RAG-from-First-Principles: RAG from First Principles Published by Packt Pub` for the complete code).

```
from llama_index.core import SimpleDirectoryReader
documents = SimpleDirectoryReader("/data").load_data() # Load documents
len(documents)
from llama_index.core import VectorStoreIndex
index = VectorStoreIndex.from_documents(documents) # Create index
vars(index)
```

```
{'_use_async': False,
'_store_nodes_override': False,
'_embed_model': OpenAIEmbedding(model_name='text-embedding-ada-002',
embed_batch_size=100, callback_manager=<llama_index.core.callbacks.
base.CallbackManager object at 0x0000022E8FEB1730>, num_workers=None,
additional_kwargs={}, api_key='sk-8j2Vjv......', api_base='https://api.
openai.com/v1', api_version='', max_retries=10, timeout=60.0, default_
headers=None, reuse_client=True, dimensions=None),
'_insert_batch_size': 2048,
'_storage_context': StorageContext(docstore=<llama_index.core.
storage.docstore.simple_docstore.SimpleDocumentStore object at
0x0000022ECC6291C0>,
index_store=<llama_index.core.storage.index_store.simple_index_store.
SimpleIndexStore object at 0x0000022E90DE6570>,
vector_stores={'default': SimpleVectorStore(stores_text=False,
is_embedding_query=True, data=SimpleVectorStoreData(embedding_
dict={'03fa0674-d5cc-4e2b-b65d-45a36da94cb2': [-0.008005363866686821,
0.012379131279885769, 0.005627532955259085, 0.01884971372783184,
-0.02227955311536789, -0.01039039995521...]})
```

The "**index**" information in the above output is very rich, including core components for data management and organization such as **course storage** (`SimpleDocumentStore`), **index storage** (`SimpleIndexStore`), and **vector storage** (`SimpleVectorStore`). Each of these components undertakes different responsibilities and cooperates with each other throughout the data processing workflow.

- **Course storage**: Used to save and read courses, which are represented as **node objects**. Nodes are the result of chunking the original courses, containing text content and related metadata.
- **Index storage**: Contains lightweight **index metadata**, that is, additional state information created when building the index. It is used to store the index structure and related metadata to support fast retrieval and query operations.
- **Vector store**: An in-memory storage system that stores **embeddings** in the form of a dictionary, mapping node IDs to their corresponding embeddings.

In this vector index, `llama_index` automatically splits the imported course content into individual **nodes**. **Nodes** in LlamaIndex are the basic unit of vector storage.

The relationships between nodes as well as the connections between nodes and embeddings are thoroughly recorded in the index.

```
nodes = index.index_struct.nodes_dict
for node in nodes:
    print(node)
```

```
4a2aedf6-6c9e-4359-9125-786119be2b50
77f2ab3f-4ac0-433d-9b5a-f3fa442587a5
07388425-9662-4690-b0b4-6ede6943561d
```

Of course, you can also manually split the nodes (Refer to `GitHub - PacktPublishing/RAG-from-First-Principles: RAG from First Principles Published by Packt Pub` for the complete code).

```
from llama_index.core.node_parser import SentenceSplitter
text_splitter = SentenceSplitter(chunk_size=512, chunk_overlap=10)
nodes = text_splitter.get_nodes_from_documents(documents) # Split the
course into nodes (text blocks)
index = VectorStoreIndex(nodes) # Generate an index from the nodes
nodes = index.index_struct.nodes_dict
for node in nodes:
    print(node)
```

Next, use `storage_context` to save the index to disk and view the structure of the index files.

```
index.storage_context.persist(persist_dir="saved_index") # Save the index
```

In the generated `saved_index` directory, you can see the following content:

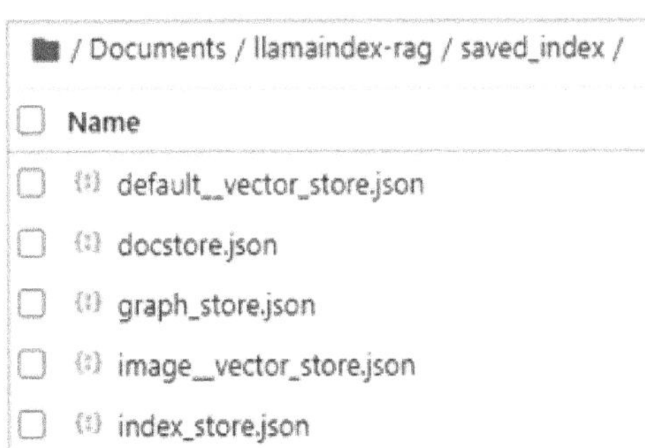

Figure 4.4: A file explorer window shows five JSON files in a folder named savedindex within llamaindexrag

This directory contains multiple JSON files used for storing indexes and related data.

- **default_vector_store.json**: Stores the default vector storage configuration or data. Used to store the embedded default vector data, such as the vectorized representations of user-uploaded texts, documents, or other resources. It is used by the system as the main vector index library during retrieval.
- **docstore.json**: Stores metadata or actual content of the document store. Stores detailed document information, such as the original content, title, and `path` of documents. During retrieval, the results returned by the vector index can use **docstore** to obtain specific document content.
- **graph_store.json**: Stores knowledge graph or relationship graph data. If the system supports **knowledge graph enhanced retrieval**, this file records the relationships between documents or vectors. It is used when reasoning based on node relationships is needed.
- **image_vector_store.json**: Stores vector data related to images. If the system supports **multimodal retrieval** (e.g., mixed text and image retrieval), this file may contain embedded image data (vectorized representations). With this file, the system can perform similarity retrieval based on image content.
- **index_store.json**: Stores the structure or meta information of the index itself. Stores metadata of all created indexes, such as the document range each index covers, embedding models, parameter configurations, etc. It is used to manage the entire index system and determine how to schedule different indexes.

Figure 4.5: Jupyter Notebook interface showing a JSON tree view of `index_store.json` *with data fields expanded*

Figure 4.6: Jupyter notebook view of a JSON structure showing metadata and text from a PDF document

The data structure information in **docstore.json** is particularly rich. For example, by expanding relationships, you can see the stored relationships between nodes.

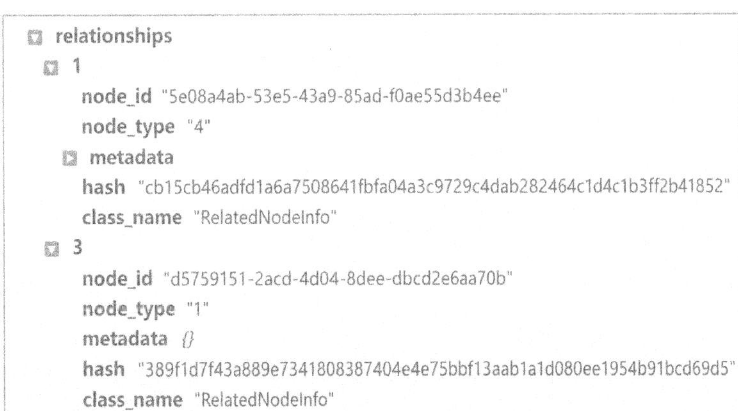

Figure 4.7: A software interface shows two relationships each with node IDs types and metadata details

Among these, **1** and **3** are the types of **relationships**, used to indicate the associations between different nodes. For example, current document nodes, previous nodes and next nodes are all connected via `node_id`. **node_type** is used to distinguish different types of nodes: **4** indicates a document node, and **1** represents a normal vector node (text chunk).

`default__vector_store.json`'s content is shown below. This file stores the **embedding vectors** of text chunks.

Here, **embedding_dict** contains the **embedding vector** for each text chunk, each being a 1536-dimensional **OpenAI embedding vector**.

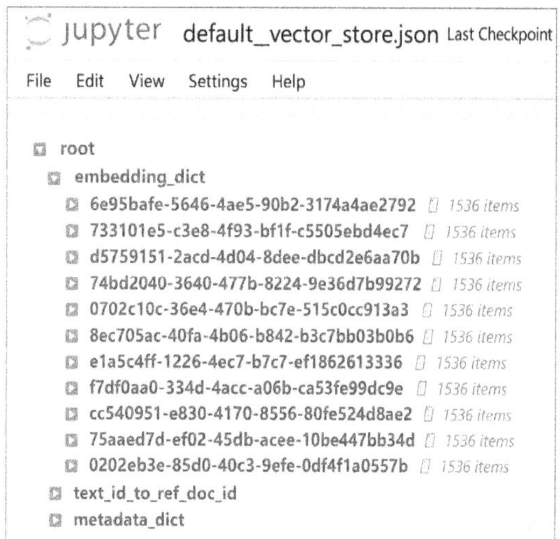

Figure 4.8: Jupyter file browser showing a JSON file with nested folders for embeddings and metadata

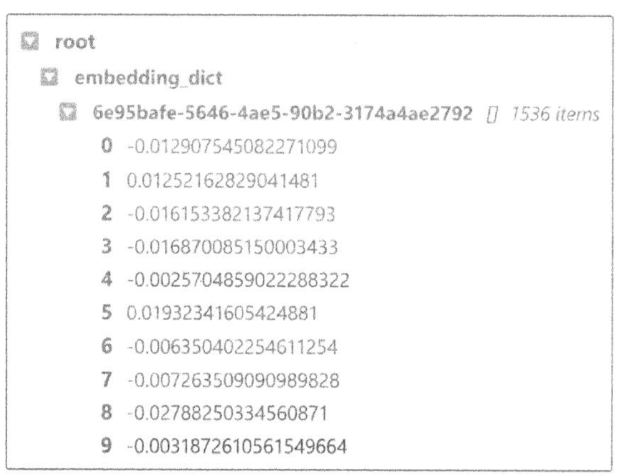

Figure 4.9: A tree view showing a dictionary with a key of numbers and floating point values

These numbers are the distilled information from the **embedding model**, known as **dense embeddings. Vector storage** or **indexing** is just the way to organize these numbers efficiently.

Alex: Lewis, I have a question here. Does the content in **embedding_dict** correspond to individual text chunks or individual tokens?

Lewis: They are **text chunks** (which are nodes in **LlamaIndex** or chunks in **LangChain**). The key (such as `6e95bafe-5646-4ae5-90b2-3174a4ae2792`) is the unique ID of the text chunk. Each text chunk (which could be a sentence, paragraph, or even a larger piece of text) will be transformed into a **1536-dimensional vector**, rather than generating a vector for each token.

> The input of an embedding model is text, not a single token. When you input a piece of text, such as a sentence or paragraph, the model first splits the text into tokens. This is only an internal computation process and does not affect the final output.
>
> Although each token is represented as a vector during the intermediate processing stage, after Transformer computation, the model ultimately generates a fixed-length vector, such as a 1536-dimensional vector, to represent the semantics of the entire input text. The model does not calculate a separate embedding for each token; instead, it calculates one embedding vector for the entire input text. Therefore, a 1536-dimensional embedding represents the semantic information of the whole text chunk, rather than the independent information of a single token.

The reason for detailing the **index construction** and **storage details** of *LlamaIndex* here is to help you understand the process of information organization in **vector storage**, that is, in a small vector database.

Components of a vector database

Alex: Lewis, since using **LlamaIndex** we can already achieve local vector storage and search, why do we still need open-source or commercial vector databases like **Milvus** or **Weaviate**?

Lewis: These **vector databases** provide more comprehensive vector data management solutions. To implement a **RAG system** in practice, the vector database needs **scalability**, allow dynamic data changes, support **metadata storage and filtering**, maintain **high availability and fault tolerance**, and offer functionalities such as **monitoring, security, access control, multi-user support**, and **data isolation**.

Next, let's use **Milvus** as an example for explanation.

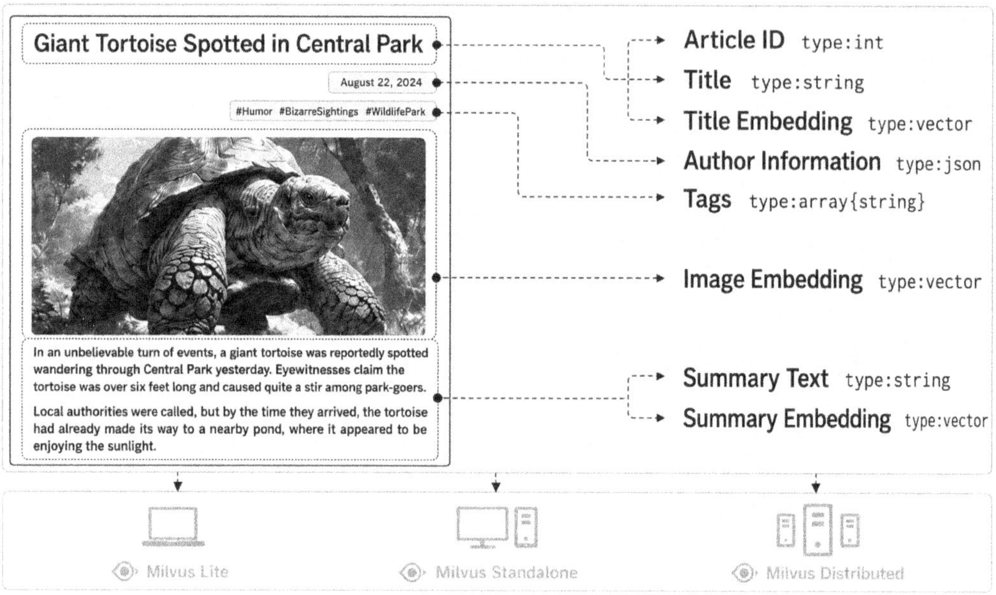

Figure 4.10: Diagram showing an article on a giant tortoise with data fields mapped for database storage

Milvus provides three deployment modes suitable for data scales ranging from simple applications to managing tens of billions of vectors in large-scale Kubernetes clusters.

- **Milvus Lite**, as a lightweight version of Milvus, is easy to integrate into applications. *This course* will introduce it as an example.
- **Milvus Standalone** is the single-server version of Milvus, with all components packaged into one **Docker image** for easy deployment.
- **Milvus Distributed** can be deployed on **Kubernetes clusters**, supporting scenarios with billions of vectors or even larger scale in a cloud-native architecture.

In practical applications, storing only vectors is not enough, as business logic usually requires additional **metadata** (such as text, time, tags, and categories). **Milvus** organizes unstructured or multi-modal data into structured **collections** and supports various data types, including common numeric and character types, a variety of vector types, arrays, sets, and JSON, thus reducing the need to maintain multiple database systems.

More importantly, vector databases create **indexes** and perform **queries** on vector embeddings using algorithms. These algorithms utilize **hash, quantization**, or **graph-based search** methods to achieve **ANN (Approximate Nearest Neighbor)** search. The goal of ANN search is to find the vectors closest to the query. While its accuracy is slightly lower than **k-NN search (exact nearest neighbor search)**, it requires less computation and is better suited for efficiently handling large, high-dimensional datasets.

In terms of performance, **Milvus** adopts hardware-aware optimizations (such as **AVX512, SIMD,** and **GPU support**), advanced search algorithms (such as **IVF**, **HNSW**, and **DiskANN**), and a high-performance search engine developed in C++, making its speed very fast. **Columnar storage** further improves query efficiency.

In terms of scalability, **Milvus** adopts a cloud-native architecture, supporting the processing of vector data at the scale of tens of billions. Its modular design enables core functionalities such as **search, data insertion**, and **index building** to be independently scaled.

In terms of features, **Milvus** supports various search methods (such as **ANN search, filtered search, range search**, etc.), provides multilingual **SDKs (Software Development Kits)**, supports multiple data types, and comes with enterprise-grade features such as **partition management, multi-tenancy support**, and **secure authorization**. In addition, **Milvus** offers a rich ecosystem of tools, such as a **visual management interface, monitoring tools**, and integration support with mainstream AI tools.

Feature	Description
Performance and fault tolerance	Sharding, partitioning data across multiple nodes; replication, creating multiple data copies on different nodes. Enables fault tolerance in case of failure to ensure stable performance
Monitoring	Monitor resource usage, query performance, and system operation status, and continuously optimize performance and fault tolerance
Access control	Ensure data security, provide compliance, accountability, and audit capabilities; protect data from unauthorized access and record user activity
Scalability and adjustability	Support horizontal scaling to accommodate different insertion rates, query rates, and hardware differences

Feature	Description
Multi-user and data isolation	Support multi-user or multi-tenancy; implement data isolation to ensure that user activities (such as insert, delete, query) do not affect the private data of other users
Backup	Periodically create data backups; support restoring the system to a previous state in case of data loss or corruption, reducing downtime
APIs and SDKs	Provide easy-to-use APIs; encapsulate multiple APIs to help developers use vector databases for specific use cases (such as semantic search, recommendation systems, etc.) without focusing on the underlying structure

Table 4.1: Core enterprise capabilities of vector databases and their operational benefits

Indexing in vector databases

Before a vector database can return relevant results efficiently, it must organize stored vectors in a way that supports fast similarity search. This is where indexing becomes essential. Instead of comparing a query vector with every vector in the database, an index provides a structured retrieval path that reduces search space and improves query performance. In this section, we examine how vector databases build and use indexes, and then introduce several common indexing approaches, including FLAT, IVF, quantization-based indexes, graph-based indexes, and hashing techniques.

The typical workflow of a **vector database** includes the following steps:

1. **Data storage:** Store high-dimensional vector data into the vector database.
2. **Index construction:** Build indexes for **vector embeddings** using techniques such as **hashing, quantization**, or **graph structures** to accelerate the query process.
3. **Query retrieval:** Upon receiving a query request, the vector database compares the query vector with the vectors in the index, using similarity measurement methods (such as **cosine similarity, Euclidean distance**, or **dot product**) to determine the nearest vectors.
4. **Post-retrieval processing:** Further filter or sort the found nearest neighbor results to optimize the query output.

Performing **vector search** in large datasets is a computationally intensive task, especially in high-dimensional spaces. To improve search efficiency, various **index structures** can be introduced to reduce the number of vectors that need to be compared, thereby lowering computational cost.

Indexing is an important concept in both vector databases and the broader RAG system. As explained previously, the purpose of indexing in a RAG system is to optimize retrieval by building an efficient storage mechanism for text chunks. This includes the process and methods used to construct document embeddings and metadata.

This definition refers to indexing at the application level. In contrast, the internal indexes discussed here for vector databases are more technical in nature. Their main purpose is to optimize the storage and retrieval performance of high-dimensional vector data, thereby improving the efficiency of similarity search. This involves various data structures and algorithms, such as FLAT, IVF, and HNSW, which are used to organize and accelerate ANN search over vectors.

This type of indexing is part of the internal implementation of the database and focuses more on low-level data processing and search optimization.

Vector indexing is a key technology that accelerates the retrieval process in vector databases. It determines how vectors are organized and the retrieval strategies used. The following sections will introduce several common vector indexing methods in detail.

We will begin with the simplest indexing method, FLAT, before moving on to more optimized approaches such as IVF, quantization-based indexing, graph indexing, and hashing.

Flat index

The **flat index** (abbreviated as **FLAT**) is the most basic indexing method. Its main feature is to compare every vector in the database one by one to ensure absolute accuracy of retrieval results. Since it does not use approximation or compression, FLAT can return exact nearest-neighbor results and achieve 100% recall, assuming the similarity metric is correctly configured.

When executing a query, **FLAT** compares by calculating the similarity or distance between the query vector and each vector in the database. However, because it needs to traverse all vectors, retrieval speed significantly decreases when the data scale is large.

One can imagine a two-dimensional space where all the vectors are distributed in this space. The **query vector** needs to compute the distance to every data point.

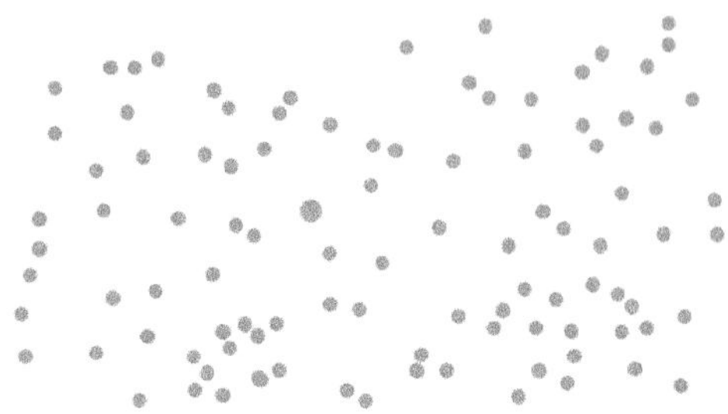

Figure 4.11: A cluster of purple dots scattered randomly with one red dot near the center on a white background

FLAT is suitable for relatively small datasets or offline evaluation scenarios where exact retrieval accuracy is more important than query speed. When the application scenario requires extremely high retrieval accuracy and can tolerate longer query times, **FLAT** is an ideal choice.

IVF index

The **Inverted File Index (IVF)** significantly accelerates retrieval speed by clustering vector data to reduce the number of vectors that need to be compared during queries. The most basic form of IVF is **IVF_FLAT**. There are also variants such as **IVF_SQ8** and **IVF_PQ**.

IVF_FLAT first clusters the vector data into several clusters, each representing a specific region in the data space. When performing a query, it first calculates the distance between the query vector and each **cluster center**, then only selects the top n clusters most similar to the query vector. Next, an exact match is performed for all vectors in these selected clusters. In the example, vectors are grouped into different clusters. The query vector only needs to be compared with vectors in these selected clusters.

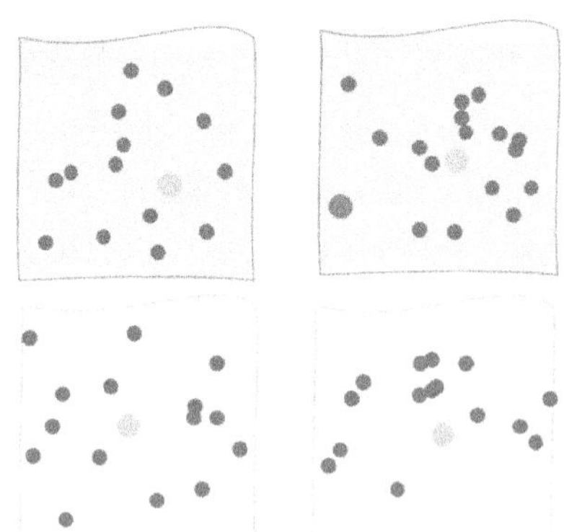

Figure 4.12: Four panels show clusters of purple dots with one large pink dot and a red dot in one panel

By searching only a portion of clusters, **IVF_FLAT** greatly reduces the number of vectors that need to be computed, improving query efficiency. Meanwhile, because exact comparison is performed within the selected clusters, the accuracy of retrieval results is ensured.

Alex: Why is it called "inverted"?

Lewis: In text retrieval scenarios, an "**inverted index**" refers to maintaining a **document list** for a given word (or keyword), listing all documents that contain that word. In this way, when searching for a word, you only need to look up related documents from this **inverted list** instead of traversing the entire document set.

IVF borrows this idea, clustering all vectors into multiple **clusters**, each recording its own **vector list**, just like inverted lists in text retrieval. When executing a query, according to the similarity between the query vector and each **cluster center**, only the most similar clusters are selected for retrieval, instead of traversing the entire dataset.

Quantization index

Quantization technology reduces storage space and computation by compressing vector data. The main quantization methods include **Scalar Quantization (SQ)**, **Product Quantization (PQ)**, and **Optimized Product Quantization (OPQ)**.

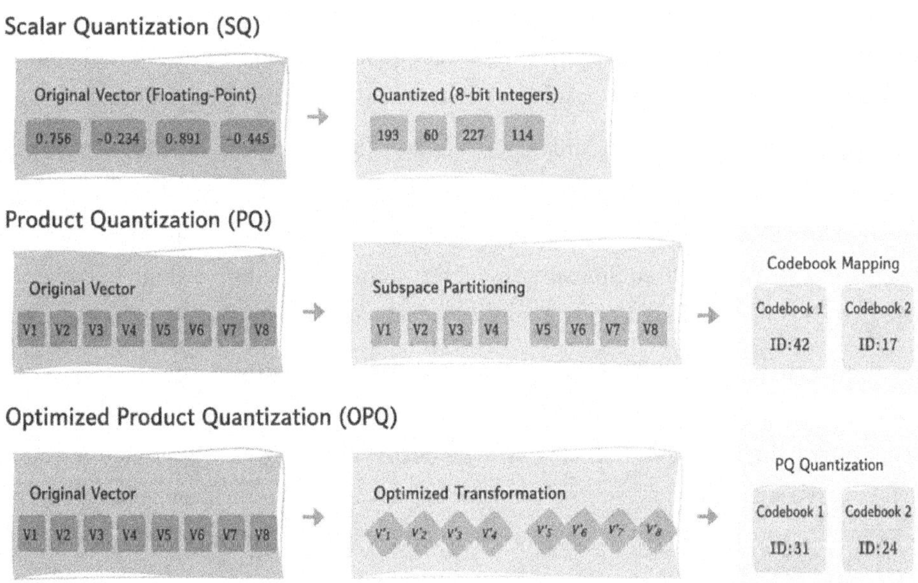

Figure 4.13: Flowchart compares three quantization methods for vectors showing stepwise transformations

> The indexing method determines how vectors are organized and retrieved, while quantization techniques focus on compressing and optimizing vector data. In practical applications, these two techniques are often used together to achieve the best results.

Scalar quantization is the simplest quantization method; it directly converts each floating-point number into a low-bit integer (such as 8-bit or 4-bit integers). This method is easy to implement, and both the quantization and dequantization processes are fast, significantly reducing storage requirements. However, it may result in a larger quantization error, thus affecting retrieval accuracy.

Product quantization splits high-dimensional vectors into several lower-dimensional parts and performs quantization on each part independently. The values in each subspace are mapped to discrete codewords represented by a pre-generated **codebook** that captures the data closest to the query vector. Since only the codeword indices need to be stored, product quantization greatly reduces storage requirements and improves query efficiency, enabling distance computation in compressed space.

Optimized product quantization improves upon product quantization by first optimizing the distribution of vectors through a linear transformation (such as rotation) before applying product quantization. This method helps to reduce quantization errors and improves retrieval accuracy. With the same compression rate, optimized product quantization can provide higher accuracy than product quantization and better adapts to the actual distribution of vector data.

IVF_SQ8 is a method that applies scalar quantization to compress vectors based on **IVF_FLAT**. In this approach, vectors are converted into low-bit representations, i.e., floating-point numbers are converted into 8-bit integers, further reducing storage needs on top of clustering, and greatly lowering memory and storage requirements, making it suitable for resource-limited environments. Although there is some quantization error, this impact is acceptable in most application scenarios.

IVF_PQ, on the other hand, combines **IVF** and product quantization: based on clustering, high-dimensional vectors are split into several low-dimensional subspaces and quantized separately, improving query efficiency and reducing storage needs. However, this approach introduces a certain loss of retrieval accuracy, so a balance between accuracy and efficiency must be struck.

Graph indexing

The **Hierarchical Navigable Small World (HNSW)** graph is an efficient graph-based indexing structure specifically designed to accelerate **ANN (Approximate Nearest Neighbor)** search for vectors. It leverages the characteristics of **small-world networks** by constructing a multi-layered graph structure, enabling fast retrieval of similar vectors in large-scale vector datasets.

In **HNSW**, the graph structure is organized into multiple layers, each with a different density. The topmost graph is very sparse, with few connections between nodes, which helps in coarse localization and rapid "jumps" during a query. Closer to the bottom, the graph becomes denser, allowing for more detailed searches. The query process starts from the top layer, where the search range can be quickly narrowed down to approximately locate the query vector. Then, the process goes deeper layer by layer, with each layer refining the search result based on the previous one until the most similar vector is found in the final layer. **HNSW** can provide extremely fast query speeds while maintaining high recall rates.

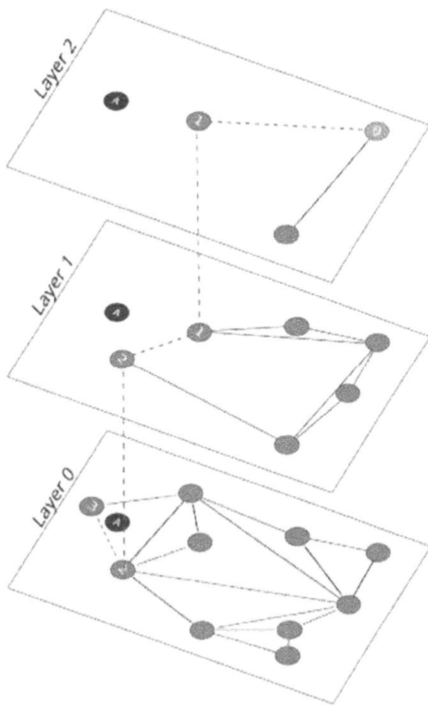

Figure 4.14: Three network layers are shown with colored nodes and edges connected by dashed lines

The advantage of **HNSW** lies in its ability to significantly improve query efficiency without sacrificing much accuracy, making it highly suitable for application scenarios that demand both fast query speed and high accuracy. However, using **HNSW** requires the system to have sufficient memory resources to store its graph structure to ensure query efficiency and result quality.

Hashing techniques

Locality Sensitive Hashing (LSH) constructs a set of **hash functions** to map similar high-dimensional vectors into the same **hash bucket**, thereby accelerating **ANN search**. When performing queries, it is only necessary to search the vectors located in the same hash bucket as the query vector, which greatly reduces computational overhead.

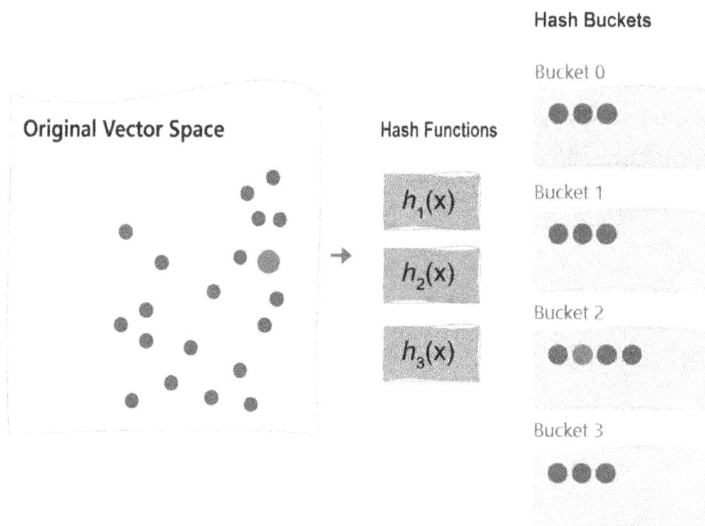

Figure 4.15: Diagram showing data points hashed from original vector space into different hash buckets

The advantages of **LSH** are fast retrieval speed, simple algorithms, and ease of implementation. However, its disadvantage is relatively lower accuracy and it is only suitable for approximate retrieval scenarios. In addition, depending on the data distribution, the performance of LSH may vary significantly.

Therefore, **LSH** is particularly suitable for application scenarios that require rapid return of approximate results, such as **recommendation systems** and **real-time queries**, as well as those applications where the data distribution is sparse and strict accuracy is not required.

Vector retrieval (similarity measurement)

In a **vector database**, the essence of retrieval or search is to find the vectors most similar to the query vector in a high-dimensional space, so it can also be referred to as **similarity measurement**. In order to achieve fast and efficient retrieval in vector databases, understanding their underlying principles is crucial.

In vector databases, there is a close relationship between **index structures** and **similarity measurements.** Similarity measurement determines how to quantify the distance or similarity between vectors, while index structures use this measurement method to organize and accelerate vector data retrieval. Choosing the appropriate similarity measurement and indexing method is critical for improving retrieval efficiency and accuracy.

Anna: You mentioned in Section 3 that measurement methods include **Euclidean distance, Manhattan distance, cosine similarity,** and **inner product.**

Lewis: Yes. **Manhattan distance** is less commonly used for vector similarity measurement. Here, I will provide the calculation formulas for several commonly used measurement methods, and also introduce the occasionally used **Hamming distance** and **Jaccard similarity.**

Euclidean distance (L2): Measures the straight-line distance between two vectors in space, suitable for continuous numerical data. The calculation formula is as follows:

$$d = \sqrt{\sum_{i=1}^{n} (a_i - b_i)^2}$$

Cosine similarity: Measures the cosine value of the angle between two vectors, reflecting the directional similarity of the vectors. The calculation formula is as follows:

$$\text{Cosine Similarity} = \frac{\sum_{i=1}^{n} a_i b_i}{\sqrt{\sum_{i=1}^{n} a_i^2}\sqrt{\sum_{i=1}^{n} b_i^2}}$$

Inner product (IP): Measures the projection relationship between two vectors, reflecting the direction and magnitude of the vectors. The calculation formula is as follows:

$$a \cdot b = \sum_{i=1}^{n} a_i \times b_i$$

Hamming distance: Measures the number of differing bits between binary vectors, suitable for binary data. The calculation formula is as follows:

$$d(a, b) = \sum_{i-1}^{n} (a_i \oplus b_i)$$

Jaccard similarity: Measures the similarity between two sets by calculating the ratio of the intersection to the union, suitable for sets or sparse data. The calculation formula is as follows:

$$\text{Jaccard Similarity} = \frac{|A \cap B|}{|A \cup B|}$$

Alex: Lewis, these **indexing methods** and **vector similarity measurements** are obviously very important. You have summarized them very clearly here, giving me a systematic understanding of this knowledge. However, I feel that in practical applications, it is still difficult to operate.

Lewis: That's true. These are core concepts of vector databases. To truly master them, you need hands-on practice and to try them out yourself. In Section 4.5, I will guide you in writing some examples of vector retrieval using these index methods, so you can more clearly understand which indexing and measurement methods to choose in different situations.

Mainstream vector databases

With the growing adoption of large language models and **vector retrieval technologies**, a variety of open-source and commercial **vector databases** have sprung up like mushrooms after the rain. These databases play an important role in the development process of AI and large model applications.

Each of these databases has its own characteristics in terms of **scalability**, **performance optimization**, deployment methods, and ecosystem. The following is a brief introduction to several commonly used vector databases.

- **Milvus:** The database most frequently used by Lewis in daily work is **Milvus**. It is an open-source, high-performance vector database that supports PB-level data and offers excellent scalability and high throughput.

  Milvus is particularly designed with the **developer experience** in mind, providing comprehensive documentation that makes it easy for learners to get started quickly. In addition, it supports **Docker deployment**, making it particularly suitable for applications adopting cloud-native architectures. For small teams and individual developers, the **local installation version** of Milvus is even easier to use. In the following examples, we will also use the local version of **Milvus** for demonstration.

  Milvus is favored for its wide range of use cases, performing exceptionally well in **cloud-native applications** that need to process large-scale vector data. It should be noted that optimization of Milvus configurations requires some experience, so its learning curve is relatively steep.

- **Zilliz Cloud: Zilliz Could** is the fully managed SaaS enterprise version based on Milvus, focusing on the commercialization of vector databases and providing managed services and advanced features for enterprise users, such as **automatic scaling** and **optimization**. After completing the development of a prototype project using Milvus, if there is a need to migrate to a larger scale production application scenario, moving from Milvus to Zilliz Cloud becomes a natural choice. Therefore, whether it is from small projects to large-scale applications, or from individual developers to enterprise users, **Milvus** and its enterprise version **Zilliz Cloud** offer a one-stop solution.
- **Weaviate:** The key feature of **Weaviate** lies in its open-source nature and its support for storing and retrieving **multimodal data** (such as text, images, and videos). It is easy to get started with quickly, making it very suitable for proof of concept and small to medium-sized projects. **Weaviate** supports **embedded mode**, making it convenient to run on local or small devices, and provides **data persistence** support, enabling integration with a variety of backend storage options (such as **S3**, **GCP**).

  Weaviate is suitable for quickly building multimodal applications, for example, intelligent Q&A systems based on images and text. However, its capabilities in large-scale scalability and performance optimization still need to be improved.
- **Qdrant: Qdrant** is renowned for its excellent performance, specifically optimized for **high-performance scenarios**. It can scale to massive vector collections containing over 50 million records and excels in **near real-time retrieval** and **dynamic writing**. However, it may face some challenges under **high concurrent write workloads**. If you need to implement **dynamic index updates**, **real-time recommendations**, or **personalized content delivery**, you may consider using Qdrant.

  Qdrant offers an **open-source version**, a **Cloud version**, and an **Enterprise version**. The **Cloud version** provides 1GB of free space, suitable for demo-level projects.
- **Faiss: Faiss**, developed by the Facebook AI Research team, is a library specially designed for efficient similarity search and dense vector clustering, mainly used for handling large-scale vector data. The library is written in C++ and provides a Python package.

  Faiss is divided into **CPU** and **GPU** versions: the **CPU version** is suitable for small-scale datasets and can run on ordinary servers; the **GPU version** utilizes **CUDA** acceleration, is suitable for large-scale datasets, and can significantly speed up search performance. It is important to note that the **GPU version of Faiss** only supports specific versions of **CUDA**, and if your CUDA version is not supported, installation will result in errors.

Faiss provides the core functions needed for **vector storage**, including **nearest neighbor search** (k-NN/ANN), **index structure optimization** (supporting algorithms such as **HNSW, IVF, PQ**), and **vector clustering**.

Although Faiss has the advantages of being lightweight and easy to start with, its functionality is relatively limited. Indexes can only be stored in memory, and it does not provide database-level storage management (such as **transactions, data persistence**). Unlike **Milvus** and **Weaviate**, it does not natively support distributed storage and queries. Therefore, Faiss is more suitable for handling million-level vector datasets, and its ability to handle billion-level vector datasets is limited. It is an ideal choice for beginners to learn from.

- **Pinecone: Pinecone** is a well-known commercial **vector storage solution** focused on managed services, aimed at reducing deployment and maintenance costs. Its advantages include ease of use and scalability, offering a one-stop solution with support for **automatic scaling** and **high availability**. Nevertheless, when it comes to certain customized performance requirements, **Pinecone** may be less capable than open-source alternatives, and it tends to be more expensive. Therefore, for organizations with high demands for **stability** and **availability** but without additional operational capabilities, **Pinecone** is a good choice.

  Pinecone's documentation is also very comprehensive, containing many valuable **RAG solution** examples that are worth studying for reference.

- **Chroma:** Similar to Faiss, the open-source library **Chroma** also provides all the basic functionalities required for **retrieval**: storing **embeddings** and their **metadata**, vector search, full-text search, file storage, metadata filtering, and multimodal retrieval.

  By default, **Chroma** uses **SQLite** for storage (with support for persistence to disk), which means it does not require an additional database management system and is very suitable for quickly setting up projects. However, this also means Chroma is not suitable for large-scale production environments and has limitations in supporting distributed systems, complex queries, and enterprise-level applications.

  Like Faiss, Chroma's advantage lies in its **ease of use**. The Chroma documentation also provides a wealth of knowledge related to **vector storage**, helping users to better understand and utilize it.

- **Elasticsearch:** As a mature distributed search engine, **Elasticsearch** has become a benchmark tool in enterprise-level search scenarios due to its near real-time retrieval capabilities, horizontal scalability, and rich query syntax. In recent years, **Elasticsearch** has introduced

vector search features (such as the `dense_vector` field type and **k-NN search** interface), enabling it to support both traditional keyword retrieval, numerical range filtering, as well as high-dimensional vector similarity calculations. This is particularly suitable for scenarios requiring **hybrid multi-modal queries**, such as e-commerce search combining text semantic vectors with product attribute filtering.

For teams that have already deeply integrated the **Elasticsearch technology stack**, existing clusters and operations systems can be directly reused, thereby reducing the marginal cost of introducing vector capabilities. **Elasticsearch**'s distributed architecture can easily handle datasets at the tens-of-billions scale, and supports enterprise-level features such as **multi-tenancy** and **fine-grained permission control**. However, in pure vector retrieval scenarios, **Elasticsearch**'s performance may not match that of dedicated vector databases, and requires optimization through **sharding strategies** or approximate algorithms to improve performance.

- **PGVector: PGVector** (a PostgreSQL extension) seamlessly integrates vector computation capabilities into relational databases by providing **vector data types** and **ANN retrieval** (such as **HNSW, IVF_FLAT**) for PostgreSQL. This design is particularly well-suited for scenarios that require handling both structured data associations and vector similarity analysis, such as linking user behavior vectors with label data in SQL tables in user profiling systems, or performing multi-condition queries that combine spatial coordinates and feature vectors in geographic information systems.

  In **PGVector**, developers can directly use standard SQL syntax to perform complex queries that **JOIN vectors with structured data**, avoiding the complexity of cross-database synchronization. Although PGVector improves performance through index optimization, its throughput and latency may still lag behind dedicated vector databases when dealing with ultra-large-scale vector datasets (e.g., tens of millions or more) or high-concurrency scenarios. The advantages of PGVector lie in its native support for transactional consistency and complex SQL operations (such as **window functions** and **stored procedures**), making it suitable for moderately sized datasets and applications requiring strong transactional guarantees, such as real-time feature comparison in financial risk control.

Selection and evaluation of vector databases

Alex: Here comes the question. With so many **vector databases** available and all seemingly similar on the surface, how should one choose?

Lewis: That is indeed a difficult question to answer. The concepts of **RAG** and **vector databases** are quite new, and currently there are not many who have thoroughly evaluated multiple vector databases in production-level projects. Practical experience in this area is also limited.

Vector database selection

Nevertheless, we can still consider the following key factors and combine them with specific needs and scenarios to make a choice.

- **Open source vs. Paid managed service**: If your team has strong DevOps capabilities, you can choose open-source databases (such as **Milvus**, **Weaviate**, **Qdrant**, etc.) for flexibility. If you want to reduce operational costs, you can opt for commercial managed services (such as **Pinecone**, **AWS Kendra**, etc.).
- **Performance (query speed)**: For scenarios requiring large-scale, high-concurrency queries, **Milvus** and **Pinecone** perform well. For latency-sensitive applications (such as recommendation systems), databases with low latency, such as **Milvus**, should be prioritized.
- **Scalability**: While the scalability of various vector databases is generally good, **Milvus** and **Pinecone** excel for massive datasets.
- **Developer experience**: Choose databases with comprehensive documentation and community support whenever possible, such as **Milvus** and **Weaviate**. If your development team is Python-friendly, select databases with simple APIs, such as **Chroma**.
- **Feature support**: If you need complex hybrid search (combining structured and vector data), **Weaviate**, **Qdrant**, and **Milvus** are good choices. For dynamic data and index updates, **Milvus** and **Qdrant** offer stronger support.
- **Cost and budget**: Using open-source tools (such as **PGVector**, **Chroma**) can reduce initial investment. Although commercial solutions (such as **Pinecone**) are more expensive, they are more suitable for enterprises seeking stability and service support.
- **Tech stack compatibility**: If your existing tech stack uses **Elasticsearch**, you can extend its vector search capabilities to reduce the learning curve. Teams using **PostgreSQL** can consider **PGVector** for easy integration of structured and vector data.

For cloud-native applications, **Vald** and **Milvus** offer better Kubernetes support. In scenarios with high demand for GPU acceleration, **Faiss** is an excellent choice.

Based on these dimensions, you can quickly match the most suitable **vector database**. For example, when developing a **real-time recommendation system**, you can choose **Milvus** or **Qdrant**;

for proof-of-concept or small project development, you can choose **Chroma** or **Weaviate**; for developing **enterprise-level search**, you can go with **Pinecone** or **Elasticsearch**; if integration with relational databases is needed, **PGVector** is a good option.

Note that as time goes on, the features and characteristics of each vector database may change.

By clearly identifying your **project requirements** and **budget**, and referring to the comparison below, you can complete the vector database selection process.

Frameworks like **LangChain** offer interfaces for almost all vector databases, so developers can freely switch between different vector databases to experience differences in performance.

Database	Open source	Self-host	Cloud	Vector-first	Dev exp.	Index types	Hybrid	Disk index	RBAC	Sharding
Pinecone	No	No	Yes	Yes	Good	Unknown	Yes	No	No	Unknown
Weaviate	Yes	Yes	Yes	Yes	Good	HNSW	Yes	Yes	No	Static only
Milvus	Yes	Yes	Yes	Yes	Very good	11 types	Yes	Yes	Yes	Yes
Qdrant	Yes	Yes	Yes	Yes	Good	HNSW	Yes	Yes	No	Yes
Chroma	Yes	Yes	No	Yes	Good	HNSW	Yes	Yes	No	Yes
Elastic-search	No	Yes	Yes	No	Average	HNSW	Yes	No	Yes	Static only
PGVector	Yes	Yes	Yes	No	Average	HNSW / IVFFlat	Yes	Yes	No	-

Table 4.2: Comparison of selected vector databases by deployment model, search capabilities, and governance features

Database	QPS	Latency (ms)	Free plan	Price 50k vectors (USD)	Price 20M vectors (USD)
Pinecone	150+ (scaled)	1	Yes	70	227 (HP: 2074)
Weaviate	791	2	Yes	From 25	1536
Milvus	2406	1	Yes	From 65	309 (HP: 2291)
Qdrant	326	4	Yes	From 9	281 (HP: 820)
Chroma	Unknown	Unknown	Yes	Self-hosted free	Self-hosted free
Elastic-search	700~100	5~10	Self-hosted free	Varies	1225
PGVector	141	8	Self-hosted free	Varies	Varies

Table 4.3: Comparison of selected vector databases by performance and estimated hosting cost

Common tools for evaluating vector databases include **ANN Benchmark** and **VectorDBBench**.

ANN Benchmark is an external tool used to evaluate the performance of **vector index algorithms** on real datasets. Since **vector indexing** is a resource-intensive core component of vector databases, its performance has a significant impact on the overall database performance. **ANN Benchmark** excels at measuring the performance of **vector index algorithms** and provides a reliable reference for selecting and comparing different **vector search libraries**. However, its limitation is that it cannot evaluate complex and mature vector database systems, nor does it cover scenarios such as **combining vector search with conditional filtering**.

In contrast, **VectorDBBench** is an open-source tool specifically designed for evaluating **vector databases**. It is suitable for open-source vector databases (such as **Milvus** and **Weaviate**) as well as fully managed services (such as **Zilliz Cloud** and **Pinecone**). It supports evaluating key metrics of the database such as **queries per second** and **recall rate**, and focuses on resource consumption, data loading capacity, and system stability. Unlike **ANN Benchmark**, **VectorDBBench** is able to simulate testing scenarios that are closer to real production environments, making it more suitable for a comprehensive evaluation of the actual performance of vector databases.

Yifan Cai used the tool **VectorDBBench** in the article *Open-Source Vector Database Performance Comparison: Milvus, Chroma, Qdrant* to evaluate three commonly used open-source vector databases.

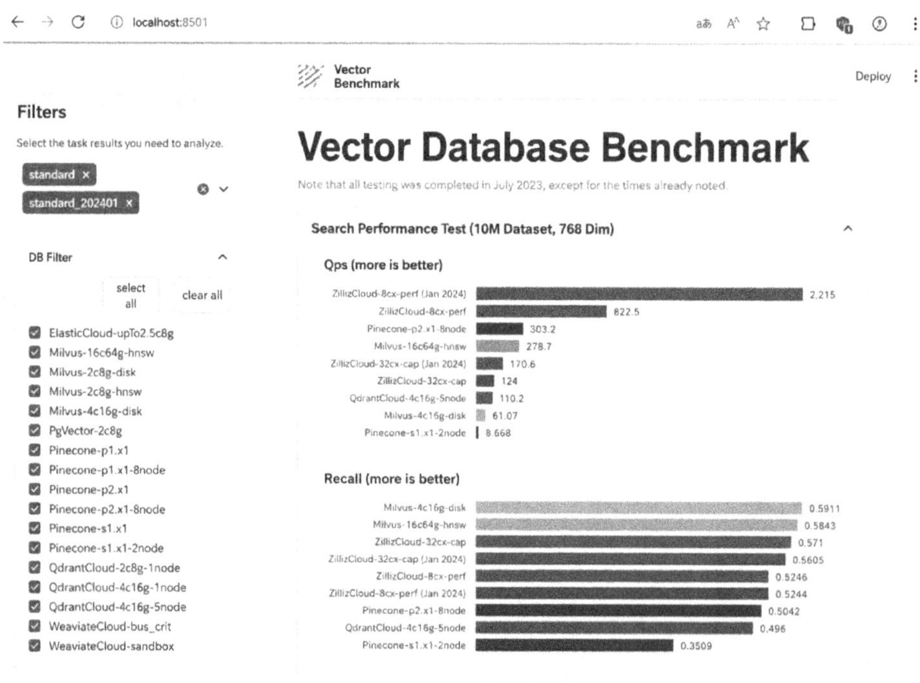

Figure 4.16: Webpage showing Vector Database Benchmark charts for search performance and recall scores

This article provides a detailed introduction to the specific steps and details of evaluating various vector databases with **VectorDBBench**. Here, we only present the final conclusions: According to the test results, **Milvus** is suitable for handling large-scale datasets and applications with high performance requirements, delivering the best performance (i.e., query speed); **Qdrant** has lower latency and is suitable for applications with a smaller scale and higher latency requirements; **Chroma** is more suitable for small-scale, low-load applications.

Index and search settings in vector databases

When using vector databases, the selection of **index** and **search metrics** is the most critical part. This section uses **Milvus** as an example to explain these two parameters in detail and their applicable scenarios.

Milvus vector operation example

The overall code workflow for operating **Milvus** is shown below. This code is completely independent of frameworks like **LangChain** or **LlamaIndex**, and is intended to clearly demonstrate how to create collections, insert vectors, and perform retrieval in Milvus.

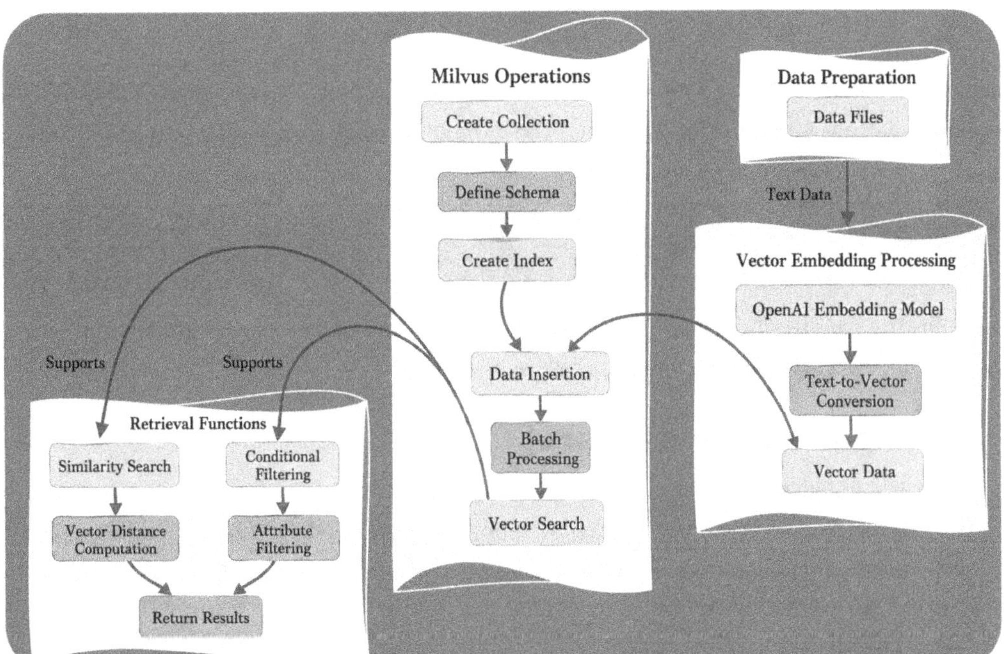

Figure 4.17: Flowchart in Chinese showing Milvus operations data prep embedding and search processes

In Milvus, data organization and management are mainly achieved through **collections** (`Collection`). Collections support various operations such as **insert, delete, index creation**, and **search**. It is the core data structure of Milvus, representing a group of data. When creating a collection, you need to specify the collection name and **schema**.

> Here, two core collection-related concepts are introduced: **FieldSchema** and **CollectionSchema**.
>
> **FieldSchema:** Defines the properties of each field in a collection. Each field represents a specific attribute of the data. Its main properties include the field name and data type, such as integer (INT64), floating point (FLOAT), string (VARCHAR), or vector type (FLOAT_VECTOR).
>
> **CollectionSchema:** Defines the structure of the entire collection, including which fields the collection contains and its description. Its main properties include the field list and descriptive information. By defining a collection schema, users can clearly specify the data structure and organization of the collection, making it easier to manage and operate the data.

Next, we will install **Milvus Lite**, which is the local version of the Milvus Python package. For beginners, **Milvus Lite** is sufficient. If you need to build a larger-scale system, you should install a more powerful version of **Milvus**.

```
pip install pymilvus
pip install pymilvus[model]
```

The following code example demonstrates how to create a Milvus vector collection from scratch with custom data and perform vector search operations.

Preparing the sample dataset

In this example, we create a small dataset containing monster information. Each record includes fields such as monster ID, name, location, difficulty level, synonyms, and description. These fields will later be stored as metadata alongside the vector embeddings (Refer to `GitHub - PacktPublishing/RAG-from-First-Principles: RAG from First Principles Published by Packt Pub` for the complete code).

```
### Prepare Sample Dataset
import pandas as pd
data_records = [
```

```
{
"monster_id": "BM001",
"monster_name": "Tiger Vanguard",
"location": "Bamboo Forest Pass",
"difficulty": "High",
"synonyms": "Fierce Tiger Demon, Tiger Demon",
"description": "A tiger-shaped monster appearing in the Bamboo Forest
checkpoint, extremely powerful."
},
{
"monster_id": "BM002",
"monster_name": "Fire Ape",
"location": "Volcano Cave",
"difficulty": "Low",
"synonyms": "Flame Ape, Blazing Ape",
"description": "A primate monster living in volcanic caves, just a minor
character."
},]
df = pd.DataFrame(data_records)
```

Creating a Milvus collection and index

After preparing the dataset, we connect to Milvus Lite and create a collection named Wukong_Monsters. The schema defines both structured metadata fields and a vector field. The vector dimension is determined by generating a sample embedding with the selected embedding model.

The collection also uses an automatically generated primary key. The `auto_id=True` setting means that Milvus will create the primary key values automatically, so users do not need to provide them during insertion.

```
### Create or Connect to Milvus
from pymilvus import MilvusClient, DataType, FieldSchema, CollectionSchema
from pymilvus import model
db_path = "./wukong.db"
client = MilvusClient(db_path)
collection_name = "Wukong_Monsters"
### Get Vector Dimension of Embedding Model
from pymilvus.model.dense import SentenceTransformerEmbeddingFunction
embedding_function = SentenceTransformerEmbeddingFunction(model_
```

```
name='BAAI/bge-large-zh')
sample_embedding = embedding_function(["Sample text"])[0]
vector_dim = len(sample_embedding)
fields = [
    FieldSchema(name="id", dtype=DataType.INT64, is_primary=True, auto_
id=True),
    FieldSchema(name="vector", dtype=DataType.FLOAT_VECTOR, dim=vector_
dim),
    FieldSchema(name="monster_id", dtype=DataType.VARCHAR, max_length=50),
    FieldSchema(name="monster_name", dtype=DataType.VARCHAR, max_
length=100),
    FieldSchema(name="location", dtype=DataType.VARCHAR, max_length=100),
    FieldSchema(name="difficulty", dtype=DataType.VARCHAR, max_length=20),
    FieldSchema(name="synonyms", dtype=DataType.VARCHAR, max_length=200),
    FieldSchema(name="description", dtype=DataType.VARCHAR, max_
length=500),
]
schema = CollectionSchema(fields, description=" Wukong Monsters", enable_
dynamic_field=True)
if not client.has_collection(collection_name):
    client.create_collection(collection_name=collection_name,
schema=schema)
index_params = client.prepare_index_params()
index_params.add_index(
    field_name="vector",
    index_type="AUTOINDEX",
    metric_type="L2",
    params={"nlist": 1024}
)
client.create_index(
    collection_name=collection_name,
    index_params=index_params
)
from tqdm import tqdm
for start_idx in tqdm(range(0, len(df)), desc="Inserting data"):
    row = df.iloc[start_idx]
    doc_parts = [str(row['monster_name'])]
    if row['synonyms']:
```

```
        doc_parts.append(f"(Alias: {row['synonyms']})")
    if row['location']:
        doc_parts.append(f"Scene: {row['location']}")
    if row['description']:
        doc_parts.append(f"Description: {row['description']}")
    doc_text = ";".join(doc_parts)
    embedding = embedding_function([doc_text])[0]
```

The index is created on the vector field. In this example, AUTOINDEX is used, which allows Milvus to automatically select an appropriate index type based on the data and configuration. The similarity metric is set to L2, which means Euclidean distance is used for vector comparison.

Example: Inserting and querying monster data with vector search

After creating the collection and index, we can insert vectorized monster data into Milvus. Each record is converted into a text representation by combining fields such as monster name, synonyms, location, and description. This text is then converted into an embedding vector and inserted into the collection along with its metadata.

```
data_to_insert = [{
"vector": embedding,
"monster_id": str(row["monster_id"]),
"monster_name": str(row["monster_name"]),
"location": str(row["location"]),
"difficulty": str(row["difficulty"]),
"synonyms": str(row["synonyms"]),
"description": str(row["description"])
}]
client.insert(collection_name=collection_name, data=data_to_insert)
## Test Search
search_query = "High difficulty monster"
search_embedding = embedding_function([search_query])[0]
search_result = client.search(
collection_name=collection_name,
data=[search_embedding.tolist()],
limit=3,
output_fields=["monster_name", "location", "difficulty", "synonyms"]
)
```

```
print(f"Search results for '{search_query}':", search_result)
## Test Conditional Query
query_result = client.query(
collection_name=collection_name,
filter="difficulty == 'Low'",
output_fields=["monster_name", "location", "difficulty", "synonyms"]
)
print(f"Monsters with difficulty Low:", query_result)
```

```
Inserting data: 100%|██████████| 2/2 [00:01<00:00,  1.68it/s]
Search result for 'high difficulty monster': data: ["[{'id':
456823454216224768, 'distance': 1.0104241371154785, 'entity':
{'difficulty': 'High', 'location': 'Bamboo Forest Pass', 'monster_name':
'Tiger Vanguard', 'synonyms': 'Ferocious Tiger Demon, Tiger Demon'}}]"]
Monster with difficulty Low: data: ["{'id': 456823565118078978,
'difficulty': 'Low', 'location': 'Volcano Cave', 'monster_name': 'Fire
Ape', 'synonyms': 'Blazing Ape, Flame Ape'}"]
```

The search example retrieves monsters that are semantically similar to the query "**High difficulty monster**." In contrast, the conditional query retrieves records based on an exact metadata condition, such as `difficulty == 'Low'`.

The output shows that Milvus can return both vector-based search results and metadata-filtered query results. For example, the vector search identifies **Tiger Vanguard** as a high-difficulty monster, while the conditional query returns **Fire Ape** as a low-difficulty monster.

This piece of code creates and connects to the local Milvus database **wukong.db**, and also creates a collection called `Wukong_Monsters` for storing vector data. In the collection's field schema, `is_primary=True` indicates that the `id` field is the **primary key**, which uniquely identifies a record. `auto_id=True` means that the primary key is automatically generated by **Milvus**, so you do not and cannot manually specify it. Therefore, when inserting data, we do not provide the `id` field, but only the other fields defined in the **Schema**. In addition, `enable_dynamic_field=True` means that when defining the collection **Schema**, the **dynamic fields** feature is enabled, allowing fields not defined in the Schema to be included when inserting data. These extra fields will not be discarded, but will instead be automatically stored in a built-in field named `$meta`.

Now, we will focus on the parameters **index_type** (index type) and **metric_type** (similarity metric) in the code, and discuss their optional values and applicable scenarios.

Choosing the appropriate index type

Indexing is the process of organizing data so that similarity search can be performed efficiently. It plays a vital role in making **similarity search** practical by significantly speeding up time-consuming queries on large datasets. **Milvus** organizes data with specialized structures and stores metadata in **index files** to enable fast retrieval of requested information during search or query operations.

Most of the **vector index types** supported by Milvus use **ANN (Approximate Nearest Neighbor)** search. Compared to **precise search**, which is often very time-consuming, the core idea of ANN search is not to return the most exact results, but to only search for the neighbors of the target. In this way, ANN search greatly improves search efficiency by sacrificing a certain degree of accuracy within an acceptable range.

According to implementation approach, ANN vector indexes can be categorized as **flat indexes, graph-based indexes, tree-based indexes, hash-based indexes**, and **quantization-based indexes.** A given vector database may not necessarily support all index types.

Index type is closely related to the type of **vector embedding. Float embeddings** (also known as float vectors or dense vectors), **binary embeddings** (also known as binary vectors), and **sparse embeddings** (also known as sparse vectors) each have their own suitable index types. To enhance query performance, an index type can be specified for each vector field. Currently, each vector field can only be assigned one index type; when switching the index type, Milvus will automatically remove the old index. In code, the `index_type` parameter of the `add_index` method specifies the index type used for vector data in Milvus. Table 4 summarizes the main Milvus index types, their applicable scenarios, and the embedding formats they support.

Index type	Category	Applicable scenarios	Embedding type
FLAT	Flat index	Relatively small datasets, 100% recall needed	Float embedding
IVF_FLAT	Tree-based index	High query speed required, needs as high recall as possible	Float embedding
IVF_SQ8	Quantization-based index	Extremely fast query speed, limited memory resources, can accept slight compromise on recall	Float embedding
IVF_PQ	Quantization-based index	Fast query speed, limited memory resources, can accept slight compromise on recall	Float embedding

Index name	Index type	Application scenarios	Supported embeddings
ScaNN	Quantization-based index	Very fast query speed; High recall required; Sufficient memory resources	Floating-point embeddings
HNSW	Graph-based index	Very fast query speed; High recall required; Relatively sufficient memory resources	Floating-point embeddings
HNSW_SQ	Graph-based index	Very fast query speed; Limited memory resources; Acceptable slight compromise on recall	Floating-point embeddings
HNSW_PQ	Graph-based index	Moderate query speed; Very limited memory resources; Acceptable slight compromise on recall	Floating-point embeddings
HNSW_PRQ	Graph-based index	Moderate query speed; Very limited memory resources; Acceptable slight compromise on recall	Floating-point embeddings
BIN_FLAT	Standard index	Small dataset size; Needs precise search results; No compression needed	Binary embeddings
BIN_IVF_FLAT	Tree-based index	High query speed required; High recall required; Large dataset size	Binary embeddings
SPARSE_INVERTED_INDEX	Standard index	Small dataset size; 100% recall required; Applicable for sparse vector search	Sparse embeddings

Table 4.4: Milvus vector index types, applicable scenarios, and supported embedding formats

Next, we will introduce in detail the index types listed above, as well as **disk indexes** and **GPU indexes**.

FLAT (Exact brute-force search)

FLAT is the simplest type of **index**. It does not construct any index structure, but rather traverses all the data and performs an exact brute-force search. This indexing method is suitable for relatively small datasets or evaluation scenarios where exact retrieval accuracy is more important than query speed.

FLAT does not compress the vectors, ensuring complete accuracy of the search results and a 100% recall rate. This makes it an ideal benchmark for measuring the performance of other indexes.

> In vector search, recall is an important metric used to measure whether the search results cover all the correct nearest-neighbor vectors. The formula is as follows:
>
> Recall = Number of correct vectors retrieved / Total number of possible correct vectors
>
> Here, the numerator represents the number of truly relevant vectors returned in the algorithm's top-k results, while the denominator represents the number of correct nearest-neighbor vectors returned by brute-force search. When the recall rate is 1.0, or 100%, it means that all correct nearest neighbors have been retrieved with no omissions. When the recall rate is less than 1.0, it means that some correct nearest neighbors were not found, indicating that the search has missed some relevant results.

The FLAT search method is exhaustive; that is, for each query vector, it will be compared with all vectors in the dataset. This indexing method does not require any parameter configuration or training data; data can be queried directly after insertion. However, as the data volume increases, the query speed will drop significantly; with very large datasets, the query speed will become slow.

Alex: Lewis, in the code you provided, the **index_type** is `AUTOINDEX`. What's going on here?

Lewis: When set to `AUTOINDEX`, **Milvus** will automatically select the most suitable index type and parameters based on the data type. For our simple application, there is no need to manually control the specific index parameters. Setting `AUTOINDEX` will actually create an index for each vector field.

IVF_FLAT (Inverted file index + Exact search)

IVF_FLAT accelerates queries by dividing vector data into **nlist** clusters and, during search, only comparing with several clusters that are most similar. Specifically, it first calculates the distance between the query vector and each cluster center, then, based on the **nprobe** parameter, selects the most similar clusters, and finally searches for target vectors only within these clusters.

By adjusting the value of **nprobe**, you can find a balance between **accuracy** and **query speed**. The larger the value of **nprobe**, the higher the accuracy, but the slower the query speed; conversely, a smaller **nprobe** results in faster query speed but potentially lower accuracy.

IVF_FLAT does not compress vectors, so the size of the index file is basically the same as the original data size. If the data volume is very large, loading the index may consume a lot of memory. The main index construction parameter for IVF_FLAT is shown below.

Parameter	Description	Value range	Default value
nlist	Number of clusters	[1, 65536]	128

The following code example demonstrates how to create an index using **IVF_FLAT**.

```
### Create IVF_FLAT Index
index_params = {
"index_type": "IVF_FLAT",
"metric_type": "L2",
"params": {"nlist": 100}  # Set 100 clusters
}
collection.create_index("vector", index_params)
### Insert Vector Data into the Collection
import numpy as np
num_vectors = 100000 # Number of vectors
dim = 128 # Dimension of vectors
vectors = np.random.random((num_vectors, dim)).astype("float32")
collection.insert([vectors.tolist()]) # Insert vectors
```

The search parameters for **IVF_FLAT** are shown below.

Type	Parameter	Description	Value range	Default value
General search	nprobe	Number of clusters to search	[1, nlist]	8
Range search	max_empty_result_buckets	During range search, if the number of consecutive "empty result clusters" reaches this value, the search will terminate early. Increasing this value can improve recall, but will increase search time	[1, 65535]	2

Table 4.5: IVF_FLAT search parameters for general and range-based vector retrieval

The following code example demonstrates how to perform a search using **IVF_FLAT**.

```
## Create IVF_FLAT Search
collection.load()
query_vectors = np.random.random((5, dim)).astype("float32")  # 5 query
vectors
search_params = {"metric_type": "L2", "params": {"nprobe": 10}}  # Search
10 clusters
results = collection.search(query_vectors.tolist(), "vector", search_
params, limit=5)
```

IVF_FLAT is suitable for medium-sized datasets containing tens of thousands to millions of entries, and can achieve a good balance between query speed and accuracy. The query speed of **IVF_FLAT** is relatively fast and performs better than **FLAT**, with relatively short index construction time. However, when using **IVF_FLAT**, it is necessary to carefully tune the **nlist** and **nprobe** parameters to obtain optimal results.

IVF_SQ8 (Inverted File Index + 8-bit Quantization)

IVF_SQ8 also builds the index based on the **IVF principle**. On the foundation of **IVF_FLAT**, it applies **8-bit SQ quantization** compression to vectors, thereby reducing memory usage.

SQ quantization can convert each floating-point value (4 bytes) into a 1-byte `UINT8`, reducing the storage requirement by 70% to 75%. Under the same **IVF strategy**, compared to **IVF_FLAT**, IVF_SQ8 generates much smaller index files, making it particularly suitable for environments with limited **disk**, **CPU**, or **GPU** resources. For example, when processing the SIFT1B dataset, after applying IVF_SQ8, the index file size can be reduced from about 470GB to 140GB.

The index construction parameters and search parameters for **IVF_SQ8** are the same as those for **IVF_FLAT**.

This indexing method is suitable for large-scale datasets containing millions to tens of millions of vectors, especially when **memory usage reduction** is desired and a slight loss in accuracy is acceptable. Using this method, memory consumption is significantly reduced and query speed is increased, but accuracy drops slightly, so a trade-off should be made based on your specific needs.

IVF_PQ (Inverted file index + Product quantization)

Before performing **IVF clustering**, **IVF_PQ** first applies **Product Quantization (PQ) sub-blocking** to the vectors. **PQ** can evenly decompose high-dimensional vectors into *m* low-dimensional subspaces and quantize each subspace. Each subvector identifies 2*nbits* centroids using k-means, and then, for each subvector, only the distance to the nearest centroid is stored, thus encoding the entire vector using *m nbits* bits. During search, it is not necessary to calculate the distance between the query vector and all cluster centers; instead, only the distances to the central points of each subspace are computed, significantly reducing both time and space complexity.

IVF_PQ achieves a higher compression ratio quantization compared to **IVF_SQ8**, resulting in smaller index files, but this also introduces a certain loss of accuracy, leading to decreased search accuracy.

The index construction parameters for **IVF_PQ** are shown below. Its search parameters are the same as those used for **IVF_FLAT**.

Parameter	Description	Value range
nlist	Number of clusters	[1, 65536]
m	Number of PQ decomposition factors (vector is divided into *m* subvectors)	Must satisfy dim mod m == 0
nbits	(Optional) Number of quantization bits for each low-dimensional vector, default is 8 bits	[1, 64] (default is 8)

Table 4.6: IVF_PQ index construction parameters and configuration constraints

IVF_PQ is suitable for ultra-large-scale datasets, especially those containing tens of millions to hundreds of millions of vectors, and for scenarios where minimizing memory usage is required. Although the main advantage of this indexing method is its low memory consumption, making it well-suited for handling extremely large datasets, its disadvantages are significant loss of accuracy and longer index construction time.

ScaNN

ScaNN (**Scalable Nearest Neighbor**) is similar to **IVF_PQ** in that it also employs **vector clustering** and **PQ (Product Quantization)** methods, and achieves efficient computation through **SIMD (Single-Instruction/Multi-data)** optimizations. However, its internal PQ implementation details and optimization techniques differ from those of IVF_PQ. ScaNN provides optimized default settings for parameters such as `m` and `nbits`, allowing it to deliver better performance in most application scenarios.

The index construction parameters for ScaNN are shown below.

Parameter	Description	Value range
nlist	Number of clusters	[1, 65536]
with_raw_data	Whether to store raw data in the index file	True or False, default is True

Table 4.7: ScaNN index construction parameters and configuration options

For parameters such as `m` and `nbits`, ScaNN adopts default values to ensure optimal performance, so explicit configuration is not required. The search parameters for ScaNN are shown below.

Search type	Parameter	Description	Value range	Default value
Standard search	`nprobe`	Number of clusters to probe during search.	`[1, nlist]`	8
Standard search	`reorder_k`	Number of candidate results considered for query reordering.	`[top_k, ∞]`	`top_k`
Range search	`max_empty_result_buckets`	During range search, if this number of consecutive clusters returns no results, the search stops early. Increasing this value can improve recall, but may increase search time.	`[1, 65535]`	2

Table 4.8: ScaNN search parameters for standard and range-based vector retrieval

HNSW

Milvus also supports the **HNSW index**. As introduced earlier, this type of index builds a multi-layered navigational graph structure for the data based on certain rules. The upper layers of the graph are more sparse, with larger distances between nodes; the lower layers are denser, with nodes closer together. The search process starts from the topmost layer of the graph, seeking the node closest to the target vector, then moves to the next layer to repeat the search. Through multiple iterations, it can quickly home in on the area containing the most similar vectors.

To enhance performance, **HNSW** limits the maximum number of connections per node per layer (**M**). In addition, you can specify the search scope using the `efConstruction` parameter (when building the index) and the `ef` parameter (when performing a search).

The index construction parameters for **HNSW** are shown below.

Parameter	**Description**	**Value range**	**Default value**
M	Maximum number of connections per node in each layer. A larger value can improve recall, but also increases computational cost when using the same `ef` or `efConstruction` settings.	`[2, 2048]`	`None`
`efConstruction`	Controls the search scope during index construction. Increasing this value improves index quality, but slows down index building.	`[1, int_max]`	`None`

Table 4.9: HNSW index construction parameters and their effects on recall, computational cost, and build speed

The search parameters for **HNSW** are shown below.

Parameter	**Description**	**Value range**	**Default value**
`ef`	Defines the search scope during query execution. Increasing this value improves recall, but slows down query speed.	[top_k, `int_max`]	None

Table 4.10: HNSW query-time search parameter and its effect on recall and query speed

HNSW is suitable for medium to large-scale datasets containing hundreds of thousands to tens of millions of vectors, and is suitable for scenarios requiring both fast query and high accuracy. Its advantage is achieving a good balance between fast queries and high accuracy retrieval, but the disadvantage is longer index building time and higher memory consumption.

HNSW_SQ, HNSW_PQ, and HNSW_PRQ

The **HNSW index family** includes derivative types such as **HNSW_SQ**, **HNSW_PQ**, and **HNSW_PRQ**. They are introduced as follows.

- **HNSW_SQ**: Based on the HNSW graph index, **SQ** is combined to discretely compress the data. For example, **SQ6** converts floating-point numbers to 2^6 (64) discrete values and encodes them using 6 bits; whereas **SQ8** quantizes them into 2^8(256) discrete values and encodes them using 8 bits. This method can significantly reduce memory usage while better preserving the structure of the data. Compared to standard HNSW, the index construction overhead of HNSW_SQ is somewhat higher, but it achieves a better balance between index size and query speed.

- **HNSW_PQ**: Based on the HNSW graph index, it uses **PQ** for compression. Compared with HNSW_SQ, with the same compression rate, the queries per second for HNSW_PQ may be lower, but its recall rate is higher. At the same time, the index construction time for HNSW_PQ is also somewhat longer than that of HNSW_SQ.
- **HNSW_PRQ**: Based on the HNSW graph index, it incorporates **PRQ** (Product Residual Quantization), providing higher accuracy and more flexible compression rate options, though the index construction time is correspondingly longer. **PRQ** is similar to PQ in that both divide the vector into *m* groups, with each group quantized using *nbits* bits. The difference is that PRQ first performs PQ, then computes the residual vector between the original and quantized vectors and applies PQ to this residual, repeating this process for *nrq* iterations. Therefore, a vector of dimension *dim* will ultimately be encoded as $m \times nbits \times nrq$ bits.

The index construction and search parameters for these derivative types are not elaborated here. For specific parameter configuration information, please refer to the official Milvus documentation.

SPARSE_INVERTED_INDEX

For **sparse vectors**, Milvus provides the **SPARSE_INVERTED_INDEX** index type. This index maintains a list for each **dimension**, recording all vectors that have non-zero values in the corresponding dimension. During query execution, the system traverses each non-zero dimension of the query vector and calculates the scores of vectors that also have non-zero values in these dimensions.

The index build parameters for **SPARSE_INVERTED_INDEX** are shown below.

Parameter	Description	Values	Default
inverted_index_algo	The relevant algorithm used during index construction and search	DAAT_MAXSCORE, DAAT_WAND, TAAT_NAIVE	DAAT_MAXSCORE

Table 4.11: SPARSE_INVERTED_INDEX algorithm options for sparse vector indexing and search

The search parameters for **SPARSE_INVERTED_INDEX** are shown below.

Parameter	Description	Value range
drop_ratio_search	The proportion of small vector values excluded during the search process	[0, 1]

Table 4.12: SPARSE_INVERTED_INDEX search parameter for controlling sparse vector pruning

It should be noted that the index for **sparse embeddings** only supports the **IP** and **BM25** (used for full-text search) metrics.

BIN_FLAT and BIN_IVF_FLAT

Milvus provides two types of indexes for binary embedding vectors – **BIN_FLAT** and **BIN_IVF_FLAT**. These two index types can be compared to the **FLAT** and **IVF_FLAT** index types for numerical vectors, respectively. Their design aims to meet the requirements of different application scenarios.

- **BIN_FLAT**: Similar to **FLAT**, BIN_FLAT performs exhaustive search on all binary vectors to ensure a 100% recall rate. This method is suitable for small-scale datasets that require precise retrieval.
- **BIN_IVF_FLAT**: Similar to **IVF_FLAT**, BIN_IVF_FLAT first divides the binary vector data into multiple clusters, with each cluster representing a group of similar vectors. When performing a query, only the clusters most similar to the query vector are searched to speed up the retrieval process. This method is suitable for large-scale binary vector datasets that require efficient queries.

For these two index types, Milvus supports **Jaccard similarity** and **Hamming distance** as distance metrics.

Disk index and GPU index

Alex: Are you done? Lewis, there are so many **index types**—my brain is going to explode after listening to all this.

Lewis: Because **index building** is critical to vector storage, I've listed them quite thoroughly here. However, this isn't an exhaustive list—the types mentioned above are all **in-memory index types**. In **Milvus**, these in-memory indexes are used to load index data into memory to enable fast queries.

However, as your dataset grows in size, if your memory resources are not sufficient to hold all the index data, you need to introduce **disk indexes** (like **DiskANN**) and store some index data on disks (such as NVMe SSDs) to handle large-scale datasets when memory is limited.

Additionally, you can also use **GPU indexes** to load vector data into GPU memory and leverage the GPU's parallel computing abilities for efficient computation. This method is suitable for scenarios that require **high throughput**, **low latency**, and **high recall**, especially under high-concurrency queries. But, limited by GPU memory capacity, it usually can't handle ultra-large-scale datasets, which means your data scale needs to fit within the GPU memory capacity.

Alex: Lewis, I also saw the following output log.

```
Database: milvus
Index Mode: flat
Total Vectors: 194
Index Size: 194
Processing Time: 0.730807s
Collection Name: ...
```

Is it normal that the number of vectors equals the number of indexes?

Lewis: Yes, that's possible. In **Milvus**, the number of vectors can equal the number of indexes. Under **FLAT mode**, Milvus does not compress or segment vector data—the number of indexes is exactly the same as the number of vectors. Each vector is stored directly in the index, so here the **Total Vectors** and **Index Size** are equal. If you use other index modes (such as **IVF**, **HNSW**), that may not be the case, since segmentation or compression can result in the number of indexes differing from the number of vectors.

As mentioned earlier, **FLAT** is an exact matching mode. It compares each vector one by one, which is suitable for high-precision searches on small datasets, but is inefficient for large datasets. If your number of vectors increases in the future, you could consider modes like **IVF_FLAT**, **HNSW**, etc. to improve search efficiency, but you'll need to accept some loss in accuracy.

Selecting the appropriate metric

In Milvus, the choice of **similarity metric** is critically important for the quality of search results. Different metrics are suitable for different types of data distributions and retrieval requirements. Selecting the correct metric can significantly improve the accuracy and efficiency of search outcomes.

Table 4.13 summarizes the similarity metrics supported by Milvus and explains how to interpret their distance or similarity values.

Type of metric	Characteristics of similarity distance value	Value range of similarity distance
Euclidean distance (L2)	Smaller values indicate greater similarity	$[0, \infty)$
Inner product (IP)	Larger values indicate greater similarity	No fixed range; depends on vector magnitude and direction

Type of metric	Characteristics of similarity distance value	Value range of similarity distance
Cosine similarity (COSINE)	Larger values indicate greater similarity	[-1, 1]
Jaccard similarity	Smaller values indicate greater similarity	[0, 1]
Hamming distance	Smaller values indicate greater similarity	[0, dim (vector dimension)]
BM25	Scores relevance based on term frequency, inverse document frequency, and document normalization	[0, ∞)

Table 4.13: Supported similarity metrics and interpretation of distance values in Milvus

For some metrics, smaller values indicate greater similarity (such as **Euclidean distance, Jaccard similarity, Hamming distance**), while for others, larger values indicate greater similarity (such as **inner product, cosine similarity, BM25**).

Table 4.14 maps Milvus vector field types to their supported and default metric types.

Vector field type	Dimension range	Supported metric types	Default metric type
`FLOAT_VECTOR`	2~32,768	Cosine similarity, Euclidean distance, inner product	Cosine similarity
`FLOAT16_VECTOR`	2~32,768	Cosine similarity, Euclidean distance, inner product	Cosine similarity
`BFLOAT16_VECTOR`	2~32,768	Cosine similarity, Euclidean distance, inner product	Cosine similarity

Vector type	Dimensions or requirements	Supported metrics	Default metric
SPARSE_FLOAT_VECTOR	No need to specify dimensions	Inner Product, BM25 (only for full-text search)	Inner product
BINARY_VECTOR	8~32,768×8 (must be a multiple of 8)	Hamming distance, Jaccard Similarity	Hamming distance

Table 4.14: Supported metric types for different Milvus vector field types

Before choosing a metric, considering the following questions:

- **Vector type**: Is your data composed of floating-point vectors or binary vectors?
- **Data characteristics**: Do you need to consider the magnitude of the vectors? Have the data already been normalized?
- **Retrieval scenario**: Is the application scenario text search, image vector search, or hash code matching, etc.?
- **Resource and performance requirements**: Can you accept extra normalization overhead? What are your requirements for accuracy and speed?

Commonly used metrics for dense floating-point vectors

Next, let's look at the three commonly used metrics for dense floating-point vectors: **Euclidean distance**, **inner product**, and **cosine similarity**.

- **Euclidean distance**: Calculates the Euclidean distance between vectors, i.e., the straight-line distance between two points. Applicable scenarios include feature vectors of continuous real numbers, such as images, audio, video, etc. The advantage is that it is commonly used and intuitive; the disadvantage is that it is sensitive to the scale of feature values and may require normalization.
- **Inner product**: Calculates the inner product between vectors, used to measure the similarity or correlation between vectors. Applicable scenarios include computing the correlation between user and item vectors in recommendation systems, or semantic comparison of text embeddings. When using **inner product**, be aware of vector normalization to ensure reasonable results.
- **Cosine similarity**: Measures the similarity of vector directions by calculating the cosine of the angle between vectors and is insensitive to the magnitude of vectors. Applicable scenarios include text analysis, such as using TF-IDF or embedding vectors to represent text, and scenarios where the length of vectors (the "modulus" or "norm" of the vector) can be ignored in text embeddings, e.g., embedding vectors generated by large models like **BERT**, **GPT**, **BGE**, etc.

Alex: Inner product and cosine similarity both seem to be able to compare text vectors, but I don't fully understand the difference between them.

Lewis: The main difference is whether vector magnitude matters. The value range of the inner product metric has no fixed bounds; it depends on the size and direction of the vectors. The larger the vector norm, the larger the value of the inner product may be; therefore, if normalization is not performed, vectors with larger norms may always produce large results. In contrast, the value range of **cosine similarity** is fixed at [-1,1] and is independent of the norm. During calculation, normalization removes the influence of vector magnitude and focuses only on the similarity of vector directions.

Here are a few examples to illustrate this point. If you are building a **recommendation system** and are calculating the size (**magnitude**) of user and item vectors via user-item matrix factorization in **collaborative filtering algorithms**, this can reflect the strength of **user preference** or **item importance**, and further be used to compute your preference score for an item. In this case, it is recommended to use the **inner product**, because recommendation systems usually need to comprehensively consider both user interest and item importance, and the result of the inner product can be used directly for recommendation ranking.

However, if you only care whether the direction of user and item features aligns, and do not consider the magnitude of the vectors—for example, in the cold start phase of a recommendation system, when there is less user data—**cosine similarity** can be used. This is because cosine similarity is more suitable in scenarios where there is a large disparity in vector magnitudes and the magnitude itself is not meaningful. If you use the inner product, it may cause certain items with larger magnitudes to always appear at the top of the recommendation list, while cosine similarity can eliminate the influence brought by magnitude.

Another example: for **text embeddings** and **semantic search**, when using large models (such as **BERT**, **OpenAI embedding models**, **BGE**, etc.) to generate embedding vectors, you usually want to ignore text length or other factors irrelevant to semantics when calculating the similarity between documents, to judge whether the semantics of two sentences are close. Cosine similarity only considers direction and can avoid bias caused by differences in text length, which is a standard practice. However, for already normalized text vectors, choosing the inner product is also feasible, since it is faster to compute and is essentially equivalent to cosine similarity after normalization.

Similarly, for **graph embeddings** and **node similarity**, if the size of your embedding vectors reflects the **influence** or **importance** of a node—such as recommending friends or community members in social network analysis—using the inner product can naturally reflect the cumulative effect of influence. Conversely, if you only want to focus on the relationship direction between nodes in the graph and ignore the weights of the nodes themselves—for instance, when looking for user groups with similar interests in social network analysis—cosine similarity after normalization can better highlight the similarity of relationships between nodes.

Alex: Oh, I understand now.

Lewis: Let me test you. If I want to compare two text vectors generated by OpenAI's embedding model, which metric should I choose?

Alex: In this case, both are feasible. This is because the result vectors returned by OpenAI's embedding model have already been **normalized**. This means that after normalization, the numerical values of the inner product and cosine similarity are completely identical. If you choose cosine similarity you can't go wrong, as it is widely regarded as the standard method for measuring semantic similarity. But if you consider efficiency, directly using the **inner product** is also a good choice, especially since it has a performance advantage due to its faster computation speed.

Lewis: Yes, in this scenario choosing **inner product** is indeed better. OpenAI's official documentation states that their **embedding models** are already normalized, so using **inner product** to calculate similarity is not only accurate but also efficient. Of course, this does not mean using **cosine similarity** is incorrect, because they are essentially equivalent. Here I provide a reference example.

```
## Create Index Parameters
index_params = client.prepare_index_params()
index_params.add_index(
    field_name="vector",
    index_type="HNSW",          # Choose HNSW or other appropriate index
type
    metric_type="IP",           # Set to inner product
    params={"M": 16, "efConstruction": 200}  # Parameters for HNSW index
)
## Create the Index
client.create_index(
    collection_name=collection_name,
    index_params=index_params
)
## Load the Collection
client.load_collection(collection_name=collection_name)
## Set Search Parameters
search_params = {
    "metric_type": "IP",        # Must be consistent with index's metric_
type
    "params": {"ef": 64}        # Query parameter for HNSW, value for ef
can be adjusted as needed
}
```

```
## Execute Search
search_result = client.search(
    collection_name=collection_name,
    data=[query_embeddings[0]],
    anns_field="vector",
    param=search_params,
    limit=5,
    output_fields=["concept_name", "synonyms", "concept_class_id", "full_
name"]
)
logging.info(f"Search result for '{query}': {search_result}")
```

Lewis: Alright, Alex, I'll continue to test you. Suppose you are handling a dataset containing millions of **text embeddings** generated by the **BERT model**, and you want to perform similarity search with high performance and high accuracy.

Alex: In this case, you should choose the **HNSW index type** because it offers a good balance between query speed and accuracy, making it very suitable for medium- to large-scale datasets. For the metric, choosing **cosine similarity** is safer, as focusing on the directional similarity of vectors is more reliable when you're not sure whether these vectors have been normalized.

```
index_params = client.prepare_index_params()
index_params.add_index(
field_name="vector",
index_type="HNSW",
metric_type="COSINE",        # Use cosine similarity
params={"M": 16, "efConstruction": 200}
)
```

After selecting a metric, it is important to use it consistently. In Milvus, the metric used during search must match the metric used when the index was created.

The metric used in search must match the index

Alex: The **index** has been created, the **vectors** have been stored, and the **metric type** has also been determined. Next, it's time to perform the **search**, right? (It can also be called a retrieval.) Can the **index type** be specified during search?

Lewis: Of course not. The **index type** is set when the index is created and cannot be changed during search. However, you can specify certain search parameters, such as `metric_type` and `params`.

Alex: Lewis, take a look at my search code, why is there an error?

```
from pymilvus import MilvusClient, DataType, FieldSchema, CollectionSchema
## Establish Milvus Connection
db_path = "./test.db"
client = MilvusClient(db_path)
## Define Collection Schema
schema = CollectionSchema(
fields=[
FieldSchema(name="id", dtype=DataType.INT64, is_primary=True),
FieldSchema(name="vector", dtype=DataType.FLOAT_VECTOR, dim=128)
]
)
## Create Collection
collection_name = "test_collection"
client.create_collection(
collection_name=collection_name,
schema=schema
)
## Create Index
index_params = client.prepare_index_params()
index_params.add_index(
field_name="vector",
index_type="IVF_FLAT",
metric_type="IP",       # Explicitly specify the metric type as Inner
Product
params={"nlist": 128}
)
client.create_index(
collection_name=collection_name,
index_params=index_params
)
## Create a Query Vector
import numpy as np
query_vector = np.random.random(128).tolist()
## Perform Search
results = client.search(
collection_name="my_collection",
```

```
data=[query_vector],
anns_field="vector",
search_params={
"metric_type": "COSINE", # Error because a different metric type from the index was specified
"params": {"nprobe": 10}
},
limit=10,
output_fields=["id"]
)
print(results)
```

```
pymilvus.exceptions.MilvusException: <MilvusException: (code=1100,
message=fail to search: metric type not match: invalid [expected=IP]
[actual=COSINE]: invalid parameter)>
```

Lewis: Oh, there is a conflict between the **metric** you specified during **search** and the one specified when creating the **index**. When the `metric_type` in the search parameters does not match the one in the index, **Milvus** may ignore the `metric_type` specified during search and continue to use the one set in the index, or throw an error indicating the **distance metric type mismatch**. To ensure correct similarity computation, the `metric_type` used during search should match the one used when creating the index. In the error example above, the index was created with IP, but the search used **COSINE**, causing a metric mismatch.

Note that if you want to change the **metric type**, you must recreate the **index**. First, delete the old index.

```
### Delete the Old Index (If It Exists)
client.drop_index(
collection_name=collection_name,
index_name="vector_index"
)
### Create a New Index
index_params = client.prepare_index_params()
index_params.add_index(
field_name="vector",
index_type="IVF_FLAT",
metric_type="COSINE",     # Use cosine similarity
params={"nlist": 128}
```

```
)
client.create_index(
collection_name=collection_name,
index_params=index_params
)
## Reload the Collection (Reloading Is Necessary After Updating the Index)
collection.release()
collection.load()
```

Next, use the matching metric_type when performing the search.

```
### Set Search Parameters
search_params = {
    "metric_type": "COSINE",    # Consistent with the metric_type in the
new index
    "params": {"nprobe": 10}
}
### Perform Search
results = collection.search(
    data=[query_vector],
    anns_field="vector",
    param=search_params,
    limit=10,
    expr=None,
    output_fields=["id"]
)
```

Next, we'll briefly introduce the tuning of **search parameters.** For **IVF_FLAT,** `nlist` controls the number of cluster centers and can be adjusted to a most suitable value based on the data scale. For example, in **HNSW,** `efConstruction` represents the search depth during queries; the larger the value, the higher the query accuracy, but the search speed may slow down. It is generally set to be several times the expected number of returned results.

```
### Create Index Parameters
index_params = client.prepare_index_params()
index_params.add_index(
    field_name="vector",
    index_type="HNSW",
    metric_type="IP",
```

```
    params={"M": 16, "efConstruction": 200} # The values of M and 
efConstruction can be adjusted as needed
)
### Create Index
client.create_index(
    collection_name=collection_name,
    index_params=index_params
)
```

Search and query: Two retrieval methods

After configuring the index and metric, Milvus provides two main ways to retrieve data: Search and Query. Although both return records from a collection, they serve different purposes.

Alex: Lewis, I noticed that in **Milvus**, we mainly use two ways to retrieve data: besides **Search**, there's also **Query**.

Lewis: These two **search methods** have different application scenarios and characteristics. **Search** is used for **vector similarity search**, finding similar entities based on vector distance, while **Query** is for **exact match retrieval**, filtering based on common fields or primary keys. Therefore, **Search** requires you to provide a **query vector**, whereas **Query** uses a **filter expression** or a list of **IDs**. **Search** results are sorted by similarity, while **Query** results are usually unsorted or sorted by **ID**. Because vector computations are involved, **Search** has higher performance overhead; in contrast, **Query** mainly involves simple filtering operations and is generally faster.

The following code examples show how to use **Search** and **Query**.

```
from pymilvus import MilvusClient
client = MilvusClient("./wukong_new.db")
from pymilvus.model.dense import SentenceTransformerEmbeddingFunction
embedding_function = SentenceTransformerEmbeddingFunction(model_
name='BAAI/bge-large-zh')
### Use Search for Vector Similarity Search
search_results = client.search(
collection_name="Wukong_Monsters",
data=embedding_function(["powerful monster"]), # Query vector
filter="difficulty == 'High'", # Filter condition can be used together
limit=2, # Number of results returned
```

```
output_fields=["monster_name", "location", "difficulty", "synonyms"]
)
### Example Use Query for Exact Match
query_results = client.query(
collection_name="Wukong_Monsters",
filter="location == 'Volcanic Cave'", # Must specify query condition
output_fields=["monster_name", "location", "difficulty", "synonyms"]
)
### Query by Primary Key
id_query_results = client.query(
collection_name="Wukong_Monsters",
ids=[1, 2], # Primary keys, must match actual primary key values to get
query results
output_fields=["vector", "monster_name", "location", "difficulty",
"synonyms"]
```

Alex: It seems that **Search** and **Query** can be used together.

Lewis: Yes. For example, when we want to find articles similar to a certain medical paper, but only search for articles published in a specific year, we can use **Search** with filtering conditions. This is exactly **conditional retrieval based on metadata filtering** in a RAG system. Similarly, in an e-commerce recommendation system, we can first use **Query** to filter out products with zero inventory, and then use **Search** to find products similar to the user's interests.

Using Milvus for hybrid search

Alex: Lewis, I already understand the basic patterns of indexing and searching, but I still have a question. In the previous examples, most vectors were **Float Vectors**, that is, **dense vectors** stored in floating-point format. So in **Milvus**, how should we understand **Sparse Float Vector** and **Binary Vector**?

Lewis: That's exactly what I'm about to introduce—the knowledge related to **hybrid search**. In some scenarios, a single retrieval method is not sufficient to meet complex query needs. In such cases, **hybrid search** can significantly improve retrieval results by combining the strengths of multiple retrieval methods.

Floating point vectors, sparse floating point vectors, and binary vectors

In Milvus, there are three types of vectors: **floating point vectors**, **sparse floating point vectors**, and **binary vectors**. These vector types support different retrieval needs: semantic matching, keyword-based matching, and fast approximate matching, and correspond to the following data types:

- **FLOAT_VECTOR (Dense floating point vector):** The most common type of vector, usually generated by deep learning models. Its dimension is fixed and each dimension has a corresponding value. It is suitable for scenarios such as **semantic search** and **image feature extraction**. The characteristics are large storage usage and strong expression capability. An example is as follows.

```
[0.2, -0.5, 0.8, ..., 0.3] # 512 dimensions
```

- **SPARSE_FLOAT_VECTOR (Sparse floating point vector): The** majority of dimensions have a value of 0—only non-zero values and their indices are stored. Although the **dimensionality** can be very high, only the **non-zero elements** are actually stored. Traditional **TF-IDF** or **BM25** representations are typical sparse vectors, suitable for scenarios such as **keyword retrieval**. The storage format is usually a key-value pair in the form of `{index: value}`. For example, a certain vector has 10,000 dimensions, but only 3 non-zero values.

```
If represented in full, it would be a 10,000-dimensional vector, but
in reality, only the following 3 non-zero values are stored
{ 15: 0.5,   # The value of dimension 15 is 0.5
128: 0.3,  # The value of dimension 128 is 0.3
945: 0.8   # The value of dimension 945 is 0.8}
```

- **BINARY_VECTOR (Binary vector):** Each dimension has only two possible values: 0 or 1. This is a simple form of **sparse vector** representation, commonly used for fast approximate matching. It is suitable for scenarios such as **image hashing**, **fast similarity search**, and **binarized feature representation.** Its features include small storage requirements and high computational efficiency, but possibly lower precision. Example:

```
[1, 0, 1, 1, 0, 0, 1, 0] # 500 dimensions
```

These vector types differ in expressive power, storage cost, and computational complexity. `FLOAT_VECTOR` provides the strongest semantic representation but uses the most storage and computation. `SPARSE_FLOAT_VECTOR` is more efficient when most dimensions are zero, making it suitable for keyword-based retrieval. `BINARY_VECTOR` is the most compact and fastest to compare, but it usually provides lower precision.

The choice of which vector storage type to use depends on the specific use case and speed requirements. For scenarios requiring precise **semantic understanding**, consider using `FLOAT_VECTOR`. For **keyword matching** scenarios, consider using `SPARSE_FLOAT_VECTOR`. For scenarios requiring fast rough ranking, consider using `BINARY_VECTOR`.

Not only **Milvus**, but many modern vector databases (such as **Astra DB**, **Elasticsearch**, **Neo4j**, **AzureSearch**, **Qdrant**, etc.) support hybrid vector storage, leading to multiple retrieval approaches.

The following simplified example shows how a **Milvus** collection can contain dense, sparse, and binary vector fields at the same time. This enables a multi-stage retrieval pipeline in which different vector types are used for different retrieval purposes.

```
### Define a Collection Containing All Three Kinds of Vectors
fields = [
FieldSchema(name="id", dtype=DataType.INT64, is_primary=True),
### Semantic Vector
FieldSchema(name="dense_vec", dtype=DataType.FLOAT_VECTOR, dim=768),
### Keyword Vector
FieldSchema(name="sparse_vec", dtype=DataType.SPARSE_FLOAT_VECTOR),
### Fast Matching Vector
FieldSchema(name="binary_vec", dtype=DataType.BINARY_VECTOR, dim=256)
]
### Multi-Stage Retrieval Strategy
def multi_stage_search(query, collection):
### Use BINARY_VECTOR for Fast Rough Ranking
stage1_results = collection.search(
binary_vectors,
"binary_vec",
limit=1000
)
### Use SPARSE_VECTOR for Keyword Filtering
stage2_results = collection.search(
sparse_vectors,
"sparse_vec",
expr=f"id in {[r.id for r in stage1_results]}",
limit=100
)
### Use DENSE_VECTOR for Precise Semantic Matching
final_results = collection.search(
```

```
    dense_vectors,
    "dense_vec",
    expr=f"id in {[r.id for r in stage2_results]}",
    limit=10
)
```

Hybrid retrieval strategy implementation

Hybrid retrieval combines multiple retrieval methods to improve both efficiency and relevance. A common pattern is to use a faster method first to narrow the candidate set, and then apply more precise semantic matching to rerank the results. In modern information retrieval systems, **hybrid retrieval strategies** are very common. For example, in compliance document retrieval, efficient **keyword matching** is used in the pre-filtering layer for preliminary filtering; in the exact match layer, methods such as **BM25** are used for relevance ranking; and in the semantic understanding layer, **vector similarity** is used for deeper semantic matching. This strategy is also called **cascaded fusion** or **multi-level retrieval**, meaning the result of one retrieval method serves as the input for another method. In this way, retrieval efficiency is preserved while also improving the relevance and accuracy of the results.

Alex: I always hear you mention **BM25**. How exactly is it related to sparse vectors? I kind of forgot.

Lewis: **BM25** generates vectors by calculating the importance of each word in a document (combining **term frequency** and **inverse document frequency**), where each dimension corresponds to a word in the vocabulary. Since most words do not appear in a single document, this vector is naturally **sparse**. For example, if the vocabulary size is 10,000, and a document uses only 50 words, then only those 50 positions in the BM25 vector will have non-zero values (these values are computed according to the BM25 formula), while the remaining 9,950 positions are all 0. This forms a **sparse vector**. Therefore, **BM25** is essentially a special type of sparse vector representation. When we say "using BM25," we are actually referring to using a specific formula to compute the weights of the non-zero values in the sparse vector.

The official *Milvus* documentation provides an example, showing that under different vector types and retrieval methods, different answers may be obtained for the same question.

Figure 4.18: Milvus hybrid search demo with search results in dense sparse and hybrid columns

Dense retrieval mainly focuses on **semantic similarity**, while **sparse retrieval** puts more emphasis on whether keywords match. **Hybrid retrieval** seeks a balance between the two.

Building a hybrid retrieval system using Milvus

This section will demonstrate how to build a **hybrid retrieval system** for the *Chronicles of the Godslayer: Housun* game content, combining **semantic search** and **keyword matching** to achieve more precise content retrieval. In this system, we will use the **BGE-M3 model** mentioned in Section 3, which is capable of generating multiple formats of vectors.

The example follows four main steps: preparing the dataset, generating dense and sparse embeddings, creating the Milvus collection and indexes, and executing a weighted hybrid search.

First, install the necessary dependencies.

```
pip install --upgrade pymilvus "pymilvus[model]" pandas numpy pillow
```

Next, load our prepared dataset of the *Chronicles of the Godslayer: Housun* game (Refer to `GitHub - PacktPublishing/RAG-from-First-Principles: RAG from First Principles Published by Packt Pub` for the complete code).

```
import json
from typing import Optional, Dict
with open("data/Chronicles_of_the_Godslayer/Battle_Scenes.json", 'r',
encoding='utf-8') as f:
    dataset = json.load(f)
    docs = []
    metadata = []
    for item in dataset['data']:
        text_parts = [item['title'], item['description']]
        if 'combat_details' in item:
            text_parts.extend(item['combat_details'].get('combat_style',
[]))
            text_parts.extend(item['combat_details'].get('abilities_used',
[]))
        if 'scene_info' in item:
            text_parts.extend([
                item['scene_info'].get('location', ''),
                item['scene_info'].get('environment', ''),
                item['scene_info'].get('time_of_day', '')
            ])
        docs.append(' '.join(filter(None, text_parts)))
        metadata.append(item)
```

Next, use the BGE-M3 model to generate dense vectors and sparse vectors.

```
from milvus_model.hybrid import BGEM3EmbeddingFunction
ef = BGEM3EmbeddingFunction(use_fp16=False, device="cpu")
docs_embeddings = ef(docs)
```

```
start to install package: datasets
```

```
successfully installed package: datasets
start to install package: peft
successfully installed package: peft
start to install package: FlagEmbedding>=1.3.3
successfully installed package: FlagEmbedding>=1.3.3
sentencepiece.bpe.model: 100%|█████| 5.07M/5.07M [00:00<00:00, 113MB/s]
tokenizer.json: 100%|█████| 17.1M/17.1M [00:00<00:00, 168MB/s]
colbert_linear.pt: 100%|█████| 2.10M/2.10M [00:00<00:00, 50.5MB/s]
bm25.jpg: 100%|█████| 132k/132k [00:00<00:00, 30.1MB/s]
sentence_bert_config.json: 100%|█████| 54.0/54.0 [00:00<00:00, 218kB/s]
pytorch_model.bin: 100%|█████| 2.27G/2.27G [00:15<00:00, 149MB/s]
Starting to generate vector embeddings......99%|█████| 2.25G/2.27G
[00:14<00:00, 236MB/s]
You're using a XLMRobertaTokenizerFast tokenizer. Please note that with a
fast tokenizer, using the `__call__` method is faster than using a method
to encode the text followed by a call to the `pad` method to get a padded
encoding.
Vector generation completed, dense vector dimension: 1024
```

Upon first run, the system will prompt you to install a series of packages related to the **BGE embedding model**, as well as download various associated models.

Next, connect to **Milvus**, create a Milvus collection, and the corresponding indexes.

```
## Import Milvus and Connect to the Service
from pymilvus import (
    connections,
    utility,
    FieldSchema,
    CollectionSchema,
    DataType,
    Collection
)
collection_name = "wukong_hybrid"
connections.connect(uri="./wukong.db")
## Create Milvus Collection and Indexes
fields = [
    FieldSchema(name="pk", dtype=DataType.VARCHAR, is_primary=True, auto_
id=True, max_length=100),
```

```
    FieldSchema(name="text", dtype=DataType.VARCHAR, max_length=2048),
    FieldSchema(name="id", dtype=DataType.VARCHAR, max_length=100),
    FieldSchema(name="title", dtype=DataType.VARCHAR, max_length=256),
    FieldSchema(name="category", dtype=DataType.VARCHAR, max_length=64),
    FieldSchema(name="location", dtype=DataType.VARCHAR, max_length=128),
    FieldSchema(name="environment", dtype=DataType.VARCHAR, max_
length=64),
    FieldSchema(name="sparse_vector", dtype=DataType.SPARSE_FLOAT_VECTOR),
    FieldSchema(name="dense_vector", dtype=DataType.FLOAT_VECTOR, dim=ef.
dim["dense"])
]
schema = CollectionSchema(fields)
if utility.has_collection(collection_name):
    utility.drop_collection(collection_name)
collection = Collection(name=collection_name, schema=schema, consistency_
level="Strong")
collection.create_index("sparse_vector", {"index_type": "SPARSE_INVERTED_
INDEX", "metric_type": "IP"})
collection.create_index("dense_vector", {"index_type": "AUTOINDEX",
"metric_type": "IP"})
collection.load()
```

Afterwards, insert the documents and vectors into the **Milvus collection**.

```
batch_size = 50
for i in range(0, len(docs), batch_size):
    end_idx = min(i + batch_size, len(docs))
    batch_data = []
    for j in range(i, end_idx):
        item = metadata[j]
        batch_data.append({
            "text": docs[j],
            "id": item["id"],
            "title": item["title"],
            "category": item["category"],
            "location": item.get("scene_info", {}).get("location", ""),
            "environment": item.get("scene_info", {}).get("environment",
""),
            "sparse_vector": docs_embeddings["sparse"]._getrow(j),
```

```
                "dense_vector": docs_embeddings["dense"][j]
            })
        collection.insert(batch_data)
```

Next, perform a **hybrid search** and display the search results.

```
### Define and Perform a Hybrid Search
from pymilvus import AnnSearchRequest, WeightedRanker
query = "battle scene in the snowfield"
category = "combat"
environment = "snowfield"
limit = 5
search_type = "hybrid"
weights = {"sparse": 0.7, "dense": 1.0}
query_embeddings = ef([query])
### Build Filter Expression
expr = None
conditions = []
if category:
    conditions.append(f'category == "{category}"')
if environment:
    conditions.append(f'environment == "{environment}"')
if conditions:
    expr = " && ".join(conditions)
search_params = {
    "metric_type": "IP",
    "params": {}
}
if expr:
    search_params["expr"] = expr
if search_type == "hybrid":
    dense_req = AnnSearchRequest(
        data=[query_embeddings["dense"][0]],
        anns_field="dense_vector",
        param=search_params,
        limit=limit
    )
    sparse_req = AnnSearchRequest(
```

```
        data=[query_embeddings["sparse"]._getrow(0)],
        anns_field="sparse_vector",
        param=search_params,
        limit=limit
    )
)
rerank = WeightedRanker(weights["sparse"], weights["dense"])
results = collection.hybrid_search(
reqs=[dense_req, sparse_req],
rerank=rerank,
limit=limit,
output_fields=["text", "id", "title", "category", "location",
"environment"]
)[0]
else:
field = "dense_vector" if search_type == "dense" else "sparse_vector"
vec = query_embeddings["dense"][0] if search_type == "dense" else query_
embeddings["sparse"]._getrow(0)
results = collection.search(
data=[vec],
anns_field=field,
param=search_params,
limit=limit,
output_fields=["text", "id", "title", "category", "location",
"environment"]
)[0]
## Display Search Results
print(f"\nQuery: {query}")
print("\nSearch Results:")
for i, hit in enumerate(results):
    print(f"\n{i+1}. {hit.entity.title}")
    print(f"ID: {hit.entity.id}")
    print(f"Category: {hit.entity.category}")
    print(f"Location: {hit.entity.location}")
    print(f"Environment: {hit.entity.environment}")
    print(f"Similarity Score: {hit.distance:.4f}")
    print(f"Text: {hit.entity.text[:200]}...")
```

```
Query: Combat scene in the snow
Search results:
Battle with the White Bone Spirit on the Snowy Mountain
ID: 455509357906362369
Category: combat
Location: Snowy mountain summit
Environment: Snow field
Similarity score: 1.0097
Text: Battle with the White Bone Spirit on the snowy mountain summit.
On the snow-covered peak, Wukong and the White Bone Spirit engage in an
intense showdown. Amidst the howling cold wind......
Monkey form combat demonstration......
Fiery Eyes Golden Gaze......
```

The above code uses the **BGE-M3 model** to convert the user's query "combat scene in the snow" into dense and sparse vector representations, then constructs **Milvus Boolean filter expressions** (filtering results where category is `"combat"` and environment is `"snowfield"`. Next, when the search type is set to `hybrid`, it creates both dense and sparse vector search requests, and uses **WeightedRanker** to set the weights (e.g., sparse vector weight 0.7, dense vector weight 1.0) for weighted fusion ranking. Finally, it calls the `collection.hybrid_search` method to execute the retrieval in Milvus and returns the top 5 most relevant results. During the retrieval process, structured field filtering is also integrated, achieving a typical **hybrid RAG retrieval** method of "semantic search + rule-based constraints."

Vector databases and multimodal retrieval

Data of different modalities such as **text**, **images**, **audio**, etc. can all be represented as vectors to support more generalized similarity search. This enables vector databases to support multi-modal retrieval, where results can be found by comparing text, image, or combined image-text embeddings.

In this example, the system simultaneously retrieves **text** and **image vectors**, and uses result fusion strategies such as **RRF** (reciprocal rank fusion) to assign weights to the retrieval results from both paths, ultimately producing ranked results.

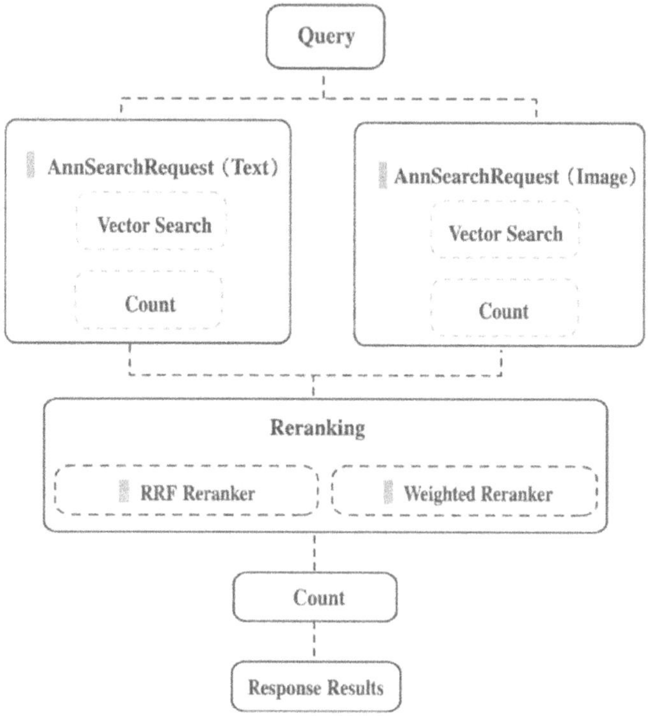

Figure 4.19: Flowchart showing query process for text and image leading to reranking and response output

This section introduces two methods for multimodal and image-based retrieval. The first method uses the Visualized BGE model for image-text embedding and matching. The second method uses ResNet-34 to extract image features for visual similarity retrieval.

Using the visualized BGE model for multimodal retrieval

This section will demonstrate how to build a multimodal retrieval system using the **Visualized BGE model** and **Milvus**. This system supports combined queries based on images and text, allowing learners to search for similar scenes in the game, specific battle moments, and more.

Here, a sample dataset containing images related to the game *Black Myth: Wukong* is used. The dataset can also be found in **Lewis's GitHub** repository.

The example follows five main steps: loading the multimodal embedding model, preparing the image dataset, generating image embeddings, storing the vectors in Milvus, and performing image-text similarity search.

Loading the visualized BGE model

First, load the Visualized BGE model to generate image-text embeddings.

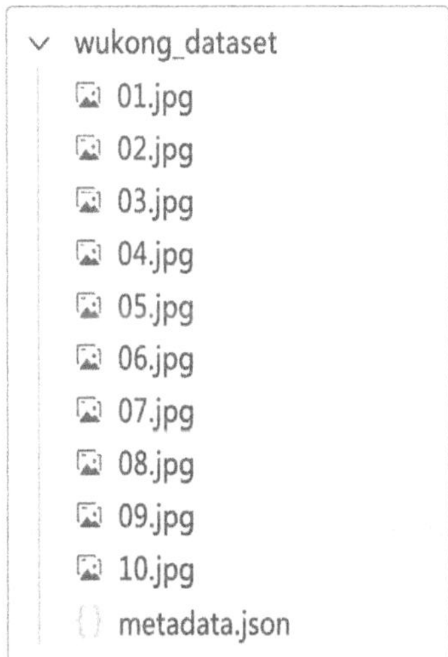

Figure 4.20: A folder named `wukong_dataset` *contains ten JPG image files and one meta-datajson file*

```
import torch
from visual_bge.modeling import Visualized_BGE
from dataclasses import dataclass
from typing import List, Optional
import json
from tqdm import tqdm
import numpy as np
import cv2
from PIL import Image
from pymilvus import MilvusClient
class WukongEncoder:
    """Multimodal encoder: encodes images and text into vectors"""
    def __init__(self, model_name: str, model_path: str):
        self.model = Visualized_BGE(model_name_bge=model_name, model_
weight=model_path)
        self.model.eval()
    def encode_query(self, image_path: str, text: str) -> list[float]:
        """Encode a combined image and text query"""
```

```
        with torch.no_grad():
            query_emb = self.model.encode(image=image_path, text=text)
        return query_emb.tolist()[0]
    def encode_image(self, image_path: str) -> list[float]:
        """Encode image only"""
        with torch.no_grad():
            query_emb = self.model.encode(image=image_path)
        return query_emb.tolist()[0]
### Initialize Encoder
model_name = "BAAI/bge-base-en-v1.5"
model_path = "./Visualized_base_en_v1.5.pth"
encoder = WukongEncoder(model_name, model_path)
```

Creating the image dataset

After loading the model, define a dataset class to manage image metadata. Each image record includes information such as the image path, title, category, description, tags, game chapter, location, characters, abilities, environment, and time of day.

```
@dataclass
class WukongImage:
    """Image metadata structure"""
    image_id: str
    file_path: str
    title: str
    category: str
    description: str
    tags: List[str]
    game_chapter: str
    location: str
    characters: List[str]
abilities_shown: List[str]
environment: str
time_of_day: str
class WukongDataset:
    """Image dataset management class"""
    def __init__(self, data_dir: str, metadata_path: str):
```

```
        self.data_dir = data_dir
        self.metadata_path = metadata_path
        self.images: List[WukongImage] = []
        self._load_metadata()
    def _load_metadata(self):
        """Load image metadata"""
        with open(self.metadata_path, 'r', encoding='utf-8') as f:
            data = json.load(f)
        for img_data in data['images']:
            self.images.append(WukongImage(**img_data))
### Initialize the Dataset
dataset = WukongDataset("data/multimodal", "data/multimodal/metadata.
json")
```

This dataset class makes it easier to keep each image and its metadata together before inserting them into Milvus.

Generating image embeddings

Once the metadata is loaded, generate image embeddings for all images in the dataset. Each image is converted into a vector representation that can later be stored and searched in Milvus.

```
### Generate Embedding Vectors for All Images
image_dict = {}
for image in tqdm(dataset.images, desc="Generating image embeddings"):
    try:
        image_dict[image.file_path] = encoder.encode_image(image.file_
path)
    except Exception as e:
        print(f"Failed to process image {image.file_path}: {str(e)}")
        continue
print(f"Successfully encoded {len(image_dict)} images")
```

```
Generating image embeddings: 100%|██████████| 10/10 [00:00<00:00,
29.35it/s]
Successfully encoded 10 images
```

At this stage, each image has been converted into a vector and stored temporarily in `image_dict`.

Storing image vectors in Milvus

After generating the embeddings, create a Milvus collection to store the image vectors and their metadata. This allows each image vector to be searched along with fields such as title, category, location, characters, and environment.

```
## Connect or Create Milvus
collection_name = "wukong"
milvus_client = MilvusClient(uri="./wukong_images.db")
## Create Vector Collection
dim = len(list(image_dict.values())[0])
milvus_client.create_collection(
    collection_name=collection_name,
    dimension=dim,
    auto_id=True,
    enable_dynamic_field=True
)
## Insert Data into Milvus
insert_data = []
for image in dataset.images:
    if image.file_path in image_dict:
        insert_data.append({
            "image_path": image.file_path,
            "vector": image_dict[image.file_path],
            "title": image.title,
            "category": image.category,
            "description": image.description,
            "tags": ",".join(image.tags),
            "game_chapter": image.game_chapter,
            "location": image.location,
            "characters": ",".join(image.characters),
            "abilities": ",".join(image.abilities_shown),
            "environment": image.environment,
            "time_of_day": image.time_of_day
        })
result = milvus_client.insert(
    collection_name=collection_name,
    data=insert_data
```

```
)
print(f"Index building completed, {result['insert_count']} records
inserted in total")
```

```
Index construction complete, 10 records inserted in total
```

Next, Now the image vectors and their metadata are stored in Milvus and can be used for similarity search.

Creating a multimodal search function

With the vectors stored in Milvus, define a search function for multimodal queries. The function takes both a query image and query text, converts them into a query vector, applies optional metadata filters, and returns the most similar images.

```
def search_similar_images(
    query_image: str,
    query_text: str,
    limit: int = 9,
    filters: Optional[dict] = None
) -> List[dict]:
    # Generate query vector
    query_vec = encoder.encode_query(query_image, query_text)
    # Build search parameters
    search_params = {
        "metric_type": "COSINE",
        "params": {"nprobe": 10}
    }
    # Add filter conditions
    if filters:
        filter_conditions = []
        for key, value in filters.items():
            if isinstance(value, list):
                filter_conditions.append(f"{key} in {value}")
            else:
                filter_conditions.append(f"{key} == '{value}'")
        search_params["expr"] = " and ".join(filter_conditions)
    # Execute the search
    results = milvus_client.search(
        collection_name=collection_name,
```

```
            data=[query_vec],
            output_fields=[
                "image_path", "title", "category", "description",
                "tags", "game_chapter", "location", "characters",
                "abilities", "environment", "time_of_day"
            ],
            limit=limit,
            search_params=search_params
        )[0]
        return results
```

This function performs the core multimodal retrieval operation: it combines the image and text query into one vector, then searches for similar vectors in Milvus.

Executing a sample image search query

Now execute a sample query using an image and the text prompt "**Find similar snowy combat scenes.**" In this example, the search is filtered to return results where the environment is snow and the category is combat.

```
## Execute Query
query_image = "data/multimodal/query_image.jpg"
query_text = "Find similar snowy combat scenes"
filters = {
    "environment": "snow",
    "category": "combat"
}
results = search_similar_images(
    query_image=query_image,
    query_text=query_text,
    limit=9,
    filters=filters
)
## Output Detailed Information
print("\nSearch results:")
for idx, result in enumerate(results):
    print(f"\nResult {idx}:")
    print(f"Image: {result['entity']['image_path']}")
    print(f"Title: {result['entity']['title']}")
    print(f"Description: {result['entity']['description']}")
```

```
    print(f"Similarity score: {result['distance']:.4f}")
```

```
Results have been saved to search_results.jpg
Search results:
Result 0:
Image: ./wukong_dataset/01.jpg
Title: Battle on the Snow Mountain
Description: Wukong on the snow mountain, gazing into the distance,
attempting to unleash the ultimate skill
Similarity score: 0.9454
Result 1:
Image: ./wukong_dataset/09.jpg
Title: Mountain Temple
Description: Ancient temple deep in the mountains, covered in snow,
appearing to be an exceptionally tranquil place
Similarity score: 0.8567
...
```

Create The returned results show the most similar images based on the combined image-text query. For example, the top result is a snowy battle scene involving Wukong, which matches the query intent.

Visualizing the search results

To make the retrieval results easier to inspect, create a visualization function that displays the query image alongside the top retrieved images.

```
import numpy as np
import cv2
from PIL import Image
from typing import List, Dict
def visualize_results(query_image: str, results: List[dict], output_path:
str):
    # Set image size and grid parameters
    img_size = (300, 300)
    grid_size = (3, 3)
    # Create canvas
    canvas_height = img_size[0] * (grid_size[0] + 1)
    canvas_width = img_size[1] * (grid_size[1] + 1)
    canvas = np.full((canvas_height, canvas_width, 3), 255, dtype=np.
```

```
uint8)
    # Add query image
    query_img = Image.open(query_image).convert("RGB")
    query_array = np.array(query_img)
    query_resized = cv2.resize(query_array, (img_size[0] - 20, img_size[1]
- 20))
    bordered_query = cv2.copyMakeBorder(
        query_resized, 10, 10, 10, 10,
        cv2.BORDER_CONSTANT,
        value=(255, 0, 0)
    )
    canvas[:img_size[0], :img_size[1]] = bordered_query
    # Add result images
    for idx, result in enumerate(results[:grid_size[0] * grid_size[1]]):
        row = (idx // grid_size[1]) + 1
        col = idx % grid_size[1]
        img = Image.open(result["entity"]["image_path"]).convert("RGB")
        img_array = np.array(img)
        resized = cv2.resize(img_array, (img_size[0] - 4, img_size[1] -
4))
        y_start = row * img_size[0]
        x_start = col * img_size[1]
canvas[y_start:y_start + img_size[0], x_start:x_start + img_size[1]] =
resized
## Add Similarity Score
score_text = f"Score: {result['score']:.2f}"
cv2.putText(
    canvas,
    score_text,
    (x_start + 10, y_start + img_size[0] - 10),
    cv2.FONT_HERSHEY_SIMPLEX,
    0.5,
    (0, 0, 0),
    1
)
cv2.imwrite(output_path, canvas)
## Visualize Results
visualize_results(query_image, results, "search_results.jpg")
```

After visualization, the images most similar in style and content to the query image are ranked at the top. The first result may be the query image itself, which is expected when the query image is also part of the indexed dataset (refer to `https://github.com/PacktPublishing/RAG-from-First-Principles` for the complete code).

Figure 4.21: Collage of fantasy warrior scenes in snowy landscapes and dramatic battles with mythical beasts

Using ResNet-34 to extract image features and perform retrieval

You can also extract image features using a traditional **deep learning** model, instead of relying on a multimodal embedding model. In this approach, **ResNet-34** is used to generate image-only feature vectors, which are then stored in Milvus for similarity search.

Unlike the **Visualized BGE** approach, ResNet-34 extracts image-only features. This means it can retrieve visually similar images, but it does not support combined text-image queries.

Extracting image features with ResNet-34

First, install the required dependencies and define a feature extractor based on ResNet-34. The model processes each image and converts it into a normalized feature vector.

```
pip install pymilvus>=2.4.2 timm torch numpy sklearn pillow
```

```
import torch
from PIL import Image
import timm
from sklearn.preprocessing import normalize
from timm.data import resolve_data_config
from timm.data.transforms_factory import create_transform
class WukongFeatureExtractor:
    def __init__(self):
        # Load ResNet-34
        self.model = timm.create_model('resnet34', pretrained=True, num_
classes=0)
        self.model.eval()
        # Configure image preprocessing
        config = resolve_data_config({}, model='resnet34')
        self.preprocess = create_transform(**config)
    def extract_features(self, image_path):
        # Process the game scene image
        image = Image.open(image_path).convert("RGB")
        input_tensor = self.preprocess(image).unsqueeze(0)
        # Extract features
        with torch.no_grad():
            features = self.model(input_tensor)
        return normalize(features.squeeze().numpy().reshape(1, -1)).
flatten()
```

This feature extractor converts each image into a fixed-length visual feature vector.

Storing scene features in Milvus

Next, create a Milvus collection to store the extracted scene features. Each record stores the feature vector along with metadata such as filename, scene type, and location.

```
from pymilvus import MilvusClient
### Connect or Create Milvus
```

```
client = MilvusClient(uri="wukong_images.db")
### Create Game Scene Collection
client.create_collection(
collection_name="wukong_scenes",
dimension=512,
auto_id=True,
enable_dynamic_field=True,
metric_type="COSINE"
)
```

After creating the collection, process each image in the dataset and insert its feature vector into Milvus.

```
import os
extractor = WukongFeatureExtractor()
scenes_dir = "data/multimodal"
### Index Each Scene
for scene in os.listdir(scenes_dir):
if scene.endswith(('.jpg', '.png')):
path = os.path.join(scenes_dir, scene)
features = extractor.extract_features(path)
### Add Scene Metadata
client.insert(
"wukong_scenes",
{
"vector": features,
"filename": path,
"scene_type": "combat" if "battle" in scene else "environment",
"location": scene.split('_')[0]  # Assuming filename format is location_
scenetype_id
}
)
```

The collection now contains image feature vectors that can be searched using visual similarity.

Searching for similar scenes

Finally, define a search function that extracts features from a query image and retrieves visually similar scenes from Milvus. Optional filters, such as scene_type, can be used to restrict the search results.

```
def find_similar_scenes(query_image, top_k=5, scene_type=None):
### Extract Features from the Query Image
query_features = extractor.extract_features(query_image)
### Prepare Search Parameters
search_params = {"metric_type": "COSINE"}
### Add Filter If a Scene Type Is Specified
if scene_type:
search_params["expr"] = f"scene_type == '{scene_type}'"
### Search for Similar Scenes
results = client.search(
"wukong_scenes",
data=[query_features],
output_fields=["filename", "scene_type", "location"],
search_params=search_params,
limit=top_k
)
return results[0]  # Return the result of the first query
```

Now run a sample search for similar **combat scenes**.

```
from IPython.display import display
## Search for Similar Combat Scenes
combat_scene = "data/multimodal/query_image.jpg"
results = find_similar_scenes(combat_scene, scene_type="combat")
## Display Results
print("Query scene:")
display(Image.open(combat_scene).resize((200, 200)))
print("\nSimilar combat scenes:")
for hit in results:
    scene_path = hit["entity"]["filename"]
    similarity = hit["distance"]
    print(f"\nSimilarity: {similarity:.2f}")
    print(f"Scene location: {hit['entity']['location']}")
```

```
    display(Image.open(scene_path).resize((200, 200)))
```

```
Similar combat scene: 09.jpg (snowy mountain)
Similarity: 1.00
```

With this image-feature-based method, the system can retrieve identical or visually similar image content. However, because ResNet-34 only extracts visual features, this approach is limited to image similarity retrieval and is not a full multimodal retrieval solution.

Data maintenance and vector storage CRUD operations in RAG systems

After **vectorizing** and storing data, the work is not complete. In a RAG system, the knowledge base must be maintained over time so that embeddings, metadata, and indexes remain consistent as source data changes. This section explains key **data maintenance** principles and demonstrates common insert, update, delete, and collection-management operations in Milvus.

Data flow maintenance and management in RAG systems

Whether traditional data or vector data, the core principles of data flow maintenance are as follows.

- **Consistency**: Vector embeddings, metadata, and indexes of the data should always be kept in sync. After every **CRUD operation**, ensure that the data state in the database and retrieval system is consistent.
- **Real-time capability**: For dynamic scenarios (such as **Q&A systems** or **recommendation systems**), data needs to be added or updated in real time to reduce latency. Asynchronous tasks or batch processing can be used to enhance performance.
- **Data auditing and traceability**: Log each CRUD operation to ensure that data changes are traceable, making error troubleshooting easier.
- **Automation**: Use automated scripts or services to detect and clean up or update expired data, avoiding the inefficiency of manual operations.

Periodic task scheduling is the foundation of data flow maintenance. Through tools (such as `cron` or *Airflow*), the system's data flow status can be regularly checked, such as cleaning up expired data or rebuilding indexes. This approach not only ensures long-term stable operation of the system, but also reduces the complexity of manual maintenance.

For real-time update requirements, message queue technologies such as *Kafka* or *RabbitMQ* can be used to listen for data CRUD events. Once a change is detected, the system will automatically trigger relevant operations to realize real-time updates of the knowledge base.

To further optimize the update process, **incremental index update** techniques can be adopted, updating only the affected parts of the data instead of rebuilding the entire index. This method significantly improves efficiency and saves system resources.

Performance optimization can be approached on multiple levels. For example, batch processing of additions or deletions can not only reduce frequent access to the database but also significantly increase operational efficiency and lower system load. Adjusting index parameters (such as `nlist` and `nprobe`) according to business needs allows a balance between retrieval speed and accuracy, thereby improving user experience. For data accessed with high frequency, enabling a caching mechanism to store it in memory or high-speed cache can reduce the query load on the database and speed up system response. These measures help ensure that the system continues to run efficiently and stably as it scales.

RAG system data management requires a hierarchical strategy, dividing data into two categories: **core data** and **dynamic data**. **Core data** is usually stable and valid for the long term, without the need for frequent modifications; **dynamic data**, on the other hand, needs to be frequently updated according to business requirements. By managing data in layers and focusing add, delete, and update operations on **dynamic data**, overall efficiency can be improved.

To enhance system reliability, a **version control mechanism** can be introduced for data updates. Each update retains a historical version, allowing for quick rollback in case of errors. Performing regular multi-replica backups is equally important. By regularly backing up knowledge base data, data loss caused by hardware failures or human errors can be effectively prevented, ensuring the security and availability of the system.

Vector insert, delete, and update operations in Milvus

When the original data source in a **RAG system** changes, it is necessary to ensure that **embeddings**, **metadata**, and **retrieval indexes** are updated synchronously. The **Insert** (add, meaning insert) data operation can be used to expand the system knowledge base, correct errors, improve existing data, or adjust content based on new requirements. Additionally, it helps clear expired, irrelevant, or incorrect data.

Inserting vector entities

The following code example demonstrates how to insert new **embedding vector data** into an existing **vector database collection**.

```
from pymilvus import MilvusClient
import numpy as np
## Connect to Existing Milvus Using Local SQLite Mode
db_path = "./test_vector.db"
client = MilvusClient(db_path)
## Collection Name
collection_name = "my_collection"
data_insert = [
{"id": 100001, "vector": np.random.random(128).astype("float32").
tolist()},
{"id": 100002, "vector": np.random.random(128).astype("float32").tolist()}
]
res = client.insert(collection_name=collection_name, data=data_insert)
```

Upserting vector entities

In Milvus, you can use the **Upsert** operation (insert or update, meaning "insert if it does not exist, update if it does") to combine the functionality of updating and inserting data.

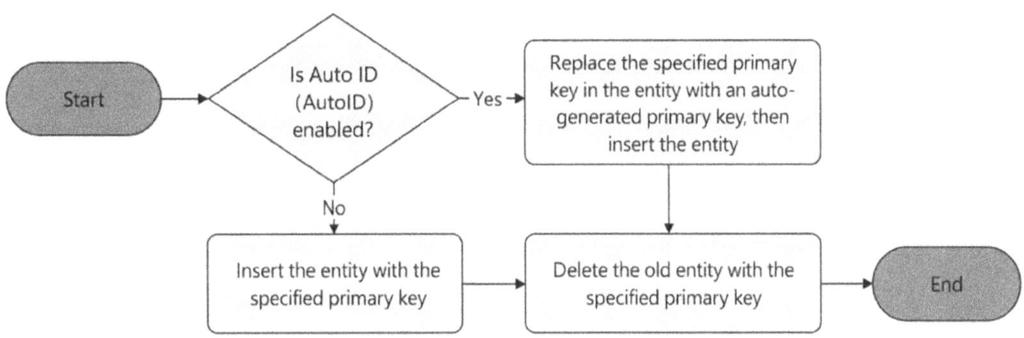

Figure 4.22: AutoID process branching based on whether AutoID is enabled

Milvus determines whether to perform an update or insert operation by checking whether the **primary key** exists. When using this operation, you must ensure that the vector entities included in the Upsert request (in Milvus, a vector entry is referred to as an **Entity**) contain a primary key, otherwise an error will occur. After receiving the Upsert request, Milvus executes the following process.

- Check whether the primary field of the collection has **AutoId** enabled.
- If it is enabled, Milvus will replace the entity's primary key with an automatically generated primary key and insert the data.
- If it is not enabled, Milvus will use the primary key provided by the entity to insert the data.
- Perform a deletion operation based on the primary key values of the entities included in the Upsert request.

```
data_upsert = [
{"id": 100001, "vector": np.random.random(128).astype("float32").
tolist()}, # Update existing ID
{"id": 100010, "vector": np.random.random(128).astype("float32").tolist()}
# Insert new ID
]
res = client.upsert(collection_name=collection_name, data=data_upsert)
```

Deleting vector entities

If you need to delete data, you can specify the entities that are no longer needed by **primary key** or **filter conditions.**

```
## Delete Entities by Primary Key
res = client.delete(
collection_name=collection_name,
ids=[100002, 100010]
)
## Delete Entities by Filter Condition
res = client.delete(
collection_name=collection_name,
filter="difficulty == 'high'"
)
```

For the complete program, please visit Lewis's GitHub repository.

Collection operations in vector databases

In vector databases, **collections** are the fundamental units of data storage and management, similar to tables in traditional databases. **Collection operations** include creating, deleting, viewing, cleaning, and **index management**, running through all stages of the vector data lifecycle.

Viewing collection information

After creating a collection, you can list all collections and inspect the structure of a specific collection.

```
## List All Current Collections
collections = client.list_collections()
print("Current collection list:", collections)
```

The following example views detailed collection information, including field structure and metadata.

```
info = client.describe_collection(collection_name)
print("\nBasic collection information:")
print("Collection name:", info["collection_name"])
print("Description:", info["description"])
print("Field information:")
for field in info["fields"]:
    print(f" - {field['name']} ({field['type']})")
```

Example output:

```
Basic collection information:
Collection name: my_collection
Description:
Field information:
- id (5)
- vector (101)
```

Load collection into memory

Before performing **vector search**, you need to first load the **collection** into memory.

```
client.load_collection(collection_name)
print(f"Collection '{collection_name}' has been loaded into memory")
```

Release memory resources

When you no longer need to use the **collection**, you can release its occupied memory to save resources.

```
client.release_collection(collection_name)
print(f"Collection '{collection_name}' has been released from memory")
```

Deleting a collection

Deleting a collection will permanently remove the **collection** and all its data. Please proceed with caution.

```
client.drop_collection(collection_name)
print(f"Collection '{collection_name}' has been permanently deleted")
```

For the complete program, please visit **Lewis's GitHub repository** (Refer to `GitHub - PacktPublishing/RAG-from-First-Principles: RAG from First Principles Published by Packt Pub` for the complete code).

Summary

Vector stores are optimized for storing and retrieving high-dimensional vectors efficiently. Unlike traditional scalar-based databases, vector stores are designed to manage complex vector embeddings and support fast similarity search, enabling rapid query responses and improved data retrieval performance.

In this chapter, we first explored the default vector storage mechanism in **LlamaIndex** and examined how vector indexes are constructed in RAG systems. We then introduced the main components of vector databases, compared several mainstream vector database solutions, and used Milvus as a practical example to explain index types, similarity metrics, and search configurations.

We also discussed how vector storage extends beyond dense vectors to include sparse vectors and binary vectors. These different vector formats provide the foundation for hybrid retrieval, where semantic search and keyword-based retrieval can be combined to improve search relevance. In addition, we explored multimodal retrieval by embedding images and demonstrated how Milvus can be used with models such as BGE and ResNet-34 to support image-based and image-text retrieval scenarios.

Finally, we covered data maintenance and CRUD operations in RAG systems, including how to insert, update, delete, inspect, load, release, and manage vector collections in Milvus. In the next chapter, we will move on to retrieval techniques, focusing on pre-retrieval processing, retrieval optimization, and post-retrieval methods in RAG systems.

5

Pre-Retrieval Processing

By the time you've studied this section, you will have already learned how to load data, chunk text, generate **embedding vectors**, and store these vectors in a **vector database**, thereby successfully building an efficient knowledge base. Next, we will explore **pre-retrieval processing techniques**, revealing how to construct appropriate queries before performing retrieval, and how to optimize these queries to enhance the system's overall execution efficiency and accuracy.

Why pre-retrieval processing matters

Before looking at specific techniques, it is useful to understand why pre-retrieval processing is needed in a RAG system.

Alex: Lewis, why do we need to do pre-retrieval processing?

Lewis: Let me explain with an analogy. I highly recommend the course *The 7 Habits of Highly Effective People*. One of the core principles of the course is: human reactions are not simply stimulus-driven; rather, there is a space of autonomous choice between "stimulus" and "response." This concept is similar to what Viktor Frankl proposed in *Man's Search for Meaning*, and was emphasized and promoted by Stephen Covey and others as the advanced intelligence's freedom to choose. I call this the **preprocessing before response**.

The following figure illustrates the analogy Lewis uses to explain the space between receiving a stimulus and producing a response.

Figure 5.1: Stimulus-choice-response sequence illustrating how an external stimulus is processed through free choice to produce a behavioral response

When a **RAG system** receives a user's initial query request, it can introduce a **preprocessing before response** through preset rules (relatively fixed) or by using a **large model** (relatively flexible). This process allows the query to be optimized and filtered before retrieval and content generation. This mechanism provides the system with a **pre-retrieval thinking space**, enabling it to more intelligently filter information, optimize queries, or decide on the next step. This not only improves the system's flexibility and retrieval efficiency, but also enhances the quality and accuracy of the output.

In a RAG system, this same idea appears as a preprocessing stage before retrieval. The following workflow shows how query construction, query routing, query translation, and evaluation can fit into this stage.

Alex: Lewis, I noticed that pre-retrieval processing includes multiple facets, such as **query construction**, **query translation**, and **query routing**.

Techniques included in pre-retrieval processing

Pre-retrieval processing is not a single technique. It includes several methods that prepare the user's query before the system performs retrieval.

Lewis: Indeed, pre-retrieval processing covers the following three techniques.

1. **Query construction:** `Query construction` involves converting user-proposed natural language questions into data query forms suitable for retrieval systems. This includes reading data from relational databases, as well as automatically converting natural language questions into SQL queries, which is known as **Text-to-SQL** (often also written as **Text2SQL**). In addition, there are scenarios where natural language questions are converted into graph database query languages to query complex entity relationships, namely **Text-to-Cypher**. For vector databases, although you can directly perform embedding queries on natural language, this section also introduces a way to build metadata filters from queries, which is a simplified version similar to **Text-to-SQL**.

2. **Query translation:** `Query translation`, also known as query rewriting or query optimization, is a stage where the system restructures the user's input question to enhance retrieval effectiveness. Specific methods include replacing, decomposing, abstracting, or expanding the original question, converting it into multiple sub-queries, or even into hypothetical questions, etc.
3. **Query routing:** `Query routing` determines which type of database or retrieval path the system selects to execute the query. It is mainly divided into **logical routing** and **semantic routing**.

The core goal of the above three techniques is to accurately convert the user's question into a form that is more suitable for system retrieval and to select the optimal retrieval path, thereby making the subsequent retrieval and generation processes more accurate, comprehensive, efficient, and smooth.

Query construction: Asking questions in natural language

Query construction is one of the main techniques used in pre-retrieval processing. It is the process of converting a user's natural language question into a form that a retrieval system can execute or apply directly. Instead of relying only on semantic similarity, the system may transform the question into SQL for relational databases, Cypher for graph databases, or metadata filters for vector stores. In this way, query construction acts as a bridge between human language and the structured or semi-structured query formats required by different data sources.

Modern enterprise knowledge bases are vast and complex systems. The ultimate goal for enterprises and individuals is to access and retrieve information in a more convenient way. This information may be stored as **unstructured vectors**, in **structured format** within traditional databases, or even in **graph databases**.

Whether it's **SQL** or **Cypher**, each has its own specific syntax and query logic. Directly writing these queries usually requires some understanding of the database structure and syntax. **Query construction** (i.e., **Text-to-Query technology**) greatly lowers the technical threshold of this process by allowing learners to ask questions in natural language and have the system automatically generate the corresponding database queries or vector searches.

The following three techniques show how natural language questions can be transformed for different types of data sources:

1. **Text-to-SQL**: Responsible for converting natural language questions into **SQL queries** suitable for relational databases (such as **MySQL**, **PostgreSQL**, **SQL Server**, etc.). For example, converting the question "Find the best-selling product" into the following SQL query.

   ```
   SELECT product_name FROM sales ORDER BY total_sold DESC LIMIT 1
   ```

2. **Text-to-Cypher**: Used to translate natural language questions into **Cypher query language** for **graph databases** (like **Neo4j**). For example, converting the question "Find the management relationship of employees" into the following Cypher query.

   ```
   MATCH (e:Employee)-[:MANAGES]->(m:Manager) RETURN e, m
   ```

3. **Self-query retriever**: A pre-retrieval tool provided by **LangChain** that can automatically generate metadata filter conditions based on the user's query before the retrieval step. This way, when generating embedding vectors and retrieving based on learner questions, it can further filter results by specifying conditions. This is an advanced query construction and retrieval technique. For example, for the query "Find videos with more than 100,000 views," the following filter condition can be generated.

   ```
   "filter": "gt(\"view_count\", \"100000\")"
   ```

Text-to-SQL: Transforming natural language into SQL

The first query construction technique is Text-to-SQL, which is used when the target data is stored in relational databases.

Text-to-SQL is one of the most common forms of query construction. It allows users to ask questions in natural language while the system generates the corresponding SQL query in the background. This is especially useful in RAG systems that need to retrieve information from relational databases, where answers often depend on structured fields, table relationships, filters, sorting, and aggregation rather than semantic similarity alone.

Why Text-to-SQL matters in RAG

In most discussions about **RAG systems**, the focus is usually on the retrieval of unstructured data (such as text, images, etc.). However, enterprises often possess various types of data assets: on the one hand, there are unstructured documents; on the other, there are various relational databases (such as **MySQL**, **PostgreSQL**, **SQL Server**, etc.), data warehouses, and so on.

Therefore, while performing vector retrieval on unstructured data, **RAG systems** also need to provide solutions for structured data. By incorporating **Text-to-SQL** into the RAG workflow, users can express their needs in natural language, and the system will automatically execute the query and integrate the results with unstructured knowledge to generate answers. This enables retrieval and computation logic to be performed within structured data sources, thereby integrating structured datasets into the overall RAG workflow. This helps to build a unified Q&A and reasoning platform that integrates both unstructured and structured data—one of the future development directions for intelligent information systems.

In fact, **Text-to-SQL** is not a new concept that emerged with the advent of RAG systems. Research and applications related to conversational database interfaces and template-based **NL2SQL (natural language to SQL)** systems existed long before the rise of deep learning. However, with the growing popularity and adoption of **large models** and **RAG** in recent years, the functionality of Text-to-SQL has gained renewed attention within unified RAG frameworks, and has achieved significant performance improvements thanks to new technologies.

> Lewis: Text-to-SQL is a specialized field with evaluation datasets such as WikiSQL, which contains a large number of single-table query examples. Because it is relatively simple, it is often used for preliminary experiments. In contrast, the Spider dataset, released by a team from Yale University, covers complex queries involving multiple tables, multiple databases, and multiple relationships. It is currently one of the most challenging open-source datasets and more realistically reflects the difficulty and diversity of real database environments. At present, researchers commonly use Spider as the main evaluation benchmark for Text-to-SQL.

Traditional Text-to-SQL implementation

Traditional **Text-to-SQL systems** use rule-based or template matching approaches to handle queries in relatively fixed or restricted domains. These systems usually include the following key steps.

1. **Natural language understanding (NLU)**: Perform operations such as word segmentation, named entity recognition, and dependency parsing on users' natural language questions to extract user intent, for example, "query sales revenue," **Return Product Names**, or **Sort By** a certain metric.
2. **Database schema mapping**: Map database table names and field names to concepts mentioned in natural language. For example, **product** corresponds to the `product_name` field, while **sales revenue** may correspond to the `sales` or `total_sold` field.

3. **SQL structure generation**: Generate relevant clauses such as **SELECT**, **FROM**, **WHERE**, **GROUP BY**, **ORDER BY**, and **LIMIT** based on user intent and the database schema. If multi-table queries are involved, **JOIN** conditions or subqueries need to be generated.
4. **SQL statement validation and execution**: The system may choose to perform simple syntax or logic checks after generation, or directly submit the SQL to the database engine to run and return the query results.

Traditional Text-to-SQL methods rely heavily on manual configuration, especially in the process of matching natural language to the database schema. For example, for the question "Among the sales records, which product has the highest sales volume?", the system needs to determine whether **sales volume** corresponds to the `sales_table.total_sold` field or the `sales_table.sales_amount` field, and whether data needs to be queried from the `orders_table`. This matching process mainly relies on **named entity recognition (NER)**, and then determines the best mapping by calculating cosine similarity between word vectors or entries in a dictionary. This approach lacks deep contextual understanding, is prone to errors, and is difficult to adapt to complex database structures or variable user queries.

Text-to-SQL in the deep learning era

With the development of deep learning technologies, **transformer-based neural network methods** have gradually become the mainstream solution for **Text-to-SQL** tasks. Early neural-network-based systems often adopted **Seq2Seq** or **encoder-decoder architectures**, encoding natural language inputs into vector representations and then directly decoding them into SQL token sequences.

Later, research focused more on representing natural language descriptions and field names via **embeddings**, and incorporating **attention mechanisms** to optimize this process. This approach improved, to some extent, the mapping between natural language and database schemas. However, it still involved a significant amount of manual feature engineering and remained limited when handling complex queries or cross-domain application scenarios.

To further enhance model performance, researchers fine-tuned models on domain-specific Text-to-SQL datasets (such as **Spider** and **WikiSQL**), enabling models to better adapt to the structural characteristics and query patterns of different databases. Fine-tuned models exhibited more precise understanding of domain-specific terminology and relationships among table fields, thus generating SQL statements that better meet real-world requirements. This made the models especially effective in handling complex multi-table or nested query problems.

Large language model-based Text-to-SQL implementation

The emergence of large language models such as *ChatGPT* and *GPT-4* has completely reshaped the implementation of **Text-to-SQL**. Through large-scale pre-training, these models have learned the complex mapping between natural language and SQL, and can generate high-quality SQL statements even without specialized fine-tuning.

Compared to the traditional "stepwise" approach—which requires manual implementation of **natural language understanding**, **schema mapping**, **SQL structure generation**, etc.—few-shot learning and in-context learning in the era of large models provide new possibilities for **Text-to-SQL**. By simply providing the **database schema**, explanatory information, and corresponding SQL query examples in the prompt, large models can quickly adapt to new database structures and query types.

Example: Building a simple Text-to-SQL workflow

Suppose we have two tables, with their structures as follows:

Field Name	Data type	Description	Example value
`scenic_id`	INT	Primary key, unique identifier of the scenic spot	1
`scenic_name`	VARCHAR	Name of the scenic spot	Jinci
`city`	VARCHAR	City located	Taiyuan City
`level`	VARCHAR	Scenic spot grade	AAAAA level
`monthly_visitors`	INT	Number of visitors in the current month	50000

Table 5.1: Structure of the `scenic_spots` table, including scenic spot identifiers, names, locations, ratings, and monthly visitor counts

Field name	Data type	Description	Example value
`city_id`	INT	Primary key, unique identifier of the city	1
`city_name`	VARCHAR	City name	Taiyuan City
`annual_tourism_income`	INT	Annual cultural and tourism income (unit: yuan)	200000000

Table 5.2: Structure of the `city_info` table, including city identifiers, city names, and annual tourism income

famous_dish	Type	Category	Example
VARCHAR	Local Specialty/Snack		Knife-cut Noodles

Table 5.3: Field description for `famous_dish`, representing the local specialty or snack associated with a city

First, create these two database tables with the following code:

```
## Connect to SQLite Database
import sqlite3
conn = sqlite3.connect('data/tourism.db')
cursor = conn.cursor()
## Create the Scenic Spots Table
cursor.execute('''
    CREATE TABLE IF NOT EXISTS scenic_spots (
        scenic_id INTEGER PRIMARY KEY,
        scenic_name VARCHAR(100) NOT NULL,
        city VARCHAR(50) NOT NULL,
        level VARCHAR(20),
        monthly_visitors INTEGER
    )''')
## Create the City Information Table
cursor.execute('''
    CREATE TABLE IF NOT EXISTS city_info (
        city_id INTEGER PRIMARY KEY,
        city_name VARCHAR(50) NOT NULL,
        annual_tourism_income INTEGER,
        famous_dish VARCHAR(100)
)''')
## Insert Sample Data Into the Scenic Spots Table
sample_scenic_spots = [
     (1, 'Jinci Temple', 'Taiyuan City', 'AAAAA', 50000),
     (2, 'Mount Wutai', 'Xinzhou City', 'AAAAA', 80000),
     (3, 'Yungang Grottoes', 'Datong City', 'AAAAA', 70000),
     (4, 'Pingyao Ancient City', 'Jinzhong City', 'AAAAA', 90000),
     (5, 'Qiao Family Compound', 'Jinzhong City', 'AAAAA', 45000)
]
cursor.executemany(
```

```
    'INSERT OR REPLACE INTO scenic_spots VALUES (?, ?, ?, ?, ?)',
    sample_scenic_spots)
## Insert Sample Data Into the City Information Table
sample_city_info = [
     (1, 'Taiyuan City', 200000000, 'Knife-cut Noodles'),
     (2, 'Datong City', 180000000, 'Datong Vinegar'),
     (3, 'Jinzhong City', 150000000, 'Daozi Noodles'),
     (4, 'Xinzhou City', 120000000, 'Youmian Kaolao Lao'),
     (5, 'Yuncheng City', 130000000, 'Yuncheng Boiled Cake')
]
cursor.executemany('INSERT OR REPLACE INTO city_info VALUES (?, ?, ?, ?)',
    sample_city_info)
## Commit Changes and Close Connection
conn.commit()
conn.close()
print("Database tables created and sample data inserted.")
```

With the database tables in place, you can now build the **Text-to-SQL** program accordingly (refer to `https://github.com/PacktPublishing/Generative-AI-at-AWS` for the complete code).

```
## Connect to the SQLite Database
import sqlite3
conn = sqlite3.connect('data/tourism.db')
cursor = conn.cursor()
## Prepare Schema Description
schema_description = """
    You are accessing a database containing two tables:
    1. scenic_spots (Scenic Spot Information Table)
    - scenic_id (INT): Primary key, unique identifier for the scenic spot
    - scenic_name (VARCHAR): Name of the scenic spot
    - city (VARCHAR): City where it is located
    - level (VARCHAR): Scenic spot rating
    - monthly_visitors (INT): Number of visitors this month
    2. city_info (City Information Table)
    - city_id (INT): Primary key, unique identifier for the city
    - city_name (VARCHAR): Name of the city
    - annual_tourism_income (INT): Annual tourism income (unit: RMB)
```

```
    - famous_dish (VARCHAR): Local famous dish/special snack
"""

## Initialize the OpenAI Client
from openai import OpenAI
import os
client = OpenAI(
    base_url="https://api.deepseek.com",
    api_key=os.getenv("DEEPSEEK_API_KEY")
)
## Set Up Query
user_query = "Query the AAAAA-rated scenic spots in Taiyuan City and their
monthly visitors"
## Prepare Prompt for SQL Generation
prompt = f"""
    The following is the structural description of the database:
    {schema_description}
    The user's natural language question is as follows:
    \"{user_query}\"
    Please note:
    1. The 'city' field in the scenic_spots table stores the city name,
corresponding to the city_name field in the city_info table
    2. The association between the two tables should use city_name and
city for matching
    3. Please return SQL query statement only, do not include any
explanation, comments, or formatting marks (such as ```sql)
    """
## Call the Large Model to Generate SQL Statement
response = client.chat.completions.create(
    model="deepseek-chat",
    messages=[
            {"role": "system", "content": "Only return the SQL statement,
do not include any Markdown formatting or other notes."},
            {"role": "user", "content": prompt}
        ],
    temperature=0
)
## Clean Up SQL Statement, Remove Possible Markdown Tags
sql = response.choices[0].message.content.strip()
```

```
sql = sql.replace('```sql', '').replace('```', '').strip()
print(f"\nGenerated SQL query statement:\n{sql}")
SELECT scenic_name, monthly_visitors
FROM scenic_spots
WHERE city = 'Taiyuan' AND level = 'AAAAA';
```

Next, execute the SQL statement generated by the large model and retrieve the results.

```
## Execute the SQL Statement and Retrieve Results
cursor.execute(sql)
results = cursor.fetchall()
print(f"Query results: {results}")
conn.close()
## Query Results
Query results: [('Jinci Temple', 50000)]
```

Then, we pass these data back to the large model to output in natural language form.

```
## Generate Natural Language Description
if results:
    # Get column names
    column_names = [description[0] for description in cursor.description]
    # Convert results into a list of dictionaries
    results_with_columns = [dict(zip(column_names, row)) for row in
results]
    nl_prompt = f"""
Query results are as follows:
{results_with_columns}
Please convert these data into a natural language description that is easy
to understand.
The original question is: {user_query}
Requirements:
1. Use simple and easy-to-understand language
2. Include all queried data information
3. If there are numbers, please use Chinese numeral expressions
"""

    response_nl = client.chat.completions.create(
        model="deepseek-chat",
        messages=[
```

```
            {"role": "system", "content": "You are responsible for
converting query results into easy-to-understand natural language
descriptions."},
            {"role": "user", "content": nl_prompt}
        ],
        temperature=0.7
    )
    description = response_nl.choices[0].message.content.strip()
    print(f"Natural language description:\n{description}")
else:
    print("No relevant data found.")
## Close Database Connection
conn.close()
```

According to the query results, among the AAAAA-level scenic spots in Taiyuan, the current month's number of visitors to Jinci reached fifty thousand.

This shows that in a simple Q&A system, learners do not need to have deep knowledge of **database structure** or **SQL syntax** to quickly obtain the information they want.

Solution combining agent, SQL data function, and tool calls

The previous example shows direct SQL generation. In more complex business scenarios, however, a more controlled approach is often needed.

Anna: Lewis, the previously introduced **Text2SQL** approach performs well in simple scenarios. However, when dealing with complex business logic, this approach often fails to generate effective queries, or its stability cannot be guaranteed. In practice, do you think there are more stable technical routes?

Lewis: I've discussed this issue with friends from the industry. Indeed, as you pointed out, this is a challenge faced by **Text2SQL**. After multiple iterations, we gradually formed an intermediate solution that balances efficiency and stability, mainly by leveraging the **Tool Calls** capability of **Agents**, together with pre-defined **Data-Function templates** (which contain `SQL statements` inside), as well as **metadata extraction** to achieve a safe transition from natural language to structured database table operations.

How to understand metadata extraction

Anna: How should we understand metadata extraction?

Lewis: Here it refers to extracting **database metadata**, including **field information**, **table structure**, and **view descriptions**, and manually supplementing necessary resource documentation. Only processed metadata can be embedded into vectors.

What are data functions

Anna: So, what are data functions?

Lewis: **Data functions** are a system of function templates aimed at establishing generic data functions to support common query scenarios. Developing data functions for specific businesses is similar to developing template mechanisms for traditional **ORM frameworks** (such as **MyBatis** and **Hibernate**). By encapsulating complex SQL logic into templates, we improve code reusability.

Next comes the intelligent scheduling process, which utilizes the **function call mechanism** to handle processing and rerouting duties. The large model collaborates to understand user intent, retrieves relevant metadata and applicable data functions, and performs single-step or multi-step SQL assembly and querying.

The following code example demonstrates how to use **Agent**, **SQL-Data-Function**, and **Tool Calls** in combination. The code adds tool descriptions through modular tool definition and defines implementation functions to provide specific functionality for the tools.

Next, inject the **database structure description** into the system prompt, including the business meanings of table fields and their relationships.

```
import sqlite3
from typing import Dict, Any, List
import json
from openai import OpenAI
import os
def load_schema_metadata() -> str:
    """Load the description of the database metadata"""
    return ''
### Database Structure Metadata
scenic_spots (Tourist Attractions Information Table)
- scenic_id: Primary Key
- scenic_name: Name of the tourist attraction (e.g. "Jinci Temple")
```

```
  - city: City where it is located (associated with city_info.city_name)
  - level: Attraction level (AAAA/AAAAA)
  - monthly_visitors: Number of visitors this month
city_info (City Information Table)
  - city_name: Primary Key
  - annual_tourism_income: Annual cultural tourism income (unit: Yuan)
  - famous_dish: Specialty cuisine
'''
```

Next, use the execute_sql function to implement the **fundamental query layer** for the entire program. This function uniformly handles SQL execution, parameterized queries, error handling, and result formatting, thereby ensuring the security and standardization of data access. Then, encapsulate common query requirements into three core functions:

- The query_scenic_spots function supports multi-condition combination queries on attractions (such as filtering by location city, attraction level, and monthly number of visitors).
- The query_city_info function enables flexible queries on city information (supports sorting).
- The cross_table_query function encapsulates the logic for association queries between the attractions information table and the city information table.

These functions are SQL-Data-Function predefined by business logic.

```
def execute_sql(db_path: str, sql: str, params: tuple = ()) -> Dict:
    """Basic method for executing SQL queries"""
    print("\n=== SQL Execution Details ===")
    print(f"SQL Statement: {sql}")
    print(f"Parameters: {params}")
    try:
        with sqlite3.connect(db_path) as conn:
            conn.row_factory = sqlite3.Row
            cursor = conn.cursor()
            cursor.execute(sql, params)
            results = [dict(row) for row in cursor.fetchall()]
            print(f"Execution results: {results}")
            print("=== Execution Successful ===\n")
            return {"success": True, "data": results, "message":
"Execution Successful"}
```

```
    except Exception as e:
        print(f"Execution Failed: {str(e)}")
        print("=== Execution Failed ===\n")
        return {"success": False, "data": None, "message": f"Execution
Failed: {str(e)}"}
def query_scenic_spots(db_path: str, city: str = None, level: str = None,
min_visitors: int = None) -> Dict:
    """Predefined function for querying tourist attractions"""
    conditions = []
    params = []
    if city:
        conditions.append("city = ?")
        params.append(city)
    if level:
        conditions.append("level = ?")
        params.append(level)
    if min_visitors:
        conditions.append("monthly_visitors >= ?")
        params.append(min_visitors)
    where_clause = " AND ".join(conditions) if conditions else "1=1"
    sql = f"SELECT scenic_name, city, level, monthly_visitors FROM scenic_
spots WHERE {where_clause}"
def query_city_info(db_path: str, city_name: str, order_by: str = None) ->
Dict:
    """Predefined function to query city information"""
    order_clause = ""
    if order_by:
        order_clause = f" ORDER BY {order_by} DESC"
    sql = f"SELECT * FROM city_info WHERE city_name LIKE ?{order_clause}"
    return execute_sql(db_path, sql, (f"%{city_name}%",))
def cross_table_query(db_path: str, target_city: str, min_income: int) ->
Dict:
    """Predefined cross-table join query function"""
    sql = """
    SELECT s.scenic_name, s.level, c.annual_tourism_income
    FROM scenic_spots s
    JOIN city_info c ON s.city = c.city_name
```

```
    WHERE s.city = ? AND c.annual_tourism_income >= ?
    """
    return execute_sql(db_path, sql, (target_city, min_income))
```

The above functions use **parameterized queries** for security to prevent **SQL injection**, and strictly constrain parameter values through enumerations (such as limiting **scenic spot levels** to AAAA or AAAAA). In addition, the `QueryResult` object is used to uniformly format the return structure, ensuring it includes execution status (`success`), data (`data`), and message (`message`), accompanied by detailed execution log output. Unified handling of execution exceptions is implemented, while preserving the original error messages. This design makes the query process more transparent and easier to debug.

Next, use the **Tool Calls** feature of the large model to implement **tool routing**, where each tool corresponds to a predefined **SQL-Data-Function template**. The results of tool calls will be automatically added to the conversational context, making it easier to handle follow-up questions.

Among them, the `define_tools` function defines three structured query tools: `query_scenic_spots` is used to query scenic spot information, supporting filtering by city, scenic level, and the number of monthly visitors; `query_city_info` is used to query city information, supporting sorting by annual tourism revenue or specialty dishes; `cross_table_query` is used for cross-table queries, enabling the association of scenic and city information.

The `process_query` function implements a two-turn conversational query process.

Two-turn conversational query process

First turn: The user's question and database schema information are sent to the GPT model so that it can choose a suitable query tool; then, the corresponding database query is executed according to the tool selected by GPT.

Second turn: The query results are sent to the GPT model to generate a natural language answer.

```
def define_tools() -> List[Dict]:
    """Define the basic functions for structured data access"""
    return [
        {
            "type": "function",
            "function": {
                "name": "query_scenic_spots",
                "description": "Query scenic spot information based on
conditions",
```

```
                "parameters": {
                    "type": "object",
                    "properties": {
                        "city": {"type": "string", "description": "The
name of the city where it is located"},
                        "level": {"type": "string", "enum": ["AAAA",
"AAAAA"]},
                        "min_visitors": {"type": "number", "description":
"Minimum threshold of visitors"}
                    }
                }
            }
        },
        {
            "type": "function",
            "function": {
                "name": "query_city_info",
                "description": "Query city cultural tourism information",
                "parameters": {
                    "type": "object",
                    "properties": {
                        "city_name": {"type": "string", "description":
"City name"},
                        "order_by": {"type": "string", "enum": ["annual_
tourism_income", "famous_dish"]}
                    }
                }
            }
        },
        {
            "type": "function",
            "function": {
                "name": "cross_table_query",
                "description": "Cross-table joint query for scenic spot
and city information",
                "parameters": {
                    "type": "object",
```

```
                    "properties": {
                        "target_city": {"type": "string", "description":
"Target city name"},
                        "min_income": {"type": "number", "description":
"Minimum annual tourism income"}
                    }
                }
            }
        }
    ]
def process_query(db_path: str, user_input: str) -> str:
    """Complete process for handling user queries"""
    client = OpenAI(
        base_url="https://api.deepseek.com",
api_key = os.getenv("DEEPSEEK_API_KEY")
)
tools = define_tools()
schema_metadata = load_schema_metadata()
system_prompt = f"""
You can select the appropriate **data access method** according to the
user's question.
The current **database structure** is as follows:
{schema_metadata}
Please give priority to using **predefined functions** to access data.
Note:
- **City names** must be an exact match (e.g., 'Taiyuan City')
- **Scenic spot grades** must use the standard format (e.g., 'AAAA')
- **Numeric parameters** must be converted to integer type
"""
messages = [
    {"role": "system", "content": system_prompt},
    {"role": "user", "content": user_input}
]
### First Call Select a Tool
response = client.chat.completions.create(
    model="deepseek-chat",
    messages=messages,
    tools=tools,
```

```
        tool_choice="auto"
    )
    tool_calls = response.choices[0].message.tool_calls
    if not tool_calls:
        return response.choices[0].message.content
    ### Execute Tool Call
    messages.append(response.choices[0].message)
    for tool_call in tool_calls:
        func_name = tool_call.function.name
        kwargs = json.loads(tool_call.function.arguments)
        if func_name == "query_scenic_spots":
            result = query_scenic_spots(db_path, **kwargs)
        elif func_name == "query_city_info":
            result = query_city_info(db_path, **kwargs)
        elif func_name == "cross_table_query":
            result = cross_table_query(db_path, **kwargs)
        messages.append({
            "role": "tool",
            "tool_call_id": tool_call.id,
            "name": func_name,
            "content": json.dumps(result, ensure_ascii=False)
        })
    ### Generate a Natural Language Answer
    final_response = client.chat.completions.create(
    model="deepseek-chat",
    messages=messages,
    temperature=0.3
    )
    return final_response.choices[0].message.content
```

At this point, everything is ready, and we can start making natural language queries. The **large language model** will first convert our natural language input into a **tool invocation**, then execute the **SQL statement** inside the **Data-Function template**, and return the query result as the answer (refer to `https://github.com/PacktPublishing/RAG from First-Principles` for the complete code).

```
db_path = "data/tourism.db"
query = "Please help me find all AAAAA-level scenic spots in Taiyuan City
```

```
and list the attractions with more than 40,000 visitors."
print("\n=== User Query ===")
print(f"Query Content: {query}")
result = process_query(db_path, query)
print("\n=== Final Result ===")
print(result)
```

```
=== User Query ===
Query Content: Please help me find all AAAAA-level scenic spots in Taiyuan
City and list the attractions with more than 40,000 visitors.
=== SQL Execution Details ===
SQL Statement: SELECT scenic_name, city, level, monthly_visitors FROM
scenic_spots WHERE city = ? AND level = ? AND monthly_visitors >= ?
Parameters: ('Taiyuan City', 'AAAAA', 40000)
Execution Result: [{'scenic_name': 'Jinci', 'city': 'Taiyuan City',
'level': 'AAAAA', 'monthly_visitors': 50000}]
=== Execution Successful ===
=== Final Result ===
Among the AAAAA-level scenic spots in Taiyuan City, the attractions with
more than 40,000 visitors this month are:
- Jinci, with 50,000 visitors this month.
```

The execution process of the above program is as follows.

1. The **large model** analyzes the user's intent and chooses to call the **query_scenic_spots** tool.
2. **Parameter conversion**: `city="Taiyuan City"`, `level="AAAAA"`, `min_visitors=40000`.
3. Execute the predefined **SQL query**: `SELECT ... WHERE city = 'Taiyuan City' AND level = 'AAAAA' AND monthly_visitors >= 40000`.
4. Inject the query results into the context.
5. The **large model** generates the final answer based on the original question and the query results.

This solution, by using predefined **data functions** and strict **parameter control**, effectively manages query risks while ensuring flexibility. Combined with **metadata descriptions** and **tool invocation mechanisms**, it retains the convenience of natural language interaction and enables precise access to structured data. Although creating **SQL-Data-Functions** requires some initial investment, this method achieves more stable and reliable execution. For enterprise users, system stability and controllability often take precedence over development convenience, so this compromise solution has received positive practical feedback.

Text-to-cypher: From natural language to graph database queries

After relational databases, another important structured data source for RAG systems is the graph database.

Understanding graph databases

A **graph database** is a form of data storage based on graph structures. As enterprise data shifts from structured to multimodal, networked, and complex associations, graph databases, thanks to their powerful relationship modeling capabilities, are particularly suitable for representing complex entity relationship networks, making them one of the preferred tools for handling these intricate data relationships.

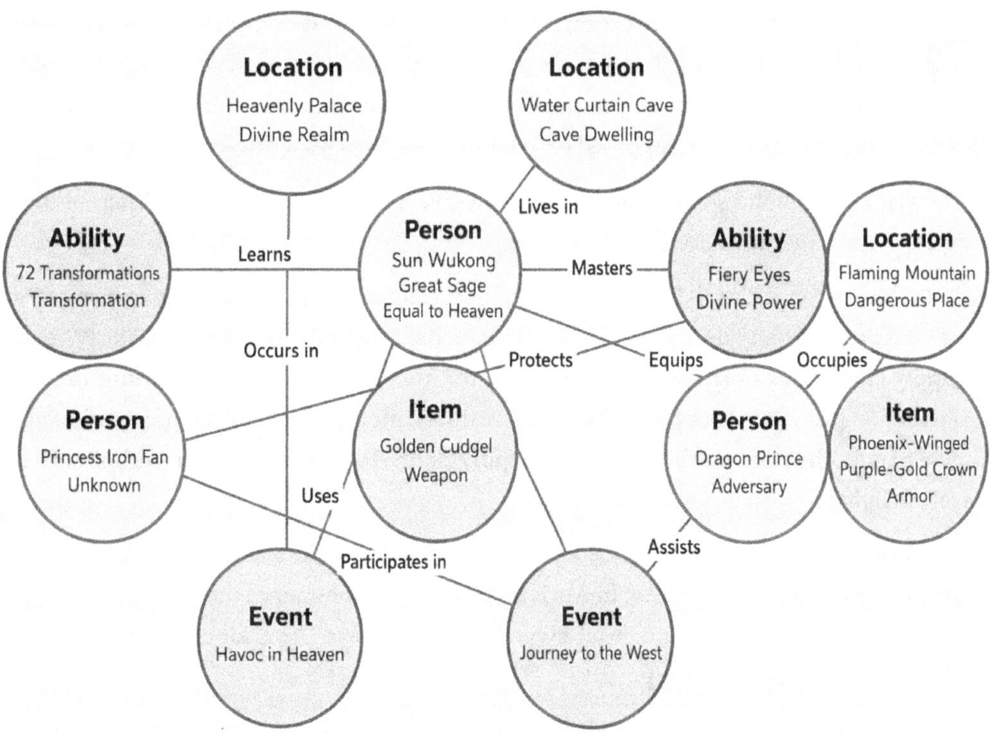

Figure 5.2: A concept map connecting characters, items, abilities, events, and locations through their semantic relationships

Core components of a graph database

The core components of a graph database are as follows.

- **Node**: Represents entities in the data, such as "Employee," "Customer," "Product," etc.
- **Edge**: Describes how nodes are connected, such as "manages," "purchases," "depends on," and so on.
- **Property**: Provides detailed additional information for nodes or edges, such as "Name," "Age," "Price," "Time," etc.

Why graph databases matter in RAG

In an **RAG system**, connecting to a graph database enables efficient querying and reasoning over entity relationship networks. For example, in scenarios such as social network relationship analysis, understanding corporate organizational structures, and optimizing logistics network routes, the application of graph databases is particularly effective. The introduction of graph databases allows the system to not only retrieve isolated texts or data, but also to perform in-depth reasoning and generate responses based on relationships between entities.

Alex: Lewis, I understand somewhat, but can you give a concrete example to illustrate the importance of graph databases?

Lewis: Of course. Let me explain with a hypothetical example. Suppose in a certain project, you help a logistics company design a question-answering system. When a user asks, "What are the supply chain risks of Huaguoshan Fresh Fruit?" the initial **RAG system** cannot provide a satisfactory answer. This is because the search results contain only product information about Huaguoshan Fresh Fruit and the company's supply chain risk documentation, without offering valuable insights.

The **RAG system** without the Text-to-Cypher step would provide the answer: "Huaguoshan Fresh Fruit typically enters its sales peak in April to May. It is recommended to notify suppliers in advance to coordinate supply and ensure warehouse readiness." This kind of answer does not actually address the user's inquiry.

However, after adding the **Text-to-Cypher** step for graph database queries, the **RAG system** uses the relationships in the graph database to effectively connect products with suppliers. It also links relevant local weather conditions through the suppliers' knowledge graph, thus providing a much more accurate answer: "Huaguoshan Fresh Fruit is supplied by Supplier A Pantao Yuan (located in Shanghai, with sunny weather) and Supplier B Wuzhuangguan (located in Guangdong, with heavy rainstorms). Currently, Wuzhuangguan may face supply risks due to storms.

It is recommended to monitor their inventory and consider backup suppliers." This is an answer with real business insight.

By applying graph analysis algorithms such as **community detection**, we can identify "subgroups" within the graph structure, namely clusters whose internal nodes are closely connected but have loose connections with other groups. By combining **graph databases** and **community detection techniques**, RAG systems are not only capable of simple text matching but can also deeply understand associations within the data, providing richer content and more intelligent decision support.

Alex: Lewis, I think I get it now. **Community detection** is like helping us find "friend circles" in the data! This way, the system can discover those key relationships, not just isolated pieces of information.

Lewis: That's right. A typical representative of graph databases is *Neo4j*, and **Cypher** is a widely used query language for graph databases like *Neo4j*. **Cypher** is designed similarly to SQL but is dedicated to handling nodes, relationships, and properties in graph data.

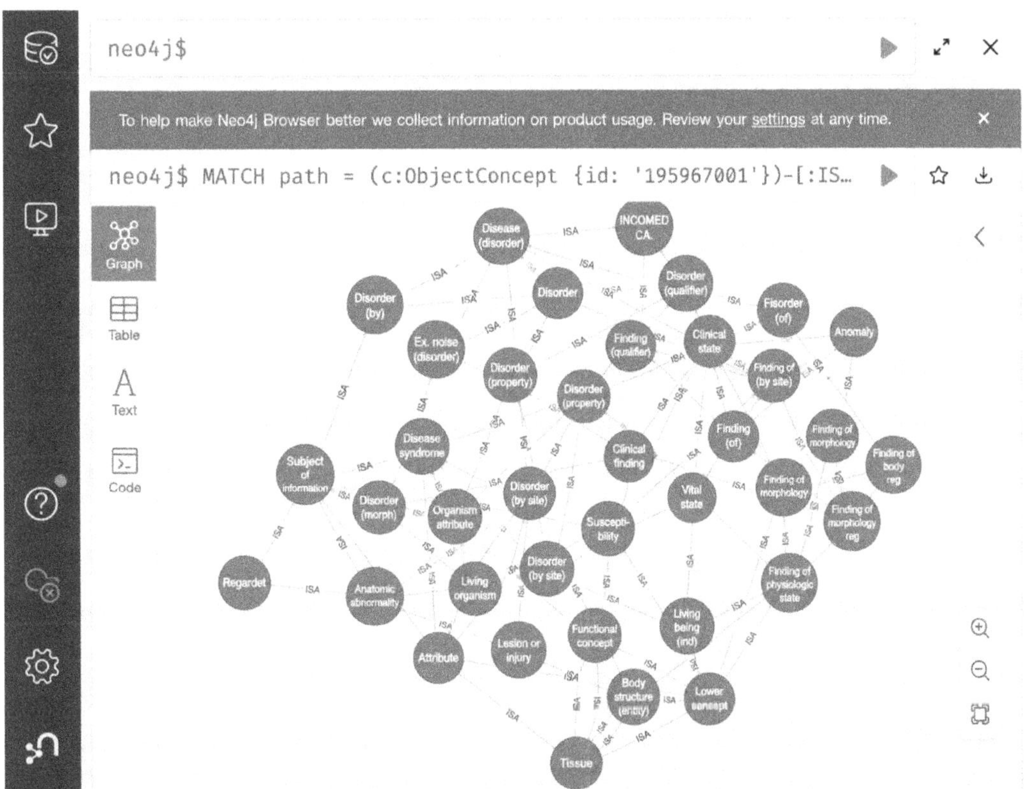

Figure 5.3: A Neo4j browser window showing a complex graph of purple nodes and labeled connections

Basic Cypher syntax

The basic syntax of **Cypher** is as follows:

- Node matching: `(n:Label)` represents matching a node with label Label.
- Relationship matching: `(a)-[r:RELATIONSHIP]->(b)` indicates there is a relationship of type RELATIONSHIP from node a to node b.
- Property filtering: Use the `WHERE` clause to filter properties of nodes or relationships.

For example, to find all direct subordinates of a certain employee, you can use the following **Cypher** query.

```
MATCH (e:Employee)-[:MANAGES]->(sub:Employee)
WHERE e.name = "Alice"
RETURN sub.name;
```

This query searches in the graph for all employees who are directly managed by an employee named Alice.

Text-to-Cypher workflow

The architecture of **Text-to-Cypher** is similar to **Text-to-SQL** and includes the following main steps.

- **Natural language understanding**: Parse user questions to extract intent, entities, and relationships.
- **Schema matching**: Map entities or relationships in natural language to node labels, relationship types, and properties in the graph database.
- **Cypher generation**: Dynamically generate Cypher queries based on parsing results.
- **Query validation and execution**: Check whether the generated Cypher query is syntactically correct and submit it to the graph database for execution.

The key difference is that **Cypher queries** usually need to consider more complex multi-hop relationships. In addition, the schema of a **graph database** is typically flexible, which brings greater uncertainty to query generation.

Due to space limitations, we cannot delve into all the details regarding **graph databases, Neo4j**, and the **Cypher language** here. Next, let's inspire your understanding of the process of transforming natural language into Cypher queries through a simple example.

Example: Generating a Cypher query from natural language

Suppose the following node types exist.

- **Yokai**: Contains attributes **name** (yokai name) and **strength** (yokai combat power).
- **BattleScene**: Contains attributes **location** (scene location) and **difficulty** (scene difficulty).
- The relationship types are as follows.
- **[:PARTICIPATES_IN]**: Indicates that a yokai participated in a certain battle scene.
- **[:LOCATED_IN]**: Indicates that a battle scene is located at a specific location.

The schema of the graph database is as follows.

```
Nodes:
(Yokai {name: "Bull Demon King", strength: 900})
(Yokai {name: "Lady White Bone", strength: 750})
(Yokai {name: "King Golden Horn", strength: 850})
(BattleScene {location: "Flaming Mountain", difficulty: "Hard"})
(BattleScene {location: "White Bone Cave", difficulty: "Normal"})
Relationships:
(Yokai {name: "Bull Demon King", strength: 900})-[:PARTICIPATES_IN]-
>(BattleScene {location: "Flaming Mountain", difficulty: "Hard"})
(Yokai {name: "Lady White Bone", strength: 750})-[:PARTICIPATES_IN]-
>(BattleScene {location: "Flaming Mountain", difficulty: "Hard"})
(Yokai {name: "King Golden Horn", strength: 850})-[:PARTICIPATES_IN]-
>(BattleScene {location: "White Bone Cave", difficulty: "Normal"})
(BattleScene {location: "Flaming Mountain", difficulty: "Hard"})-
[:LOCATED_IN]->("Flaming Mountain")
(BattleScene {location: "White Bone Cave", difficulty: "Normal"})-
[:LOCATED_IN]->("White Bone Cave")
```

Below is a prompt designed to help large models understand the structure of a **graph database** and generate **Cypher queries.**

```
You are a Text-to-Cypher expert. Below is the schema of a graph database.
Nodes:
- Yokai: Properties: name (string), strength (integer)
- BattleScene: Properties: location (string), difficulty (string)
Relationships:
- PARTICIPATES_IN: From Yokai to BattleScene
- LOCATED_IN: From BattleScene to Location
```

```
User question: "Find all yokai that participate in scenes with a
difficulty of 'hard', and return their strength."
Please generate a Cypher query.
Based on the above prompt, the large model will generate the following
Cypher query.
MATCH (yokai:Yokai)-[:PARTICIPATES_IN]->(scene:BattleScene {difficulty: "
困难"})
RETURN yokai.name, yokai.strength;
```

SQL query vs Cypher query

The following table summarizes the main differences between SQL and Cypher queries.

Query type	Data model	Query target	Syntax style	Complex relationship modeling capability
SQL query	Tabular (such as tables, rows, columns)	Rows and columns	Natural language-like declarative	Relies on multi-table JOIN
Cypher query	Graph structure (such as nodes, relationships, properties)	Nodes and relationships	Declarative + graph pattern matching	Natively supports nodes and relationships, more efficient for complex queries

Table 5.4: Comparison between SQL and Cypher queries in terms of data model, query target, syntax style, and complex relationship modeling capability

One of the advantages of **Text-to-Cypher** is its support for multi-hop queries and reasoning. When a user poses a question involving multiple nodes and relationships, such as "Find the department budgets of employees managed by Alice," **Text-to-Cypher** can generate a query spanning multiple nodes—first determining which departments are relevant to the query, then further checking the specific budget of those departments.

The integration of **knowledge graphs** and **question answering systems** is currently a very important application direction. By incorporating knowledge graphs into **RAG systems**, more intelligent semantic Q&A and deep reasoning can be achieved, thereby providing stronger technical support for intelligent enterprise decision-making.

Self-query retriever automatically generating metadata filter conditions from queries

For **vector data**, natural language queries can be directly embedded and used to retrieve relevant information, without the need to construct specific query statements as in **Text-to-SQL** or **Text-to-Cypher**. This process includes several pre-retrieval optimization techniques, one of which is the **Self-query Retriever** technique. This technology can automatically extract information from natural language queries, generate metadata filter conditions, and thus help **vector stores** preliminarily filter documents through keywords.

Alex: Lewis, your explanation isn't very clear. What is a **Self-query Retriever**? What does it mean to automatically generate **metadata filter conditions** from a natural language query? And, how exactly is filtering through keywords done?

Lewis: I think I was quite clear. Anyway, let's use a concrete example to explain this design concept more clearly.

Metadata fields for video retrieval

The following code example demonstrates how to build an intelligent video retrieval system using the **LangChain** framework. Here, we'll use **Shanxi culture and tourism** as an example. Suppose we've loaded videos introducing scenic spots, cities, etc. When crawling these videos, we naturally obtain the following **metadata fields**, which will serve as the basis for metadata filtering.

- **title**: Document title.
- **description**: Document description.
- **view_count**: Number of document views.
- **publish_date**: Date of publication.
- **length**: Document length (seconds).

Figure 5.4: Entrance of Shanxi cultural relics digital experience museum

Combining vector retrieval and metadata filtering

By using the **Self-query Retriever** technique, the key retrieval points in a natural language query can be converted into a structured query and accurately filtered based on the video's metadata. This approach combines **vector retrieval** and **metadata filtering**, forming a **hybrid retrieval method** that supports querying video attributes across multiple dimensions. This process perfectly demonstrates the combination of vector retrieval and structured retrieval and is well worth delving deeper into.

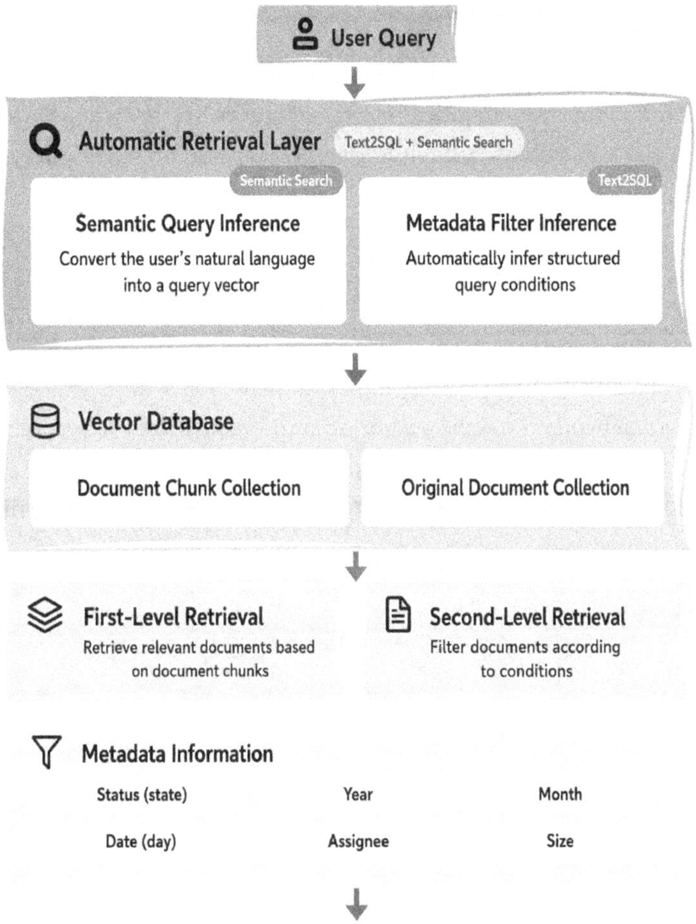

Figure 5.5: Flowchart in showing a multilayered automated query system for document searching

Lewis: My guess is that LangChain classifies the Self-query Retriever as a query construction technique in its RAG documentation because the process of generating metadata and filter expressions effectively constructs structured retrieval elements. Of course, in essence, this technique also belongs to hybrid retrieval, as discussed in the next chapter.

Installing required libraries

First, install some necessary libraries. **pytube** and **youtube-transcript-api** are used to connect to **YouTube**, **Chroma** supports metadata filters in **Self-query Retriever** as a vector database (the author also tried **Faiss** and **Milvus**, but found that neither supports **Self-query Retriever**), and **lark** is the Python API interaction pacLewis for **Feishu**.

```
pip install pytube
pip install youtube-transcript-api
pip install langchain-chroma
pip install lark
```

After installing these dependencies, the author encountered an error when trying to connect to the video website via script. On related forum posts, someone suggested changing the value of `client` from `ANDROIDMUSIC` to `WEB` in the `InnerTube` class of the `innertube.py` file in the **pytube** pacLewis. After making this change, the issue was resolved.

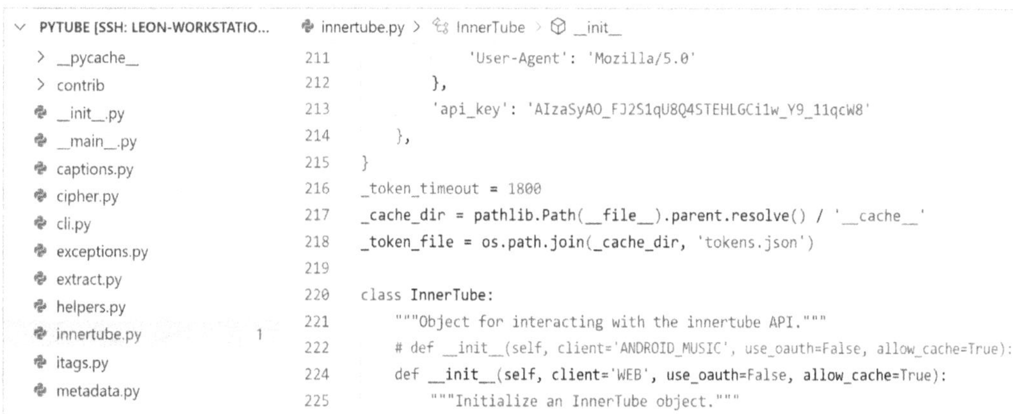

Figure 5.6: Code editor showing a Python class InnerTube with initialization and file path variables set

Loading documents with metadata

The following is an example of loading documents using the `YoutubeLoader` class from **LangChain**.

```
from langchain_community.document_loaders import YoutubeLoader
### Load Documents with Metadata
docs = YoutubeLoader.from_youtube_url(
" https://www.youtube.com/watch?v=zDvnAY0zH7U",
```

```
add_video_info=True).load()
### View the Metadata of the First Loaded Document
print(docs[0].metadata)
```

```
{'source': 'zDvnAY0zH7U',
'title': '...Tang Dynasty Wooden Architecture...in the Mountains of Shanxi...A Must-Visit Place in One's Lifetime',
'description': "The Tang Dynasty was the heyday of China's feudal society, with many Tang Dynasty stone architectural works across the country...
At Mount Wutai, Shanxi, there is a grand Tang Dynasty wooden structure preserved, which is the largest and best preserved Tang Dynasty wooden structure in China.",
'view_count': 81598,
'publish_date': '2024-04-08 00:00:00',
'length': 1394,
'author': 'On the Journey'
```

These metadata fields are exactly the **fields** we use for query filtering. Calculating **view counts**, comparing **publish dates**, etc. are exactly the strengths of traditional database **fields**, not those of **vector semantic retrieval**.

Building the self-query retriever

The following code builds the retriever in stages: loading videos, creating embeddings, configuring metadata fields, and initializing the retriever.

Below is a complete example of the `Self-query Retriever` code.

```
### Import Required Libraries
from langchain_core.prompts import ChatPromptTemplate
from langchain_deepseek import ChatDeepSeek
from langchain_community.document_loaders import YoutubeLoader
from langchain.chains.query_constructor.base import AttributeInfo
from langchain.retrievers.self_query.base import SelfQueryRetriever
from langchain_chroma import Chroma
from langchain_huggingface import HuggingFaceEmbeddings
from pydantic import BaseModel, Field
### Define Video Metadata Model
class VideoMetadata(BaseModel):
    """Video metadata model, defining the video attributes to extract"""
```

```
    source: str = Field(description="Video ID")
    title: str = Field(description="Video title")
    description: str = Field(description="Video description")
    view_count: int = Field(description="View count")
    publish_date: str = Field(description="Publish date")
    length: int = Field(description="Video length (seconds)")
    author: str = Field(description="Author")
### Load Video Data
video_urls = [
    "https://www.youtube.com/watch?v=zDvnAY0zH7U",  # Foguang Temple,
Shanxi
    "https://www.youtube.com/watch?v=iAinNeOp6Hk",  # China's Largest
Compound
    "https://www.youtube.com/watch?v=gCVy6NQtk2U",  # Song Dynasty
Underground Palace
]
### Load Video Metadata
videos = []
for url in video_urls:
    try:
        loader = YoutubeLoader.from_youtube_url(url, add_video_info=True)
        docs = loader.load()
        doc = docs[0]
videos.append(doc)
print(f"Loaded: {doc.metadata['title']}")
except Exception as e:
print(f"Failed to load {url}: {str(e)}")
```

Create vector store:

```
embed_model = HuggingFaceEmbeddings(model_name="BAAI/bge-small-zh")
vectorstore = Chroma.from_documents(videos, embed_model)
```

Configure metadata fields for the retriever

The **metadata fields** are set as follows:

```
metadata_field_info = [
    AttributeInfo(
        name="title",
```

```
    description="Video title (string)",
    type="string",
    ),
    AttributeInfo(
        name="author",
        description="Video author (string)",
        type="string",
    ),
    AttributeInfo(
        name="view_count",
        description="Video view count (integer)",
        type="integer",
    ),
    AttributeInfo(
        name="publish_date",
        description="Video publish date, a string in the format YYYY-MM-
DD",
        type="string",
    ),
    AttributeInfo(
        name="length",
        description="Video length, an integer in seconds",
        type="integer",
    ),
]
#Create SelfQueryRetriever:
llm = ChatDeepSeek(model="deepseek-chat", temperature=0) # Deterministic
output
retriever = SelfQueryRetriever.from_llm(
    llm=llm,
    vectorstore=vectorstore,
    document_contents= "Video metadata including title, author, view
count, publish date, and other information",
    metadata_field_info=metadata_field_info,
    enable_limit=True,
    verbose=True )
```

Execute example query:

```
queries = [
"Find two videos with more than 100,000 views",
"Show the most recently published video"
]
## Execute the Queries and Output the Results
for query in queries:
    print(f"\nQuery: {query}")
    try:
        results = retriever.invoke(query)
        if not results:
            print("No matching videos found")
            continue
        for doc in results:
            print(f"Title: {doc.metadata['title']}")
            print(f"Views: {doc.metadata['view_count']}")
            print(f"Publish Date: {doc.metadata['publish_date']}")
    except Exception as e:
        print(f"Query error: {str(e)}")
        continue
```

```
Loaded: ' ......Tang Dynasty Wooden Architecture in the Mountains of Shanxi......A must-visit place in one's lifetime'
Loaded: ' ......Private mansion, owner started out selling tofu......Twice the size of the Forbidden City'
Loaded: ' ......Live footage of a Song Dynasty underground palace......An internal refrigerator used for 2,000 years'
Query: Find videos with more than 100,000 views
Title: ' ......Live footage of a Song Dynasty underground palace......An internal refrigerator used for 2,000 years'
Views: 263138
Publish Date: 2024-01-27 00:00:00
Title: ' ......Private mansion, owner started out selling tofu......Twice the size of the Forbidden City'
Views: 907279
Publish Date: 2023-11-11 00:00:00
Query: Show the most recently published video
```

```
Title: ' ......Live footage of a Song Dynasty underground palace......An
internal refrigerator used for 2,000 years'
Views: 263138
Publish Date: 2024-01-27 00:00:00
```

Self-query retriever enables the transformation from natural language to structured queries through **metadata configuration**, converting requests like "Find videos with more than 100,000 views" into structured query conditions.

The internally generated parsed text is as follows, where the **field name** (`view_count`), **condition** (`gt`), and **value** (`100000`) are automatically extracted by the large language model from the user's question.

```
{ "query": "Find two videos with more than 100,000 views", "filter":
"gt(\"view_count\", \"100000\")", "limit":2 }
```

From the output results, we can see that the **Self-query Retriever** is not only able to accurately identify videos that meet the criteria, but can also filter for the most recently published videos.

Limitations of Self-query retriever

However, the performance of the Self-query retriever is not stable; for some queries (such as "Find videos published in January 2024"), Lewis found during testing that its answers are inaccurate.

When errors occur, users need to dive deep into the **LangChain** codebase for debugging. This is one of the criticisms of **LangChain**: it offers a useful tool, but the tool is not entirely reliable. As such, the tools in these frameworks may serve more as sources of inspiration; in production environments, we need to implement more robust solutions on our own based on these concepts.

Query translation: Better explaining user questions

The **query construction methods** introduced earlier generate various structured query statements through the capabilities of large models, differing from **vector search**, to access structured data sources. In contrast, the **query translation** to be discussed next focuses mainly on semantically reconstructing user input through **prompt engineering**.

Specifically, when the quality of a query is low—potentially containing noise or ambiguous terms, or failing to cover all aspects of the required information retrieval—a series of optimization techniques need to be employed, such as **rewriting**, **decomposition**, **clarification**, and **expansion**, to improve the query and make it more complete, thereby achieving better retrieval results.

Query rewriting: Reformulating the original question into an appropriate form

Query rewriting refers to the process of reformulating the original question into an appropriate form to improve the accuracy of the system's retrieval results.

Guiding large language models to rewrite queries via prompts

The most straightforward method is to use custom **prompt templates** with **large language models** to rewrite user queries. Below is a simple example of **query rewriting**.

```
from openai import OpenAI
import os
client = OpenAI(
base_url="https://api.deepseek.com",
api_key=os.getenv("DEEPSEEK_API_KEY"),
)
def rewrite_query(question: str) -> str:
    """Use a large language model to rewrite the query"""
    prompt = """As a game customer service representative, you need to
help users rewrite their questions.
Rules:
1. Remove irrelevant information (e.g., personal situations, chit-chat)
2. Use accurate gaming terminology
3. Preserve the core intent of the question
4. Convert vague questions into specific queries
Original question: {question}
Please provide the rewritten query directly (do not add any prefixes or
explanations)."""
    # Rewrite the query using the DeepSeek model
    response = client.chat.completions.create(
        model="deepseek-chat",
        messages=[
            {"role": "user", "content": prompt.format(question=question)}
        ],
    )
    return response.choices[0].message.content.strip()
query = "Well, I just started playing this game, it feels really hard,
I can't get past the Putuo Mountain level no matter what. Which skills
```

```
should I learn first? Any tips for beginners!"
print(f"\nOriginal query: {query}")
print(f"Rewritten query: {rewrite_query(query)}")
```

```
Original query: Um, I just started playing this game, and it feels really
hard. I'm stuck at the Putuo Mountain level and just can't get through.
Which skills should I learn first? Beginner seeking advice!
Rewritten query: For the Putuo Mountain level, which skills should
beginners prioritize learning?
```

With the query rewritten by a large language model, the new query becomes clearer and more concise. It not only saves token count but also retrieves results more effectively for players.

Optimizing queries with RePhraseQueryRetriever

LangChain provides an out-of-the-box tool, **RePhraseQueryRetriever**, to perform **query rewriting**. It leverages **large language models** and internally set prompts to make queries more succinct and clear.

The following code sample demonstrates how to use **RePhraseQueryRetriever** to optimize queries.

```
import logging
from langchain_chroma import Chroma
from langchain_community.document_loaders import TextLoader
from langchain_deepseek import ChatDeepSeek
from langchain_huggingface import HuggingFaceEmbeddings
from langchain_text_splitters import RecursiveCharacterTextSplitter
from langchain.retrievers import RePhraseQueryRetriever
### Set Up Logging
logging.basicConfig()
logging.getLogger("langchain.retrievers.re_phraser").setLevel(logging.
INFO)
loader = TextLoader("data/Destruction of Gods/setup.txt",
encoding='utf-8')
data = loader.load()
text_splitter = RecursiveCharacterTextSplitter(chunk_size=500, chunk_
overlap=0)
all_splits = text_splitter.split_documents(data)
embed_model = HuggingFaceEmbeddings(model_name="BAAI/bge-small-zh")
vectorstore = Chroma.from_documents(documents=all_splits, embedding=
embed_model)
```

```
### Set Up RePhraseQueryRetriever to Reconstruct Queries With a Large Language Model
llm = ChatDeepSeek(model="deepseek-chat", temperature=0)
retriever_from_llm = RePhraseQueryRetriever.from_llm(
    retriever=vectorstore.as_retriever(),
    llm=llm
)
query = "Well, I just started playing this game, it feels really hard, I'm stuck on the Putuo Mountain level and just can't get through. Which skills should I learn first? Any tips for a beginner?"
### Using RePhraseQueryRetriever for Query Rewriting
docs = retriever_from_llm.invoke(query)
```

```
INFO: langchain.retrievers.re_phraser: Re-phrased question: Vectorstore query: "Putuo Mountain level beginner skill recommendations game guide" Explanation: - Removed conversational fillers ("Well", "just") and emotional expressions ("feels really hard", "just can't get through", "Any tips for a beginner"). - Kept key game-specific terms: Location: "Putuo Mountain" (level implied), Core need: "skill recommendations", Context: "beginner" and "game guide". - Structured for optimal retrieval of strategy guides or skill trees relevant to the early-game hurdle.
```

From the log information, we can see that the rewritten **query** is more concise and clear, and unnecessary content has also been removed, which helps improve retrieval efficiency and accuracy. Of course, this new **Query** is in English because the default prompt inside LangChain's `RePhraseQueryRetriever` class is in English.

We can customize the prompt and pass it to the `from_llm` method of **RePhraseQueryRetriever** to ensure the rewritten result is in Chinese. However, as for the specific code implementation, I'll leave that as homework for you, because reading the LangChain documentation (`langchain\retrievers\re_phraser.py`) and understanding class design details are essential skills for technical personnel.

Query decomposition: Breaking down queries into multiple subproblems

Query rewriting aims to make queries more standardized, while **query decomposition** goes a step further by breaking a **query** down into multiple subproblems. This allows exploration of different aspects of the query from various perspectives, making the retrieved content richer.

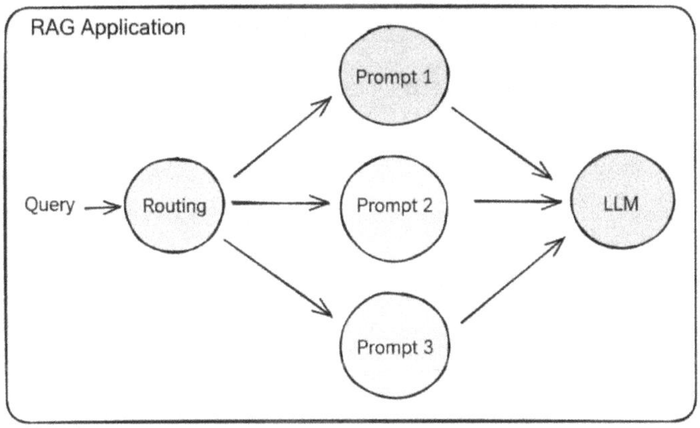

Figure 5.7: A flowchart showing a query routed to three prompts each leading to a large model in RAG apps

It is not difficult to guide large language models to decompose queries through prompts, so prompt examples will not be given here. You can also use the **MultiQueryRetriever** tool provided by **LangChain** to have the large language model generate multiple queries from different perspectives.

For each generated query, the **retriever** will obtain the corresponding document set from the vector database. Then, all documents from all query results are deduplicated and merged into a richer result set, thus providing more relevant content.

Using MultiQueryRetriever

The following example shows how MultiQueryRetriever generates several related queries from one complex user question.

```
import logging
from langchain_chroma import Chroma
from langchain_community.document_loaders import TextLoader
from langchain_deepseek import ChatDeepSeek
from langchain_huggingface import HuggingFaceEmbeddings
from langchain_text_splitters import RecursiveCharacterTextSplitter
from langchain.retrievers.multi_query import MultiQueryRetriever
### Set Up Logging
logging.basicConfig()
logging.getLogger("langchain.retrievers.multi_query").setLevel(logging.
INFO)
loader = TextLoader("data/灭神纪/设定.txt", encoding='utf-8')
data = loader.load()
```

```
text_splitter = RecursiveCharacterTextSplitter(chunk_size=500, chunk_
overlap=0)
splits = text_splitter.split_documents(data)
embed_model = HuggingFaceEmbeddings(model_name="BAAI/bge-small-zh")
vectorstore = Chroma.from_documents(documents=splits, embedding=embed_
model)
### Generate Multi-Perspective Queries Using MultiQueryRetriever
llm = ChatDeepSeek(model="deepseek-chat", temperature=0)
retriever_from_llm = MultiQueryRetriever.from_llm(
retriever=vectorstore.as_retriever(),
llm=llm
)
question = "Well, I just started playing this game and it feels very
difficult. How would you rate the difficulty of this game, how many levels
are there, and in the Putuo Mountain level, hmm, I just can't get through.
Which skills should I learn first? Any tips for beginners?"
docs = retriever_from_llm.invoke(question)
INFO:langchain.retrievers.multi_query:Generated queries: ['What is the
difficulty level of this game? How many levels are there? Are there
any tips you can share for the Putuo Mountain stage?', 'For beginners,
which skills should be learned first to better tackle the challenges
in the game?', 'I find it difficult when playing this game. Are there
any suggestions or tips to help me successfully pass the Putuo Mountain
stage?']
```

The above process automatically generates multiple forms of queries and returns the combined result of all queries (the number of documents may be greater than that from a single query).

If you want more complex query expressions, you can also customize the prompt template. For example, generate 5 different versions of the query, and make the queries have a specific tone.

```
### Load Game-Related Documents and Build the Vector Database
...
### Custom Output Parser
class LineListOutputParser(BaseOutputParser[List[str]]):
def parse(self, text: str) -> List[str]:
    lines = text.strip().split("\n")
    return list(filter(None, lines))  # Filter empty lines
output_parser = LineListOutputParser()
### Custom Query Prompt Template
```

```
QUERY_PROMPT = PromptTemplate(
    input_variables=["question"],
    template="""You are an experienced game customer service agent. Please 
rewrite the user's query from 5 different perspectives
to help the user obtain more detailed game guidance.
Make sure each query focuses on a different aspect, such as skill 
selection, combat strategy, equipment matching, etc.
User's original question: {question}
Please provide 5 different queries, one per line.""",
)
### Set the Large Model Processing Pipeline
llm = ChatDeepSeek(model="deepseek-chat", temperature=0)
llm_chain = QUERY_PROMPT | llm | output_parser
### MultiQueryRetriever Using Customized Prompt Template
retriever = MultiQueryRetriever(
    retriever=vectorstore.as_retriever(),
    llm_chain=llm_chain,
    parser_key="lines"
)
### Perform Multi-Angle Queries
custom_docs = retriever.invoke("For the Putuo Mountain level, which skills 
should beginners prioritize learning?")
INFO:langchain.retrievers.multi_query:Generated queries: ['In the Putuo 
Mountain checkpoint, which skills should beginners prioritize learning to 
enhance survivability?', 'In the Putuo Mountain checkpoint, which skills 
should beginners prioritize learning to improve output damage?', 'In 
the Putuo Mountain checkpoint, which skills should beginners prioritize 
learning to enhance team support capabilities?', 'In the Putuo Mountain 
checkpoint, which skills should beginners prioritize learning to enhance 
control ability?', 'In the Putuo Mountain checkpoint, which skills should 
beginners prioritize learning to deal with specific enemies or combat 
scenarios?']
```

The **MultiQueryRetriever** is suitable for scenarios requiring multi-perspective queries, such as complex problems or ambiguous queries. It can enhance the richness and diversity of retrieval results.

Query clarification: Step-by-step refinement and clarification of user questions

In the paper *"Tree of Clarifications: Using Retrieval-Augmented Large Language Models to Answer Ambiguous Questions"*, researchers proposed a framework called **Tree of Clarifications (ToC)**. This framework gradually refines and clarifies user questions by recursively constructing a **question clarification tree.** For an ambiguous question like "Which country has won the most medals in Olympic history?", the system generates a series of clarification questions, such as **In which edition of the Olympics?** or **In which sport?**, to obtain more contextual information.

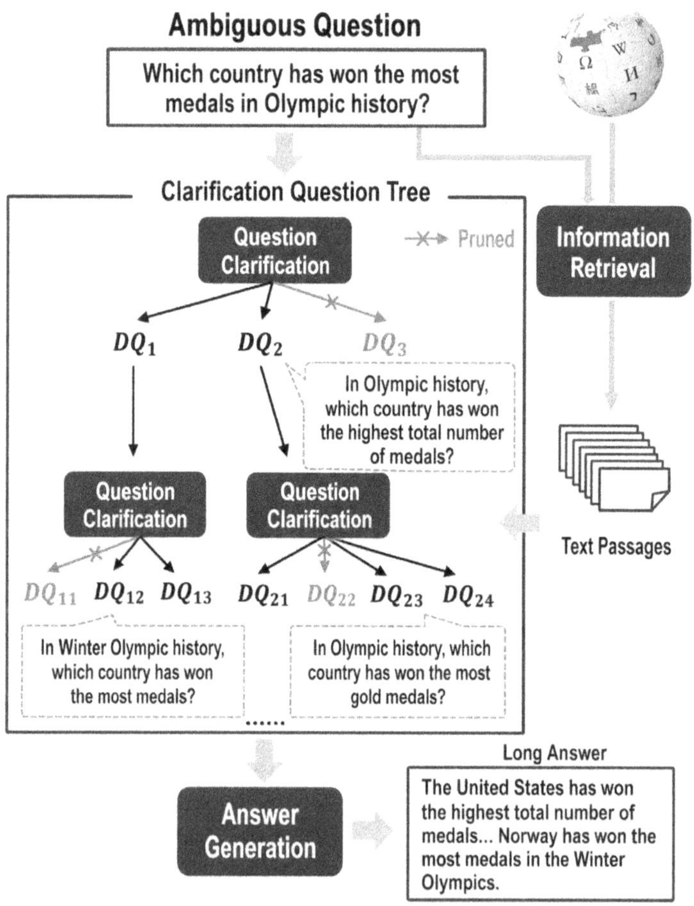

Figure 5.8: Workflow for answering ambiguous questions using a clarification question tree, where the original query is decomposed into more specific sub-questions, irrelevant branches are pruned, relevant text passages are retrieved, and a final answer is generated

Below is a code example of a question clarification tree. This example uses a **tree structure** to explore multiple possible interpretations of the question and leverages **external knowledge retrieval** to improve answer accuracy. At the same time, it uses **few-shot prompting** to generate comprehensive answers.

```
import pandas as pd
import networkx as nx
import matplotlib.pyplot as plt
from typing import List, Dict, Set, Optional
from dataclasses import dataclass
## Define the Data Structure for a Clarification Node
@dataclass
class ClarificationNode:
    """Data structure for a clarification node"""
    id: str
    text: str
    aspect: str
    depth: int
    parent_id: Optional[str] = None
    answers: Optional[List[str]] = None
## Construct Knowledge Base Data
def create_knowledge_base() -> Dict:
    """Create knowledge base"""
    return {
        "abilities": {
            "combat": {
                "physical": ["Invulnerability", "Superhuman Strength",
"Iron-like Muscles"],
```

Management question template:

```
def create_question_templates(character_name: str) -> Dict[str, Dict[str,
str]]:
    """Create question templates"""
    return {
        "abilities": {
            "root": f"Which type of abilities would you like to know about
regarding {character_name}?",
```

```
            "combat": f"In terms of combat abilities, which skill of 
{character_name} are you most interested in?",
            "perception": f"Regarding the perception abilities of 
{character_name}, which specific aspects do you want to learn about?"
        },
        "relationships": {
            "root": f"Whose relationship with {character_name} would you 
like to know about?",
            "allies": f"Among the allies of {character_name}, which type 
of relationship interests you?",
            "enemies": f"Regarding {character_name}'s opponents, which 
faction are you interested in?"
        }
    }
```

Conducting question analysis:

Refer to `https://github.com/PacktPublishing/Generative-AI-at-AWS` for the complete code.

```
def identify_main_aspects(question: str) -> Set[str]:
    """Identify the main aspects of the question"""
    aspects = set()
    keywords = {
        "abilities": ["abilities", "talents", "skills", "magic", 
"powers"],
        "relationships": ["relationships", "friends", "enemies", "master-
disciple", "making friends"]
    }
    for aspect, words in keywords.items():
        if any(word in question for word in words):
            aspects.add(aspect)
    if not aspects:
        aspects.add("abilities")
return aspects
def identify_character(question: str, characters: List[str]) -> 
Optional[str]:
    """Identify the character mentioned in the question"""
    for character in characters:
        if character in question:
            return character
```

```
        return None
### Build a Question Clarification Tree
def build_clarification_tree(
    question: str,
    character: str,
    knowledge_base: Dict,
    templates: Dict[str, Dict[str, str]]
) -> nx.DiGraph:
    G = nx.DiGraph()
    # Add root node
    root_id = "root"
    G.add_node(root_id, text-question, depth-0)
    # Analyze main aspects of the question
    main_aspects = identify_main_aspects(question)
    # Build each layer of the tree
    for aspect in main_aspects:
        if aspect not in knowledge_base:
            continue
        # First layer: main aspects
        node_id = f"{aspect}_root"
        G.add_node(node_id,
                   text=templates[aspect]["root"],
                   depth=1)
        G.add_edge(root_id, node_id)
        # Second layer: sub-aspects
        for sub_aspect, sub_data in knowledge_base[aspect].items():
            sub_node_id = f"{aspect}_{sub_aspect}"
            template_text = templates[aspect].get(
                sub_aspect,
                f"What do you want to know about {sub_aspect}?"
            )
            G.add_node(sub_node_id, text=template_text, depth=2)
            G.add_edge(node_id, sub_node_id)
            # Third layer: specific details
            for detail_type, details in sub_data.items():
                detail_node_id = f"{aspect}_{sub_aspect}_{detail_type}"
```

```
                detail_text = f"Do you want to know about these related to
{detail_type}: {', '.join(details)}?"
                G.add_node(detail_node_id,
                           text=detail_text,
                           depth=3,
answers=details)
G.add_edge(sub_node_id, detail_node_id)
return G
## Visualization of the Clarification Tree
def visualize_tree(G: nx.DiGraph, figsize=(15, 10)):
    """Visualize the clarification tree"""
    plt.figure(figsize=figsize)
    pos = nx.spring_layout(G, k=2, iterations=50)
    depths = nx.get_node_attributes(G, 'depth')
    colors = ['lightblue', 'lightgreen', 'lightyellow', 'lightpink']
    for depth in range(max(depths.values()) + 1):
        nodes_at_depth = [node for node, d in depths.items() if d ==
depth]
        nx.draw_networkx_nodes(G, pos,
                               nodelist=nodes_at_depth,
                               node_color=colors[depth],
                               node_size=2000)
    nx.draw_networkx_edges(G, pos, edge_color='gray', arrows=True)
    labels = nx.get_node_attributes(G, 'text')
    nx.draw_networkx_labels(G, pos, labels, font_size=8, font_
weight='bold')
    plt.title("Clarification Tree")
    plt.axis('off')
    plt.tight_layout()
    plt.show()
## Using the Clarification Tree
kb = create_knowledge_base()
templates = create_question_templates("Sun Wukong")
tree = build_clarification_tree(question, "Sun Wukong", kb, templates)
visualize_tree(tree)
```

The generated question clarification tree is shown below.

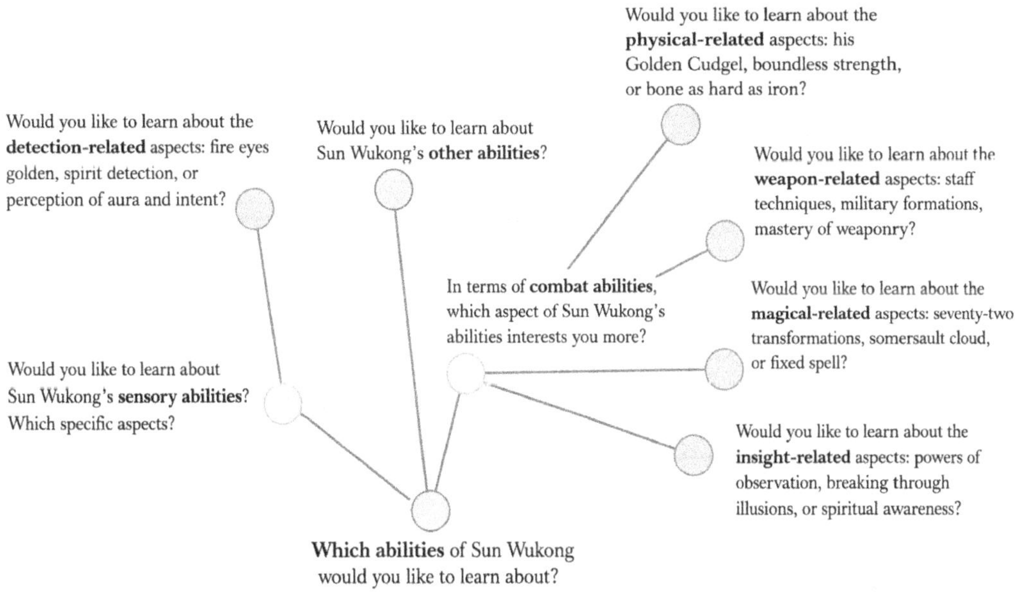

Figure 5.9: Query graph illustrating the hierarchical decomposition of questions about Sun Wukong's abilities

Query expansion using HyDE to generate hypothetical documents

Hypothetical Document Embeddings (HyDE) technology originates from a paper at the Language Technologies Institute, Carnegie Mellon University, titled *Precise Zero-Shot Dense Retrieval without Relevance Labels.*

The core of this method lies in creating a **hypothetical answer document** for a given query, embedding the document, and then using this embedding as the representation for the final query.

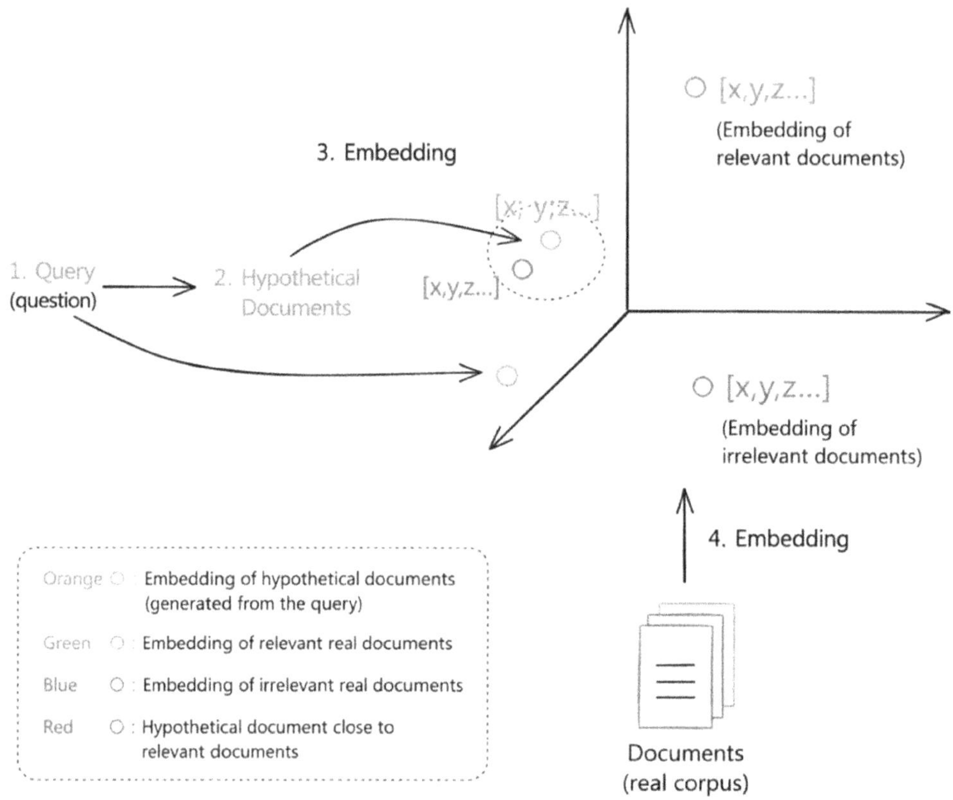

Figure 5.10: Diagram showing how questions and documents are embedded as vectors in a 3D space for comparison

The highlight of this innovative approach is that it does not learn **relevance** directly, but instead builds a query-aligned embedding by generating a hypothetical document. This means that before **retrieval**, the system first generates a hypothetical piece of content. This new paradigm performs retrieval by comparing the similarity between the generated hypothetical document and actual answer documents. This approach is highly creative and provides a novel perspective for the field of **information retrieval**.

The implementation of HyDE is quite straightforward and only requires a basic **embedding model** and a large model for generating hypothetical documents.

```
from langchain.prompts import ChatPromptTemplate
from langchain_core.output_parsers import StrOutputParser
from langchain_deepseek import ChatDeepSeek
from langchain_huggingface import HuggingFaceEmbeddings
```

```
from langchain_community.document_loaders import TextLoader
from langchain_text_splitters import RecursiveCharacterTextSplitter
from langchain_chroma import Chroma
loader = TextLoader("data/灭神纪/情节片段.txt", encoding='utf-8')
data = loader.load()
text_splitter = RecursiveCharacterTextSplitter(chunk_size=500, chunk_
overlap=0)
splits = text_splitter.split_documents(data)
embed_model = HuggingFaceEmbeddings(model_name="BAAI/bge-small-zh")
vectordb = Chroma.from_documents(documents=splits, embedding= embed_model)
### HyDE Document Generation Template
template = """Please write a piece of game content related to the
following question:
Question: {question}
Content:"""
prompt_hyde = ChatPromptTemplate.from_template(template)
llm = ChatDeepSeek(model="deepseek-chat")
### Create a Chain to Generate Hypothetical Documents
generate_docs_for_retrieval = (prompt_hyde | llm | StrOutputParser())
```

Example RAG workflow code:

```
question = "What are the main skills of the protagonist in 'Myth of Demon
Extinction: Hu Sun'?"
generated_doc = generate_docs_for_retrieval.invoke({"question": question})
print("\n=== Generated Hypothetical Document ===")
print(generated_doc)
retriever = vectordb.as_retriever()
retrieval_chain = generate_docs_for_retrieval | retriever
retrieved_docs = retrieval_chain.invoke({"question": question})
print("\n=== Retrieved Relevant Documents ===")
for i, doc in enumerate(retrieved_docs, 1):
    print(f"\nDocument {i}:")
    print(doc.page_content)
answer_template = """Answer the question based on the following content:
{context}
Question: {question}
Answer:"""
```

```
answer_prompt = ChatPromptTemplate.from_template(answer_template)
final_rag_chain = (answer_prompt | llm | StrOutputParser())
final_answer = final_rag_chain.invoke({"context": retrieved_docs,
"question": question})
print("\n=== Final Answer ===")
print(final_answer)
```

Generated hypothetical document: In the game *Myth of Demon Extinction: Hu Sun*, the protagonist possesses a variety of core skills, including the **Golden Cudgel Skill** for melee attacks using the **Golden Cudgel**, the **Flame Skill** for unleashing powerful fire attacks, the **Lightning Skill** for summoning lightning to deal area damage, as well as the **Wind Skill** utilizing the power of wind for ranged strikes, among others.

Retrieved relevant documents: Chaos splits the sky, dark clouds roll. Hu Sun stands atop the heavens, eyes like burning torches, wielding the **Golden Cudgel** with ease, bringing everything to stillness. An army of a million is instantly frozen in the wind. With a low shout: "Transformation!" he instantly multiplies into thousands, reality and illusion indistinguishable, as if a god descended to earth. The **Seventy-Two Transformations** are dreamlike and elusive, reality and falsehood impossible to tell, leaving enemy generals astonished: "How can this monkey possess such magical powers!" But Hu Sun has already soared on clouds, riding the **Somersault Cloud** straight up to the sky, his wild laughter echoing across mountains and rivers...

Final answer: The main skills of the protagonist in *Myth of Demon Extinction: Hu Sun* include the **Seventy-Two Transformations**, **Somersault Cloud**, and the **Golden Cudgel**.

The advantage of the **HyDE** method lies in its context awareness; it captures the **context** and **potential intent** of the query by generating hypothetical documents. This approach allows for customization to meet the needs of different domains through custom prompt templates, and can also expand retrieval coverage and enhance the relevance of results by generating multiple hypothetical documents.

However, it is worth noting that generating hypothetical documents requires additional computational resources and time, and the effectiveness of **HyDE** is highly dependent on the quality of the large model used. Therefore, when deciding whether to adopt the **HyDE** technique in practical applications, one must carefully weigh the performance gains it brings against the costs required.

Query routing finding the right data source

After constructing or translating a query, the system may still need to decide where the query should go.

Lewis: Alex, can you tell me why a **RAG system** needs **query routing**?

Alex: I think it might be related to **hybrid vector storage**. In complex **RAG systems**, vector storage in the vector database can take various forms, and there may be multiple **vector databases** in use, or even different types of databases storing different formats of data. After our complex query is broken down into sub-problems, we need to efficiently route the query to the correct data source.

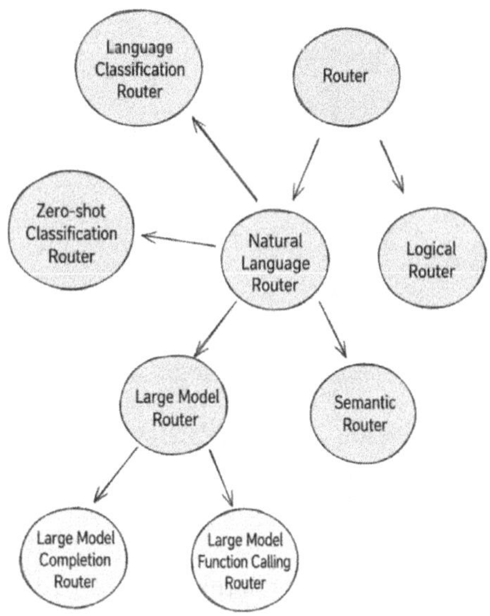

Figure 5.11: Relationships between various router types

Anna: That's right. And it's not just because of the **data sources**; the way we handle different types of questions may also vary. For example, if a user asks about the content of a game or makes a complaint to **customer service**, the subsequent handling methods could be very different.

Lewis: Exactly, this is the process of "routing requests to the most appropriate place," which is actually **intent recognition**. As the system scales up, using **routing mechanisms** to distribute user input ensures that different **data sources** or processing flows can all be seamlessly integrated through **query routing**.

Logical routing determining the path of the query

Logical Routing is responsible for determining where the query should be sent. The system starts from the user's input question, analyzes and semantically understands the question through a large model, and categorizes it based on the characteristics of the question, generating structured output to guide the selection of the **retriever**.

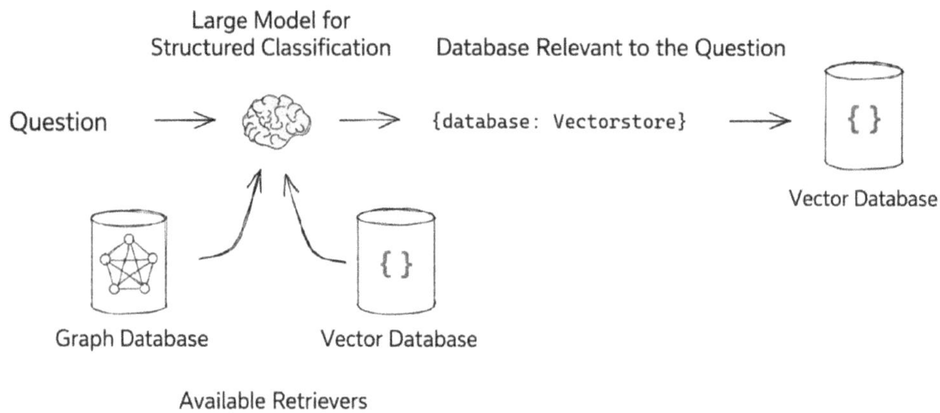

Figure 5.12: Diagram showing a process where a question is classified by a model to query graph or vector databases

For example, the question is first classified to determine whether it is related to a **graph database** or to a **vector database**. At the retrieval stage, the system can choose different databases, such as graph databases or vector databases.

When the question involves complex entity relationships or structured data, such as querying organizational structures or associations between entities, the system will choose the **graph database** to execute the query and return the result; whereas when the question requires retrieval based on semantic similarity, such as finding content semantically similar to a document, the system will select the **vector database**, convert the query and data into vectors, and use vector similarity to find related content.

Another example, if we have built three vector databases for different scenarios, namely `python_docs`, `js_docs`, and `golang_docs`, and want to route the current user's question to one of `python_docs`, `js_docs`, or `golang_docs`, we can first classify the question to determine which programming language category it belongs to; then perform the corresponding downstream processing based on the classification result (select the handling logic for **Python**, **JavaScript**, or **Go**).

Example: Routing to different data sources

Below is a code example of logical routing provided by **LangChain**.

```
from typing import Literal
from langchain_core.prompts import ChatPromptTemplate
from langchain_core.pydantic_v1 import BaseModel, Field
from langchain_deepseek import ChatDeepSeek
### Data Model
class RouteQuery(BaseModel):
    """Route the user's query to the most relevant data source"""
    datasource: Literal["python_docs", "js_docs", "golang_docs"] = Field(
        ...,
        description="Select the most suitable data source to answer the
question based on the user's query",
    )
### Large Model with Function Calling
llm = ChatDeepSeek(model="deepseek-chat", temperature=0)
structured_llm = llm.with_structured_output(RouteQuery)
system = """You are an expert at routing user questions to the appropriate
data source.
Route them to the relevant data source according to the programming
language involved."""
prompt = ChatPromptTemplate.from_messages(
    [
        ("system", system),
        ("human", "{question}"),
    ]
)
### Define the Router
router = prompt | structured_llm
```

For a complete example of accessing different data sources via the **Function/Tool Calls** functionality after routing queries, please visit Lewis's GitHub repository.

Semantic routing: Selecting relevant prompts

Logical routing refers to choosing the appropriate data source or retrieval method based on the user's question, while **semantic routing** selects targeted prompt templates according to the "semantics" of the user's question.

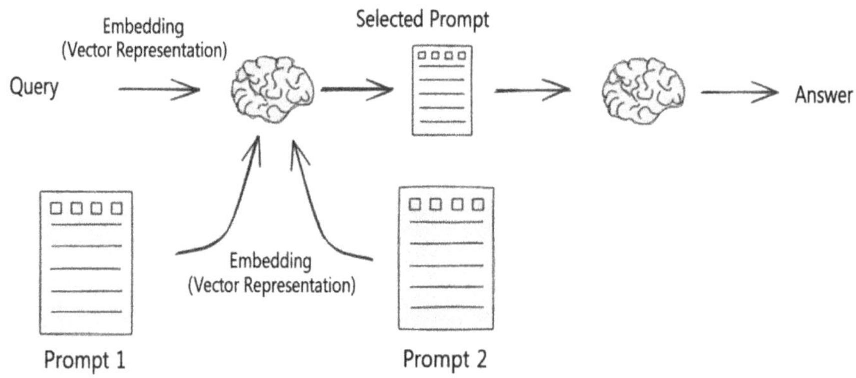

Figure 5.13: Diagram showing how a question and prompts are embedded selected and lead to an answer

Example: Routing to prompt templates

Below is a simple code example for semantic routing.

```
from langchain.utils.math import cosine_similarity
from langchain_core.output_parsers import StrOutputParser
from langchain_core.prompts import PromptTemplate
from langchain_core.runnables import RunnableLambda, RunnablePassthrough
from langchain_deepseek import ChatDeepSeek
from langchain_huggingface import HuggingFaceEmbeddings
### Define Two Prompt Templates
combat_template = """You are an expert proficient in game combat skills.
You excel at answering questions about game combat in a concise and easy-to-understand manner.
When you don't know the answer to a question, you will admit it honestly.
Here is a question:
{query}"""
story_template = """You are an expert familiar with game storylines.
You are good at breaking down complex plots and explaining them in detail.
When you don't know the answer to a question, you will admit it honestly.
```

```
Here is a question:
{query}"""
embed_model = HuggingFaceEmbeddings(model_name="BAAI/bge-small-zh")
prompt_templates = [combat_template, story_template]
prompt_embeddings = embed_model.embed_documents(prompt_templates)
### Define the Routing Function
def prompt_router(input):
    query_embedding = embed_model.embed_query(input["query"])
    similarity = cosine_similarity([query_embedding], prompt_embeddings)
[0]
    most_similar = prompt_templates[similarity.argmax()]
    ## Select the most similar prompt template
    print("Using combat skills template:" if most_similar == combat_
template else "Using story template:")
    return PromptTemplate.from_template(most_similar)
chain = (
    {"query": RunnablePassthrough()}
    | RunnableLambda(prompt_router)
    | ChatDeepSeek(model="deepseek-chat")
)
StrOutputParser()
print(chain.invoke("How does the monkey defeat his enemies?"))
```

Using the combat skills template: In battle, the monkey mainly focuses on using **instant movement** and powerful **punching and kicking skills** to defeat his enemies. He can also release his **aura** to enhance his combat power. Through continuous training and relentless effort, the monkey is able to quickly adapt to different opponents' fighting styles and find effective ways to deal with them. Ultimately, his calmness and strong will to fight are also important factors that allow him to defeat his enemies.

Summary

Although various techniques in the pre-retrieval stage are not indispensable components of a **RAG system**, they provide significant inspiration for us to optimize **RAG system performance** and design more complex systems.

Integrating **structured data** into RAG systems is a key challenge. In actual business applications, scenarios that rely solely on **unstructured data** are limited. Learners often need to connect with existing **relational databases** or query **Excel** or **CSV** files. Therefore, when introducing structured data into RAG systems, our core approach is to maintain the original structural clarity of the data without disruption.

Directly embedding structured data for retrieval often yields unsatisfactory results, frequently resulting in data loss or difficulties dealing with **time series data**. **Text-to-Query** technology can help the large model or rules engine understand **entities**, **intents**, and **conditions** in the question, and map them to the database's **table structure**, **fields**, **relationships**, and **query logic**, thereby enabling effective structured data querying within the RAG system workflow. As Lewis emphasized, it is hoped that everyone will understand its underlying meaning. This is also why the demand for **Text-to-SQL** is so significant—after all, operations involving internal databases ultimately require **SQL** to resolve, and vector retrieval alone cannot meet this need.

However, technologies such as **Text-to-SQL** and **Text-to-Cypher** perform well in simple scenarios but lack stability in complex logic situations. Therefore, a compromise approach is to first extract database metadata, including **field information**, **table structure**, and **view descriptions**, supplement with necessary manual explanations, and then embed them; next, to establish general and specific **data functions** to predefine complex query logic; and finally, to combine the **Agent's Tool Calls** function so that after the large model understands the learner's intent, it dynamically assembles **SQL statements** and executes queries based on metadata and data functions.

Of particular note is the **Self-query Retriever** method for automatically generating metadata filter conditions from queries. First, the **metadata** is defined to inform the retriever of the type and meaning of each **field**, enabling it to accurately interpret query intent. Then, it automatically generates a series of metadata-based conditional filtering statements to perform structured filtering before retrieval. This establishes a dual filtering mechanism: on the one hand, **vector storage** is used to perform semantic search on content; on the other hand, exact filtering is performed based on the extracted metadata conditions (such as "view count greater than 100000"). This design enables queries to capture both semantic relevance and precise condition filtering. Automatically generating these metadata filters is the additional work that **Self-query Retriever** performs during query construction, combining **key field-based retrieval** with **semantic retrieval** and embodying the characteristics of **hybrid retrieval**.

Through the processing in the **pre-retrieval stage**, the system can construct queries more accurately, decompose problems, and filter out noise, thus generating better queries with a wider coverage or more precise content.

Finally, **query routing** is the foundation of hybrid queries in complex systems. If there are multiple data sources in the system, one should first use **routing** or **intent recognition** to filter target data sources and then locate the appropriate path. For example, it could determine whether to use **Text-to-SQL** or **Text-to-Cypher** to query relevant structured databases, thereby improving the accuracy and efficiency of subsequent retrieval and generation tasks. These technologies lay the foundation for intelligent **hybrid query** scenarios across structured and unstructured data sources, or diversified and multi-level vector database data sources, demonstrating more advanced system designs.

6

Index Optimization

Lewis: The various techniques mentioned earlier lay the groundwork for retrieval implementation. In this section, our core focus is on how to make **retrieval** more accurate, but there are many reasons why retrieval may be inaccurate.

Anna: Lewis, you've got right to the point. Indeed, in actual projects, even though we want to improve **retrieval accuracy**, we often feel at a loss as to where to start.

Figure 6.1: Key directions for improving retrieval accuracy

Lewis: The **RAG process** contains multiple stages, and there are many possible points of failure. Similarly, optimizing any of these can potentially improve the accuracy of the entire **RAG system**.

In this section, we will provide a series of concrete strategies to improve retrieval quality from the perspective of optimizing **text block indexing**.

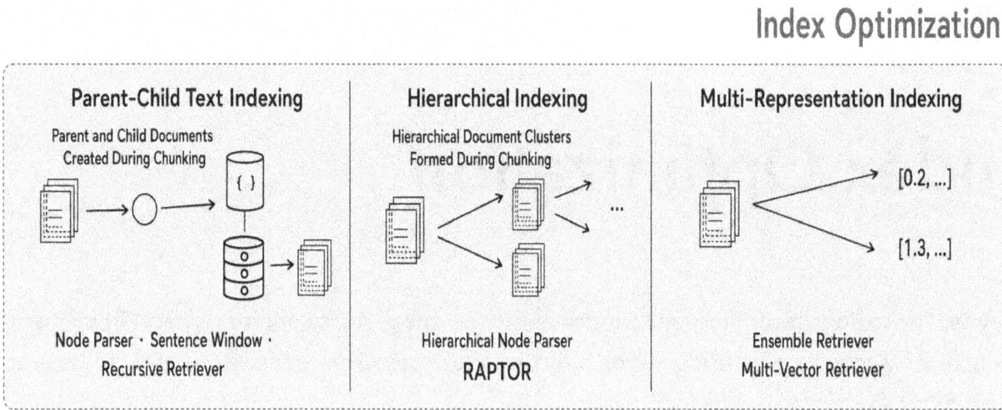

Figure 6.2: Overview of index optimization strategies for improving RAG retrieval quality

From small to large node-sentence sliding window and parent-child text chunks

In general, the smaller the **text chunk**, the more precise the retrieval result. If a **text chunk** is too large, embedding it for retrieval and content synthesis may obscure semantic details due to containing too much irrelevant information, thus affecting retrieval effectiveness. Therefore, we sometimes choose to use a **sentence** as the basic unit for **text chunks**. However, if we only pass a single **sentence** as a retrieval result to a large model, the generated answer may be incomplete or inaccurate due to a lack of sufficient **context**.

The following **"small-to-big" strategy** addresses this issue. The core of this strategy lies in decoupling the **retrieval** and **generation** processes (**Decoupling chunks used for retrieval/chunks used for synthesis**, where "**Synthesis**" refers to text generation, sometimes called composition, that is, integrating information from various text chunks to form the final answer). Specifically, it means first using smaller **text chunks** for retrieval (to increase retrieval precision), and then referencing larger, more complete **text chunks** during the **generation stage**, thereby providing the model with more **contextual information**.

Both LlamaIndex and LangChain offer ways to implement the "small-to-big" retrieval strategy.

- **LlamaIndex's node-sentence sliding window retrieval:** Only a single **sentence** is used during the retrieval stage, and the window of text containing that sentence is returned to provide context for the model.
- **LangChain's child-parent recursive retrieval:** Smaller **child text chunks** are used in the retrieval stage; once relevant child chunks are found, their corresponding **parent text chunks** are cited for synthesis.

In short, the **"small-to-big" retrieval strategy** improves retrieval precision through fine-grained chunking, while retaining sufficient context during the generation process.

Node-sentence sliding window retrieval

Let's first look at **LlamaIndex's node-sentence sliding window retrieval strategy** (introduced in *Chapter 2*). In the example below, the area inside the red box represents the "small text block" that is retrieved; the combination of the purple and red blocks represents the "large context" passed to the large model.

Figure 6.3: Node-sentence sliding window retrieval uses a precise sentence match while passing surrounding context to the LLM

Each **node** is parsed into a single sentence, and the node's metadata contains a certain number of sentences before and after it, thus forming a so-called **window**. During retrieval, by using **metadata replacement**, the entire sentence is replaced with the context in this window, thereby leveraging the extended context for large model processing.

Next, we will use `LlamaIndex's` `SentenceWindowNodeParser` and `MetadataReplacementNodePostProcessor` to implement the "from small to large" strategy. Here, **SentenceWindowNodeParser** is responsible for parsing the course into nodes at the granularity of a single sentence; while **MetadataReplacementNodePostProcessor** is used to replace the retrieved single sentence with a window containing its surrounding sentences.

In the program, two types of **indexes** will be built: one using the "from small to large" strategy, and a regular index for comparison of retrieval performance.

```
from llama_index.core import  VectorStoreIndex, Settings, Document
from llama_index.core.node_parser import  SentenceWindowNodeParser,
SentenceSplitter
from llama_index.llms.deepseek import DeepSeek
from llama_index.embeddings.huggingface import HuggingFaceEmbedding
from llama_index.core.postprocessor import
MetadataReplacementPostProcessor
### Configure Global Settings
Settings.llm = DeepSeek(model="deepseek-chat", temperature=0.1)
Settings.embed_model = HuggingFaceEmbedding(model_name="BAAI/bge-small-
zh")
Settings.text_splitter = SentenceSplitter(separator="\n",  chunk_size=50,
chunk_overlap=0)
### Prepare Knowledge Text and Create Document Object
game_knowledge = """
"Myth of Extermination: Monkey King" is an action role-playing game. The
game is set in a fictional mythological world.
Players take on the role of the Monkey King, Sun Wukong, embarking on an
adventure in a world full of Eastern mythological elements.
The game's combat system is unique, featuring a distinctive
"transformation system." Wukong can switch between different forms during
battles.
Each form has its own unique combat style and skill combinations. The
Vajra form emphasizes power strikes, delivering overwhelming destructive
force.
```

```
The Demon Buddha form focuses on magic attacks, capable of unleashing
powerful spell damage.
The game world is filled with iconic mythological characters. In addition
to the protagonist Wukong, there are also gods and demons from Buddhism,
Taoism, and other factions.
These characters may be Wukong's allies or formidable opponents to be
defeated.
The equipment system offers a variety of weapons. In addition to the
famous Ruyi Jingu Bang, Wukong can also use other powerful divine
artifacts.
Different weapons have their own unique effects, and players must choose
flexibly according to the battle scenario.
The visual presentation of the game is highly characteristic of Eastern
aesthetics. The scenes blend with the style of ink painting, perfectly
presenting elements such as mountains, rivers, and architecture.
Combat special effects incorporate both traditional Chinese cultural
elements and modern game's visual impact.
In terms of difficulty design, boss battles are highly challenging and
require players to precisely master the rhythm of combat and skill usage.
At the same time, the game offers multiple difficulty levels, catering to
players of different skill levels."""
### Create Document Object
documents = [Document(text=game_knowledge)]
Create a sentence parser with context window (i.e., window parser, each
target sentence retains 2 sentences on each side as context)
node_parser = SentenceWindowNodeParser.from_defaults(
window_size=4,
window_metadata_key="window",
original_text_metadata_key="original_text"
)
### Process Documents Using the Window Parser
nodes = node_parser.get_nodes_from_documents(documents)
### Process Documents Using the Basic Parser (For Comparison)
base_nodes = Settings.text_splitter.get_nodes_from_documents(documents)
### Construct Two Types of Indexes for Comparison
sentence_index = VectorStoreIndex(nodes)
base_index = VectorStoreIndex(base_nodes)
### Create Query Engine With Context Window
```

```
window_query_engine = sentence_index.as_query_engine(
similarity_top_k=2,
node_postprocessors=[
MetadataReplacementPostProcessor(target_metadata_key="window")
]
)
```

Create base query engine:

```
base_query_engine = base_index.as_query_engine(
    similarity_top_k=2
)
## Test Q&A
test_questions = [
    "What transformations does Wukong have in the game?",
    # "What is the game's visual style?",
    # "How is the game's difficulty designed?"
]
print("=== Retrieval Results Using Window Parser ===")
for question in test_questions:
    print(f"\nQuestion: {question}")
    window_response = window_query_engine.query(question)
    print(f"Answer: {window_response}")
## Display Retrieved Original Sentences and Window Content
print("\nRetrieval Details:")
for node in window_response.source_nodes:
    print(f"Original sentence: {node.node.metadata['original_text']}")
    print(f"Context window: {node.node.metadata['window']}")
    print("---")
print("\n=== Retrieval Results Using Base Parser (Comparison) ===")
for question in test_questions:
    print(f"\nQuestion: {question}")
    base_response = base_query_engine.query(question)
    print(f"Answer: {base_response}")
```

=== Retrieval Results Using Window Parser === Question: What transformations does **Wukong** have in the game? Answer: **Wukong** switches between the **Vajra form** and the **Demon Buddha form** in the game. Retrieval Details: Original sentence: Wukong can change into different forms during battle, Context window: Players will play as Sun Wukong, the Great Sage Equal to Heaven, embarking on an adventure in a world full of Eastern mythological elements. The battle system of the game is unique, adopting a special "**transformation system.**" Wukong can change into different forms in combat, each with its own combat style and set of skills. The **Vajra form** focuses on power strikes, delivering overwhelming destructive force; the **Demon Buddha form** specializes in magical attacks, — Original sentence: These characters may be Wukong's allies, Context window: able to unleash powerful magic damage. The game world is full of iconic mythological characters. In addition to the protagonist **Sun Wukong**, there are gods and demons from Buddhist, Taoist, and other sects. These characters may be Wukong's allies, or could be formidable opponents that must be defeated. The equipment system includes a variety of weapons. Besides the famous **Ruyi Jingu Bang**, Wukong can also use other divine weapons and treasures. — === Retrieval Results Using Base Parser (Comparison) === Question: What transformations does **Wukong** have in the game? Answer: Wukong has various forms in the game.

It is not difficult to see that the combination of **SentenceWindowNodeParser** and **MetadataReplacementNodePostProcessor** clearly stands out here.

Parent-child text chunk retrieval

Next, let's introduce the **parent-child text chunk retrieval strategy** provided by **LangChain**. The sub-chunks (called **sub-documents**) formed after preprocessing the original document are stored in a **vector store** for semantic retrieval. When a query is input, relevant content is retrieved from the vector store. At the same time, the complete original document (called the **parent document**) is also stored in the **document store**.

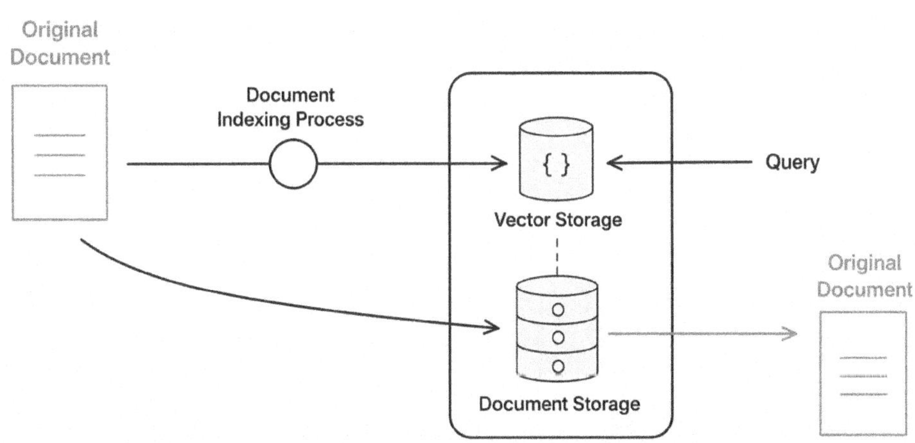

Figure 6.4: Retrieving indexed chunks while preserving the original document for context

Based on this mechanism, the **vector store** is responsible for similarity matching and semantic retrieval, while the **document store** preserves the complete contextual information. When a retrieval operation is performed, relevant segments are first located via the vector store, and then the document store is used to obtain the full content to which these segments belong. This approach also achieves "small chunk retrieval, large chunk return," ensuring that while the system improves retrieval accuracy, it also provides sufficient contextual information support.

The **parent document** mentioned here can be the complete original document before segmentation, or a parent chunk composed of larger text blocks.

The following code sample demonstrates how to use LangChain's parent-child text chunk retrieval strategy.

In this example, the **parent text chunk** is set to a larger chunk than the sub-chunks. We use a two-level splitter: the **parent text splitter** is used to create larger chunks to maintain context integrity; the **child text splitter** is used to create smaller chunks to improve retrieval precision.

For storage, a **dual-layer storage strategy** is adopted. The **vector store** (such as **Chroma**) is used to store the smaller sub-chunks for similarity retrieval, enabling precise matching; while a **document store** (such as **InMemoryStore**) stores the larger parent chunks to provide complete contextual information.

```
from langchain_deepseek import ChatDeepSeek
from langchain_huggingface import HuggingFaceEmbeddings
### Initialize Language Model and Vector Embedding Model
llm = ChatDeepSeek(model="deepseek-chat", temperature=0.1)
embed_model = HuggingFaceEmbeddings(model_name="BAAI/bge-small-zh")
### Prepare Game Knowledge Text, Create Document Object
from langchain.schema import Document
game_knowledge = """
 'Chronicles of Godslayer: Monkey' is an action role-playing game......
"""

## Create Document Object
documents = [Document(page_content=game_knowledge)]
from langchain_text_splitters import RecursiveCharacterTextSplitter
## Parent Text Chunk Splitter (Larger Chunks)
parent_splitter = RecursiveCharacterTextSplitter(
    chunk_size=1000,
    chunk_overlap=200,
```

```
    separators=["\n\n", "\n", "。", "！", "？", "；", "，", " ", ""]
)
## Child Text Chunk Splitter (Smaller Chunks)
child_splitter = RecursiveCharacterTextSplitter(
    chunk_size=200,
    chunk_overlap=50,
    separators=["\n\n", "\n", "。", "！", "？", "；", "，", " ", ""]
)
## Create Parent and Child Text Chunks
parent_docs = parent_splitter.split_documents(documents)
child_docs = child_splitter.split_documents(documents)
## Create Storage and Retriever, Establish Two-Level Storage System
from langchain.retrievers import ParentDocumentRetriever
from langchain.storage import InMemoryStore
from langchain_community.vectorstores import Chroma
vectorstore = Chroma(
    collection_name="game_knowledge",
    embedding_function=embed_model
)
store = InMemoryStore()
retriever = ParentDocumentRetriever(
    vectorstore=vectorstore,
    docstore=store,
    child_splitter=child_splitter,
    parent_splitter=parent_splitter,
)
## Add Text Chunks
retriever.add_documents(documents)
## Custom Prompt Template
from langchain.prompts import PromptTemplate
from langchain.chains import RetrievalQA
prompt_template = """Answer the question based on the following context information. If you cannot find the answer, please say 'I cannot find relevant information.'
Context:
{context}
Question: {question}
```

```
Answer:"""
PROMPT = PromptTemplate(
    template=prompt_template,
    input_variables=["context", "question"]
)
```

Create the Q&A chain:

```
qa_chain = RetrievalQA.from_chain_type(
    llm=llm,
    chain_type="stuff", # Q&A chain type
    retriever=retriever, # Retriever
    return_source_documents=True, # Whether to return source documents
    chain_type_kwargs={"prompt": PROMPT}
)
## Test the System with Actual Questions
test_questions = [
    "What forms does Wukong have in the game?",
    "What is the visual style of the game?",
]
for question in test_questions:
    print(f"\nQuestion: {question}")
    result = qa_chain({"query": question})
    print(f"\nAnswer: {result['result']}")
    print("\nSource documents used:")
    for i, doc in enumerate(result["source_documents"], 1):
        print(f"\nRelevant document {i}:")
        print(f"Length: {len(doc.page_content)} characters")
        print(f"Content snippet: {doc.page_content[:150]}...")
        print("---")
```

Alex: Lewis, here the **bottom-up** strategy is implemented using tools provided by **LangChain** and **LlamaIndex**. Can I design a similar indexing structure myself?

Lewis: Of course you can. Alex, what you need to learn here is the methodology. In real projects, we usually no longer rely on frameworks, but instead take control of every aspect ourselves.

Building summary-to-detail indexes with IndexNode and RecursiveRetriever

Next, we will explore a strategy that complements but appears opposite to the **bottom-up** approach—**Summary-to-Detail**. The core of this strategy is to first organize high-level information, using hierarchical indexing and recursive retrieval, so that search and generation processes can progressively drill down as needed, transitioning from overview-level information to detailed information.

The design concept of the **Summary-to-Detail** strategy is as follows.

- **Coarse granularity**: The main index contains summary information that enables quick location of target scenarios or topics.
- **Fine granularity**: When more detailed information is needed, secondary indexes (or even deeper indexes) linked to the main index can be recursively searched for detailed content.

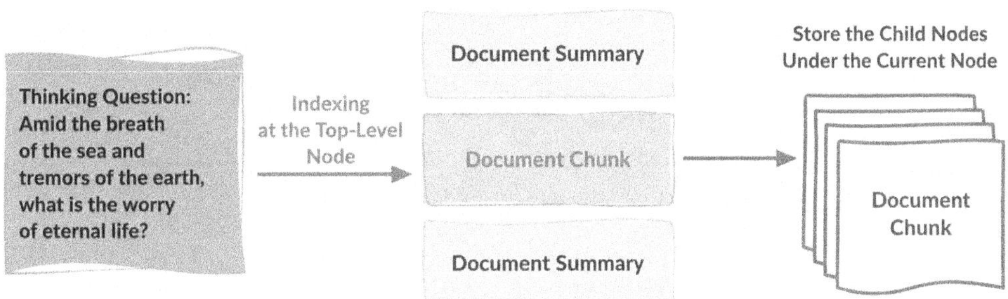

Figure 6.5: Summary-guided retrieval from top-level nodes to child document chunks

Unlike the **bottom-up** strategy, the **Summary-to-Detail** approach emphasizes the hierarchical relationships between indexes, and achieves multi-level index collaboration through the **RecursiveRetriever** tool, rather than just controlling block sizes within a single index.

Specifically, this hierarchical structure allows users to progressively dig into different levels of requirements. For example, if a knowledge base stores world countries' GDP information by year, the coarse-grained nodes are responsible for locating the overall explanation for each year to determine which year it is; the specific GDP figures are then stored in secondary indexes under that node. In this example, without a hierarchical arrangement, directly retrieving a country's GDP information might yield results unrelated to a specific year.

Implementation of the Summary-to-Detail strategy in LlamaIndex

In **LlamaIndex**, the concrete implementation of the "Summary-to-Detail" strategy is as follows.

- **Building hierarchical indexes through IndexNode**: The main index contains summary nodes and some lightweight text content; sub-indexes create independent vector indexes for each `IndexNode` in the main index, storing in-depth information related to that topic.
- **Recursive retrieval logic**: `RecursiveRetriever` is key to implementing the "Summary-to-Detail" strategy. It allows dynamic hopping to relevant secondary indexes within a single query, recursively retrieving the required information.

The following code example demonstrates how to use the **IndexNode** and **Recursive-Retriever** modules in LlamaIndex for recursive retrieval.

```
from llama_index.core import VectorStoreIndex, Settings
from llama_index.core.schema import IndexNode, Document
from llama_index.llms.deepseek import DeepSeek
from llama_index.embeddings.huggingface import HuggingFaceEmbedding
from llama_index.core.retrievers import RecursiveRetriever
from llama_index.core.query_engine import RetrieverQueryEngine
from llama_index.core import get_response_synthesizer
from typing import List
## Configure Global Settings
Settings.llm = DeepSeek(model="deepseek-chat", temperature=0.1)
Settings.embed_model = HuggingFaceEmbedding(model_name="BAAI/bge-small-
zh")
## Create Descriptions of Game Scenes
scene_descriptions = [
""""
Huaguo Mountain: This is the birthplace of the Great Sage Equal to Heaven,
Sun Wukong. Mist shrouds the mountain year-round, and a waterfall plunges
down from a height of a thousand meters,
forming the "Heavenly River Waterfall." Various magical herbs and elixirs
grow in the mountain, and many animals that have attained spirit forms
reside here.
"""",
""""
```

```
Shuilian Cave: Located at the peak of Huaguo Mountain, there is a
naturally formed curtain of water in front of the cave, making it a sacred
place for cultivation.
"""",
""""
Dragon Palace of the East Sea: A magnificent palace at the bottom of the
East Sea, decorated with coral and luminous pearls. This is where Sun
Wukong obtained the Ruyi Jingu Bang.
""""
]
## Convert Scene Descriptions Into Document Objects
documents = [Document(text=desc) for desc in scene_descriptions]
## Use the Node Parser to Convert Documents Into Nodes
doc_nodes = Settings.node_parser.get_nodes_from_documents(documents)
Create IndexNode representing hierarchical relationships: Create scene
details (simulate detailed documents)
scene_details = [
""""
Detailed Setup of Huaguo Mountain
1. Geographical Location: Within the borders of Aolai Country, Dongsheng
Divine Continent
2. Natural Environment: Exotic flowers and plants that bloom year-round,
clear mountain springs and waterfalls, dense ancient forests
3. Special Areas: Immortal Fruit Garden, where various spiritual fruits
are cultivated; Training Ground, a flat and open area for cultivation;
Rest Area, a place for the Monkey Tribe to rest
"""",
""""
Detailed Setup of Shuilian Cave
1. Architectural Structure: Exterior—a huge natural rock cave; Entrance—a
30-zhang-high water curtain; Interior—a maze of interconnected caves
2. Functional Areas: Cultivation Hall—equipped with all kinds of training
apparatus; Treasure Chamber—stores various magical treasures and elixirs,
protected by powerful arrays;
Council Hall—can accommodate hundreds of monkeys, a place for important
meetings
"""",
""""
```

```
Detailed Setup of the Dragon Palace of the East Sea
1. Architectural Features: Materials—coral, pearls, luminous pearls;
Scale—covering dozens of miles; Style—an underwater palace complex
2. Important Areas: Dragon King's Treasury—stores countless treasures such
as luminous pearls, and sacred objects like the Ruyi Jingu Bang; Armory—a
variety of aquatic magical artifacts and divine weapons; Main Hall—the
main hall for receiving guests and holding gatherings of the aquatic
tribes
"""
]
## For Each Detail, Create a Corresponding IndexNode and Create the
Associated Query Engine
index_nodes = []
index_id_query_engine_mapping = {}
for idx, detail_text in enumerate(scene_details):
    # Create IndexNode, process the text before putting it into the
f-string
    index_id = f"detail{idx}"
    first_line = detail_text.split('\n')[1].strip()
    index_node = IndexNode(text=f"This node contains {first_line}", index_
id=index_id)
    index_nodes.append(index_node)
    # Create the corresponding TextNode, and build a separate index and
query engine
    detail_node = Document(text=detail_text)
    detail_index = VectorStoreIndex.from_documents([detail_node])
    detail_query_engine = detail_index.as_query_engine()
## Add the Query Engine to the Mapping
index_id_query_engine_mapping[index_id] = detail_query_engine
## Output the Current Mapping Status
print(f"\nCurrent index ID: {index_id}")
print(f"Index node text: {index_node.text}")
print(f"Length of detailed scene information: {len(detail_text)}
characters")
print(f"Query engine type: {type(detail_query_engine).__name__}")
## Merge Document Nodes and Index Nodes
all_nodes = doc_nodes + index_nodes
## Build the Main Vector Index
```

```
vector_index = VectorStoreIndex(all_nodes)
vector_retriever = vector_index.as_retriever(similarity_top_k=2)
## Create RecursiveRetriever Object
recursive_retriever = RecursiveRetriever(
    "vector",  # ID of the root retriever
    retriever_dict={"vector": vector_retriever},  # Retriever mapping
    query_engine_dict=index_id_query_engine_mapping,  # Query engine
mapping
    verbose=True,  # Enable verbose output
)
## Create a RetrieverQueryEngine and Set the Response Mode to "Compact"
response_synthesizer = get_response_synthesizer(response_mode="compact")
## Create a RetrieverQueryEngine Passing in the RecursiveRetriever and the
Response Synthesizer
query_engine = RetrieverQueryEngine.from_args(
    recursive_retriever,
    response_synthesizer=response_synthesizer,
)
## Define the Query Function
def query_scene(question: str):
    print(f"Question: {question}\n")
    response = query_engine.query(question)
    print(f"Answer: {str(response)}\n")
## Sample Queries
if __name__ == "__main__":
    questions = [
        "What is special about Huaguo Mountain?",
        "Describe in detail the internal structure of the Water Curtain
Cave.",
        "What treasures are stored in the Dragon Palace of the East Sea?",
    ]
    for q in questions:
        query_scene(q)
Out
```

The main feature of the above program lies in its **multi-level knowledge organization.** It establishes hierarchical connections through **IndexNode**, forming a tree-like **knowledge graph.** The top level is the **scene summary** (basic descriptions of Huaguo Mountain, Water Curtain Cave, and Dragon Palace), while the bottom level contains **scene details** (such as architectural structures, functional divisions, and other detailed settings).

Through a **dynamic routing mechanism,** the main retriever (`similarity_top_k=2`) first conducts a **coarse-grained search,** automatically identifies the **IndexNode** to trigger detailed retrieval, and routes to the corresponding **sub-query engine** according to the `index_id`.

This architecture is especially suitable for handling **complex Q&A** that require combining summaries and details. It is particularly effective when the knowledge system has a natural **hierarchical structure,** allowing for precise deep information localization. The system can quickly respond to general questions and also handle complex queries that require in-depth details, achieving a balance between efficiency and accuracy.

Hierarchical merging HierarchicalNodeParser and RAPTOR

After understanding the "from small to large" and "coarse with details" strategies, let's take a look at another equally flexible and ingenious approach: first, divide text blocks into multiple levels, then index them to form various vector representations, and finally integrate them during the retrieval process.

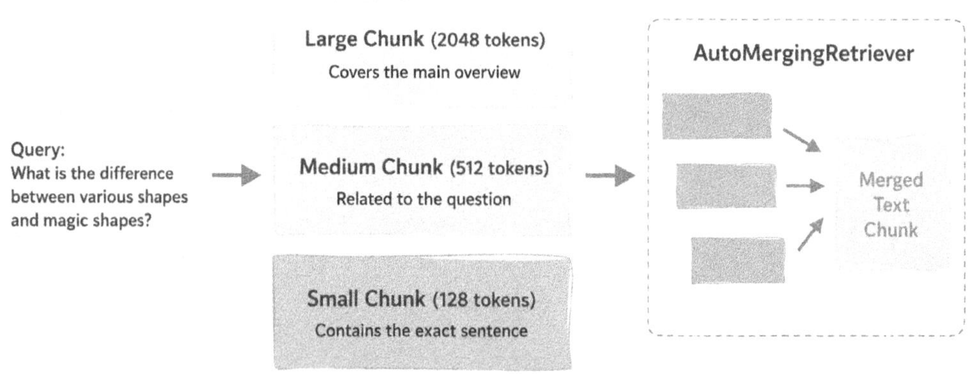

Figure 6.6: Hierarchical chunks are retrieved at different granularities and merged to provide a more complete context

Creating hierarchical indexes with HierarchicalNodeParser

Suppose a player asks: **What are the differences between the Vajra Form and the Demon Buddha Form.** Traditional vector retrieval may accurately locate the specific sentences describing these two forms, such as "Under the Vajra Form, Wukong's strength increases dramatically" and "The Demon Buddha Form grants Wukong powerful magical abilities." However, such an answer is evidently incomplete because the differences between forms are not only found in those two sentences but also include information like **combo characteristics** and **weapon synergy**, which are scattered across different parts of the text.

In **LlamaIndex**, you can use the **HierarchicalNodeParser** to divide the entire game knowledge text into three levels: large blocks (2048 characters) to preserve complete thematic paragraphs, medium blocks (512 characters) to hold several related sentences, and small blocks (128 characters) for precise descriptions. This is like dividing a game guide first into sections, then paragraphs, and finally sentences.

During retrieval, the system will first use the **vector index** to find the most relevant small blocks, ensuring precision in retrieval. But the system doesn't stop there. It uses **AutoMergingRetriever** to automatically find the "root node" of these small blocks (also known as **leaf nodes**), that is, the larger text block containing these small blocks. If it finds that multiple small blocks come from the same larger block, the system will automatically merge them to provide more complete contextual information.

For example, when answering questions about the differences between forms, the system may find that the sentences describing basic attributes, **combo characteristics**, and **weapon coordination**, although scattered in different places, are all discussing the features of combat forms. At this point, the system will automatically merge this information to provide a more comprehensive answer.

The following code example demonstrates how to use **HierarchicalNodeParser** and **AutoMergingRetriever** to build a hierarchical game knowledge retrieval system. We will create both a **base retriever** and an **auto-merging retriever**, and compare the retrieval results of the two (refer to `https://github.com/PacktPublishing/RAG-from-First-Principles` for the complete code).

```
## Import Necessary Libraries and Configure Basic Settings
from llama_index.core import VectorStoreIndex, StorageContext, Document,
Settings
from llama_index.core.node_parser import HierarchicalNodeParser, get_leaf_
nodes, get_root_nodes
from llama_index.core.storage.docstore import SimpleDocumentStore
```

```
from llama_index.core.retrievers import AutoMergingRetriever
from llama_index.llms.deepseek import DeepSeek
from llama_index.embeddings.huggingface import HuggingFaceEmbedding
## Configure Global Settings
Settings.llm = DeepSeek(model="deepseek-chat", temperature=0.1)
Settings.embed_model = HuggingFaceEmbedding(model_name="BAAI/bge-small-
zh")
## Prepare Game Knowledge Text
game_knowledge = """The combat system of 'Legend of the Demon God: Monkey
King' is ingeniously designed. Players can freely switch between multiple
combat forms during battle, each with its own unique advantage. In Vajra
form... in Demon Buddha form..."""
## Create Document Object
documents = [Document(text=game_knowledge)]
Create hierarchical node parser and process document: Use
HierarchicalNodeParser to create the text hierarchy
node_parser = HierarchicalNodeParser.from_defaults(
chunk_sizes=[256, 128, 64]  # Chunk sizes from root node to leaf node
)
nodes = node_parser.get_nodes_from_documents(documents)
## Get Leaf Nodes (Finest Granularity Text Chunks) and Root Nodes
leaf_nodes = get_leaf_nodes(nodes)
root_nodes = get_root_nodes(nodes)
## Build Storage and Index Create Document Store and Add All Nodes
docstore = SimpleDocumentStore()
docstore.add_documents(nodes)
## Create Storage Context
storage_context = StorageContext.from_defaults(docstore=docstore)
## Create Vector Index for Leaf Nodes
base_index = VectorStoreIndex(
    leaf_nodes,
    storage_context=storage_context
)
## Create Base Retriever and Auto Merging Retriever
base_retriever = base_index.as_retriever(similarity_top_k=6)
auto_merging_retriever = AutoMergingRetriever(
    base_retriever,
    storage_context,
```

```
    verbose=True  # Show merging process
)
## Prepare Test Questions
test_questions = [
    "What are the characteristics of the Golden Cudgel in its different
forms?",
]
print("=== Results from Auto Merging Retriever ===")
for question in test_questions:
    print(f"\nQuestion: {question}")
    # Retrieve using auto merging retriever
    merge_nodes = auto_merging_retriever.retrieve(question)
    print(f"Retrieved {len(merge_nodes)} merged nodes:")
    for node in merge_nodes:
        print(f"\nSimilarity: {node.score}")
        print(f"Content: {node.node.text}")
        print("-" * 50)
print("\n=== Results from Base Retriever (Comparison) ===")
for question in test_questions:
    print(f"\nQuestion: {question}")
    # Retrieve using base retriever
    base_nodes = base_retriever.retrieve(question)
    print(f"Retrieved {len(base_nodes)} base nodes:")
    for node in base_nodes:
        print(f"\nSimilarity: {node.score}")
        print(f"Content: {node.node.text}")
        print("-" * 50)
```

This design is very suitable for complex game systems like *The Legend of Godslayer: Monkey*, because many features in the game are interconnected, and players' questions often require synthesizing information from multiple aspects to provide a complete answer. For example, the characteristics of a certain **form** may involve basic attributes, combo systems, weapon features, and other aspects. Through **automatic retrieval merging**, the system can maintain the accuracy of the answer while providing more complete and coherent information.

```
=== Results of the Automatic Merged Retriever ===
Question: What are the characteristics of the Ruyi Jingu Bang in different
forms?
```

```
> Merging 3 nodes into parent node.
> Parent node id: cbb37aab-f161-4bb4-a1aa-f2adf47687a7.
> Parent node text: Exhibits different effects with different forms.
In the Vajra Form, the Ruyi Jingu Bang becomes heavy and thick, and every
hit is full of power. In the Demon Buddha Form, the staff can extend and
become slender, combining with spells to form long-range attacks. Besides
the Ruyi Jingu Bang, there are various divine artifacts and treasures in
the game that can be equipped and switched.
> Merging 1 nodes into parent node.
> Parent node id: 7b1eff02-fdfb-4dfb-81cd-0d75bf7868bc.
> Parent node text: The Vajra Form is adept at breaking enemy defenses
with continuous heavy attacks, creating openings.
Retrieved 4 merged nodes:
Similarity: 0.8093140209301627
Content: Exhibits different effects with different forms. In the Vajra
Form, the Ruyi Jingu Bang becomes heavy and thick, and every hit is full
of power. In the Demon Buddha Form, the staff can extend and become
slender, combining with spells to form long-range attacks. Besides the
Ruyi Jingu Bang, there are various divine artifacts and treasures in the
game that can be equipped and switched.
--------------------------------------------------
Similarity: 0.7931933447011333
Content: The Vajra Form is adept at breaking enemy defenses with
continuous heavy attacks, creating openings.
--------------------------------------------------
Similarity: 0.7830123004681626
Content: Each form has its own unique advantages.
In the Vajra Form, Wukong's strength surges, allowing for high physical
damage, suitable for close combat.
--------------------------------------------------
Similarity: 0.7490986271802448
Content: The weapon system is also full of variety. The iconic Ruyi Jingu
Bang can change its length and thickness at will,
--------------------------------------------------
=== Results of the Basic Retriever (Comparison) ===
Question: What are the characteristics of the Ruyi Jingu Bang in different
forms?
```

```
Retrieved 3 basic nodes:
Similarity: 0.8440463514850339
Content: Exhibits different effects with different forms. In the Vajra
Form, the Ruyi Jingu Bang becomes heavy and thick, and every hit is full
of power. In the Demon Buddha Form,
--------------------------------------------------
Similarity: 0.817276846713401
Content: Besides the Ruyi Jingu Bang, there are various divine artifacts
and treasures in the game that can be equipped and switched.
--------------------------------------------------
Similarity: 0.7931933447011333
Content: The Vajra Form is adept at breaking enemy defenses with
continuous heavy attacks, creating openings.
```

For basic retrievers, if the retrieval scope is set too small, the information may be incomplete; if the retrieval scope is set too large, irrelevant information may be introduced. In contrast, the **AutoMergingRetriever** can automatically identify and merge relevant text segments, intelligently determining which information should be integrated together, thereby providing a more complete context. This method is particularly effective for answering **complex questions** that require synthesizing information from multiple places.

Using RAPTOR to recursively generate multi-level indexes

RAPTOR (Recursive Abstractive Processing for Tree-Organized Retrieval) is a complex multi-level indexing structure proposed by the Stanford University team. Through carefully designed strategies, it fully explores and utilizes information at each level.

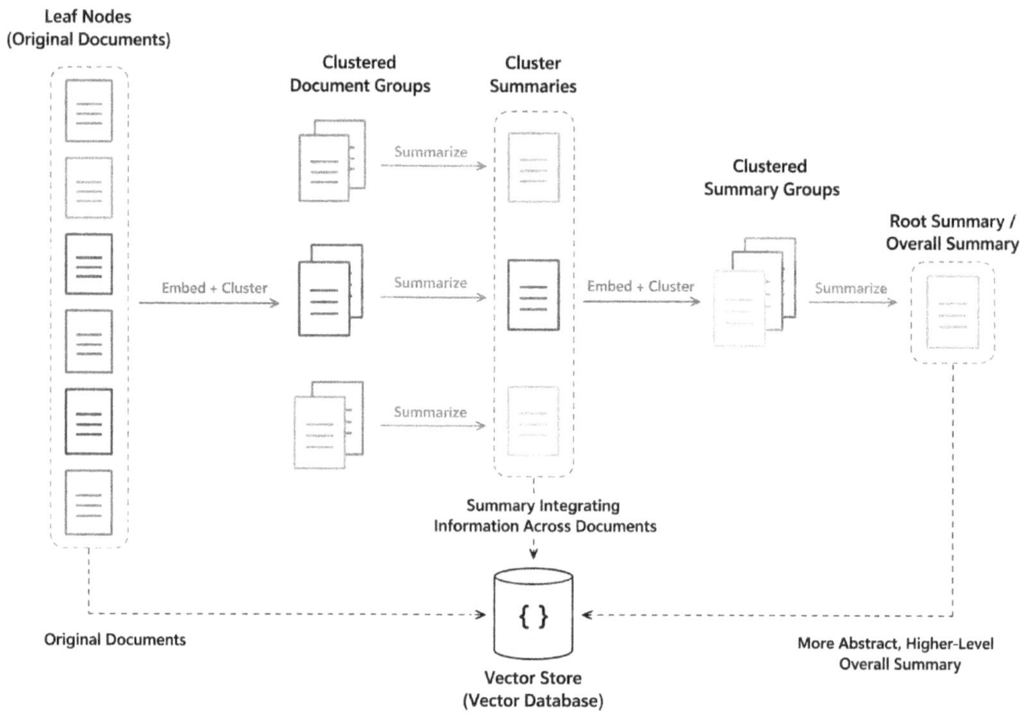

Figure 6.7: RAPTOR-style recursive clustering and summarization for multi-level retrieval

RAPTOR's retrieval and generation steps are the same as those of regular **RAG**. Its core algorithm mainly lies in the **index creation** part, which includes hierarchical document representation and level-wise recursive summarization.

- **Leaf nodes** represent the chunks of the original document or the entire document. Embeddings for the leaf nodes are computed and clustered (using **GMM** and **UMAP**).
- After lower-level documents (i.e., leaf nodes) are clustered, each cluster generates a **summary**.
- These summaries are then used as the next higher level input, which are clustered and summarized recursively until the final tree structure is formed.
- The final tree structure is then flattened into a **retrieval corpus**, using vector search for efficient information lookup.

It is like an inverted tree, with the **root** at the top and the **leaves** at the bottom, where each layer represents a different abstraction level of information. The higher the level, the more generalized and abstract the information. Each node can connect to relevant nodes in the upper and lower layers, allowing navigation from macro to micro levels of information.

The pseudocode for RAPTOR's index generation strategy is as follows.

```
def recursive_embed_cluster_summarize(text_chunks, level=1, max_levels=3):
"""
Recursively perform embedding, clustering, and summarization on the given
text chunks.
Each layer represents an abstraction level.
Parameters:
text_chunks: text chunks at the current layer (e.g., document chunks or
higher-level summaries)
level: current layer
max_levels: maximum recursion depth
Returns:
List of summaries generated at this layer (to serve as input for the upper
layer)
"""
### Embed the Text Chunks at the Current Layer
embeddings = embed_texts(text_chunks)
### If the Maximum Level Is Reached or Further Clustering Is Not Possible,
End Recursion
if level >= max_levels or len(text_chunks) <= 1:
    return text_chunks
### Cluster the Embedding Results (GMM+UMAP or K-Means Optionally)
clusters = cluster_embeddings(embeddings)
### Generate Summaries for Each Cluster
summaries = []
for cluster in clusters:
    cluster_texts = [text_chunks[i] for i in cluster.indices]
    summary = summarize_texts(cluster_texts)
    summaries.append(summary)
### Recursive Call, Entering the Next Layer
return recursive_embed_cluster_summarize(summaries, level + 1, max_levels)
```

Anna: Can it be understood this way: by having the large model summarize and abstract the lower-level content, with each ascending layer, the summary becomes more general, retaining key information while removing minor details? This is similar to the hierarchical relationship when writing an article: **section outline → paragraph outline → specific content**. For example, an overall **product line introduction → product category overview → multiple product documentation**. At the same time, lower-level content is grouped according to similarity to ensure that similar items are categorized together; for instance, gathering all documents related to **game mechanics**.

Lewis: Yes. The authors of the paper believe that the main advantage of this structure is that it enables more targeted **information retrieval** through hierarchical organization. Multi-level summarization helps access information at different **granularities**, and the combination of **global** and **local clustering** improves the quality of document organization, while the final **flattened vector storage** ensures retrieval efficiency, supporting information retrieval from different levels and perspectives.

Since the implementation in this paper is relatively complex, a detailed example is not provided here. Interested learners can refer to the **LangChain** reproduced code and the documentation explaining this paper.

Forward/backward linking connecting related nodes by forward/backward extension

Next, we will explore a technique called **Forward/Backward Augmentation** (Lewis calls it **forward/backward linking**). This technique leverages the relationships between **nodes** in a document, especially the contextual connections between adjacent nodes, to augment the retrieval context.

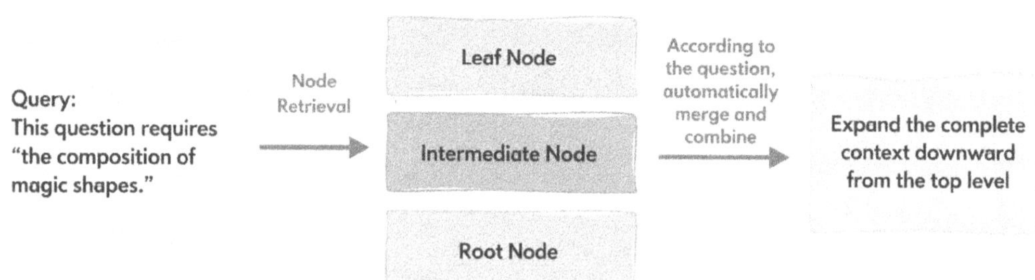

Figure 6.8: Query-based node expansion across leaf, intermediate, and root levels

In **question answering tasks** that require coherent context (such as analyzing an article or understanding a storyline), when a query involves information "after a certain event" or "before a certain event," the retrieval system can automatically infer and return the previous or next content related to the queried node. This enhances the contextual information in retrieval results, providing more comprehensive and coherent answers.

For the forward/backward extension technique, **LlamaIndex** provides the following two implementation tools:

- **PrevNextNodePostprocessor**: Allows retrieval of a specified number of nodes before and after the current node during retrieval. By setting the number of nodes to expand (`num_nodes` parameter), you can control the degree of enhancement.
- **AutoPrevNextNodePostprocessor**: Can infer from the query content whether forward/backward extension retrieval is needed. For example, if the query contains keywords like **"after"** or **"before"**, the postprocessor will automatically adjust the mode and choose **"next"** (backward retrieval), **"previous"** (forward retrieval), or **"none"** (no forward/backward extension retrieval).

Alex: Huh, Lewis, isn't this technique very similar to **node-sentence sliding window retrieval**?

Lewis: Haha, there is indeed a similarity in approach. But I was just about to ask you, can you tell what differences there are between the two?

Alex: Hmm. **Forward/backward extension retrieval** is a post-retrieval processing step; it doesn't involve index construction. So unlike **node-sentence sliding window retrieval**, it doesn't necessarily require the document to be split into sentences when segmenting vectors. Moreover, **AutoPrevNextNodePostprocessor** can automatically determine whether expansion is needed based on the query content, which increases flexibility.

Lewis: That's right. In **LlamaIndex**, the metadata of each node stores the IDs of the preceding and following nodes, which means any node can be automatically expanded as needed during retrieval. By understanding the specific content of the query, the system can decide whether to retrieve adjacent nodes, providing richer and more relevant information without overly sacrificing efficiency. Also, since this expansion is implemented as a **retrieval post-processing step** (in **LlamaIndex**, tools with the `Postprocessor` suffix are retrieval post-processing tools), it is relatively independent, making it easier to integrate into existing **RAG** workflows without needing to rebuild the index.

The following code example demonstrates an **intelligent game story retrieval system** that can provide complete story information by analyzing **contextual relationships** (refer to `https://github.com/PacktPublishing/RAG-from-First-Principles` for the complete code).

```
from llama_index.core import VectorStoreIndex, StorageContext, Document, Settings
from llama_index.core.node_parser import SentenceSplitter
from llama_index.core.storage.docstore import SimpleDocumentStore
from llama_index.core.postprocessor import PrevNextNodePostprocessor, AutoPrevNextNodePostprocessor
from llama_index.llms.deepseek import DeepSeek
from llama_index.embeddings.huggingface import HuggingFaceEmbedding
### Configure Global Settings
Settings.llm = DeepSeek(model="deepseek-chat", temperature=0.1)
Settings.embed_model = HuggingFaceEmbedding(model_name="BAAI/bge-small-zh")
Settings.node_parser = SentenceSplitter()
### Prepare the Game Story Text
game_story = """When Wukong first awakens, he finds himself trapped in an ancient cave. With blurred memories, he only remembers that he is the Great Sage Sun Wukong, but cannot recall why he is there. Inside the cave is a broken mirror; through it, he sees himself covered in wounds, and his legendary golden cudgel is now just a broken hilt. After leaving the cave, Wukong encounters a mysterious old monk. The old monk tells him that this is the 'Illusory Realm', a special space between reality and illusion. 500 years ago, Heaven suffered an unprecedented catastrophe: the gods fell, and the celestial world collapsed. At that time, Wukong was wreaking havoc in Heaven but was swept into the disaster, losing most of his powers and memories, and sealed in this world. The old monk suggests Wukong find the scattered fragments of his memory across the Illusory Realm. His first stop is the Wangchuan Temple in the east, where a Mirror of Memory is enshrined, which may help him recover some memories. However, the temple has been occupied by a group of evil demons, so Wukong must defeat them first. Within Wangchuan Temple, Wukong witnesses scenes from the Heaven Catastrophe through the Mirror of Memory. It turns out that a mysterious ancient force was manipulating everything behind the scenes, using the power of 'the wishes of all beings' to distort the rules of the universe. Although Wukong was mighty at the time, he still couldn't prevent the disaster from happening. After regaining these memories, the old monk tells him that the next stop should be the Fiery Mountain in
```

```
the west. There, a transformed demon clan holds even more truths. But
Fiery Mountain is surrounded by blazing flames year-round, making it
inaccessible to ordinary beings. Wukong must first find the legendary
Samadhi Fire Armor to enter safely. In his search, Wukong reunites with
his old friend, the Demon King. The Demon King tells him that after the
collapse of Heaven, chaos erupted in the Six Realms, with various factions
rising up—some in the name of rebuilding Heaven, others seeking to create
new order. A greater disaster is brewing. After obtaining the Samadhi Fire
Armor, Wukong successfully infiltrates Fiery Mountain. In a confrontation
with the demon clan leader, he finally recalls more truths. The ancient
force's goal was not mere destruction, but to reshape the rules of the
world. They believed there were fundamental flaws in the current order
that bring suffering to all beings. Returning to the old monk, Wukong
says he wants to unite all forces to fight against the power behind the
scenes. But the old monk warns him that things may not be as simple as
they appear. Whether the world order should be remade is a question
without a standard answer. The old monk advises Wukong to seek more truth
before making a decision. Wukong decides to set out for the Southern
Sinking Star Sea, where, according to legend, there is an ancient library
containing classics about the world's origin. However, before he departs,
the Illusory Realm suddenly shudders violently, as if some great upheaval
is about to occur..."""
### Create Document Object
documents = [Document(text=game_story)]
### Build Document Storage and Index and Parse Documents Using node_parser
in Settings
nodes = Settings.node_parser.get_nodes_from_documents(documents)
### Add Nodes
docstore = SimpleDocumentStore()
docstore.add_documents(nodes)
### Create Storage Context
storage_context = StorageContext.from_defaults(docstore=docstore)
### Build Vector Index
index = VectorStoreIndex(nodes, storage_context=storage_context)
### Create Different Query Engines Basic Query Engine
base_engine = index.as_query_engine(
similarity_top_k=1,
response_mode="tree_summarize"
)
```

```
### Query Engine with Fixed Previous and Next Context
prev_next_engine = index.as_query_engine(
similarity_top_k=1,
node_postprocessors=[
PrevNextNodePostprocessor(docstore=docstore, num_nodes=2)
],
response_mode="tree_summarize"
)
### Query Engine with Automatic Previous and Next Context
auto_engine = index.as_query_engine(
similarity_top_k=1,
node_postprocessors=[
AutoPrevNextNodePostprocessor(
docstore=docstore,
num_nodes=2,
verbose=True
)
],
response_mode="tree_summarize"
)
### Test Different Types of Questions and Different Query Engines
test_questions = [
"What happened after Wukong regained his memory at Wangchuan Temple?", #
Should look for later context
"How did Wukong reach the Fire Mountain?", # Should look for both
previous and next context
"Why did Wukong wake up in the cave?", # Should look for earlier context
]
```

Although the example storyline is very simple, a **plotline** was deliberately designed around uncovering the truth and searching for memories to better demonstrate how the system handles **causes and consequences** in the text. When the player asks, **What happened before/after a certain event?**, complete context is needed, as a single fragment may not provide enough information.

```
Question: Why did Wukong wake up in the cave?
> Postprocessor Predicted mode: previous
Answer: Wukong woke up in the cave because during the upheaval in Heaven
five hundred years ago, when he caused havoc in the Heavenly Palace, the
celestial court suffered a catastrophe, the gods fell, and the Heavenly
```

```
Realm collapsed. Wukong was also swept into it, losing most of his magical
power and memory, and was eventually sealed within this special space—the
Illusory Realm.
```

You can balance the context range by adjusting parameters such as **chunk_size** and **num_nodes**, or modify the story content to test the system's performance in different scenarios.

Anna: The **forward/backward expansion technique** here focuses more on the logical order of the document content, while the **parent-child text block indexing technique** mainly relies on hierarchical structure (**child text blocks** and **parent text blocks**) to return context, and does not depend on the sequential relationship of the content. From the perspective of automation, the `AutoPrevNextNodePostprocessor` in the forward/backward expansion technique can infer whether expansion is needed based on the query, whereas both the **node-sentence sliding window retrieval technique** and the parent-child text block indexing technique are based on preset ranges and do not have automated judgment capabilities.

Hybrid retrieval improving retrieval accuracy and expanding coverage

In the previous sections, we have repeatedly discussed the concept and implementation methods of **hybrid indexing** (the prerequisite and foundation for **hybrid retrieval**). When there are multiple types of databases or indexes within a database, **hybrid retrieval** can be used to improve retrieval accuracy, expand coverage, and enhance system capabilities.

Combining BM25 and semantic retrieval with ensemble retriever

In this section, we will use **LangChain's Ensemble Retriever** to combine the results of different types of retrievers. The process of implementing hybrid retrieval is shown below:

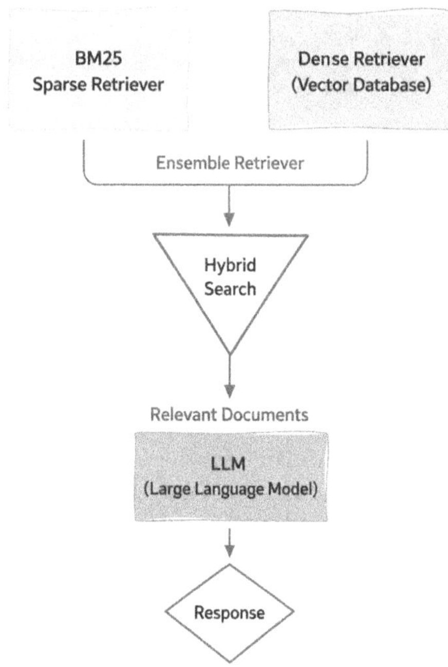

Figure 6.9: Hybrid retrieval combining BM25 keyword search with dense vector retrieval

The two retrievers operate in parallel: on the left is the **BM25 sparse retriever** based on keyword matching; on the right is the **dense retriever** performing semantic similarity search. The **Ensemble Retriever** combines the results from the two retrievers, integrates them using a hybrid retrieval strategy, and finally passes the relevant documents to the generator for output.

The advantage of this architecture is that it combines the precision of keyword matching with the flexibility of semantic retrieval. **BM25** excels at capturing exact text matches, making it ideal for finding documents containing precise terms or closely related words; while the **dense retriever** can understand the underlying context or meaning of the query, providing a deeper level of semantic similarity. Therefore, in many application scenarios, adopting a **hybrid retrieval strategy** can yield better results than using a single retriever alone.

The following code example uses the `BM25 retriever` for keyword matching and employs vector storage for semantic retrieval. The `EnsembleRetriever` then combines these two retrieval methods (the weights of BM25 and semantic retrieval can be adjusted as needed to optimize retrieval performance) to implement hybrid retrieval.

```
from langchain_huggingface import HuggingFaceEmbeddings
from langchain_deepseek import ChatDeepSeek
```

```
from langchain.chains import RetrievalQA
### System Definition Documents Focus on Specific Game Mechanics and
Systems
system_docs = [
""The Legend of Exorcising the God·Husun" features a unique transformation
system as the core combat mechanic",
"In Vajra Form, heavy weapons can be used, increasing attack and defense",
"In Demon Buddha Form, magic attacks are emphasized, unleashing powerful
spell damage",
"Different forms can be switched at any time in battle for combos",
"The game has three difficulty levels: Normal, Hard, and Asura"
]
### Lore Documents Focus on Story and Background Setting
lore_docs = [
"The game is set in a fictional mythical world, blending elements of
Eastern mythology",
"Sun Wukong is reawakened after being sealed for 500 years in the game",
"There exist multiple factions of gods and demons in the world, such as
Buddhism and Daoism",
"The player controls Sun Wukong to uncover the truth among the various
forces",
"Scenes include ink-painting-style mountains and architecture"
]
### Create Two Different Retrievers: BM25 and Vector Retriever
from langchain_community.retrievers import BM25Retriever
from langchain_community.vectorstores import FAISS
from langchain.retrievers import EnsembleRetriever
### Create BM25 Retriever
bm25_retriever = BM25Retriever.from_texts(
system_docs + lore_docs,
metadatas=[{"source": "system" if i < len(system_docs) else "lore"}
for i in range(len(system_docs) + len(lore_docs))]
)
bm25_retriever.k = 2
### Create Vector Retriever
embed_model = HuggingFaceEmbeddings(model_name="BAAI/bge-small-zh")
vectorstore = FAISS.from_texts(
system_docs + lore_docs,
```

```
embed_model,
metadatas=[{"source": "system" if i < len(system_docs) else "lore"}
for i in range(len(system_docs) + len(lore_docs))]
)
faiss_retriever = vectorstore.as_retriever(search_kwargs={"k": 2})
### Create Hybrid Retriever
ensemble_retriever = EnsembleRetriever(
retrievers=[bm25_retriever, faiss_retriever],
weights=[0.5, 0.5]
)
Create a QA chain using the hybrid retriever and a QA chain using a single
retriever (for comparison)
llm = ChatDeepSeek(model="deepseek-chat")
## Create a Hybrid Retrieval QA Chain
ensemble_qa = RetrievalQA.from_chain_type(
    llm=llm,
    retriever=ensemble_retriever,
    return_source_documents=True
)
## Create a Separate Vector Retrieval QA Chain for Comparison
vector_qa = RetrievalQA.from_chain_type(
    llm=llm,
    retriever=faiss_retriever,
    return_source_documents=True
)
## Test Different Types of Queries
test_queries = [
    "What is the transformation system like in the game?",  # System
settings query
    "What is the world background of the game?",        # Background setting
query
    "What combat forms does Wukong have?"              # Hybrid query
]
for query in test_queries:
    print(f"\nQuery: {query}")
    print("\n1. Hybrid Retrieval Results:")
    ensemble_docs = ensemble_retriever.invoke(query)
    print("Retrieved documents:")
```

```
    for i, doc in enumerate(ensemble_docs, 1):
        print(f"{i}. [{doc.metadata['source']}] {doc.page_content}")
    print("\n2. Vector Retrieval Results (Comparison):")
    vector_docs = faiss_retriever.invoke(query)
    print("Retrieved documents:")
    for i, doc in enumerate(vector_docs, 1):
        print(f"{i}. [{doc.metadata['source']}] {doc.page_content}")
## Test QA Performance
print("\n=== QA Performance Test ===")
test_questions = [
    "What are the characteristics of the Vajra form?",
    "How are the factions distributed in the game?",
]
for question in test_questions:
    print(f"\nQuestion: {question}")
    print("\n1. Answer using Hybrid Retrieval:")
    ensemble_result = ensemble_qa.invoke({"query": question})
    print(f"Answer: {ensemble_result['result']}")
    print("\nSource documents used:")
    for i, doc in enumerate(ensemble_result['source_documents'], 1):
        print(f"{i}. [{doc.metadata['source']}] {doc.page_content}")
print("\n2. Answer using pure vector retrieval (for comparison):")
vector_result = vector_qa.invoke({"query": question})
print(f"Answer: {vector_result['result']}")
print("\nSource documents used:")
for i, doc in enumerate(vector_result['source_documents'], 1):
    print(f"{i}. [{doc.metadata['source']}] {doc.page_content}")
```

```
Query: What is the transformation system like in the game?
Hybrid Retrieval Results:
Documents Retrieved:
[lore] The game scenes include ink-painting style mountains and
architecture
[system] "Annihilation God Chronicle: Housun" uses a unique transformation
system as the core combat mechanic
[lore] The player, as Sun Wukong, must seek the truth among various
factions
[system] In combat, you can switch between different forms at any time to
```

```
execute combos
Vector Retrieval Results (comparison):
Documents Retrieved:
[system] "Annihilation God Chronicle: Housun" uses a unique transformation
system as the core combat mechanic
[system] In combat, you can switch between different forms at any time to
execute combos
Question: What are the features of the Vajra Form?
Answer using hybrid retrieval:
Answer: In **Vajra Form**, you can use heavy weapons, increasing attack
and defense power.
Source documents used:
[lore] The game scenes include ink-painting style mountains and
architecture
[system] In **Vajra Form**, you can use heavy weapons, increasing attack
and defense power
[lore] The player, as Sun Wukong, must seek the truth among various
factions
[system] **Demon Buddha Form** focuses on magical attacks and can unleash
powerful spell damage
Answer using pure vector retrieval (comparison):
Answer: In **Vajra Form**, you can use heavy weapons, increasing attack
and defense power.
Source documents used:
[system] In **Vajra Form**, you can use heavy weapons, increasing attack
and defense power
[system] **Demon Buddha Form** focuses on magical attacks and can unleash
powerful spell damage
```

In this way, you can clearly observe the specific documents returned by each **retriever**, and understand how the final **ensemble retriever** balances and selects these results. This is especially helpful for debugging and optimizing retrieval strategies. During testing, the **hybrid retrieval method** demonstrated its ability to consider both keyword matching and semantic relevance, thereby providing more comprehensive and accurate search results. This approach is suitable for a variety of application scenarios, such as finding resources in digital libraries and efficiently searching large document collections.

When we compare the above code with the hybrid retrieval implementation in *Chapter 4*, we find that using the **LangChain** framework greatly simplifies this process. Specifically, the two components, **BM25Retriever** and `vectorstore.as_retriever`, encapsulate the complex logic behind information embedding, vector storage, and retrieval, allowing developers to efficiently implement information retrieval without delving into the details. The key functionality of integrating different retrievers is mainly realized by the **EnsembleRetriever** class, which is responsible for combining results from different retrievers and conducting a comprehensive evaluation based on preset weights, in order to optimize retrieval performance.

Next, let's take a look at the core logic of the **EnsembleRetriever** class.

```
class EnsembleRetriever(BaseRetriever):
    retrievers: List[RetrieverLike]
    weights: List[float]
    c: int = 60
    id_key: Optional[str] = None
    def weighted_reciprocal_rank(
        self, doc_lists: List[List[Document]]
    ) -> List[Document]:
        rrf_score: Dict[str, float] = defaultdict(float)
        for doc_list, weight in zip(doc_lists, self.weights):
            for rank, doc in enumerate(doc_list, start=1):
                rrf_score[
                    doc.page_content
                    if self.id_key is None
                    else doc.metadata[self.id_key]
                ] += weight / (rank + self.c)
        all_docs = chain.from_iterable(doc_lists)
        sorted_docs = sorted(
            unique_by_key(
                all_docs,
                lambda doc: doc.page_content
                if self.id_key is None
                else doc.metadata[self.id_key],
            ),
            reverse=True,
            key=lambda doc: rrf_score[
```

```
                doc.page_content if self.id_key is None else doc.
metadata[self.id_key]
            ],
        )
        return sorted_docs
```

The key point here is **Weighted Reciprocal Rank Fusion**, which is the core algorithm of ensemble retrieval. It is implemented in the `weighted_reciprocal_rank` method.

The score calculation statement is as follows.

```
rrf_score[doc_key] += weight / (rank + self.c)
```

For each document, a score is calculated based on its ranking in the results of various retrievers. The higher the rank (i.e., the smaller the rank number), the higher the score. The **weight** is used to adjust the importance of different retrievers. Afterwards, the `unique_by_key` function is used to remove duplicate documents, and then the documents are sorted according to the calculated **RRF scores**. The sorted and deduplicated document list is then returned. More details about the **RRF algorithm** will be introduced later in the course.

This implementation combines the results of multiple retrievers, takes into account the **weight** of each retriever and the **ranking** of the document in each retriever, and can effectively fuse the advantages of different retrieval strategies to improve the overall retrieval quality. When using it, you only need to initialize `EnsembleRetriever` and provide a list of retrievers and their corresponding weights.

```
ensemble_retriever = EnsembleRetriever(
retrievers=[bm25_retriever, faiss_retriever],
weights=[0.6, 0.4])
```

This setting gives the **BM25 retriever** a higher weight, which may be more suitable for handling keyword-matching queries, while also leveraging the semantic understanding abilities of the **Faiss retriever**.

Using MultiVectorRetriever to implement multi-representation indexing

Multi-representation indexing is a technique that improves retrieval effectiveness by creating multiple representations for documents. In fact, in previous sections, we have implemented various types of multi-representation indexing multiple times. For example, the **parent-child text blocks** mentioned in *Parent-child text chunk retrieval* and the **HierarchicalNodeParser** introduced in *Creating hierarchical indexes with HierarchicalNodeParser* can both be used to generate multiple representations for the same document.

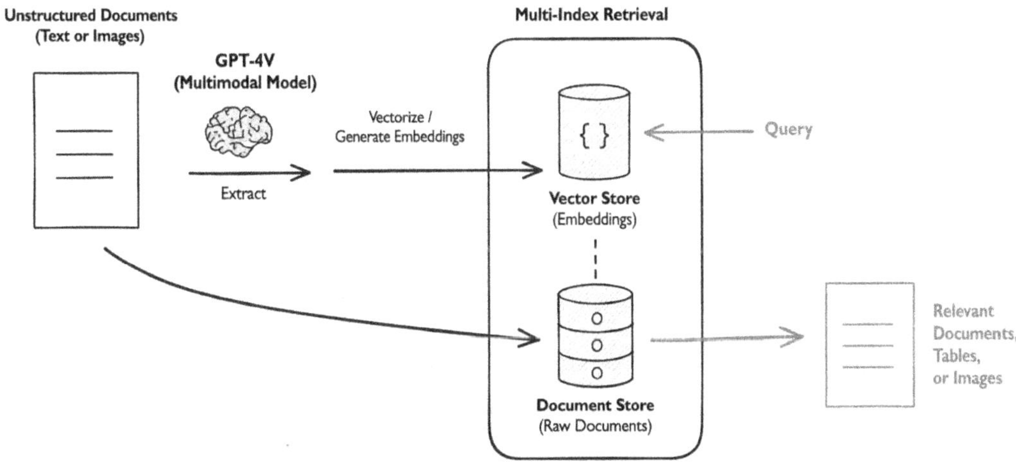

Figure 6.10: Multi-index retrieval for unstructured documents, tables, and images

The following code example demonstrates how to quickly implement multi-representation indexing using **MultiVectorRetriever** in **LangChain**.

```
### Load Documents
from langchain_community.document_loaders import WebBaseLoader
loader = WebBaseLoader("https://lilianweng.github.io/posts/2023-06-23-
agent/")
docs = loader.load()
### Create Document Summaries
from langchain_core.prompts import ChatPromptTemplate
from langchain_deepseek import ChatDeepSeek
from langchain_core.output_parsers import StrOutputParser
chain = (
{"doc": lambda x: x.page_content}
| ChatPromptTemplate.from_template("Summarize the following document:\n\
n{doc}")
| ChatDeepSeek(model="deepseek-chat")
| StrOutputParser()
)
summaries = chain.batch(docs, {"max_concurrency": 5})
### Set Up the Multi-Vector Retriever
```

```
from langchain.storage import InMemoryByteStore
from langchain_huggingface import HuggingFaceEmbeddings
from langchain_community.vectorstores import Chroma
from langchain.retrievers.multi_vector import MultiVectorRetriever
embed_model = HuggingFaceEmbeddings(model_name="BAAI/bge-m3")
vectorstore = Chroma(collection_name="summaries", embedding_function=
embed_model)
store = InMemoryByteStore()
id_key = "doc_id"
retriever = MultiVectorRetriever(
vectorstore=vectorstore,
byte_store=store,
id_key=id_key,
)
### Add Documents and Summaries to the Retriever
import uuid
from langchain_core.documents import Document
doc_ids = [str(uuid.uuid4()) for _ in docs]
summary_docs = [
Document(page_content=s, metadata={id_key: doc_ids[i]})
for i, s in enumerate(summaries)
]
retriever.vectorstore.add_documents(summary_docs)
retriever.docstore.mset(list(zip(doc_ids, docs)))
### Query the Retriever
query = "Memory in agents"
retrieved_docs = retriever.get_relevant_documents(query,n_results=1)
```

In this multi-representation index, **similarity search** is performed through summaries (which is more time-efficient and yields more precise results). After finding the relevant summaries, you can quickly locate the original document using the document's `doc_id`. This design is particularly useful when handling long documents because it allows us to maintain retrieval efficiency without losing the complete information of the original document.

Hybrid querying and query routing

Now, looking back at the **query routing** technique, we will realize that both **integrated retrieval** and **multi-representation retrieval** are closely related to **logical routing**. Once multiple types or levels of indexes are built, the key is to determine which type of **representation** is most suitable for a specific query.

For example, for queries like "Help me find battle data about Wukong," it might be more appropriate to prioritize **keyword** or **structured representations** for retrieval, as such queries typically require precisely matched specific information or data points. In contrast, for queries such as "Why is 'Chronicle of the Godslayer: Monkey' popular among players?" it is more appropriate to use **semantic representations** for retrieval, since it focuses on understanding the intent behind the query and finding more relevant content.

The process of selecting the most suitable retrieval path based on the characteristics of the query is essentially a **query routing** process. In complex scenarios, it may be necessary to utilize multiple **representations** simultaneously and merge their retrieval results. This forms a **hybrid query system** that can dynamically decide the weight distribution of different retrieval paths according to the characteristics of the query.

Summary

The technologies discussed in this section are mostly closely related to the generation of **structured text blocks** and **retrieval optimization**, aiming to provide fundamental ideas to inspire deeper applications and innovation. Below is an overview of several key technologies and their roles.

- **Small to large**: This technique combines the precision of retrieval with the large context of generation, thereby improving the accuracy and relevance of the model's answers to questions.
- **Coarse to fine**: This technique constructs hierarchical indexes and generates text summaries for each node, achieving a retrieval process that moves from coarse to detailed granularity.
- **Hierarchical merging**: By creating multiple types of indexes for the same text block, this technique enhances the comprehensiveness of retrieval and expands coverage.

- **Sequential chaining**: This technique dynamically expands the context based on the query, especially suitable for handling documents with strong causal relationships and temporal associations.
- **Hybrid retrieval**: This technique integrates multiple data sources or storage representations and is a common retrieval optimization strategy in practical applications.

It is worth noting that although the above techniques provide valuable methodological guidance, the key in actual projects is to identify the **bottlenecks** that affect the quality of retrieval and the entire **RAG system**.

It is hoped that through understanding these techniques, you can flexibly apply them in your own projects, without being constrained by existing patterns, and create **index construction** approaches and efficient **retrieval mechanisms** that best fit your needs.

Subscribe for a free eBook

New frameworks, evolving architectures, research drops, production breakdowns – *AI_Distilled* filters the noise into a weekly briefing for engineers and researchers working hands-on with LLMs and generative AI systems. Subscribe now and receive a free eBook, along with weekly insights that help you stay focused and informed.

Subscribe at `https://packt.link/8Oz6Y` or scan the QR code below.

7

Retrieval Post-Processing

After learning about **retrieval pre-processing** and **index optimization** techniques, Alex, Anna, and Lewis discussed **retrieval post-processing techniques**, but Anna still had some questions.

Figure 7.1: Lewis and Anna deep in conversation about retrieval pre-processing techniques

Anna: Could you talk about the key differences between retrieval pre-processing, index optimization, and retrieval post-processing techniques?

Lewis: **Retrieval pre-processing** and **index optimization** techniques focus on improving the efficiency of the retrieval process, while **retrieval post-processing techniques** aim to enhance the quality of the retrieval results. Since the initial retrieval results are often not ideal, further optimization and processing are needed to ensure that the **generative model** can produce high-quality answers.

Retrieval post-processing employs a series of steps to place the most relevant text chunks at the top of the result list while reducing redundant information and improving content quality. This enhances overall system performance, making the generated content more accurate and closely related to the context.

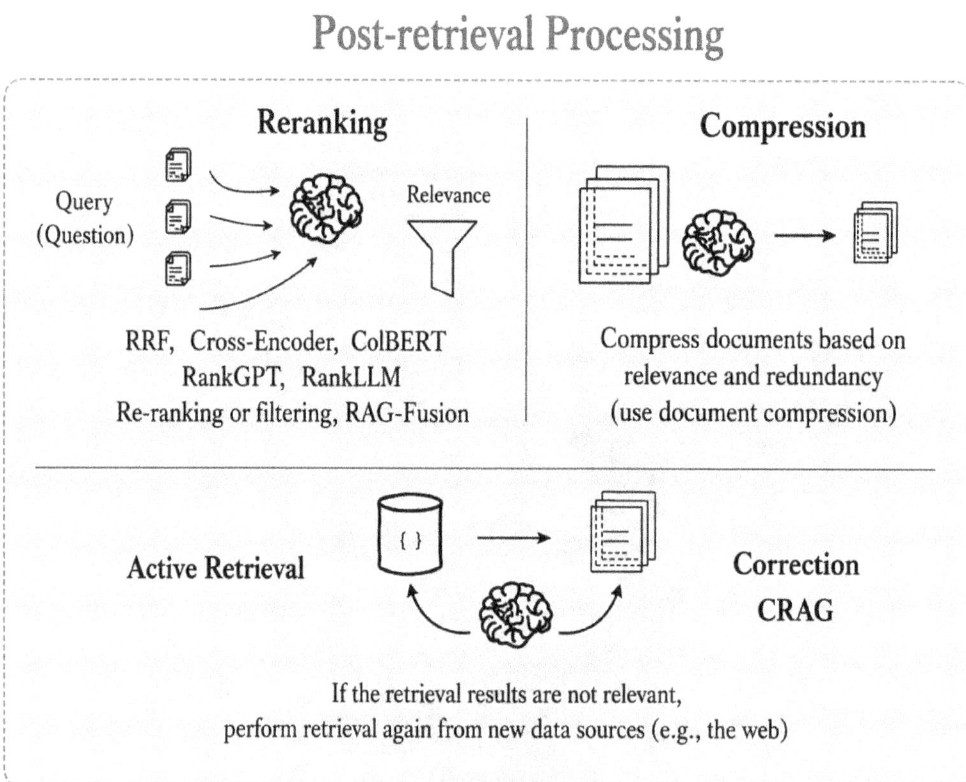

Figure 7.2: Post search processing

Common retrieval post-processing techniques

Common retrieval post-processing techniques include the following:

- **Re-ranking**: In the initial retrieval results, there may be a large number of text chunks with varying degrees of relevance to the query. By evaluating these results, the most relevant ones are placed at the front. Note that re-ranking will increase the demand for additional computing resources.
- **Compression**: Retrieved text chunks may be long and complex. Compressing them can reduce the computational burden on the generator and speed up the generation process.
- **Correction**: Results are checked and revised after generation to ensure the accuracy and coherence of the output. This is especially important in high-risk or high-standard fields (such as healthcare and law). The correction process usually also increases system complexity and resource requirements.

These techniques can be manually integrated into the **RAG workflow** by developers. Some retrievers in **LangChain** also have certain post-retrieval processing techniques built-in. In **LlamaIndex**, retrieval post-processing is usually accomplished through **node post-processors**.

Reranking

When a learner raises a question, even if the correct answer exists within a certain **text block**, if that block does not rank high enough in the retrieval results and is not passed to the large model for response generation (for example, the system only considers the **Top 3 text blocks** while the text block containing the correct answer is ranked 4th), the system will not be able to provide the correct answer.

The purpose of **reranking** is to improve the ordering quality of initially retrieved candidate text blocks. By applying a more refined scoring mechanism, reranking ensures the most relevant documents appear at the top. There are multiple ways to implement reranking, which we will explain sequentially from simple to complex approaches.

RRF re-ranking

In **hybrid retrieval**, you can obtain diverse retrieval results from multiple retrieval paths (or multiple retrievers). These paths can be a combination of **keyword search** and **vector search**, a combination of **vector store** and **structured database storage**, or a combination of different **retrieval strategies** (such as different chunking strategies and indexing strategies).

The core idea of hybrid retrieval is to complement each other's strengths. For example, **keyword retrieval** excels at exact matches, while **semantic retrieval** is good at capturing semantic relevance. By combining the results of these two retrieval methods, both recall rate and precision can be improved. However, this also brings about new issues:

- **Result redundancy**: Different retrieval methods may return the same or similar text chunks, causing duplication in the results.
- **Inconsistent ranking**: Different retrieval methods use different scoring standards (for example, BM25 scores are based on keyword matches, while semantic retrieval uses cosine similarity). Directly merging these may not yield the optimal result.
- **Efficiency issues:** Hybrid retrieval may produce a large number of candidate text chunks, making it a major challenge to filter out the most relevant documents.

To address the above issues, the most common solution is to apply **Reciprocal Rank Fusion (RRF)** re-ranking to the candidate text chunks obtained from the initial retrieval. This reduces result redundancy and unifies the scoring standards of different retrieval methods.

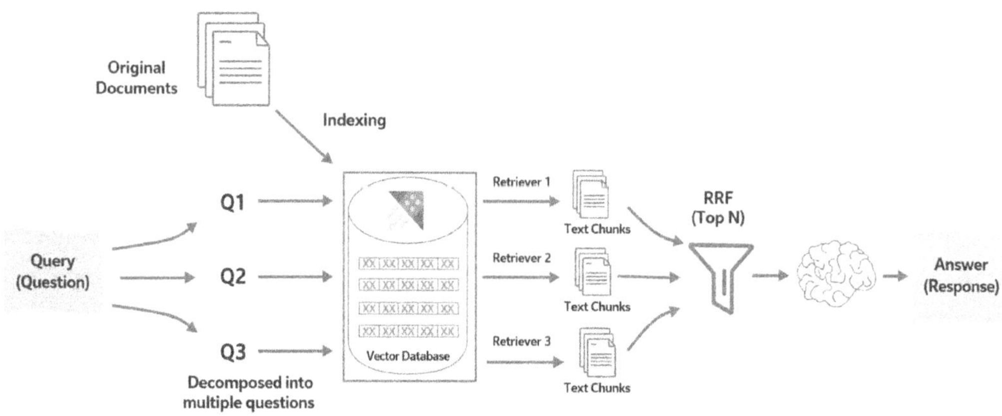

Figure 7.3: A flowchart shows questions split and processed through document blocks for generating answers

RRF merges result lists from multiple retrievers and assigns a fused score to each result. If a text chunk ranks highly in multiple result lists, it will have a higher RRF total score. This approach embodies the idea of **ensemble learning**.

The key re-ranking formula of the RRF algorithm is as follows:

$$\text{Score}_{RRF}(d) = \sum_{i=1}^{N} \frac{1}{rank_i(d) + k}$$

Figure 7.1: Mathematical formula for RRF score as a sum of one over rank plus k across N results

Where *d* represents a specific text chunk, `ScoreRRF(d)` is the fused score of that text chunk; *N* is the number of rankers (i.e., the number of input retrieval result lists); `ranki(d)` is the ranking of text chunk *d* in the *i*th ranker (starting from 1); and *k* is a smoothing parameter used to control the influence of ranking on the score, usually set as a constant (such as 60).

In this way, the final score of each text block is the accumulated sum of the scores contributed by all **rankers**. Text blocks with higher rankings (i.e., lower numbers) receive higher contribution scores. If a text block ranks higher in some **rankers** but does not appear in others, this approach adjusts its ranking to balance the weights of all **rankers**. Therefore, even if a text block does poorly in one **ranker**, **RRF** can correct the result through its performance in other **rankers**, making the method robust.

How should I understand the smoothing parameter?

Alex: How should I understand the smoothing parameter?

Lewis: The **smoothing parameter** is mainly used to solve the issue where high-ranked text blocks have too great an influence on the final score. By increasing the smoothing parameter *k*, you can further diminish the influence of those very high-ranking text blocks. In other words, a higher *k* value dilutes the impact of these top documents, thereby enhancing the overall smoothness of the ranking. This makes **RRF** more inclined to fuse the "long-tail contributions" provided by different **rankers**, rather than being overly biased toward results that are ranked especially high by a single **ranker**.

Here is a simple and intuitive example:

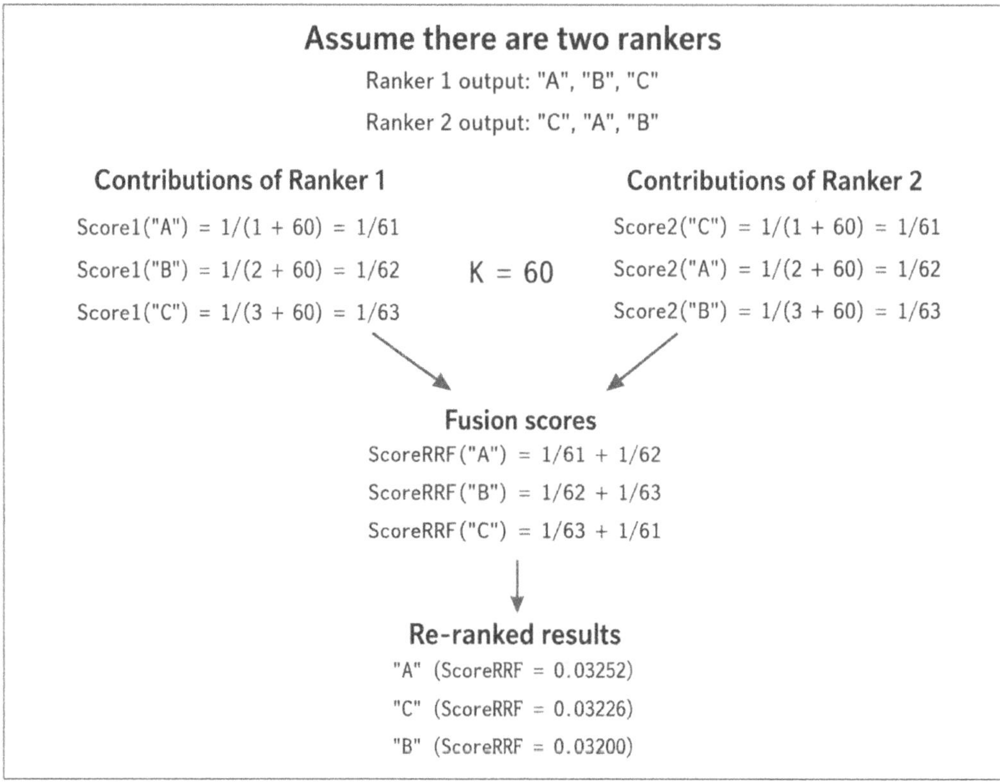

Figure 7.5: Rank fusion scoring using two rankers and showing formulas and results

From this example, you can see that because we set a relatively large *k* value, the score differences after fusion sorting are very close. Note that before re-ranking, lower scores (i.e., higher positions in the retrieval sequence) mean the text block is more important; after re-ranking, higher scores indicate more important text blocks.

Alex: Looks pretty good. **RRF** does not rely on complex hyperparameter tuning; its core logic is just simple smoothing calculations on text block rankings, allowing fusion of ranking lists in any format.

Lewis: That's true. However, genuinely valuable re-ranking still depends on the effectiveness of the original **retrievers**. If the quality of results from the original **retrievers** is not high, even after re-ranking, the outcome may still be unsatisfactory.

The following code example shows how to implement **RRF**:

```
def reciprocal_rank_fusion(results: list[list], k=60):
    """
    The RRF algorithm is used to merge retrieval results from multiple
rankers.
    Parameters:
    - results: a list containing multiple lists of retrieval results, each
sublist represents the output from one ranker.
    Each element in the sublist represents a document, sorted from highest
to lowest retrieval score.
    - k: the parameter in the RRF formula that controls the influence of
document ranking on the fusion score. Default is 60.
    Returns:
    - reranked_results: a list containing documents re-ranked by the RRF
algorithm, sorted from highest to lowest fusion score.
    """
    ## Initialize a dictionary to store the fusion score for each document
    fused_scores = {}
    ## Iterate over each ranker's retrieval results list (i.e., each
sublist in results)
    for docs in results:
        ## Iterate over each document and its rank in the result list
        for rank, doc in enumerate(docs):
            ## Serialize the document to a string so it can be used as a
dictionary key
            ## Use dumps(doc) to convert the document to a string, making
it easy to store in the dictionary
            doc_str = dumps(doc)
            ## If the document has not appeared in the dictionary,
initialize its score to 0
            if doc_str not in fused_scores:
                fused_scores[doc_str] = 0
            ## Calculate the current document's score according to the RRF
formula
            ## rank is the document's position (starting from 0), k is the
constant parameter for smoothing by rank
            fused_scores[doc_str] += 1 / (rank + k)
```

```
    ## Sort the documents in the dictionary by fusion score in descending
order, higher scores first
    reranked_results = [
        ## loads(doc) restores the serialized document string to its
original document format, along with the corresponding fusion score
        (loads(doc), score)
        ## The sorted function orders the documents in the dictionary by
score; reverse=True means descending order
        for doc, score in sorted(fused_scores.items(),
            key=lambda x: x[1], reverse=True)
    ]
    ## Return the re-ranked document list, where each element is a tuple
of (text block, fusion score)
    return reranked_results
```

The function **reciprocal_rank_fusion** accepts a list of multiple retrieval result lists and an optional parameter `k` (default value is 60). It calculates a **fusion score** for each **text chunk** from each retriever, re-ranks them based on these scores, and finally returns a new list sorted by the fusion score in descending order. Each element is a tuple containing the text chunk and its corresponding fusion score.

The following code example demonstrates how to use **LangChain** to implement **RRF re-ranking** in combination with **HuggingFace embeddings** and the **Chroma** vector database. In this example, the "Shanxi Culture and Tourism" directory contains a wealth of information about tourism in Shanxi (refer to `https://github.com/PacktPublishing/RAG-from-First-Principles` for the complete code):

```
import os
from langchain.text_splitter import RecursiveCharacterTextSplitter
from langchain_community.document_loaders import PyPDFLoader, TextLoader
from langchain_huggingface import HuggingFaceEmbeddings
from langchain_community.vectorstores import Chroma
from langchain.prompts import ChatPromptTemplate
from langchain_core.output_parsers import StrOutputParser
from langchain_deepseek import ChatDeepSeek
from langchain.load import dumps, loads
doc_dir = "./data/山西文旅"
def load_documents(directory):
```

```
    """Read all documents in the directory (including PDF, TXT, DOCX)"""
    documents = []
    for filename in os.listdir(directory):
        filepath = os.path.join(directory, filename)
        if filename.endswith(".pdf"):
            loader = PyPDFLoader(filepath)
        elif filename.endswith(".txt"):
            loader = TextLoader(filepath)
        else:
            continue  # Skip unsupported file types
        documents.extend(loader.load())
    return documents
docs = load_documents(doc_dir)
text_splitter = RecursiveCharacterTextSplitter(
    chunk_size=300,
    chunk_overlap=50
)
splits = text_splitter.split_documents(docs)
embed_model = HuggingFaceEmbeddings(model_name="all-MiniLM-L6-v2")
vectorstore = Chroma.from_documents(documents=splits, embedding=embed_
model)
retriever = vectorstore.as_retriever()
def reciprocal_rank_fusion(results: list[list], k=60):
fused_scores = {}
for docs in results:
    for rank, doc in enumerate(docs):
        doc_str = dumps(doc)
        if doc_str not in fused_scores:
            fused_scores[doc_str] = 0
        fused_scores[doc_str] += 1 / (rank + k)
reranked_results = [
    (loads(doc), score)
    for doc, score in sorted(fused_scores.items(), key=lambda x: x[1],
reverse=True)
]
return reranked_results
```

Generate multiple search queries:

```
template = """You are an assistant that helps users generate multiple
search queries.\n
Please generate several related search queries based on the following
question: {question} \n
Output (4 queries):"""
prompt_rag_fusion = ChatPromptTemplate.from_template(template)
llm = ChatDeepSeek(model="deepseek-chat")
generate_queries = (
    prompt_rag_fusion
    | llm
    | StrOutputParser()
    | (lambda x: x.split("\n"))
)
```

Example questions:

```
questions = [
    "What are some famous tourist attractions in Shanxi?",
    "What is the historical background of the Yungang Grottoes?",
    "What is the cultural and religious significance of Mount Wutai?"
]
```

Retrieve and process with RRF:

```
for question in questions:
    retrieval_chain_rag_fusion = generate_queries | retriever.map() |
reciprocal_rank_fusion
    docs = retrieval_chain_rag_fusion.invoke({"question": question})
    print(f"\n[Question] {question}")
    print(f"Number of documents: {len(docs)}")
    for doc, score in docs[:3]:  # Show top 3 results
        print(f"Document content: {doc.page_content[:200]}...")  # Only
show first 200 characters
```

Historical background of the Yungang Grottoes:

- Number of documents: 6.
- Document 1: Yungang Grottoes.
- The Yungang Grottoes are located on the southern foot of Wuzhou Mountain, 17 kilometers west of Datong City, Shanxi Province, northern China. The grottoes are carved into the mountain.
- Document 2: Yungang Wuhua Caves.
- Located in the central part of the Yungang Grottoes, Caves 9 to 13 are named for their richly adorned appearance after being coated and painted during the Qing Dynasty to depict scenes from the Yungang Grottoes. The decorative carvings are splendid.

Cross-encoder re-ranking

RRF re-ranking is a method similar to **ensemble learning**; it does not involve the semantic relationships between the retrieval results and the query. In contrast, the **Cross-Encoder re-ranking** (Cross-Encoder Re-ranking) introduced below is based on the **Cross-Encoder** model and performs re-ranking at the semantic level.

The idea of **Cross-Encoder** originates from Google's 2018 release of **BERT**. As a bidirectional Transformer model, **BERT** aims to learn universal language representations from a large corpus of unlabelled text data, and is not specifically designed for semantic matching or ranking tasks between queries and documents. In 2019, Nogueira et al. introduced the concept of using the pretrained language model **BERT** for passage re-ranking tasks in their paper *Passage Re-ranking with BERT*.

`Cross-Encoder` directly concatenates the query and the retrieved candidate text block, separated by a special separator `[SEP]`, and inputs them into a pretrained language model (such as `BERT`, `RoBERTa`, or other **Transformer models**). Through the **Transformer self-attention mechanism**, the query can fully interact with every token in the text block, and the model can understand their semantic associations. Finally, the output of the `CLS` token is fed into a classification layer to directly output the relevance score, enabling high-precision ranking of text blocks.

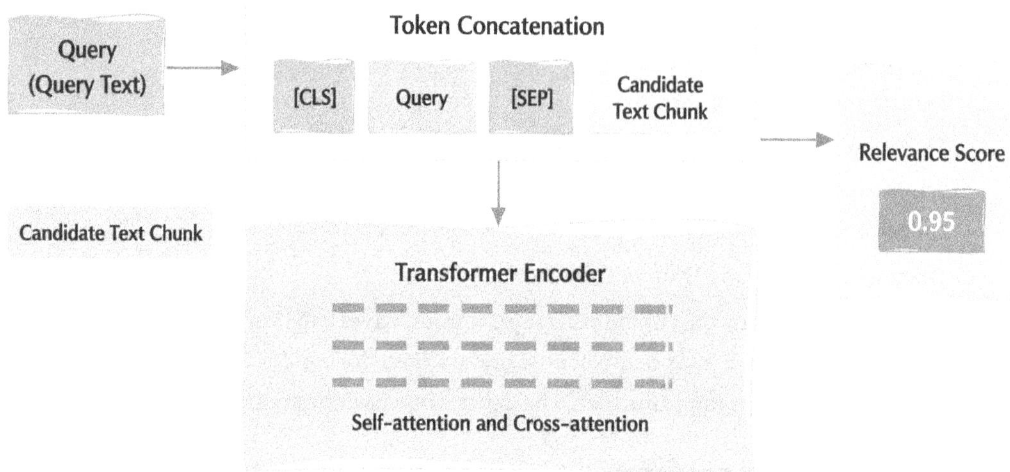

Figure 7.6: A flowchart showing how a question and a candidate text block go through a transformer to get a relevance score

In **RAG systems**, `Cross-Encoder` is usually configured as a fine-grained re-ranking module after the initial sorting. First, the **Bi-Encoder** is used for a rapid initial retrieval, and then `Cross-Encoder` is used to finely re-rank the initially selected collection of text blocks (e.g., Top-100), ultimately returning the most relevant text blocks (e.g., Top-10).

Tips from Lewis

The Bi-Encoder retrieval mentioned here actually refers to a common dense vector-based retrieval method.

Before various embedding models emerged, researchers typically used two identical or different neural networks (usually Transformer or LSTM models) to independently encode queries and documents into fixed-length embedding vectors.

These embedding vectors were then used to retrieve relevant chunks through similarity matching methods such as cosine similarity or dot product.

Alex: Isn't this just the retrieval process of **RAG**? It's just that the modern **embedding model** is replaced with the traditional **BERT model** to generate vectors.

Lewis: Exactly.

The following code example demonstrates how to implement **Cross-Encoder re-ranking** (refer to `https://github.com/PacktPublishing/RAG-from-First-Principles` for the complete code):

```
from transformers import Autotokenizer, AutoModelForSequenceClassification
import torch
### Load the Pre-Trained BERT Model for Sentence Pair Relevance
Calculation
model_name = "cross-encoder/ms-marco-MiniLM-L-12-v2"  # Suitable for
retrieval tasks
tokenizer = Autotokenizer.from_pretrained(model_name)
model = AutoModelForSequenceClassification.from_pretrained(model_name)
### Query Documents Related to Shanxi's Culture and Tourism
query = "What are some famous tourist attractions in Shanxi?"
documents = [
"Mount Wutai is one of the four great Buddhist mountains in China,
renowned as the bodhimanda of Manjushri.",
"Yungang Grottoes is one of China's three largest grottoes, famous for its
exquisite Buddhist sculptures.",
"Pingyao Ancient City is one of the best-preserved ancient county towns in
China, listed as a World Cultural Heritage site."]

### Compute Relevance Scores
def encode_and_score(query, docs):
    scores = []
    for doc in docs:
        inputs = tokenizer(query, doc, return_tensors="pt",
truncation=True, max_length=512, padding="max_length")
        with torch.no_grad():
            outputs = model(**inputs)
            score = outputs.logits[0][0].item()
        scores.append(score)
    return scores

### Get Ranking Results
scores = encode_and_score(query, documents)
ranked_docs = sorted(zip(documents, scores), key=lambda x: x[1],
reverse=True)
### Output Results
```

```
print("Query:", query)
print("\nRanking results:")
for rank, (doc, score) in enumerate(ranked_docs, start=1):
    print(f"{rank}. Relevance Score: {score:.4f} | Document: {doc}")
```

```
Query: What are some famous tourist attractions in Shanxi?
Sorting results:
Relevance score: 7.1072 | Document: Pingyao Ancient City is one of the
best-preserved ancient county towns in China and has been listed as a
World Cultural Heritage Site.
Relevance score: 7.0976 | Document: Mount Wutai is one of the Four Sacred
Buddhist Mountains in China and is renowned as the bodhimanda of Manjushri
Bodhisattva.
Relevance score: 5.8538 | Document: Yungang Grottoes is one of the
three major grottoes in China and is famous for its exquisite Buddhist
sculptures.
```

For application scenarios that require precise ranking, such as question-answering systems in the legal, medical, or financial fields, using a **Cross-Encoder** for reranking is a very suitable choice. In addition, it supports fine-tuning for different tasks and can be trained according to specific application scenarios to improve reranking performance. The drawback of the **Cross-Encoder** is that it has a high computational cost. As a result, in traditional document retrieval systems, it is usually used at the reranking stage rather than the initial retrieval stage. When the initial retrieval stage can effectively narrow down the range of candidate text blocks, the computational cost of the **Cross-Encoder** is acceptable.

ColBERT re-ranking

Contextualized Late Interaction over BERT (**ColBERT**) is a **dense vector retrieval** technique proposed by Stanford University at the SIGIR conference in 2020. The innovation of this technique lies in its introduction of the concept of **late interaction**.

Unlike **Cross-Encoder**, which directly enables full interaction between queries and documents, ColBERT first encodes the query and text chunk separately to obtain their respective representations, and then only performs token-level interaction in the final layer. At this stage, each token vector in the query and text chunk interacts one by one via **dot product**, and the results are then aggregated to generate a relevance score.

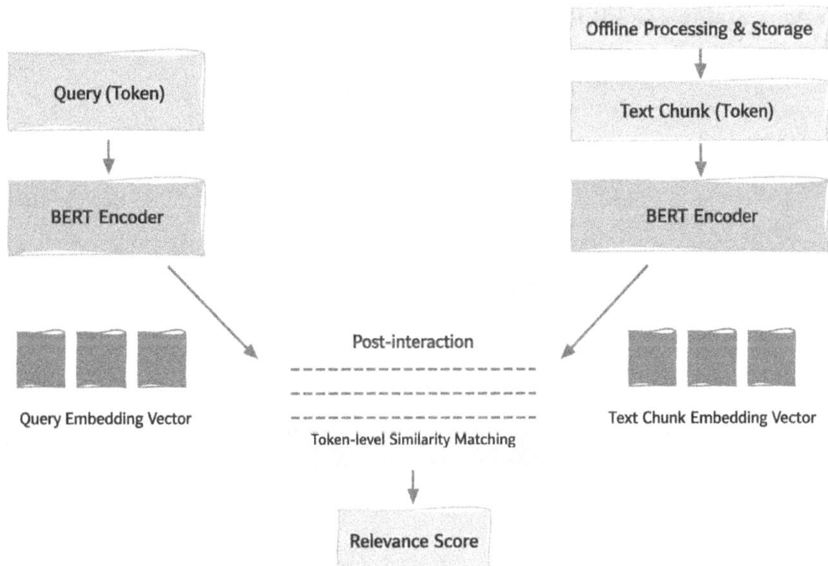

Figure 7.7: A flowchart showing a BERT-based process for token similarity and relevance scoring

Alex: ColBERT looks like it's just a regular **cosine similarity** comparison. Why do we need it? Didn't traditional retrievers already do similar work with cosine similarity comparisons?

Lewis: Although ColBERT may appear similar to traditional **cosine similarity-based methods** on the surface, its core difference lies in the level of **granularity**. Traditional methods directly compute the cosine similarity between query and document vectors; in contrast, ColBERT preserves the vectors for all tokens in both the query and the text chunk, determining relevance through interactive computation. This approach enables more **fine-grained semantic matching**, capable of capturing **local alignment relationships** and thus providing more accurate matching results.

Alex: So how is it different from Cross-Encoder?

Lewis: In ColBERT, the encoding of the query and text chunk is separated, which means that text chunks can be **pre-encoded** and stored. During retrieval, only token-level interactions need to be computed. In contrast, Cross-Encoder requires every **query-text chunk pair** to be processed holistically, including comprehensive interaction among all tokens in the sentence. Therefore, ColBERT offers higher **computational efficiency** in the re-ranking stage, as it directly uses the **embedding vector** of each token for similarity computation. However, this method also results in larger storage overhead, since it is necessary to store a large number of **token-level representations**.

The following is a sample **ColBERT** code (refer to `https://github.com/PacktPublishing/RAG-from-First-Principles` for the complete code):

```
from transformers import AutoTokenizer, AutoModel
import torch
import faiss
### Load ColBERT Model and Tokenizer
model_name = "bert-base-uncased"  # Can be replaced with a ColBERT fine-tuned model
tokenizer = AutoTokenizer.from_pretrained(model_name)
model = AutoModel.from_pretrained(model_name)
### Query and Document Collection
query = "What are some famous tourist attractions in Shanxi?"
documents = [
"Mount Wutai is one of the Four Sacred Buddhist Mountains in China, renowned as the bodhimanda of Manjushri Bodhisattva.",
"Yungang Grottoes is one of the three major grottoes in China, famous for its exquisite Buddhist sculptures.",
"Pingyao Ancient City is one of the best preserved ancient counties in China and has been listed as a World Cultural Heritage site."]
### Encoding Function
def encode_text(texts, max_length=128):
    inputs = tokenizer(
        texts,
        return_tensors="pt",
        padding=True,
        truncation=True,
        max_length=max_length
    )
    with torch.no_grad():
        outputs = model(**inputs)
    return outputs.last_hidden_state  # Return [CLS] and other token embeddings
### Encode Query and Documents
query_embeddings = encode_text([query])  # Query vector
doc_embeddings = encode_text(documents)  # Document vectors
### Compute Cosine Similarity
```

```
def calculate_similarity(query_emb, doc_embs):
    ## ColBERT uses late interaction (i.e., token-wise comparison). Here
we simplify to use cosine similarity for comparison
    query_emb = query_emb.mean(dim=1)  # Average pooling for query vector
    doc_embs = doc_embs.mean(dim=1)    # Average pooling for document
vectors
    query_emb = query_emb / query_emb.norm(dim=1, keepdim=True)  #
Normalize
    doc_embs = doc_embs / doc_embs.norm(dim=1, keepdim=True)
    scores = torch.mm(query_emb, doc_embs.t())  # Compute cosine
similarity
    return scores.squeeze().tolist()
### Sort Documents
scores = calculate_similarity(query_embeddings, doc_embeddings)
ranked_docs = sorted(zip(documents, scores), key=lambda x: x[1],
reverse=True)
### Output Sorted Results
print("Query:", query)
print("\nRanked Results:")
for rank, (doc, score) in enumerate(ranked_docs, start=1):
    print(f"{rank}. Score: {score:.4f} | Document: {doc}")
```

```
Query: What are some famous tourist attractions in Shanxi?
Ranked Results:
Score: 0.9420 | Document: Yungang Grottoes is one of China's three major
grottoes, famous for its exquisite Buddhist sculptures.
Score: 0.9158 | Document: Pingyao Ancient City is one of the best-
preserved ancient county-level cities in China and is listed as a World
Cultural Heritage site.
Score: 0.9132 | Document: Wutai Mountain is one of China's four major
Buddhist sacred mountains, renowned as the bodhimanda of Manjushri
Bodhisattva.
```

To simplify the example, we use **average pooling** combined with **cosine similarity** to replace ColBERT's's original method of scoring based on interaction between each token of the query and document. Although this approach simplifies implementation, it may not fully capture **ColBERT's** advantage in capturing fine-grained semantic information. For large-scale document collections, it is recommended to use a **vector database** to build an index for accelerating vector retrieval.

Additionally, in actual production environments, it is recommended to use a **ColBERT model** trained or fine-tuned on domain-specific data rather than the general **bert-base-uncased** model.

Feature	ColBERT	Cross-encoder	RRF
Design goal	Efficient dense retrieval + fine re-ranking	Deep semantic matching for fine re-ranking	Lightweight re-ranking by merging multi-model results
Semantic interaction	Token-level interaction, capturing fine-grained semantics	Full sentence interaction between query and document, precise semantic matching	No semantic interaction, ranking-based fusion
Computational cost	Medium (separate encoding for query and document + dot product)	High (full model inference for every query-document pair)	Low (directly fuse existing ranking scores)
Applicable scenario	Dense retrieval or top-k document re-ranking	Top-k document fine re-ranking	Signal fusion or lightweight re-ranking
Contextual awareness	Strong (based on token-level embeddings)	Very strong (full-sentence semantic modeling)	Weak
Suitable for large-scale retrieval	Yes (supports precomputed document vectors)	No (computational cost too high)	Yes

Table 7.1: A comparison of ColBERT, cross-encoder, and RRF

Since the **Cross-Encoder** achieves full interaction between the query and document, it usually provides better performance, but it comes with a high computational cost and requires recalculation each time. In contrast, **ColBERT**, through its late interaction design, allows for precomputing and storing document vector representations, and only computes similarity during querying, greatly improving efficiency. Therefore, in practical applications, if precise re-ranking is needed on a small scale, the **Cross-Encoder** can be chosen; for large-scale document retrieval and re-ranking tasks, **ColBERT** may be the better choice.

Cohere re-ranking and Jina re-ranking

Alex: Lewis, besides RRF, Cross-Encoder, and ColBERT, I've also heard of other re-ranking techniques, such as **Cohere re-ranking** and **Jina Re-ranking**. How are they different?

Lewis: Both Cohere re-ranking and Jina Re-ranking are methods based on **large models**. Let's talk about **Cohere re-ranking** first.

Cohere (similar to **OpenAI**, one of the large model service providers that offers large model services via API) has launched the **Rerank API** specifically designed for enterprise-level search needs. It is based on Cohere's self-developed **Command series large models** (like **Command R**), leveraging the powerful semantic comprehension capabilities of large models and using a **Cross-Encoder architecture** to achieve deep semantic understanding of documents, thus enabling fine grained re-ranking of candidate documents.

As we know, **Cross-Encoder** concatenates the query and the document, then inputs them into the same model for joint encoding to directly compute the relevance score between the two, thereby capturing fine-grained semantic matching relationships.

Since Cohere's **Rerank API** is a commercial API, users do not need to train their own models. They only need to send the existing retrieval results (such as the Top-100 results returned by **BM25** or vector search) to the Cohere re-ranking tool via the API to obtain optimized ranking results. Even without domain-specific training data, Cohere's model can be directly applied to different ranking tasks and demonstrates strong adaptability.

Cohere re-ranking supports multiple languages, with English supported by default. To support Chinese and other languages, you need to apply for a customized model. In addition, this service is optimized for high concurrency and low latency scenarios. According to official data, when processing 100 candidate documents, the average response time is less than 300 ms.

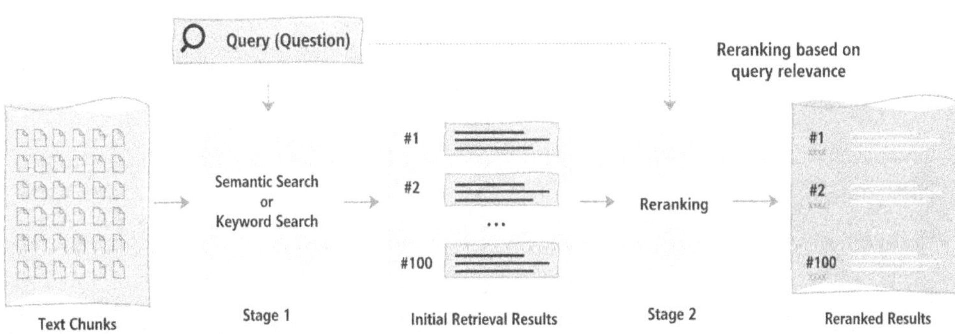

Figure 7.8: A flowchart shows how a query retrieves documents reranks them and displays sorted results

The following code example shows how to use the LangChain framework combined with the Cohere re-ranker to re-rank documents that have been initially ranked by BM25.

First, install the **LangChain** and **Cohere interface** packages, and configure your **Cohere API Key**:

```
pip install langchain-cohere
export CO_API_KEY="Your Cohere API Key"
```

The complete code is as follows:

```
## Import the Necessary Libraries
from langchain_cohere import CohereRerank
from langchain_core.documents import Document
from langchain_community.retrievers import BM25Retriever
## Prepare Example Documents
documents = [
    Document(
        page_content="Mount Wutai is one of China's four great Buddhist mountains, renowned as Manjusri Bodhisattva's sacred site.",
        metadata={"source": "Shanxi Travel Guide"}
    ),
    Document(
        page_content="The Yungang Grottoes are one of China's three major grottoes, famous for their exquisite Buddhist sculptures.",
        metadata={"source": "Shanxi Travel Guide"}
    ),
    Document(
        page_content="Pingyao Ancient City is one of the best-preserved ancient county towns in China and is listed as a World Cultural Heritage site.",
        metadata={"source": "Shanxi Travel Guide"}
    )
]
## Create a BM25 Retriever
retriever = BM25Retriever.from_documents(documents)
retriever.k = 3  # Set to return the top 3 results
## Set Up the Cohere Reranker
reranker = CohereRerank(model="rerank-multilingual-v2.0")
## Execute Query and Rerank First Get the Initial Retrieval Results
initial_docs = retriever.invoke(query)
```

```
## Use the Reranker to Reorder the Results
reranked_docs = reranker.compress_documents(documents=initial_docs,
query=query)
## Print the Reranked Results
print(f"Query: {query}\n")
print("Reranked results:")
for i, doc in enumerate(reranked_docs, 1):
    print(f"{i}. {doc.page_content}")
```

Query: What are some famous tourist attractions in Shanxi?

1. Pingyao Ancient City is one of the best-preserved ancient county towns in China and is listed as a World Cultural Heritage site
2. Mount Wutai is one of the four sacred Buddhist mountains in China, renowned as the bodhimanda of Manjushri Bodhisattva
3. Yungang Grottoes is one of China's three major grottoes, famous for its exquisite Buddhist sculptures

Introduction to Jina reranker v2

The **Jina Reranker v2 model** boasts excellent multilingual support, **function call comprehension**, code retrieval performance, and extremely fast inference speed. Compared with the previous generation, its throughput has increased sixfold, and its task understanding capability has been enhanced, making it one of the top general-purpose rerankers available today.

The Jina Reranker v2 model supports over 100 languages and can accurately comprehend user queries and rerank documents across languages. Whether in the **MKQA** multilingual QA task or in retrieval benchmarks such as **BEIR** and **AirBench**, the `jina-reranker-v2-base-multilingual` model outperforms competing models like the `bge-reranker-v2-m3` model (according to evaluation results provided on the Jina official website).

Applications and capabilities

The Jina Reranker v2 model further expands the range of **agent applications**, especially excelling in **function call** and **structured data retrieval scenarios**. It can not only recognize function call intents in natural language, but also sort SQL table structures or external APIs based on queries and select the most appropriate call item, making it highly suitable for agent applications with function-aware capabilities. Additionally, in code retrieval tasks such as **CodeSearchNet**, the model supports semantic pairing and reranking between docstrings and code snippets, providing strong support for building intelligent code assistants.

Performance and efficiency

In terms of speed, the Jina Reranker v2 model also stands out. By employing **Flash Attention 2** technology and a **lightweight architecture**, it significantly improves inference efficiency while maintaining high accuracy. For example, on the **RTX 4090**, the number of documents it can process every 50ms far exceeds that of competing models. This performance boost is not only ideal for API calls but also offers a very high cost-performance ratio for private deployments.

Integration and access

The Jina Reranker v2 model provides **API access**, **open source models**, and integration with multiple frameworks (such as **LangChain**, **LlamaIndex**, **Haystack**), making it easy for developers to flexibly use according to various scenarios. You can visit the **Jina official website** to find relevant API call code. In addition, Jina has also made the `jina-reranker-v2-base-multilingual` model accessible on the Hugging Face community for research and evaluation purposes.

RankGPT and RankLLM

Whether it is **Cross-Encoder re-ranking** or **ColBERT re-ranking**, both are re-ranking methods based on classical deep learning models, and the relevant papers were also published prior to the advent of **ChatGPT** in 2022. Entering the era of large language models, **re-ranking technology** has also made new progress.

RankGPT was proposed by Weiwei Sun et al. in the paper *Is ChatGPT Good at Search? Investigating Large Language Models as Re-Ranking Agents*. This method leverages the powerful semantic understanding capabilities of large models (such as **ChatGPT** or **GPT-4**) to finely sort the initially retrieved candidate documents in a zero-shot manner, thereby improving the relevance and accuracy of retrieval results. **RankGPT** generates different permutations of the candidate documents and rearranges the paragraphs efficiently using a **sliding window strategy**. The advantage of this method is that it does not require specialized fine-tuning of the model. Highly efficient re-ranking can be achieved directly using a pre-trained large model.

RankLLM, on the other hand, is a Python toolkit developed by the open-source community (such as **Castorini**) aiming to provide reusable re-ranking tools for **information retrieval research**, with a particular focus on list-style re-ranking tasks. Similar to **RankGPT**, **RankLLM** also utilizes large models to perform re-ranking tasks, but it focuses more on using fine-tuned, open-source models optimized specifically for re-ranking tasks (such as **RankVicuna** and **RankZephyr**) to improve performance.

The following code example demonstrates how to use GPT models for **RankLLM** re-ranking in **LangChain** (refer to `https://github.com/PacktPublishing/RAG-from-First-Principles` for the complete code):

```
from langchain_community.document_loaders import TextLoader
from langchain_community.vectorstores import FAISS
from langchain_huggingface import HuggingFaceEmbeddings
from langchain_text_splitters import RecursiveCharacterTextSplitter
from langchain.retrievers.contextual_compression import
ContextualCompressionRetriever
from langchain_community.document_compressors.rankllm_rerank import
RankLLMRerank
import torch
### Load Documents and Perform Segmentation
documents = TextLoader("data/ShanxiCultureAndTourism/YungangGrottoes.
txt").load()
text_splitter = RecursiveCharacterTextSplitter(chunk_size=500, chunk_
overlap=100)
texts = text_splitter.split_documents(documents)
for idx, text in enumerate(texts):
    text.metadata["id"] = idx
### Generate Embeddings and Create Retriever
embed_model = HuggingFaceEmbeddings(model_name="BAAI/bge-small-zh")
retriever = FAISS.from_documents(texts, embed_model).as_retriever(search_
kwargs={"k": 20})
### Set Up RankLLM Re-Ranker
compressor = RankLLMRerank(top_n=3, model="gpt", gpt_model="gpt-4o-mini")
### Create Contextual Compression Retriever
compression_retriever = ContextualCompressionRetriever(
    base_compressor=compressor,
    base_retriever=retriever
)
### Execute Query and Get Re-Ranked Documents
query = "What are the famous statues in Yungang Grottoes?"
compressed_docs = compression_retriever.invoke(query)
### Output Results
def pretty_print_docs(docs):
    print(
        f"\n{'-' * 100}\n".join(
```

```
            [f"Document {i+1}:\n\n" + d.page_content for i, d in
enumerate(docs)]
        )
    )
```

Expected output:

```
pretty_print_docs(compressed_docs)
Document 1: Yungang Grottoes
The Yungang Grottoes are located on the southern foot of Mount Wuzhou, 17
kilometers west of Datong City, Shanxi Province, northern China......
```

LlamaIndex's LLM Reranker also provides a similar reranking function. The **LLM Reranker** is a **node post-processor** in LlamaIndex and can be used in combination with other retrieval modules.

Both **RankGPT** and **RankLLM** demonstrate the potential of applying large models to **reranking tasks**, but they adopt different approaches. **RankGPT** emphasizes its **zero-shot capability**, meaning it can directly utilize **pre-trained models** to perform **reranking tasks** without any additional training steps. In contrast, **RankLLM** focuses more on adapting to specific needs by **fine-tuning open-source models.**

Time-weighted re-ranking

The **time-weighted vector store retriever** provided by LangChain can be broadly regarded as a **re-ranking mechanism.** It not only considers the **semantic similarity** between documents and queries, but also incorporates **temporal factors** to adjust the document's relevance score. This method mimics the characteristics of **human memory**: information that is accessed frequently remains "fresh," while information that is rarely used is gradually "forgotten."

This algorithm constructs a **decay function** based on the document's last access time. Its basic formula is as follows:

$$score = semantic\_similarity + (1.0 - decay\_rate)^{hours\_passed}$$

Here, **semantic_similarity** is the semantic similarity score between the document and the query. **hours_passed** is the number of hours passed since the document was last accessed, rather than the time since the document was created. Each time the document is accessed, **hours_passed** is reset to 0 to maintain the document's "freshness." **decay_rate** is the decay rate parameter (ranging from 0 to 1), which determines how quickly the score decays over time. A higher value means the document becomes "outdated" more quickly, while a lower value means the document can stay "fresh" for a longer period of time.

For example, if `decay_rate=0.99`, then a document that has not been accessed in 24 hours will have a time score close to `(1-0.99)^24`, which is almost 0. Conversely, if `decay_rate=0.01`, even after a long period of time, the time score will still be close to 1. In this way, we can flexibly adjust the **decay_rate parameter** to control the balance between the system's memory persistence and timeliness.

This retriever is especially suitable for application scenarios where both **relevance** and **timeliness** need to be considered, such as **personalized recommendation systems** or **knowledge management systems**. By appropriately adjusting the **decay_rate** parameter, users can find a suitable balance between the two based on their specific needs.

The following code example demonstrates how to use the **TimeWeightedVectorStore Retriever** in LangChain to implement a retrieval method that combines semantic similarity and time decay rate (refer to `https://github.com/PacktPublishing/RAG-from-First-Principles` for the complete code):

```
from datetime import datetime, timedelta
import faiss
from langchain.retrievers import TimeWeightedVectorStoreRetriever
from langchain_community.docstore import InMemoryDocstore
from langchain_community.vectorstores import FAISS
from langchain_core.documents import Document
from langchain_openai import OpenAIEmbeddings
## Define the Embedding Model
embeddings_model = OpenAIEmbeddings()
## Initialize Vector Store
index = faiss.IndexFlatL2(1536)
vectorstore = FAISS(embeddings_model, index, InMemoryDocstore({}), {})
## Create a TimeWeightedVectorStoreRetriever With a High Decay Rate
retriever = TimeWeightedVectorStoreRetriever(
    vectorstore=vectorstore,
    decay_rate=0.999,
    k=1
)
## Set the Document's Last Accessed Time to Yesterday
yesterday = datetime.now() - timedelta(days=1)
## Add Document
retriever.add_documents(
```

```
    [Document(page_content="hello world", metadata={"last_accessed_at":
yesterday})]
)
## Add a Document Without Specifying Accessed Time; Default to Current
Time as Its Last Accessed Time
retriever.add_documents([Document(page_content="hello foo")])
Since a high decay rate is set, "hello foo" (with its more recent "access"
time) may be returned first
results = retriever.get_relevant_documents("hello world")
## Output Retrieval Results
for doc in results:
    print(f"Document Content: {doc.page_content}")
```

Expected output:

```
Document Content: hello foo
```

The key parameter adjusts the speed at which documents are **"forgotten"** through the decay rate. At a low **decay rate** (close to 0), documents are hardly ever **forgotten** due to the passage of time, which is similar to traditional vector retrieval. At a high decay rate (close to 1), documents lose their weight over time, especially those that have not been accessed for a long time; their weights will drop rapidly, causing query results to be more biased toward recently accessed documents.

To simulate queries in the future or the past, you can use the **mock_now** feature to control the time, allowing you to test retrieval results over different time periods. The following code simulates a query performed on August 8, 2028:

```
from langchain_core.utils import mock_now
import datetime
## Simulate a Future Query
with mock_now(datetime.datetime(2028, 8, 8, 10, 11)):
    print(retriever.get_relevant_documents("hello world"))
[Document(metadata={'last_accessed_at': MockDateTime(2028, 8, 8, 10, 11),
'created_at': datetime.datetime(2025, 4, 12, 14, 42, 33, 978711), 'buffer_
idx': 0}, page_content='hello world')]
```

A similar implementation exists in **LlamaIndex**, called **Recency Filtering**, which addresses the **timeliness** issue in multi-version document retrieval. When documents have different versions, it preferentially returns the **latest version** of the information. This method determines which version is the most recent based on the document's **timestamp** and increases the weight or ranking of these latest pieces of information in the retrieval results.

When the query system encounters multiple document versions containing **time metadata**, the **recency filter** checks the creation/update dates of these documents and sorts or weights them according to their time attributes, prioritizing the content of the most recent documents in the returned results.

The official **LlamaIndex** examples demonstrate two implementations of **recency filters**:

- **FixedRecencyPostprocessor**: Sorts directly based on a fixed timestamp of the document, simply prioritizing the newest document version
- **EmbeddingRecencyPostprocessor**: Combines semantic similarity of the document with temporal information, adding a time factor on top of similarity scoring

The following example presents three different versions (V1, V2, V3) of a certain blog post, with differing descriptions regarding the amount of funding raised:

- **V1 (2020-01-01)**: Mentions raising $50,000
- **V2 (2020-02-03)**: Mentions raising $30,000
- **V3 (2022-04-12)**: Mentions raising $10,000

When a user queries **How much seed funding did the author raise**, the recency filter ensures the system returns the latest version's (V3) information ($10,000) instead of outdated information from older versions.

Difference between LangChain and LlamaIndex recency weighting

Anna: Lewis, I noticed that **TimeWeightedVectorStoreRetriever** in **LangChain** uses access time weighting, while **LlamaIndex**'s **Recency Filtering** uses document creation and modification time weighting.

Lewis: That's a sharp observation. The specific mechanism to choose depends on your needs. These techniques are well-suited for scenarios that require handling frequently updated information, such as **news reporting**, **product specifications**, **financial data**, or any knowledge base content that changes over time, ensuring the latest version is always accessible while maintaining relevance, and reducing confusion caused by outdated data.

Compression

Modern **generative models** can handle significantly longer **context lengths.** If the **knowledge base** is no larger than 200,000 tokens (roughly equivalent to 500 pages of material), you can consider skipping the **retrieval step** and including the entire knowledge base directly in the prompt, without the need for **chunking**.

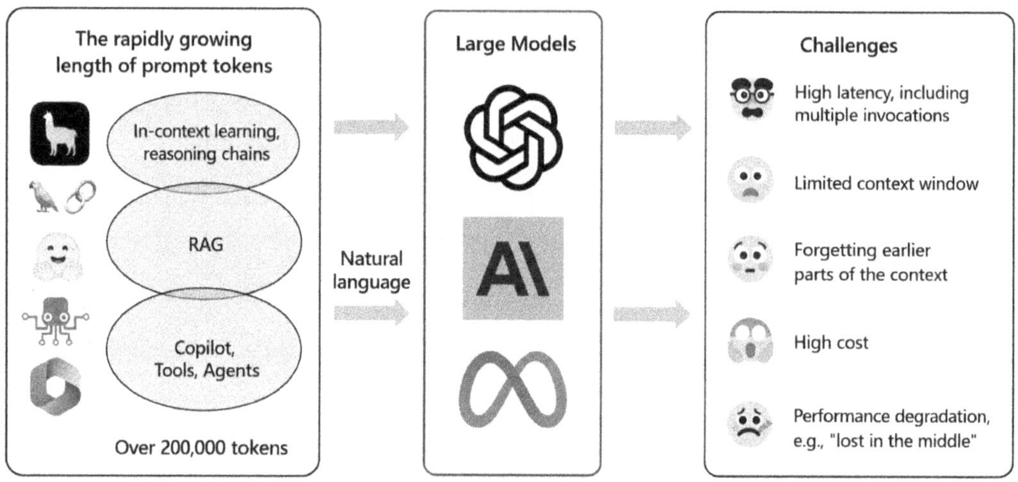

Figure 7.9: Diagram showing natural language model workflow, prompt growth, and challenges with emojis

However, when generative models are faced with overly long contexts, the problem of being **"lost in the middle"** can easily arise. This means it is necessary to effectively **compress** the knowledge base and make it more concise, so that the model can process this information more efficiently.

Contextual compression retrievers

LangChain provides a **Contextual Compression Retriever**, which includes the following two components:

- **Base retriever**: For example, **Faiss**, **ChromaDB**, used to perform standard vector retrieval
- **Document compressor**: After retrieving documents, filters or shortens the content, retaining only the most relevant information

The following code example refactors the example from Section 7.1.4. While using **Cohere re-ranking**, the **Cohere re-ranker** is also passed into LangChain's **ContextualCompressionRetriever** to compress the retrieval results (refer to `https://github.com/PacktPublishing/RAG-from-First-Principles` for the complete code):

```
## Import Required Libraries
from langchain_cohere import CohereRerank
from langchain.retrievers.contextual_compression import
ContextualCompressionRetriever
from langchain_core.documents import Document
from langchain_community.retrievers import BM25Retriever
## Prepare Sample Documents
documents = [
Document(
page_content="Mount Wutai is one of the four great Buddhist mountains in
China and is famous as the bodhimanda of Manjusri.",
metadata={"source": "Shanxi Travel Guide"}
),
Document(
page_content="The Yungang Grottoes are one of China's three major
grottoes, renowned for exquisite Buddhist sculptures.",
metadata={"source": "Shanxi Travel Guide"}
),
Document(
page_content="Pingyao Ancient City is one of the best-preserved ancient
county towns in China and is listed as a World Cultural Heritage site.",
metadata={"source": "Shanxi Travel Guide"}
)
]
## Create BM25 Retriever
retriever = BM25Retriever.from_documents(documents)
retriever.k = 3  # Set to return the top 3 results
## Set Up Cohere Reranker
compressor = CohereRerank(model="verank-multilingual-v2.0")
## Create ContextualCompressionRetriever
compression_retriever = ContextualCompressionRetriever(
base_compressor=compressor,
base_retriever=retriever
```

```
)
## Execute Query, Re-Rank, and Compress
query = "What are some famous tourist attractions in Shanxi?"
compressed_docs = compression_retriever.invoke(query)
### Output the Compressed Result
print("Re-ranked and compressed results:")
for i, doc in enumerate(compressed_docs, 1):
    print(f"{i}. {doc.page_content}")
```

Expected output:

```
Re-ranked and compressed results:
Pingyao Ancient City is one of the best-preserved ancient county-level
cities in China and is listed as a World Cultural Heritage site.
Mount Wutai is one of China's four great Buddhist mountains, famous as the
bodhimanda of Manjushri Bodhisattva.
Yungang Grottoes are one of the three major grottoes in China, renowned
for their exquisite Buddhist sculptures.
```

ContextualCompressionRetriever removes irrelevant or redundant information from the original retrieval results. For example, in a course section, only part of the content may be relevant to the query; in this case, the **compressor** retains the relevant parts. In addition, it reorders the documents based on their relevance to the query.

LangChain provides multiple **compression strategies** for the **Contextual Compression Retriever**, which can be used individually or in sequence:

- **LLMChainExtractor** (Content extraction based on large models): Uses a large language model to extract the most relevant parts from documents, removing unrelated content. Suitable for scenarios that require extracting key information from long documents.
- **LLMChainFilter** (Document filtering based on large models): Only retains documents that are highly relevant to the query, directly discarding unrelated documents instead of modifying the content. Suitable for scenarios where you need to reduce the number of documents processed by the LLM.
- **LLMListwiseRerank** (Document reranking based on large models): Re-ranks all retrieved documents and returns only the top N most relevant documents. Suitable for fine-grained selection when there are many search results.

- **EmbeddingsFilter** (Similarity filtering based on embeddings): Computes the embedding similarity between the query and documents, discarding documents below a set threshold to reduce irrelevant information. Suitable for rapid filtering without invoking a large language model.

Multiple compressors can be used in combination to process documents sequentially. For example, first use the **Embeddings-Filter** to remove irrelevant documents, then use the **LLMChainExtractor** to extract the most relevant content. In this way, documents can be efficiently cleaned, and only the most important parts are passed to the large model.

Compressing prompts with LLMLingua

LLMLingua is a technology developed by Microsoft, focused on mitigating the "midway forgetting" problem in large models and enhancing their ability to handle **long-context information**. By compressing prompts and **key-value cache (KV-Cache)**, it accelerates the reasoning process of large models, achieving up to a 20x compression rate while ensuring minimal performance loss.

> **Tips from Lewis**
>
> Key-value caching is a core optimization mechanism in the inference process of large language models. This concept originates from the attention mechanism in the Transformer architecture.
>
> When a model generates text, each token must perform attention calculations with all previously generated tokens. Without key-value caching, every time the model generates a new token, it would need to recompute the key and value vectors for all previous tokens, resulting in a large amount of redundant computation.

The functions of the **key-value cache** are as follows:

- **Caching history**: Key and value vectors of tokens that have already been computed are stored in memory
- **Incremental computation**: When generating a new token, only the key and value vectors for the new token need to be computed, which are then combined with the cached historical key and value vectors
- **Performance improvement**: Significantly reduces the need for redundant computation and can boost inference speed several times over
- **Memory trade-off**: Although extra memory is needed to store the key-value cache, in practice this trade-off is usually worthwhile

For example, suppose the model is generating the sentence "I like to eat apples." When generating the character 'ap', the model has already computed the key and value vectors for 'I', 'like', 'to', and 'eat'. With the **key-value cache**, when generating the character 'ple', there is no need to recompute the key and value vectors for the preceding characters. Instead, the cached computation results can be directly used.

The original *LLMLingua* paper proposed using compact and well-trained small models (such as **GPT2-small, LLaMA-7B**) to identify and remove unnecessary tokens from prompts, thereby reducing computational burden. This method not only avoids the need for additional training on large models but also preserves the integrity and accuracy of the original prompt information. The paper points out that **LLMLingua**, with its fast compression technology, lowers costs and boosts efficiency, achieving a 21.4% **RAG performance improvement** with only a quarter of the token count.

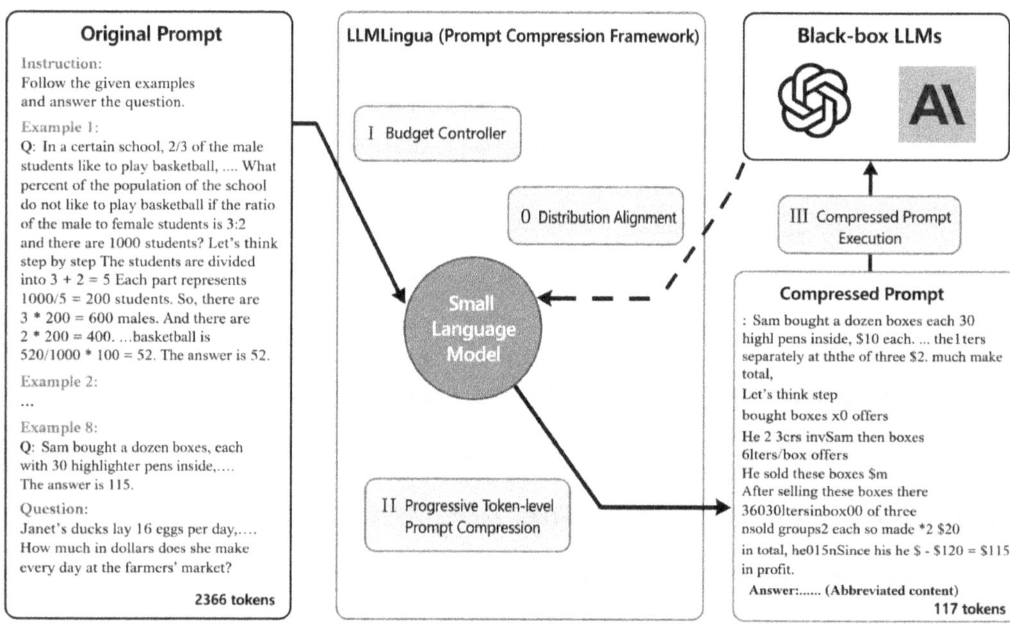

Figure 7.10: A prompt compression framework reducing lengthy prompts to concise ones for AI

Subsequently, LLMLingua launched LongLLMLingua and LLMLingua-2.

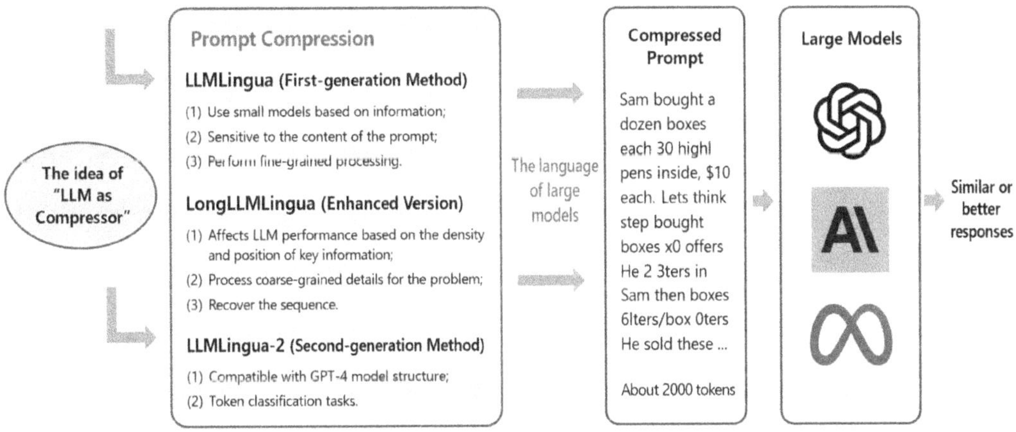

Figure 7.11: A flowchart explains compressing prompts for large language models using LLMLingua methods

LLMLingua-2 performs **data distillation training** using the **GPT-4** model and adopts a **BERT-like encoder** for **token classification**, excelling in **task-agnostic compression.** Especially when handling out-of-domain data, the performance of **LLMLingua-2** is 3 to 6 times higher than that of **LLMLingua.**

How to use LLMLingua to compress prompts

The following code example demonstrates how to use **LLMLingua** to compress prompts. In this example, the original prompt is compressed to a specified number of tokens while retaining key information.

First, install **LLMLingua:**

```
pip install llmlingua
```

Next, use the following code to compress the prompt:

```
from llmlingua import PromptCompressor
llm_lingua = PromptCompressor()
compressed_prompt = llm_lingua.compress_prompt(
context="Yungang Grottoes are located at the southern foot of Wuzhou
Mountain, 17 kilometers west of Datong City, Shanxi Province, northern
China...",
instruction="Compress and retain main content",
```

```
question="",
target_token=100  # Set the target number of tokens
)
print(compressed_prompt['compressed_prompt'])
```

You can also compress **JSON data** and control the **compression rate** for each JSON key-value pair:

```
json_data = {
"id": 1,
"name": "Wukong",
"biography": "In the beginning of the cosmos, before heaven and earth were
separated..."
}
json_config = {
"id": {"rate": 1, "compress": False, "pair_remove": False, "value_type":
"number"},
"name": {"rate": 0.7, "compress": False, "pair_remove": False, "value_
type": "string"},
"biography": {"rate": 0.3, "compress": True, "pair_remove": False, "value_
type": "string"}
}
## Example Compressing a JSON Prompt Using LLMLingua
import llm_lingua
json_data = {
    "prompt": "Write a summary of the following article...",
    "metadata": {
        "author": "John Doe",
        "date": "2023-10-01"
    }
}
json_config = {
    "keep_keys": ["prompt"],
    "compression_level": 2
}
compressed_json = llm_lingua.compress_json(json_data, json_config)
print(compressed_json['compressed_prompt'])
```

LLMLingua is currently integrated into **LangChain** and **LlamaIndex**. Learners can access its functionality by importing the relevant libraries, or find more information by visiting the **LLM-Lingua** project page on GitHub.

RECOMP method

RECOMP is a method that generates concise text summaries by compressing retrieved documents. This method introduces an **intermediate step** between retrieval and generation, specifically designed to compress key information from retrieved documents via text summarization and then append it to the model input.

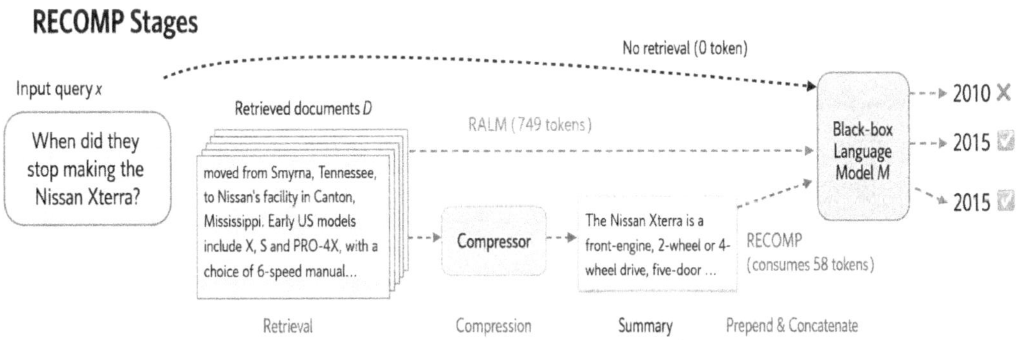

Figure 7.12: A flowchart shows how a query about when the Nissan Xterra stopped production is processed

In RECOMP, two types of **compressors** are used to achieve this goal:

- **Extractive compressor**: This type of compressor selects the most relevant sentences from the retrieved documents. To optimize sentence selection, it employs **contrastive learning** to ensure that the selected sentences maximize task performance.
- **Abstractive compressor**: Unlike the extractive compressor, the abstractive compressor generates summaries by synthesizing information from multiple documents. It utilizes a **large language model** to generate training data and trains a smaller compressor model through **knowledge distillation**.

Additionally, if the retrieved documents do not help with the current task, the compressor will intelligently return an empty string, thereby avoiding unnecessary information interference and improving the overall efficiency of the generation model.

Sentence embedding optimizer

Next, we introduce another compression technique provided by **LlamaIndex** – the **Sentence Embedding Optimizer**. This method focuses on calculating the relevance of each sentence to the query through **sentence embeddings**, thereby reducing the number of irrelevant sentences and optimizing the input content.

As a node post-processing tool, the main function of the **Sentence Embedding Optimizer** is to optimize the input content during the text retrieval process. It uses **embedding-based similarity analysis methods** to remove unrelated sentences from the text according to the user's query, thus shortening the length of the input text and improving processing efficiency and the relevance of the results. This optimization and compression are performed at the **token embedding level**, ensuring that the information remains concise and accurate.

The **Sentence Embedding Optimizer** supports the following two filtering methods:

- **Percentile cutoff**: This method retains sentences with similarity scores above a certain percentile
- **Threshold cutoff**: This method retains sentences whose similarity scores are above a certain fixed value

The following code example demonstrates how to use the **Sentence Embedding Optimizer** to optimize the query processing procedure (refer to `https://github.com/PacktPublishing/RAG-from-First-Principles` for the complete code):

```
from llama_index.core import VectorStoreIndex, SimpleDirectoryReader
from llama_index.core.postprocessor import SentenceEmbeddingOptimizer
documents = SimpleDirectoryReader("data/山西文旅").load_data()
index = VectorStoreIndex.from_documents(documents)
### Query Without Optimization
print("Without optimization:")
query_engine = index.as_query_engine()
response = query_engine.query("What are the main tourist attractions in
Shanxi Province?")
print(f"Answer: {response}")
### Query with Optimization (Percentile Cutoff)
print("\nWith optimization (percentile_cutoff=0.5):")
query_engine = index.as_query_engine(node_
postprocessors=[SentenceEmbeddingOptimizer(percentile_cutoff=0.5)])
response = query_engine.query("What are the main tourist attractions in
Shanxi Province?")
print(f"Answer: {response}")
### Query with Optimization (Threshold Cutoff)
print("\nWith optimization (threshold_cutoff=0.7):")
query_engine = index.as_query_engine(node_
postprocessors=[SentenceEmbeddingOptimizer(threshold_cutoff=0.7)])
```

```
response = query_engine.query("What are the main tourist attractions in
Shanxi Province?")
print(f"Answer: {response}")
```

Expected output:

```
Without Optimization:
Answer: The **Yungang Grottoes** are a major tourist attraction in Shanxi
Province, located at the southern foot of **Wuzhou Mountain** in the
western suburbs of Datong City. It is one of the largest ancient grotto
clusters in China. In addition, Shanxi Province also has other famous
attractions such as **Wuzhou Mountain**, which is a scenic spot in the
western mountains of Datong City.
With Optimization (percentile_cutoff=0.5):
Answer: The **Yungang Grottoes** are one of the major tourist attractions
in Shanxi Province.
With Optimization (threshold_cutoff=0.7):
Answer: The main tourist attractions in Shanxi Province include the
**Yungang Grottoes**, **Wuzhou Mountain**, and others.
```

In the above example, the **percentile truncation** setting retains sentences in the top 50% of similarity, while the **threshold truncation** is set to only keep sentences with similarity greater than 0.7.

Remembering long context through prompt caching

Alex: By the way, Lewis, after listening to your introduction of this series of **compression technologies**, I was reminded of the **Prompt Caching** concept I came across a few days ago. This is a **prompt caching** method proposed by Anthropic, aimed at reducing the processing time and cost of repetitive or similar tasks. Can this also be considered a form of **compression**?

Lewis: That's right. **Prompt Caching** can indeed be seen as an application of **context compression**. It focuses on optimizing **context management** in repetitive tasks, significantly improving system efficiency and reducing computational costs by minimizing redundant processing.

Developing **large model applications** often involves scenarios with substantial background information or requiring multiple rounds of interaction, such as long conversations or document analysis. **Prompt Caching** can intelligently cache reusable context prefixes, thus avoiding the need to reprocess large chunks of content (such as lengthy documents or background information) for every call.

In practical applications, when retrieved content or contextual information is irrelevant to the current task, **Prompt Caching** can output an empty cache.

Compared to **RAG technology**, **Prompt Caching** is more focused on **performance optimization**. It is not a direct component for retrieving or generating content, but rather provides an intelligent caching mechanism to enhance the performance and efficiency of generative models. In the post-retrieval processing stage of **RAG**, when the same context content needs to be called multiple times, the caching mechanism of **Prompt Caching** can avoid reloading and reprocessing the same background information, thereby significantly reducing the latency and cost of API calls. This optimization is especially effective in scenarios where large documents or complex user background information are frequently processed.

Correction

Correction technology introduces self-reflection and self-scoring mechanisms for retrieved documents and generated answers in **RAG systems**, allowing it to be applied both in the post-retrieval processing phase and as part of the generation process. A typical implementation of this technique is **Corrective Retrieval Augmented Generation (CRAG)**. The implementation process of CRAG is shown below.

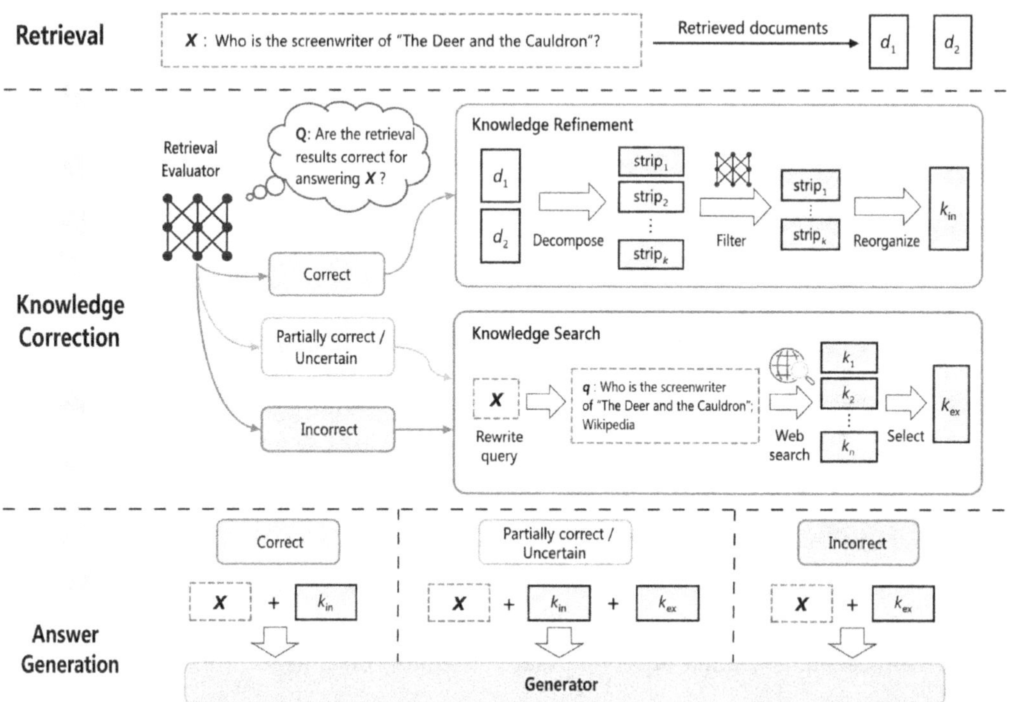

Figure 7.13: A flowchart shows a search and knowledge correction process for a question-answer system

The core concept of the **CRAG system** lies in repeatedly evaluating and re-retrieving to ensure that the information on which the generated answers are based is highly relevant. The system consists of two main components: **correction of knowledge after retrieval** and **correction during generation**.

The **retrieval assessor** is responsible for the correction of post-retrieval knowledge. If at least one document's relevance exceeds a set threshold, the system proceeds to content generation. Before generation, a **knowledge refinement process** is performed that splits documents into **knowledge fragments**, scores each fragment, and filters out irrelevant parts. If all documents' relevance is below the threshold, or if the assessor cannot determine relevance, the system seeks additional data sources to supplement the retrieval results, such as by finding more relevant documents through **web search**.

After the **generator** provides an initial answer, additional modules or steps are used to perform a second validation and optimization of the answer. For example, after generating an answer, it can be compared with the retrieved information to ensure consistency and correct errors. Furthermore, steps such as **fact-checking**, **grammatical correction**, and **semantic consistency verification** can be employed to further enhance the quality of the generated answers.

Next, we will use **LangGraph** to implement some of the ideas of CRAG.

The following code example can automatically determine the quality of retrieved results. If any irrelevant documents are found, the system will supplement the retrieval information through a **web search** (using the **Tavily Search** tool) and optimize the web search queries using **query rewriting**.

First, install the necessary packages and set the `TAVILY_API_KEY` for web search.

Subsequently, create indexes for 3 blog articles and store these fragments in a **Chroma** vector database (refer to `https://github.com/PacktPublishing/RAG-from-First-Principles` for the complete code):

```
from langchain.text_splitter import RecursiveCharacterTextSplitter
from langchain_community.document_loaders import WebBaseLoader
from langchain_community.vectorstores import Chroma
from langchain_huggingface import HuggingFaceEmbeddings
urls = [
"https://lilianweng.github.io/posts/2023-06-23-agent/",
"https://lilianweng.github.io/posts/2023-03-15-prompt-engineering/",
"https://lilianweng.github.io/posts/2023-10-25-adv-attack-llm/",
```

```
]
docs = [WebBaseLoader(url).load() for url in urls]
docs_list = [item for sublist in docs for item in sublist]
text_splitter = RecursiveCharacterTextSplitter.from_tiktoken_encoder(
chunk_size=250, chunk_overlap=0
)
doc_splits = text_splitter.split_documents(docs_list)
## Add to Vector Database
vectorstore = Chroma.from_documents(
    documents=doc_splits,
    collection_name="rag-chroma",
    embedding=HuggingFaceEmbeddings(model_name="BAAI/bge-small-en"),
)
retriever = vectorstore.as_retriever()
```

Next, set up a **retrieval evaluator** to assess the relevance of the retrieved documents to the user's question (refer to `https://github.com/PacktPublishing/RAG-from-First-Principles` for the complete code):

```
from langchain_core.prompts import ChatPromptTemplate
from langchain_core.pydantic_v1 import BaseModel, Field
from langchain_deepseek import ChatDeepSeek
### Data Model
class GradeDocuments(BaseModel):
    """Binary scoring for the relevance of retrieved documents"""
    binary_score: str = Field(
        description="If the document is relevant to the question, it is
'yes'; if not, it is 'no'"
    )
### Language Model That Supports Tool Calls
llm = ChatDeepSeek(model="deepseek-chat")
structured_llm_grader = llm.with_structured_output(GradeDocuments)
### Prompt Template
system = """You are a grader who evaluates the relevance between the
retrieved document and the user's question. \n
If the document contains keywords or semantics related to the question,
rate it as relevant. \n
Give a binary score of 'yes' or 'no' to indicate whether the document is
relevant to the question."""
```

```
grade_prompt = ChatPromptTemplate.from_messages(
    [
        ("system", system),
        ("human", "Retrieved document:\n\n {document} \n\n User question:
{question}"),
    ]
)
retrieval_grader = grade_prompt | structured_llm_grader
question = "agent memory"
docs = retriever.get_relevant_documents(question)
doc_txt = docs[1].page_content
print(retrieval_grader.invoke({"question": question, "document": doc_
txt}))
```

Next, create a **generation model** used to generate answers based on the retrieved documents and the user's question. Here, a predefined **RAG prompt template** is used:

```
from langchain import hub
from langchain_core.output_parsers import StrOutputParser
## Prompt Template
prompt = hub.pull("rlm/rag-prompt")
## Language Model
llm = ChatDeepSeek(model="deepseek-chat")
## Post-Processing
def format_docs(docs):
    return "\n\n".join(doc.page_content for doc in docs)
## Chain Call
rag_chain = prompt | llm | StrOutputParser()
## Run
generation = rag_chain.invoke({"context": docs, "question": question})
print(generation)
```

Then, create a **question rewriter** to convert the user's original question into a form more suitable for web search, so as to improve the effectiveness of web searching (refer to `https://github.com/PacktPublishing/RAG-from-First-Principles` for the complete code):

```
## Language Model
llm = ChatDeepSeek(model="deepseek-chat")
## Prompt Template
```

```
system = """You are a question rewriter, converting the input question
into a version more suitable for web search. \n
Analyze the input and try to reason out the potential semantic intent/
meaning."""
re_write_prompt = ChatPromptTemplate.from_messages(
    [
        ("system", system),
        (
            "human",
            "This is the initial question:\n\n {question} \n Please
restate it as an improved question.",
        ),
    ]
)
question_rewriter = re_write_prompt | llm | StrOutputParser()
question_rewriter.invoke({"question": question})
```

Next, set up the **Tavily search API** web search tool, which will return the top 3 most relevant search results:

```
from langchain_community.tools.tavily_search import TavilySearchResults
web_search_tool = TavilySearchResults(k=3)
```

Next, we use the *LangGraph* library to build a **CRAG-based graph structure**. Each node in the graph represents an operation, and edges represent transitions between operations. This self-correcting architecture is a typical implementation of the **Agentic pattern**. *LangGraph* is very suitable for designing such workflows.

```
from typing import List
from typing_extensions import TypedDict
class GraphState(TypedDict):
    """
    Represents the state of the graph
    Attributes:
    - question: The user's question
    - generation: The answer generated by the language model
    - web_search: Whether web search is needed to supplement information
```

```
    - documents: List of documents
    """
    question: str
    generation: str
    web_search: str
    documents: List[str]
from langchain.schema import Document
def retrieve(state):
    """
    Retrieve documents relevant to the question
    Parameters:
        state (dict): Current graph state
    Returns:
        state (dict): Updated graph state
        documents: Added retrieved relevant documents
    """
    print("---Retrieving---")
    question = state["question"]
    ## Retrieval
    documents = retriever.get_relevant_documents(question)
    return {"documents": documents, "question": question}
def generate(state):
    """
    Generate an answer
    Parameters:
        state (dict): Current graph state
    Returns:
        state (dict): Updated graph state
        generation: Contains content generated by the language model
    """
    print("---Generating---")
    question = state["question"]
    documents = state["documents"]
    ## RAG generation
    generation = rag_chain.invoke({"context": documents, "question":
question})
    return {"documents": documents, "question": question, "generation":
generation}
```

```
def grade_documents(state):
    """
    Determine whether the retrieved documents are relevant to the question
    Parameters:
    """
## Function to Check Document Relevance to the Question
def check_document_relevance(state):
    """
    Parameters:
    state (dict): current graph state
    Return:
    state (dict): updates the 'documents' key, retaining only the filtered
relevant documents
    """
    print("---Checking document relevance to the question---")
    question = state["question"]
    documents = state["documents"]
    # Score each document
    filtered_docs = []
    web_search = "No"
    has_relevant_docs = False
    for d in documents:
        score = retrieval_grader.invoke({
            "question": question, "document": d.page_content
        })
        grade = score.binary_score
        if grade == "yes":
            print("---Score: Document is relevant---")
            filtered_docs.append(d)
            has_relevant_docs = True
        else:
            print("---Score: Document is not relevant---")
    if not has_relevant_docs:
        web_search = "Yes"
    return {"documents": filtered_docs, "question": question, "web_
search": web_search}
## Function to Transform Query
```

```
def transform_query(state):
    """
    Rewrite the question based on the current state to improve search
results
    Parameters:
    state (dict): current graph state
    Return:
    state (dict): updated graph state containing the rewritten question
    """
    print("---Transforming query---")
    question = state["question"]
    documents = state["documents"]
    # Rewrite question
    better_question = question_rewriter.invoke({"question": question})
    return {"documents": documents, "question": better_question}
## Function for Web Search
def web_search(state):
    """
    Use web search tool to obtain additional information
    Parameters:
    state (dict): contains current state
        - question: the question
    """
    # Web search implementation would go here
    pass
- documents: List of **documents**
Returns:
state (dict): Update the **documents** key by appending network search
results
"""
print("---Network Search---")
question = state["question"]
documents = state["documents"]
### Network Search
search_results = web_search_tool.invoke(question)
### Convert the List of Search Results to a String
search_results_str = "\n".join([str(result) for result in search_results])
```

```
web_results = Document(page_content=search_results_str)
documents.append(web_results)
return {"documents": documents, "question": question}
### Edge Case Handling
def decide_to_generate(state):
"""
Decide the next step based on the current state: whether to generate an
answer or rewrite the question
Parameters:
state (dict): current **graph state**
Returns:
str: name of the next operation to invoke
"""
print("---Evaluate Scored Documents---")
state["question"]
web_search = state["web_search"]
state["documents"]
if web_search == "Yes":
### All Documents Have Been Filtered by check_relevance We Will Generate a
New Query
print(
"---Decision: All documents are irrelevant to the question, transforming
query---"
)
return "transform_query"
else:
### Since We Have Relevant Documents We Can Generate the Answer
print("---Decision: Generate---")
return "generate"
```

Next, define the **states** of the graph and the functions of each **node**. Each **function** represents a node in the graph and is responsible for performing a specific task, such as retrieving documents, grading documents, generating answers, and more (refer to `https://github.com/PacktPublishing/RAG-from-First-Principles` for the complete code):

```
from langgraph.graph import END, StateGraph, START
## Initialize the Workflow State Graph
workflow = StateGraph(GraphState)
```

```
## Define Nodes
workflow.add_node("retrieve", retrieve) # Retrieve documents
workflow.add_node("grade_documents", grade_documents) # Grade documents
workflow.add_node("generate", generate) # Generate answer
workflow.add_node("transform_query", transform_query) # Transform query
workflow.add_node("web_search_node", web_search) # Web search
## Build Graph Edges (Connections)
workflow.add_edge(START, "retrieve") # From start to retrieve documents
workflow.add_edge("retrieve", "grade_documents") # From retrieve
documents to grade documents
workflow.add_conditional_edges(
    "grade_documents",
    decide_to_generate,
    {
        "transform_query": "transform_query",
        "generate": "generate",
    },
)
workflow.add_edge("transform_query", "web_search_node") # From transform
query to web search
workflow.add_edge("web_search_node", "generate") # From web search to
generate answer
workflow.add_edge("generate", END) # From generate answer to end
## Compile the Entire Workflow
app = workflow.compile()
```

Finally, use the **CRAG system** to solve a specific problem. It will execute each node in the graph step by step and output the name of each node, as well as the final generated answer (refer to `https://github.com/PacktPublishing/RAG-from-First-Principles` for the complete code):

```
from pprint import pprint
## Set Input Question
inputs = {"question": "What are the types of agent memory?"}
## Run the Program and Process the Output
for output in app.stream(inputs):
    for key, value in output.items():
        # Print the current node name
        pprint(f"Node '{key}':")
```

```
    # Optional: output complete state at each node
    # pprint(value["keys"], indent=2, width=80, depth=None)
    pprint("\n---\n")
    # Output the final generated answer
    pprint(value["generation"])
```

Expected output:

```
---Retrieval---
"Node 'retrieve':"
---Check document relevance to the question---
---Score: Document Relevant---
---Score: Document Relevant---
---Score: Document Not Relevant---
---Evaluate scored documents---
---Decision: Generate---
"Node 'grade_documents':"
---Generate---
"Node 'generate':"
('The different categories of memory in agents are short-term memory and
long-term memory. Short-term memory is utilized for in-context learning,
while long-term memory allows agents to retain and recall information
over extended periods. These memory components play a crucial role in the
functioning of AI agents.')
```

Throughout the program flow, the **CRAG system** first retrieves documents related to the question and then assesses the relevance of these documents. In the example above, based on the evaluation results, the system decides to directly generate the answer.

If the question is completely unrelated to the content within the **knowledge base**, the process will move to **query transformation** (optimizing the question phrasing) and **web search** stages, only generating the final answer after obtaining relevant information:

```
inputs = {"question": "Why does Shanxi Province have abundant tourism
resources?"}
---Retrieval---
"Node 'retrieve':"
---Check document relevance with the question---
---Score: Document not relevant---
---Score: Document not relevant---
```

```
---Evaluate scored documents---
---Decision: All documents are not relevant to the question, transform
query---
"Node 'grade_documents':"
---Transform query---
"Node 'transform_query':"
---Web search---
"Node 'web_search_node':"
---Generation---
"Node 'generate':"
'The factors making Shanxi Province a region rich in tourism resources
include thousands of years of historical and cultural accumulation and
heritage, unique folk customs, as well as distinctive topography. Shanxi
has 390 A-level tourist attractions, including well-known sites such
as Mount Wutai, Yungang Grottoes, Taihang Grand Canyon, and Pingyao.
Government regulations and the support of related policies are also
important factors in the development of Shanxi's tourism industry.'
```

In the process above, if the **knowledge base** already contains enough information to answer the question, the system will proactively end the retrieval process. For questions about Shanxi province's culture and tourism that are entirely unrelated to **AI technology**, when the system detects that the initial set of retrieved documents lacks sufficient relevant information, it will automatically execute a **web search**. This mechanism demonstrates how the **CRAG system** flexibly adjusts its retrieval and generation strategies according to different types of questions to meet various needs.

CRAG represents an important evolutionary direction for **RAG systems**, namely leveraging the intelligence of large models to improve the answer quality of RAG systems. However, in practical applications, this approach may lead to increased system complexity and longer response times. Therefore, while ensuring answer quality, system efficiency also needs to be considered.

Summary

Retrieval post-processing technologies play a critical role in **RAG system architecture**, sitting between the retrieval and generation stages. Their purpose is to optimize the accuracy, relevance, and efficiency of retrieval results.

Re-ranking techniques employ various algorithms to reorder initial retrieval results in order to improve the ranking of relevant documents. For example, **RRF** is suitable for fusing results from multiple different rankers, showing remarkable performance especially when different retrieval strategies are used. It balances the results from each ranker, avoids the influence of a single ranker, and is simple and efficient. **Cross-Encoder** concatenates the query and document and inputs them into a pre-trained model (such as **BERT**), using full interaction to directly output relevance scores. **ColBERT** achieves token-level fine-grained matching via late interaction, balancing efficiency and accuracy. **Cohere/Jina** directly leverages commercial APIs (such as **Cohere re-ranking, Jina Re-ranking**), using their pre-trained large models for black-box re-ranking. **RankGPT/RankLLM** utilizes large models (like **GPT-4, Llama 3**) for instruction understanding, directly generating re-ranking results through zero-shot or few-shot prompting. In addition, by introducing temporal weighting mechanisms, the time relevance of results can be ensured, which is suitable for scenarios with high real-time requirements.

In the current era dominated by large models, manually deploying **Cross-Encoder** or **ColBERT** has become less common. For scenarios requiring simple and effective fusion of ranking results, **RRF** is a good choice. If semantic understanding and ranking of documents and queries are required and data privacy is not a major concern, for enterprises already equipped with search systems such as **Elasticsearch** and hoping to quickly enhance their semantic capabilities, especially those lacking in-house NLP engineer teams but willing to adopt an on-demand payment model, choosing **Cohere re-ranking** is more suitable. However, if business rules are special (such as medical search requiring integration with professional term libraries), the internal technical team is capable of model tuning, and there are strict data privacy requirements with reluctance to use third-party APIs, deploying open-source re-ranking models is more appropriate.

Compression techniques aim to remove redundant information while preserving the key content of retrieval results, but excessive compression may cause information loss and affect the completeness and accuracy of generation results.

Context compression technologies (such as **ContextualCompressionRetriever**, **LLMLingua**, etc.) can extract key information and reduce redundancy. **Model optimization** (such as **RECOMP**, **Sentence Embedding Optimizer**) improves efficiency through embedding optimization or enhanced retrieval techniques. The caching mechanism of **Prompt Caching** can address the issue of processing long contexts, balancing performance gains with resource consumption.

Correction techniques can fix errors that may occur during the retrieval and generation stages, ensuring that output content is more consistent with facts or specific standards, thereby enhancing the reliability of **RAG systems**. However, the correction process often increases system complexity and computational resource consumption, especially when deep semantic analysis is required.

After retrieval post-processing, the quality of information passed to the generator is improved, resulting in more refined and accurate information.

Get this book's PDF version and more

Scan the QR code (or go to `packtpub.com/unlock`). Search for this book by name, confirm the edition, and then follow the steps on the page.

UNLOCK NOW

Note: Keep your invoice handy. Purchases made directly from Packt don't require an invoice.

8

Response Generation

Alex: In my opinion, among the entire **RAG process**, the **generation step** is the one we need to worry about the least. Although it's the facade of the RAG system, it's also the part we have the least control over. It's the final content delivered to the learner. Since current **large models** are extremely capable, the generation tasks are mainly handled by these large models.

Lewis: That makes sense. However, in **RAG systems**, generation is not just a simple *output*; it's more of a *strategic expression*. Large models can generate content tailored specifically for each learner based on their individual characteristics.

Anna: Exactly! The process of generating content can be full of creativity and flexibility. From my practical experience, carefully designing prompts is crucial for improving output quality, as this can guide the large model to generate more diverse and coherent content.

Lewis: In addition to prompt design, another key aspect of the generation phase is the choice of generation model. You can choose to call an API or deploy a local model; the quality of answers provided by different models may vary significantly. Take DeepSeek as an example: it not only provides an API call method, but also offers an open-source version for local deployment. DeepSeek has tailored specialized chat models (V3) and reasoning models (R1) for different application scenarios. The chat model is more suitable for general conversation, while the reasoning model meets the needs of more complex and professional academic discussions.

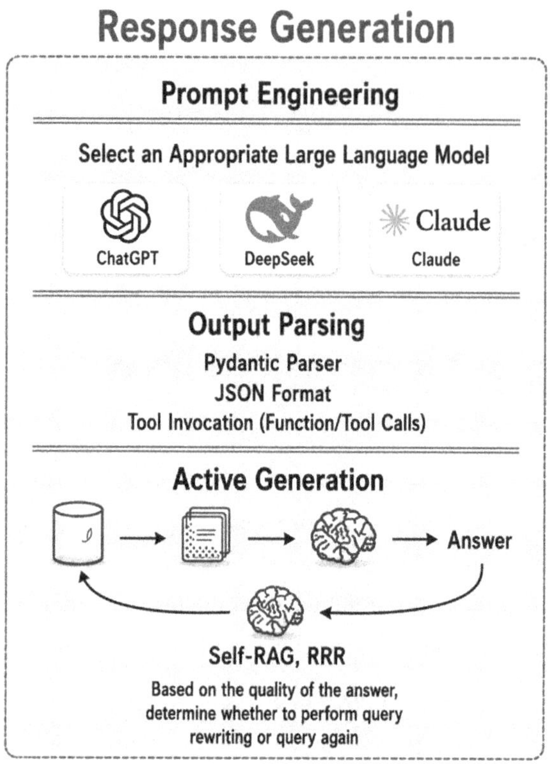

Figure 8.1: AI response generation steps

Moreover, when the actual answer is not found in the knowledge base, RAG systems tend to provide an answer that appears reasonable but is actually incorrect, rather than directly admitting they cannot answer. Similar issues also include a lack of valid content in the generated responses, and so forth. These problems can be alleviated by employing proactive optimization strategies such as **Self-RAG** and **RRR** during the generation process.

Improving LLM output quality by refining prompts

When the information in the knowledge base is insufficient and the system may provide incorrect answers, refining prompts can help improve the accuracy of generated answers. A common example is telling the model `If you are not sure of the answer, please state that you do not know`. This approach encourages the model to recognize its own limitations and express uncertainty more transparently.

Next, we will explore how to use **prompt engineering** to improve LLM output from three perspectives.

Guiding generation results with templates and examples

First, let's discuss how to guide the LLM to generate our desired result using templates and examples.

Using predefined templates can guide the LLM to produce output in a specific format. The model will generate coherent content conforming to the template description based on known information, ensuring consistency in the output.

Here is a concrete example on using predefined template:

```
from langchain import PromptTemplate
template = """
As an experienced game planner, you are skilled at constructing character
analyses based on script content.
[Background Information]
{context}
[Analysis Task]
Please write a character analysis report based on the above material in
the following format:
---
Character Name: <Fill in the character's Chinese name>
Background Story: Describe their origin, personality, key plot points, and
relationships and conflicts with other characters.
Skill Characteristics: Main abilities or skills (such as magic, weapons,
special abilities, etc.).
Combat Strategy: Recommended tactical playstyle (how players should
respond); Weakness analysis (how and under what conditions the character
is restrained).
---
Note: The content must be closely related to the material, logically
clear, and professionally worded, suitable for planning reviews or
producer briefings.
"""
prompt = PromptTemplate(input_variables=["context"], template=template)
```

Providing **examples** in prompts (such as few-shot examples) enables the LLM to imitate the format and style of the example, guiding the model to generate the expected output.

For example, in a development scenario with **RAG knowledge bases**, we may want the LLM to analyze automated test logs to help R&D personnel and test engineers identify code segments potentially related to failed test cases and provide preliminary fix suggestions, such as the following:

```
from langchain.prompts import PromptTemplate
template = """
You are responsible for analyzing the reasons for program failures from
test logs, and locating the relevant code segments.
[Example 1]
Case ID: TC_001
Execution Log Summary: Input A=5, B=0; called function **divide(a, b)**;
returned error: **ZeroDivisionError**
Analysis Conclusion:
- Root Cause: The divide function does not handle division by zero
exception
- Related Code: `math_utils.c` line 24
- Fix Suggestion: Add exception detection logic for zero divisors
[Example 2]
Case ID: TC_002
Execution Log Summary: Input user ID is empty, called function
**login(user_id)**; program returned abnormal status code **500**
Analysis Conclusion:
- Root Cause: The login API does not perform parameter validation for
empty user IDs
- Related Code: `auth.c` line 12
- Fix Suggestion: Add a non-empty check at the function entry.
[Current Task]
Please refer to the above format and analyze the following test case:
Case ID: {case_id}
Execution Log Summary:
{log}
Please output a structured analysis including root cause, related code,
and suggestions.
"""
prompt = PromptTemplate(input_variables=["case_id", "log"],
template=template)
```

Enhancing the diversity and comprehensiveness of generation

To enhance the *diversity* of large model generation, you can first generate multiple candidate answers, then compare them with retrieval results and select the optimal one; you can also encourage the large model to consider different viewpoints or possibilities in the prompt in order to generate a more comprehensive answer.

Here's a concrete example:

```
## Define Retrieved Document Content
def get_code_snippet() -> str:
    """
    Get the code snippet to be analyzed.
    Returns:
        str: String containing the code snippet
    """
    return """
def handle_request(request):
    # Check if the token is included in the request headers
    if 'token' not in request.headers:
        return {'status': 401, 'message': 'Unauthorized'}, 401
    try:
        # Check user permissions
        check_permission(request.headers['token'])
        # Process request logic
        return process_request(request)
    except AccessDenied:
        return {'status': 403, 'message': 'Forbidden'}, 403
    except Exception as e:
        return {'status': 500, 'message': str(e)}, 500
"""
retrieved_content = get_code_snippet()
## Define Prompt to Enhance Diversity and Comprehensiveness of Generation
prompt = f"""
Please describe possible error handling mechanisms based on the following
code snippet:
{retrieved_content}
```

```
Note: Please provide multiple different analytical perspectives, covering
**input exceptions**, **permission control**, **call chain**, and other
aspects."""
```

Next, we'll see how to implement fact-checking mechanisms to improve content accuracy.

Introducing fact-checking mechanisms to enhance factual accuracy

Sometimes **fact-checking** is necessary. This can be achieved by emphasizing in the prompt that responses should be based only on retrieved content, or by confining generated content to specific topics or scopes to reduce the generation of unfounded information. By comparing the consistency between the generated content and the retrieved documents, erroneous information can be effectively avoided.

For instance, consider this example:

```
### Define the Content of the Retrieved Document
retrieved_content = get_code_snippet()
### Define the Prompt, Emphasizing to Respond Only Based on the Retrieved
Content
prompt = f"""
Please identify potential flaws in the following code based on its
content:
{retrieved_content}
Note: Please analyze only based on the code above without introducing
external knowledge."""
```

Controlling output format through output parsing

In certain situations, it is necessary to output content in a very strict manner, for example, when an Agent needs to invoke functions or tools in subsequent processes. In such cases, you should clearly describe the expected output format in the prompt. For instance, when you require the large language model to present answers in the form of a list, or restrict the length and structure of the response. If the large model does not organize the information as desired, there are some methods to better guide it to understand your requirements, ensuring the output matches the desired format.

Both **LangChain** and **LlamaIndex**, as mainstream frameworks, provide corresponding components to parse the generated output after calling the large language model. This allows for standardized output formats to meet the needs of different application scenarios.

LangChain output parsing mechanisms

LangChain provides a series of **OutputParser** components used to parse the output from large models, including:

- `StrOutputParser`: The default output parser, directly returns the text output of the large model
- `JSONOutputParser`: Used to parse outputs in JSON format, ensuring that the large model's output conforms to JSON specifications
- `PydanticOutputParser`: Performs structured parsing based on Pydantic, suitable for complex data structures
- `RegexParser`: Extracts key content through regular expression matching
- `StructuredOutputParser`: Parses structured data based on JSON Schema

The following code example demonstrates how to use LangChain's `JSONOutputParser`:

```
from langchain_core.output_parsers import JsonOutputParser
from langchain_deepseek import ChatDeepSeek
from langchain.prompts import PromptTemplate
## Define Output Format
parser = JsonOutputParser()
prompt = PromptTemplate.from_template("Please return the user's
information in JSON format: {query}")
## Call the Large Model and Parse
llm = ChatDeepSeek(model="deepseek-chat")
output = llm(prompt.format(query="User ID 123"))
parsed_output = parser.parse(output.content)
print(parsed_output)
{'user_id': '123'}
```

LlamaIndex output parsing mechanisms

The output parsing of LlamaIndex is mainly reflected in two components: response synthetization and structured output parsing.

After retrieval, LlamaIndex performs response synthetization. That is, it first recalls relevant documents, then processes the recalled data using `response_synthesizer`, and finally uses a large model to generate the final answer. Here's a nice example showing the parsing mechanism:

```
from llama_index.core import VectorStoreIndex, SimpleDirectoryReader
from llama_index.core.response_synthesizers import get_response_
```

```
synthesizer
from llama_index.core.response_synthesizers.type import ResponseMode
from llama_index.core.prompts import PromptTemplate
from pydantic import BaseModel, Field
from typing import List
## Define the Game Information Structure
class GameInfo(BaseModel):
    title: str = Field(description="Game title")
    developer: str = Field(description="Developer")
    release_date: str = Field(description="Release date")
    platforms: List[str] = Field(description="Supported platforms")
    main_features: List[str] = Field(description="Main features")
    story_summary: str = Field(description="Story summary")
    reception: str = Field(description="Market reception")
## Load Data
documents = SimpleDirectoryReader("data/黑神话").load_data()
index = VectorStoreIndex.from_documents(documents)
## Basic Parsing Mode Using COMPACT Mode
print("=== Basic Parsing Mode ===")
synthesizer = get_response_synthesizer(
    response_mode=ResponseMode.COMPACT,
    verbose=True    # Show detailed information
)
query_engine = index.as_query_engine(response_synthesizer=synthesizer)
response = query_engine.query("Please summarize the main content of the
game 'Black Myth: Wukong'")
print(response)
## Structured Parsing Mode Using REFINE Mode
print("\n=== Structured Parsing Mode ===")
synthesizer = get_response_synthesizer(
    response_mode=ResponseMode.REFINE,
    output_cls=GameInfo,  # Specify output class
    verbose=True
)
query_engine = index.as_query_engine(response_synthesizer=synthesizer)
response = query_engine.query("Please extract the key information of
'Black Myth: Wukong'")
## Handle the Response Safely
```

```
if hasattr(response, 'response'):
    print(response.response)
else:
    print(response)
## Table Format Parsing Using TREE_SUMMARIZE Mode
print("\n=== Game Features Table Parsing ===")
table_prompt = PromptTemplate(
    template="Please present the following game features in table form:\
n{query_str}\nFormat requirements:\n| Category | Content |\n|--|--|\n"
)
synthesizer = get_response_synthesizer(
    response_mode=ResponseMode.TREE_SUMMARIZE,
    summary_template=table_prompt,
    verbose=True
)
query_engine = index.as_query_engine(response_synthesizer=synthesizer)
response = query_engine.query("Please summarize the main features of
'*Black Myth: Wukong*' in table form")
print(response)

## Bullet Point Analysis Mode Using COMPACT_ACCUMULATE Mode
print("\n=== Game Highlights Bullet Point Analysis ===")
bullet_prompt = PromptTemplate(
    template="Please present the following game highlights in bullet point
form:\n{query_str}\nFormat requirements:\n1. \n2. \n3. "
)
synthesizer = get_response_synthesizer(
    response_mode=ResponseMode.COMPACT_ACCUMULATE,
    text_qa_template=bullet_prompt,
    verbose=True,
    use_async=True  # Enable asynchronous processing
)
query_engine = index.as_query_engine(response_synthesizer=synthesizer)
response = query_engine.query("Please summarize the highlights of '*Black
Myth: Wukong*' in bullet point form")
print(response)
```

```
## Storyline Analysis Using SIMPLE_SUMMARIZE Mode
print("\n=== Game Storyline Analysis ===")
story_prompt = PromptTemplate(
    template="Please present the following game story as a timeline:\
n{query_str}\nFormat requirements:\n- Time point: Event\n"
)
synthesizer = get_response_synthesizer(
    response_mode=ResponseMode.SIMPLE_SUMMARIZE,
    text_qa_template=story_prompt,
    verbose=True
)
query_engine = index.as_query_engine(response_synthesizer=synthesizer)
response = query_engine.query("Please summarize the story development of
'*Black Myth: Wukong*' in timeline form")
print(response)
```

Let's dissect the preceding code, by understanding each function one-by-one.

Basic parsing mode

Black Myth: Wukong is an action role-playing game developed and published by Game Science. It is praised as China's first AAA game and is based on the classic Chinese novel *Journey to the West*. In this game, the learners control a character called **The Destined One** who embarks on a journey to find and revive *Sun Wukong* by collecting his lost body parts known as *Root Vessels*. The course features a **combat system** with various staff fighting styles, resource management mechanics, and incorporates Chinese cultural and natural landmarks, along with elements of Buddhism and Taoism. The story takes place after the events of *Journey to the West* and includes references to the Hong Kong film *A Chinese Odyssey*.

Structured parsing mode

The structured parsing mode consists of parameters such as `title`, `release_date`, `story_summary`, and `reception`. Learners play as `Lingming Stone Monkey` who is *The Destined One* from Mount Huaguo, embarking on a journey to retrieve lost Root Vessels, rescue, and revive Sun Wukong. In the process of searching for Root Vessels, *The Destined One* defeats various demon kings and bosses to recover Wukong's Root Vessels.

The following table represents the game features:

Category	Content
Game Type	Action-adventure game
Game Style	Chinese mythology theme, combined with Eastern cultural elements
Gameplay	Unique combat system, including combinations of weapons, skills, and ultimate moves
Game World	Open world with free exploration and puzzles
Role-playing	Learners can play as Sun Wukong, experiencing his adventure story
Art Style	Exquisite visuals and animation, showcasing the style of traditional Chinese painting
Music Score	Original music, complementing game scenes, enhancing the atmosphere
Game Difficulty	Relatively high challenge, requiring learners to use combat skills flexibly

Here are the game highlights with point-by-point analysis:

1. Unique Chinese mythology theme: The course is based on Chinese mythological stories, letting learners experience a unique Eastern mythological worldview
2. Open world with free exploration: Learners can freely explore the game world, discovering hidden quests and secrets
3. Innovative combat system: The course adopts real-time combat, allowing learners to use various weapons and skills in battle, providing different fighting experiences

Analyzing the game storyline, you can note that:

- **Ancient times: Sun Wukong** is sealed within mountains
- **Tang dynasty**: A stele sealing **Sun Wukong** is discovered in the mountains
- **Tang dynasty: Sun Wukong** regains his freedom and begins his adventure

In addition, **LlamaIndex** also supports integration with other output parsing frameworks. For example, final output safety protection and value alignment can be achieved through **GuarDrails**. Please refer to its official documentation for specific usage instructions.

OpenAI's JSON mode and structured output

OpenAI's traditional **JSON mode** allows you to activate the JSON response mode by setting `response_format` to `{ "type": "json_object" }`. When this mode is enabled, the system will only generate strings that can be parsed as valid JSON objects. It is important to note that although this mode specifies that the output format must be **JSON**, it does not ensure that the content conforms to a specific type. For example, the name and type of each field may not always be exactly as expected.

In OpenAI's latest (at the time of writing this book) **Responses API Structured Outputs** feature, the model is further ensured to generate responses that match the **JSON schema** provided by the user. This means you no longer need to worry about the model missing required keys or generating invalid enumeration values, and there's no need to use strongly worded prompts to enforce consistent formatting requirements. For weaker models, well-crafted prompts are still essential.

Here's a sample of structured output for the Responses API:

```
from openai import OpenAI
import json
client = OpenAI()
response = client.responses.create(
    model="gpt-4o",
    input=[
        {"role": "system", "content": "Extract the event information."},
        {"role": "user", "content": "Alice and Bob are going to a science 
fair on Friday."}
    ],
    text={
        "format": {
            "type": "json_schema",
            "name": "calendar_event",
            "schema": {
                "type": "object",
                "properties": {
                    "name": {
                        "type": "string"
                    },
                    "date": {
                        "type": "string"
```

```
                    },
                "participants": {
                    "type": "array",
                    "items": {
                        "type": "string"
                    }
                },
            },
            "required": ["name", "date", "participants"],
            "additionalProperties": False
            },
        "strict": True
        }
    }
)
event = json.loads(response.output_text)
```

In the preceding example, the "`type`": "`json_schema`" and "`schema`" parameters explicitly specify the exact format of the output JSON file.

Pydantic parsing

Pydantic provides a versatile framework capable of transforming input text into structured Pydantic objects. LlamaIndex offers several types of Pydantic programs, each with specific application scenarios. Let's name a few here:

- **LLM Text Completion Pydantic Programs**: These programs process input text and convert it into user-defined structured objects. They combine the text completion API and output parsing functionality.
- **LLM Function Calling Pydantic Programs**: Depending on user requirements, these programs convert input text into specific structured objects. This process relies on the LLM function calling API.
- **Prepackaged Pydantic Programs**: These programs are designed to convert input text into pre-defined structured objects.

Here's an example of a Pydantic program:

```
from pydantic import BaseModel, Field
from typing import List, Optional
from llama_index.program.openai import OpenAIPydanticProgram
```

```
### Define the Code Issue Model
class CodeIssue(BaseModel):
    """Problems present in the code"""
    line_number: int = Field(..., description="Line number where the issue 
is located")
    issue_type: str = Field(..., description="Type of issue, such as 
security vulnerability, performance issue, code style, etc.")
    description: str = Field(..., description="Detailed description of the 
issue")
    severity: str = Field(..., description="Severity of the issue: high/
medium/low")
### Define the Code Analysis Report Model
class CodeAnalysis(BaseModel):
    """Code analysis report"""
    file_name: str = Field(..., description="File name being analyzed")
    issues: List[CodeIssue] = Field(default_factory=list, 
description="List of identified issues")
    overall_quality: str = Field(..., description="Overall code quality 
assessment: excellent/good/fair/poor")
    recommendations: List[str] = Field(default_factory=list, 
description="Suggestions for improvement")
### Create OpenAI Pydantic Program
program = OpenAIPydanticProgram.from_defaults(
    output_cls=CodeAnalysis,
    prompt_template_str="""
    Please analyze the following code and generate a detailed analysis 
report:
    {code}
    Requirements:
    1. Identify potential issues in the code
    2. Assess code quality
    3. Provide suggestions for improvement
    """,
    verbose=True
)
### Sample Code
sample_code = """
def process_data(data):
```

```
if data is None:
return
for item in data:
if item > 100:
print("Large value found")
else:
print("Small value")
```

Let's run the following code snippet to obtain the quality analysis:

```
try:
analysis = program(code=sample_code)
print(f"File Analysis Report: {analysis.file_name}")
print(f"Overall Quality: {analysis.overall_quality}")
print("\nIssues Found: ")
for issue in analysis.issues:
print(f"- Line {issue.line_number}: {issue.issue_type}")
print(f"  Description: {issue.description}")
print(f"  Severity: {issue.severity}")
print("\nImprovement Suggestions: ")
for rec in analysis.recommendations:
print(f"- {rec}")
except Exception as e:
print(f"Error occurred during analysis: {e}")
```

The preceding code will produce the following output:

```
File Analysis Report: code.py
Overall Quality: fair
Issues Found:
```

Alex, you can make the following observations from the preceding output:

- **In line 3, there's a potential bug.** The function returns without processing data if it is None, which may lead to unexpected behavior. However, the severity is medium.
- **Similarly, there's another potential bug in line 5. Here,** comparison of item with 100 may not be appropriate. Hence, you should consider using > instead of >. The severity of this bug is still low.

What I would suggest for improvement, is:

- Handle the case when data is None more appropriately
- Consider using > instead of > for comparison with 100

Function call parsing

By using **Function Calling** or **Tool Calling**, large language models can return structured data and parse the `function_call` field to dynamically generate the name and parameters for subsequent function calls.

The following code example demonstrates how to use **Function Calling** for parsing:

```
from langchain_deepseek import ChatDeepSeek
from pydantic import BaseModel, Field
## Define Tool Schema
class get_weather(BaseModel):
    “””Get weather information”””
    location: str = Field(..., description=”City name”)
    temperature: float = Field(..., description=”Temperature”)
## Initialize the Large Model
llm = ChatDeepSeek(model=”deepseek-chat”)
## Bind Tool
llm_with_tools = llm.bind_tools([get_weather])
## Send Request
response = llm_with_tools.invoke(“Please tell me the weather in Shanghai”)
## Parse Output
if response.tool_calls:
    for tool_call in response.tool_calls:
        print(f”Tool name: {tool_call[‘name’]}”)
        print(f”Parameters: {tool_call[‘args’]}”)
else:
    print(“No tool call”)
Tool name: get_weather
Parameters: {‘location’: ‘Shanghai’, ‘temperature’: 25}
```

Although the preceding example is simple, it forms the starting point for **Agentic intelligent systems.** When large models are able to autonomously determine which tool or function needs to be called next, and output the data in a format that meets the function's parameter interface requirements based on either retrieved knowledge or the user's input, it is equivalent to equipping these systems with a pair of hands that can flexibly use a variety of tools.

In the future, through **MCP**, **RAG**, and **Agent**, applications will be able to connect with external systems to achieve more powerful functionalities. An accurate parsing mechanism is the prerequisite for enabling smooth interconnection between large model applications and external systems.

Improving output quality through model choice

There are various ways to call large models, generally falling into three categories—API calls, deployment on open-source model platforms, and local deployment:

- Using APIs to access large models (such as OpenAI's **GPT-4** model, Anthropic's **Claude** model, etc.) is a common way for developers to quickly integrate large model capabilities. This approach allows users to directly call APIs via cloud services without requiring local deployment. However, this method depends on network connectivity and is relatively costly.
- **Hugging Face** and **ModelScope** are open-source model platforms, each with its own advantages. The former provides a rich library of pre-trained models (such as **transformers**) and easy-to-use toolchains, supporting developers for model fine-tuning and deployment; the latter, promoted by **Alibaba Cloud**, focuses on Chinese scenarios, offering localized models and computing power support, thereby lowering the threshold for Chinese NLP development.
- **Ollama** and **vLLM** are representatives among local deployment tools. Ollama is known for its lightweight design, supporting rapid startup and operation of open-source models like the Llama series, making it suitable for local debugging; **vLLM**, developed by the team at the University of California, Berkeley, optimizes memory management through efficient PagedAttention technology, significantly improving large model inference speed to meet the demands of high concurrency in production environments.

Alex, you should note that the first method is mainly used for accessing closed-source commercial models, while the latter two are commonly used to access open-source models. Following are the commonly used models, at present:

- **GPT series (OpenAI)**: As a pioneer in the era of large models, the GPT series performs excellently in all aspects, with notable strengths in logical reasoning and instruction following, making it a leader in innovation.
- **Claude series (Anthropic)**: As a new generation expert in long-context processing (supporting up to 200K tokens of long context), Claude 3 emphasizes safety and low hallucination rates. It excels in mathematical and programming benchmarks, showing a trend of surpassing GPT.

- **Gemini series (Google)**: Although Google's large model is not as striking as the first two, the Gemini series still has its own unique features. It adopts a unified multimodal architecture, supports ultra-long context, and has enhanced reasoning and coding capabilities.
- **DeepSeek series (DeepSeek)**: This is a leading domestic large model in China, utilizing the MoE architecture (Mixture of Experts), specifically optimized for mathematics and coding capabilities, and supports long context up to 128K #tokens. `DeepSeek-R1` is open-source and available for commercial use. In addition, DeepSeek has released an easy-to-deploy small distilled version.
- **Llama series (Meta)**: This is an open-source large model with parameter sizes ranging from 8B to 70B. Llama is known for its high inference efficiency and long context support, and comes with a rich ecosystem of tools.
- **Qwen (Alibaba Cloud)**: This is significantly optimized for Chinese language processing, covering parameter sizes from 1.8B to 72B, and supports multi-turn dialogue and plugin extensions.
- **Mixtral (Mistral AI)**: This utilizes the **MoE architecture** to achieve high performance with a relatively small number of active parameters, is open-source and commercially available.

These models generally pursue lower inference costs, larger context lengths, and multimodal expansion, while promoting parallel development of open-source and commercial ecosystems, aiming for the democratization of technology.

Different models have slight differences in performance, efficiency, and application scenarios. The key considerations when choosing a model are as follows:

- **Model scale and performance**: Generally speaking, larger models have stronger generative abilities and can understand more complex contexts. However, as the model size increases, the demand for computing resources and inference time also rises significantly. Therefore, while pursuing high performance, it is necessary to find a balance between performance and resource consumption.
- **Task adaptability**: Different models may perform better on specific tasks. For example, some models excel in code generation, while others may be better at natural language understanding or dialogue generation. Choosing models based on specific task requirements helps improve output quality.

- **Fine-tuning and customization**: By using fine-tuning techniques, pre-trained models can be adjusted to specific domains or tasks, thereby improving their performance in specific application scenarios. Parameter-efficient fine-tuning techniques, such as Adapter Learning and **Low-Rank Adaptation (LoRA)**, achieves efficient model customization by introducing a small number of trainable parameters.
- **Self-feedback mechanism**: Introducing a **self-feedback mechanism** that allows the model to self-evaluate and revise its initial output can further improve the accuracy and consistency of generated content. Specifically, this process includes having the model first generate an initial output, then review that output and provide feedback, and finally optimize the initial output based on the feedback.

Now that you know how to choose a model, let's see how to integrate the results.

Methods of integrating retrieved results into the generation process

Alex: Lewis, besides improving the output quality by adjusting prompts and switching to different large models, are there more sophisticated and advanced **generation techniques**?

Lewis: Of course there are. The traditional **RAG process** directly inputs the retrieved information into the generator (i.e., the large model). In this case, **retrieval** and **generation** are relatively independent, and the retrieval results are only used at the input stage. The quality of **retrieval** directly affects the generator's output. If retrieval fails or contains noise, the generation performance is reduced. Since this process does not modify the generator, it is relatively simple to implement.

However, this relatively independent structure between retrieval and generation is not the only way to integrate **retrievers** and **generators**. The paper *A Survey on RAG Meeting LLMs: Towards Retrieval-Augmented Large Language Models* discusses integration methods for retrieved results within the generation process. (Source: `https://arxiv.org/abs/2405.06211`)

The retrieval process is the same as in traditional RAG, but in the generation process section, three integration methods are listed:

- **Input-level integration**: This method involves passing the retrieved content along with the original query to the generator, which is similar to how traditional RAG processes operate.

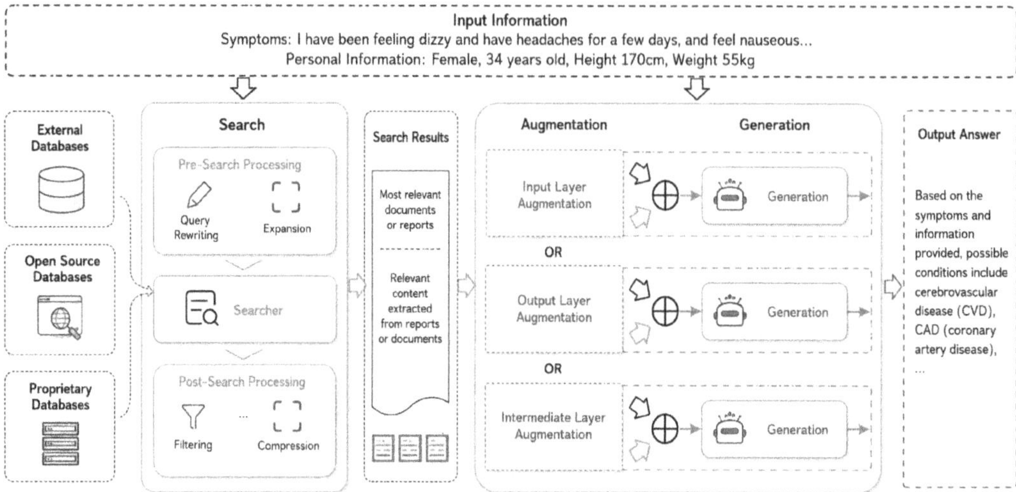

Figure 8.2: The data flow from input systems rough search enhancement and answer generation

- **Output-level integration:** The large model is first run to generate an output based on the input, then this output is combined with the retrieval results, and a weighted integration method is used to optimize and obtain the final result.
- **Intermediate-layer integration:** As the most complex integration method, this involves introducing the retrieval results directly at the internal layers of the generator, achieving a deep fusion of the retrieval results and the large model to enhance the generation performance.

Input layer integration

Input layer integration involves combining the retrieved content with the user's original query and then passing them together to the generator for processing. This process is similar to searching for answers during an open-book exam and using these references as input to help the generator produce more accurate outputs.

The generator concatenates the user's initial question with the retrieved relevant documents, passages, or entities, and then processes them through the generator. In this way, the generator can directly use this retrieved content to generate answers or text.

Retrieval-augmented language model (REALM) is a typical example of input layer integration and actually represents the standard RAG architecture. REALM introduces a retrieval mechanism during its pre-training phase, enabling real-time access to external knowledge to enhance generation performance. Specifically, the model combines the retrieved passages with the input question to improve answer accuracy.

The advantage of this approach lies in its relative simplicity and ease of implementation, while also maintaining output coherence when handling a large number of relevant documents. However, if the number of retrieved documents is too great, the concatenated input may exceed the maximum sequence length that large models can handle, making processing impossible.

Output layer integration

Output layer integration involves combining the generated content from the generator with retrieved information and applying weighted processing to produce more accurate results. This approach is similar to proofreading and optimizing an initial answer by referencing external sources after the initial response has been generated.

When generating each output, the model computes two probability distributions: one predicted by the model for the next word, and another provided by the retrieved context (such as similar text fragments). The model then performs weighted integration of these two probability distributions to generate the final answer. This integration method allows the model to incorporate retrieved information in the final stage of the generation process, thereby improving result accuracy.

K-nearest neighbor language model (kNN-LM) is a typical example of output layer integration. After generating output, the model adjusts the probability distribution for the generated word based on retrieved similar contexts, thus reducing incorrect generations and hallucinations. This method offers flexibility, as it can be applied after the generator's output without interfering with the intermediate processes of the model, and it can better handle complex contextual environments.

However, a challenge faced by output layer integration is how to effectively weight the retrieved results and the generator's output. Particularly when there are inconsistencies between the retrieved results and the generator's output, finding the appropriate trade-off becomes a difficult problem.

Intermediate layer integration

Intermediate layer integration introduces retrieved information into the internal (i.e., intermediate) layers of the generator, enabling this information to influence the model output at multiple stages during the generation process. This approach is similar to referencing materials from time to time while writing an article, constantly adjusting the content based on these materials.

In this process, the retrieved document fragments are converted into dense vectors and integrated into the generation process at a certain intermediate layer of the generator via **attention mechanisms** or other integration modules. This allows the generator to dynamically interact with the retrieved information during output generation, enhancing information interaction while maintaining a smooth generation process.

Retrieval-Enhanced Transformer (**RETRO**) is a typical example of intermediate layer integration. RETRO introduces retrieved text blocks into the intermediate layers of its generator, enabling the model to dynamically access this information during the generation process, thereby producing more coherent and accurate text.

Compared to input layer and output layer integration, **intermediate layer integration** offers more opportunities for information interaction and allows the retrieved information to be used multiple times at different stages of generation. This approach is especially suitable for tasks that require handling large amounts of retrieved information and generating high-quality long-form text.

However, this approach is relatively complex to implement, as it requires modifications to the internal structure of the model and significant computational resources to support multiple information interactions at intermediate layers.

Self-RAG generation

We covered CRAG earlier in this chapter. The **Self-reflective retrieval-augmented generation** (**Self-RAG**) has certain similarities to CRAG.

Self-RAG is a strategy that integrates a self-reflection/self-assessment mechanism into the RAG architecture, a concept originating from a paper by the University of Washington titled *Self-RAG: Learning to Retrieve, Generate, and Critique through Self-Reflection*. The core of Self-RAG lies in incrementally validating the relevance of retrieved documents and the accuracy of generated content through an automated decision-making process. This approach allows large models to dynamically decide whether to perform retrieval and to evaluate the generated content, thereby improving both the quality and factuality of the generated text and reducing biases or so-called *hallucinations*.

Self-RAG has the following three main features:

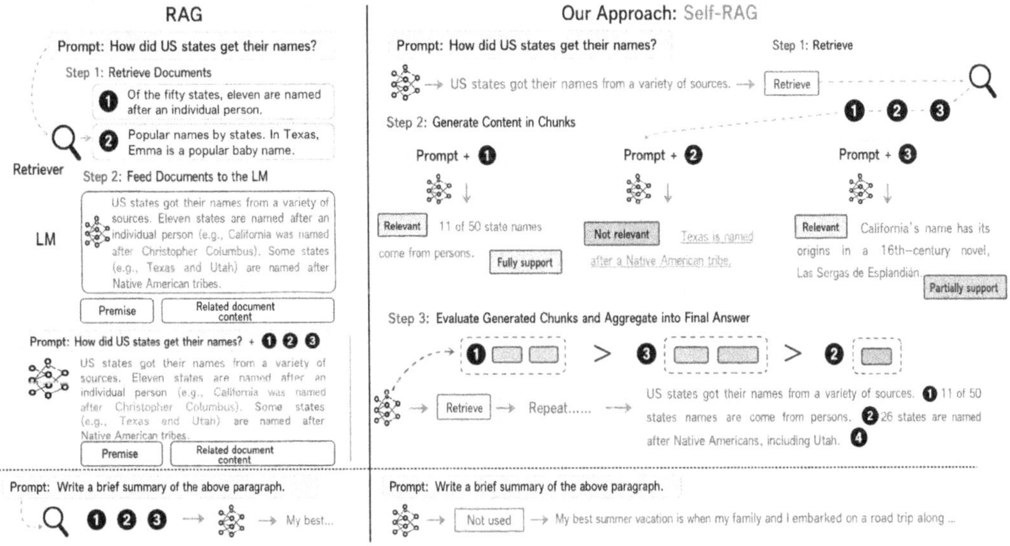

Figure 8.3: Comparison of RAG and Self-RAG methods

The preceding diagram highlights the following features:

- **On-demand retrieval**: According to the specific needs of the input question, the large model can dynamically decide whether to perform a retrieval operation, avoiding unnecessary retrieval processes.
- **Self-assessment**: During the generation process, the large model uses a special reflection token to evaluate its output, ensuring that the generated content aligns with the retrieved knowledge.
- **Multi-dimensional control**: By introducing a critic model, the generated text can be evaluated and controlled from multiple granular perspectives to improve the quality of the final output.

The main steps in **Self-RAG** include:

1. **Determining whether retrieval is needed:** First, the system decides if it is necessary to obtain information from the retriever. The input for this step is the user's query (x), and the output is a decision about whether to proceed with retrieval, including **Yes**, **No**, or **Continue**, to accommodate different processing needs.

2. **Determining the relevance of retrieved documents:** Once the need for retrieval is established, the system will evaluate the relevance of each text block *d* in the retrieved documents *D*. The inputs for this step include the original question *x* and the retrieved text block *d*. The system uses model analysis to determine whether these document contents are relevant to the question *x*. The output is either `Relevant` or `Irrelevant`.
3. **Confirming the support for the generated content**: Next, the system will check whether the generated content is supported by the retrieved documents. The input for this step includes the original question *x*, the retrieved text block *d*, and the generated content *y*. The system will evaluate whether the generated information is based on facts provided by the retrieved documents. The output will be **Fully** `Supported`, `Partially Supported`, or `No Support`.
4. **Evaluating the quality of the generated content**: Finally, the system will further assess the quality of the generated content to determine whether it effectively answers the question *x*. The input for this step includes the original question *x* and the generated content *y*. The rating ranges from `1 to 5`, reflecting the completeness and effectiveness of the generated content.

For an example of **Self-RAG** implemented in **LangGraph**, please refer to the book's GitHub repository (`https://github.com/PacktPublishing/RAG-from-First-Principles`).

RRR dynamic generation optimization

Rewrite-Retrieve-Read (**RRR**) originates from the paper *Query Rewriting for Retrieval-Augmented Large Language Models* and is a method for optimizing RAG systems. In traditional RAG systems, the user's original query is used directly to retrieve relevant documents, after which a generative model produces answers based on these documents. However, since the original query may be vague or incomplete, this can affect retrieval effectiveness. By using the RRR approach to rewrite the query before retrieval, the relevance and quality of retrieved results can be improved.

The main process of RRR is as follows:

1. **Rewrite**: Use a large model to rewrite the user's original query, producing a clearer and more specific version of the query.
2. **Retrieve**: Use the rewritten query to retrieve relevant documents from the web.

3. **Read**: Feed the retrieved documents into the generative model to produce the final answer.

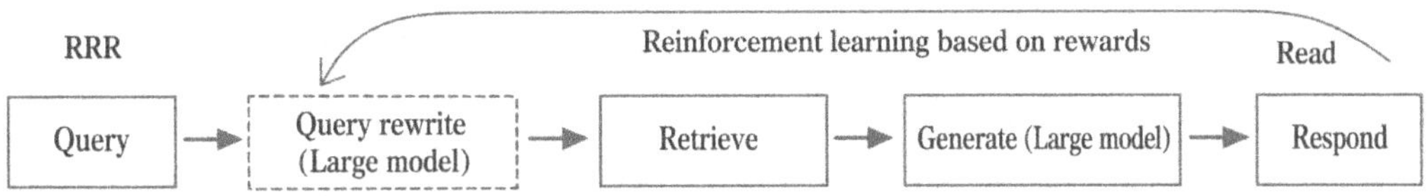

Figure 8.4: RRR stages from query to response and reinforcement learning steps

By rewriting the query before retrieval, RRR can more accurately capture the user's intent, improve the relevance of retrieval results, and thereby enhance the quality of generated answers.

A comparison of three similar methods: The retrieve-then-read method directly uses the input for retrieval, and then lets the large model read the retrieved documents to generate an answer; the RRR method first uses a large model to rewrite the input into a better retrieval query, conducts a web search using this query, and finally the large model reads the retrieved documents to generate the output; the trainable rewrite-retrieve-read method first uses a small pretrained language model to rewrite the query, then performs web retrieval to obtain documents, and finally the large model reads the retrieved documents to generate the output. The so-called *trainable* aspect refers to the introduction of a reinforcement learning reward mechanism to optimize the rewriter.

The following figure shows a comparison of the three methods:

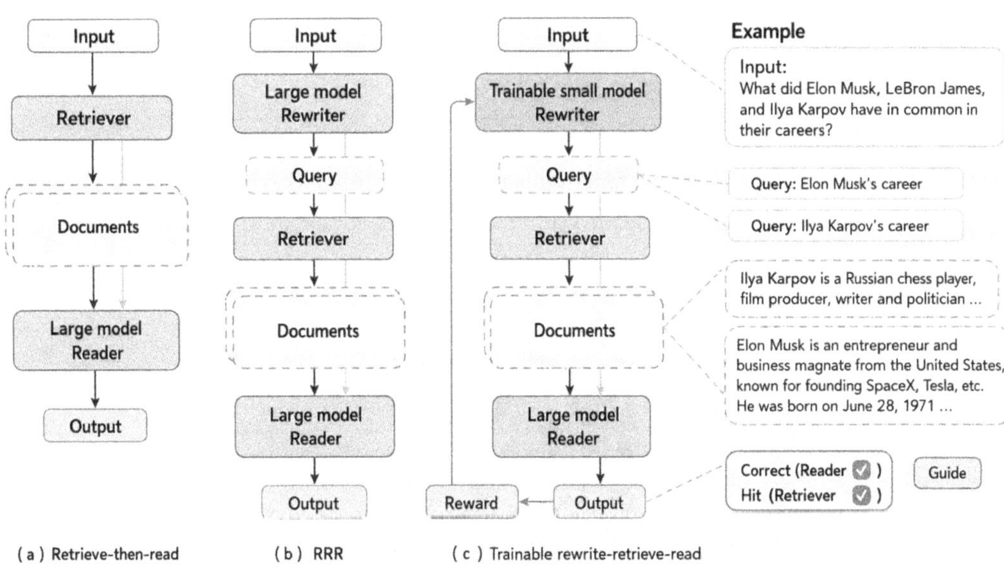

Figure 8.5: Comparison of three methods of RRR dynamic generation

The core of **RRR** lies in improving the quality of generated results through a cyclical process of optimization, rewriting, and retrieval. The output is evaluated based on the initially generated content, and if the answer is incomplete or inaccurate, more relevant documents are retrieved to modify and enhance the initial generated content accordingly.

This approach is similar to the self-reflection mechanism in **Self-RAG**, ensuring that the final generated answer is based on sufficient information and supported by high-quality documents.

Summary

Response generation is a stage in the entire RAG process with a relatively limited operational space. This chapter explored methods to improve the quality of generated content through prompt optimization, how to use output parsing mechanisms to control the format of generated content, and how to improve output quality by selecting large models, among others.

During the generation process, there are three ways to integrate retrieval results—input-layer integration, output-layer integration, and intermediate-layer integration.

In addition, the application of technologies such as Self-RAG and dynamic generation optimization can further improve the accuracy and controllability of the generated content.

In the next chapter, we will explore how to evaluate **Retrieval-Augmented Generation** (**RAG**) systems.

9

System Evaluation

Anna: Lewis, the evaluation of traditional machine learning models is relatively straightforward. For example, **classifiers** or **object detection systems** have clear criteria for right and wrong. However, unlike these models, when it comes to **RAG systems**, if a client asks about its performance, I have a hard time giving a definitive answer.

Lewis: That's true. The way **RAG systems** are evaluated differs from traditional machine learning models. Traditional model evaluations usually rely on clear quantitative metrics, such as **classification accuracy**, **object detection precision**, **Gini coefficient**, R-squared, **F1 score**, and **confusion matrix**, etc. In contrast, evaluating a **RAG system** requires separately assessing its two core components: the **retriever** and the **generator**. This not only involves evaluating the relevance of retrieved content but also whether the generated answers meet the user's needs.

Figure 9.1: Conversation between Lewis and Anna on RAG systems

The goal of the **retriever** is to find the most relevant documents. Although evaluation of the retriever (also called **retrieval evaluation**) carries some subjective factors, we can still use several metrics from the field of information retrieval to measure it, such as **Precision**, **Recall**, and **ranking accuracy**.

Anna: That's fairly easy to understand. So what about evaluating the generator?

Lewis: Evaluation of the **generator** (also called **response evaluation**, which is actually an overall assessment of the final result delivered by the **RAG system**) is more complex. It not only requires checking if the generated answer is factually grounded (i.e., contextually relevant) and whether it effectively answers the user's question (i.e., query relevance), but also whether the answer is fluent, safe, and aligned with human values. To assess the quality of generation, we use a combination of quantitative metrics (such as **BLEU** or **ROUGE**) and qualitative indicators (such as answer relevance, semantic consistency, contextual fit, robustness, and faithfulness). In addition, due to the complexity of these factors, human subjective assessment is also needed to assist throughout the evaluation process.

Combining **retrieval evaluation** and **response evaluation** forms the evaluation framework for **RAG systems**.

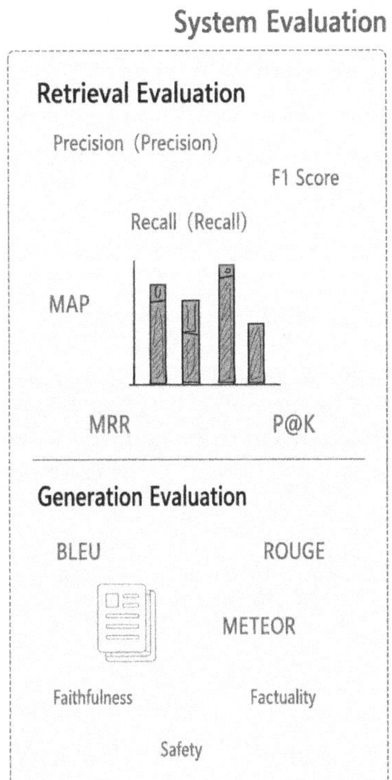

Figure 9.2: Diagram of a system evaluation process

Evaluation system for RAG systems

Anna: Since evaluating **RAG systems** is much more complex and also involves a lot of subjective factors, where should we start when implementing a project?

Lewis: If possible, I suggest that you and the client work together to collect some typical questions and standard answers based on a portion of the most commonly used and familiar documents. Use this as a starting point to first create a high-quality **evaluation dataset** that is recognized by both parties.

Evaluation dataset for RAG

Establishing an **evaluation dataset** is crucial. In the absence of unified evaluation standards, developers and business teams may each have their own opinions when discussing the accuracy of the **Q&A system**. The completeness and diversity of the evaluation dataset directly affect the accuracy and reliability of the **RAG system**'s evaluation process. A high-quality dataset should contain a rich array of comprehensive questions and source-reliable answers that have been verified by the business team or client.

Evaluation Dataset

Query	Expected Answer (Label)	Expected Source (Document)	Expected Source (Page)
<Question 1>	<Answer 1>	[Document 1] [Document 2]	[3, 6], [23]
<Question 2>	<Answer 2>	[Document 10]	[3]
⋮	⋮	⋮	⋮
<Question N>	<Answer N>	[Document X]	[*X*1, *X*2]

Figure 9.3: A table shows evaluation datasets with columns for queries, answers, and sources

The evaluation dataset includes questions, standard answers, as well as information about the **source documents** and the **page number** of the standard answers. Based on these materials, a series of **evaluation metrics** can be established to check whether the system can accurately retrieve the standard answers. Of course, the specific format of the evaluation dataset should be determined based on the actual project requirements. The reason why the dataset in the example includes the page label is that documents in this project are mainly in PDF or Word/WPS format. If the project documents are in Markdown or web format, the page field may not be applicable.

Alex: Lewis, building a **dataset** from scratch is very resource-intensive. How large should the dataset be?

Lewis: Building a **dataset** from scratch does indeed require substantial resources. For preliminary testing, you can start by creating around **200 Q&A entries**. As the project progresses, you should gradually accumulate more content.

The format of **evaluation datasets** for different **RAG systems** may vary. Sometimes there is a precisely unique data source, while at other times the answer may come from multiple pages or documents. Therefore, it's necessary to handle these differences flexibly when implementing the project.

Retrieval evaluation and response evaluation

Retrieval evaluation and response evaluation are the two core components of the RAG system evaluation framework; let's consider them in detail:

- **Retrieval evaluation** focuses on whether the model can retrieve accurate and relevant context during a query. It assesses whether the content found by the system from the knowledge base or external resources is closely related to the user's query and can effectively support subsequent generation. Key metrics in retrieval evaluation include **context relevance**, **retrieval precision**, and **recall**. Retrieval evaluation often emphasizes assessing the quality of the **embedding model** (i.e., the core component of the **retriever**).
- **Response evaluation**, on the other hand, focuses on the quality of the answers generated by the model based on the retrieved content. Its goal is to ensure that the generated content is not only relevant to the user's query but also **faithful** to the provided context information. Response evaluation typically looks at whether the generated answer is accurate, whether it contains **"hallucinations"**, and whether it is consistent with the context. Key metrics for response evaluation include **answer relevance** and **faithfulness**, which help teams better assess whether the generated answers meet expectations. Response evaluation often emphasizes assessing the level of the **generative model** (i.e., the core component of the **generator**).

When an evaluation dataset is available, meaning some questions already have labeled standard answers and sources, for retrieval evaluation, more precise quantitative metrics such as **precision** and **recall** can be used; whereas for response evaluation, it is usually difficult to quantify answer quality with specific scores, and subjective factors play a relatively larger role.

RAG TRIAD – holistic evaluation

At present, one evaluation approach is to assess the overall effectiveness of the **Retrieval-Augmented Generation (RAG)** process. This method is known as the **RAG TRIAD framework**.

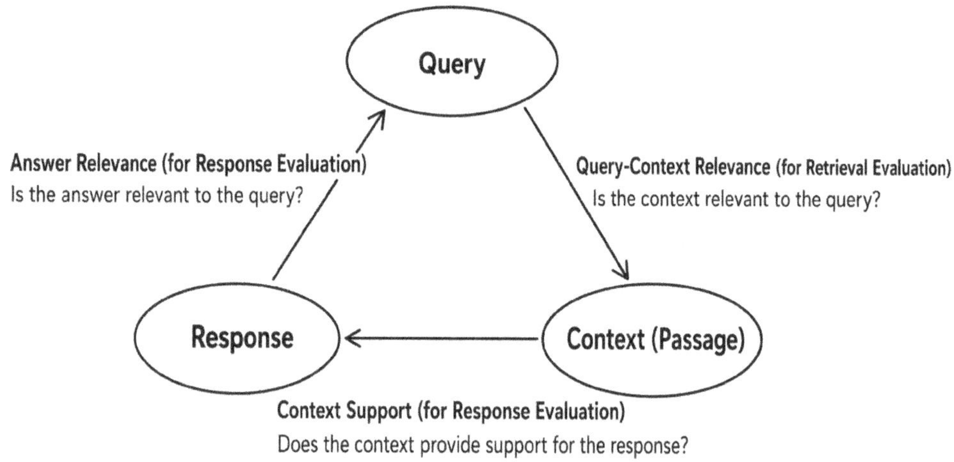

Figure 9.4: A flowchart showing relationships among query context and response

In the **RAG TRIAD framework**, evaluation is focused on three core aspects: **query**, **context**, and **response**. These three aspects are measured by the following three key evaluation metrics:

- **Contextual relevancy**: An indicator for retrieval evaluation, mainly assessing whether the text blocks returned by the retriever are relevant to the user's query and helpful for generating an ideal answer. This involves selecting hyperparameters such as **block size**, **Top-K** value, and **embedding model**. An efficient embedding model can ensure that the retrieved text blocks are semantically similar to the user's query, while an appropriate combination of block size and Top-K value helps pick out the most critical information from the knowledge base.
- **Faithfulness**: A key metric in response evaluation, used to measure whether the generated answer is based on the provided context, i.e., whether the answer has a factual basis and does not contain "hallucinations." This metric is often closely related to **model selection**. If the current model cannot generate accurate answers based on the retrieved context, it may be necessary to replace the model or fine-tune it.

- **Answer relevancy**: Also a response evaluation metric, it focuses on the degree to which the generated answer is relevant to the user's query. As the model's reasoning ability improves, this metric increasingly depends on the quality of the retrieval results rather than the capability of the model itself. If the score is low, it may be necessary to improve the retrieval process or optimize **prompts** to enhance the model's ability to generate more relevant answers.

The **RAG TRIAD framework** provides a reference-free evaluation system. Even without ready-made evaluation datasets, it is still possible to evaluate the outputs of the RAG system from the above three aspects. Therefore, this evaluation system has a certain degree of generality and flexibility. Each metric corresponds to specific components or hyperparameter settings in the RAG process. If a RAG system scores highly in these three areas, it indicates that its components or hyperparameter settings are appropriate; otherwise, further adjustment and optimization are needed.

This reference-free evaluation system saves the trouble of creating evaluation datasets, but at the same time, it also means that the evaluation metrics themselves have a certain degree of non-determinism. Therefore, the final performance of the RAG system should not only depend on these evaluation metrics but also require practical confirmation from business teams and end users.

Retrieval evaluation metrics

Retrieval evaluation is critical for **RAG systems** because it directly affects the quality of the **context** adopted by the generator, thereby indirectly impacting the relevance and accuracy of the final generated response.

MTEB provides a comprehensive benchmarking platform for evaluating text embedding models, covering tasks such as text similarity, text classification, and retrieval. **MTEB** can effectively measure the performance of **text embedding models** across multiple tasks. Therefore, **MTEB** is regarded as a means to evaluate the embedding models used in the retrieval process and is suitable for local task evaluation.

However, in practical **RAG projects**, retrieval evaluation is not limited to the direct assessment of the **embedding model**, but more broadly targets the entire **retriever component**, evaluating whether it can effectively identify and prioritize the most relevant documents. This process not only depends on the quality of the embedding model but is also influenced by factors such as **chunking strategy** and **indexing strategy**.

Retrieval evaluation mainly uses metrics such as **precision**, **recall**, **Mean Reciprocal Rank** (**MRR**), and **Mean Average Precision** (**MAP**). Before introducing these metrics, it should be noted that the text chunks retrieved by the **retriever** are usually not singular but rather one or more (this is a configurable parameter). In addition, the context text chunks relevant to a specific query are often more than one, and all relevant text chunks should be listed in the evaluation dataset.

Precision

Precision measures how many of the retrieved text blocks are relevant to the query, i.e., the proportion of relevant text blocks among all retrieved text blocks. Precision aims to answer the question: "Of all text blocks retrieved, how many are truly relevant?"

The calculation formula for **precision** is as follows:

$$\text{Precision} = \frac{\text{Number of relevant text chunks retrieved}}{\text{Total number of text chunks retrieved}}$$

Figure 9.5: Formula for precision

Suppose a scientific literature information retrieval system returns 15 text blocks, of which 12 are directly related to the query, then the **precision** is 80%. High precision means that learners can obtain the needed information more quickly without being distracted by irrelevant text blocks.

Tips from Lewis

"In the evaluation dataset, if the system can find the relevant 'text chunks,' it is considered a successful retrieval.

However, depending on the task, we may also need to locate specific pages, paragraphs, sentences, or even the original document."

High precision also means that the retrieved content is more accurate, effectively reducing unnecessary information display. This metric is especially important in avoiding the presentation of irrelevant information, in fields such as medicine and law, high precision can effectively prevent the spread of misleading information.

Recall

Recall measures the comprehensiveness with which the system retrieves relevant text blocks, that is, the proportion of relevant text blocks retrieved by the system to all relevant text blocks in the database. **Recall** aims to answer the following question: **Of all the relevant text blocks, how many did the system successfully retrieve?**

The formula for calculating **recall** is as follows:

$$\text{Recall} = \frac{\text{Number of relevant text chunks retrieved}}{\text{Total number of relevant text chunks}}$$

Figure 9.6: The ratio of retrieved relevant documents to all relevant documents

Assume that in a legal document retrieval system, the database contains 50 documents relevant to the query topic, and the system successfully retrieves 40 of them. Then the recall is 80%. In scientific research, high recall can ensure that researchers do not miss key references.

High **recall** is critical for avoiding the omission of crucial information. If recall is low, the model may generate incomplete answers or make mistakes due to missing key information. For example, in legal document retrieval, missing relevant information may affect the completeness of case analysis.

F1 score

In a **RAG system**, improving **precision** often leads to a decrease in **recall**, and vice versa. Therefore, to achieve optimal retrieval performance, it is usually necessary to find a balance between precision and recall. This balance is typically quantified using the **F1 score**, which is the harmonic mean of precision and recall, used to find the optimal point suitable for the specific application requirements.

The formula for calculating the F1 score is as follows:

$$F1\ Score = \frac{2 \times (\text{Precision} \times \text{Recall})}{\text{Precision} + \text{Recall}}$$

Figure 9.7: Equation for F1 score in showing the harmonic mean of precision and recall values

Mean reciprocal rank

Mean Reciprocal Rank (MRR) is an evaluation metric for the efficiency of retrieval systems, with a special focus on the rank of the first relevant text chunk. **MRR** helps us gauge whether a RAG system can quickly return the first relevant text chunk, and its value has a direct impact on user experience. The higher the MRR value, the faster the system is able to find the first suitable answer.

The formula for calculating **MRR** is as follows:

$$MRR = \frac{1}{Q}\sum_{q=1}^{Q}\frac{1}{rank_q}$$

Figure 9.8: Mathematical formula for MRR showing the average inverse rank over Q queries

Where **Q** represents the total number of queries. `rankq` denotes the position of the first relevant text chunk for **q** query q. The formula requires taking the reciprocal of the ranking of the first relevant text chunk, which means that **MRR** only considers the position of the first relevant text chunk returned for each query. With this calculation method, the higher the rank of the text chunk, the greater the reciprocal of `rankq`, and thus the greater the MRR.

MRR is particularly important in question-answering or information retrieval systems, as it focuses on the ability to quickly obtain the first relevant answer. For example, in a customer service Q&A system, if a user poses a question and the system can select and respond with an answer within the top 3 results, the **MRR** value will be relatively high, indicating that the system has stronger speed and accuracy in responding to user needs.

Mean average precision

Mean Average Precision (MAP) is a precision metric evaluated across multiple queries. It not only considers the precision of the retrieval results but also emphasizes the importance of document ranking. **MAP** evaluates retrieval effectiveness by calculating the precision at various ranks for each query, ensuring that important relevant documents are positioned higher, thereby optimizing the user search experience.

The calculation formula for **MAP** is as follows:

$$MAP = \frac{1}{Q}\sum_{q=1}^{Q}\text{AveragePrecision}_{\text{q}}$$

Figure 9.9: MAP equals the mean of Average Precision over Q queries

Here, Q denotes the total number of queries. **Average Precision** is the mean precision calculated for each query, taking into account the order of relevant documents.

MAP is very useful in systems where the quality of rankings is important, such as search engines, and is often used in product recommendation systems on e-commerce platforms.

P@K

P@K measures the precision of the top K retrieved results, ensuring that as many relevant pieces of information as possible are included in the first few results displayed.

$$\text{P@K} = \frac{\text{Number of relevant documents in the top K search results}}{K}$$

Figure 9.10: Mathematical formula for P@K

Here, the numerator represents the number of relevant documents among the top K results, and the K in the denominator is a fixed return count.

P@K is especially useful in scenarios where users are particularly concerned with the top few results. For example, in a news search system, **P@K** can ensure that the first few news items retrieved are highly relevant to the query topic, thereby improving reading efficiency.

Document precision, page precision, and positional document precision

Successfully retrieving relevant text blocks is not the only criterion. In certain projects, we require some different evaluation perspectives. For example, sometimes, in addition to text blocks, we also care about the positioning of courses and pages, as well as their relative positions in the retrieval results. The evaluation metrics involved are as follows:

- **Document precision**: This metric assesses whether the system has found the entire course containing the answer. It mainly focuses on **course-level accuracy**, i.e., whether the correct course has been found, but does not concern itself with the accuracy of specific pages within the course.
- **Page precision**: This metric focuses on whether the system has found the correct page within the course containing the answer.
- **Positional document precision**: This metric assigns different weights to courses based on their position in the retrieval results. The earlier the course appears, the higher the weight. This is achieved by applying a penalty factor (such as `-1.1`) to decrease the score of lower-ranked courses, ensuring that courses appearing earlier receive higher scores. The final score is normalized to the `[0, 1]` range.

Note

The previously introduced metrics (such as **precision**, **MRR**, etc.) all directly apply to specific text blocks, whereas Document Precision, Page Precision, and Positional Document Precision target the specific course and page where the text block is located. These belong to the **metadata** of the text block. Why should we pay attention to the accuracy of this metadata?

In some cases, identifying the relevant course or page is sufficient, especially when **large models** are able to generate answers based on a long context. We can use text blocks to locate a certain course or page and then pass the entire course or page to the large model.

Looking at the actual text blocks and pages retrieved by the system, among the top 5 retrieval results, although no text block matched the expected answer, there was one relevant page (**page 23**) that met the requirements. All expected courses were hit. Therefore, the **Document Precision** reached 100%, while the **Page Precision** was 33.3% (only one of the three expected pages was found).

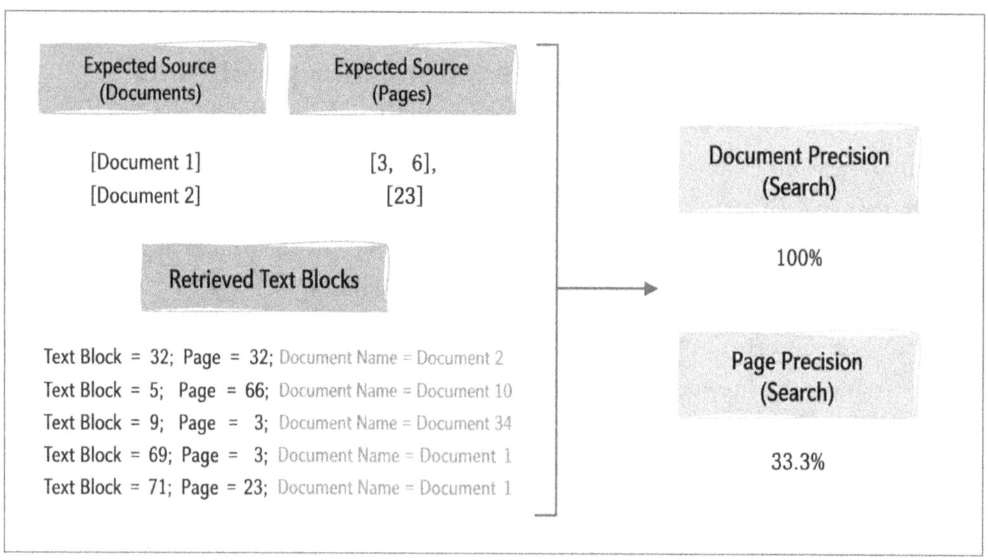

Figure 9.11: A flowchart shows expected and found documents and pages with the calculation of accuracy rates

Alex: **Lewis**, what do this example and the retrieval results indicate?

Lewis: As shown above, the system has already found two documents containing the answer (i.e., **100% expected document hit rate**), but since it failed to identify all the key pages, the answer's accuracy may be affected. In other words, if the project's goal is to retrieve relevant documents from a large number of PDF files, the system's performance is already quite impressive. However, if precise localization of the specific text content is required, the system's performance still needs significant improvement.

From the perspective of **text generation**, if we rely solely on the retrieved text blocks to generate the answer, the information might not be sufficiently accurate. However, if we consider the pages or even the entire document to which the text blocks belong, the generated text can contain some or even all of the key information. Do you remember the **parent-child text block retrieval strategy** we discussed in Section 6.1? In this respect, this retrieval can be considered a success.

Alex: I see!

Positional document precision

Positional document precision further refines the evaluation metric by considering the position of documents in the retrieval results, emphasizing that documents found earlier in the results are more valuable than those found later.

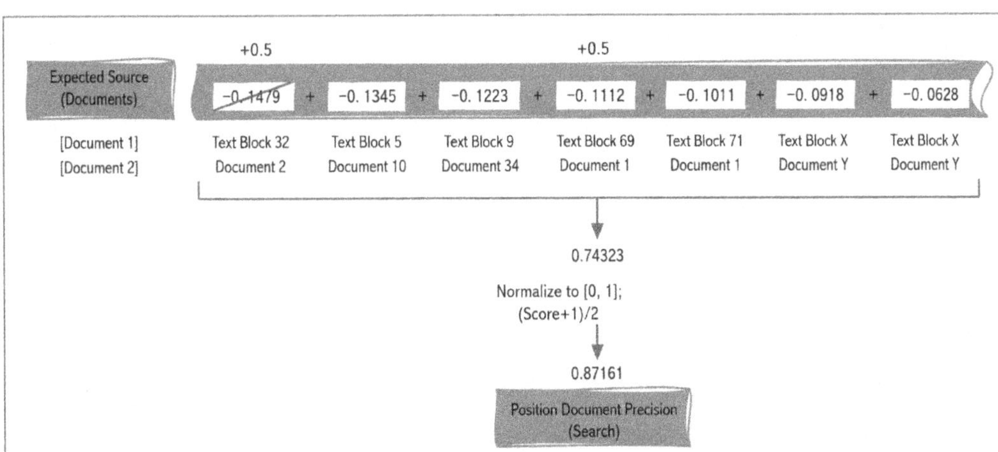

Figure 9.12: Document sources, text blocks with score normalization, and accuracy calculation

To calculate **positional document precision**, you should first record the relevant information and scores for each text block. At each position, if the correct text block is found, add 0.5 points; if not, apply a negative value vector that changes over time as a penalty factor. This means that the later the reference answer appears, the greater the penalty to the overall score.

Response evaluation metrics

Response evaluation focuses on the **generator** component in **RAG systems.** It plays an important role in assessing the **accuracy**, **coherence**, and **reliability** of large model outputs. Response evaluation metrics can generally be divided into three main categories: n-gram overlap-based metrics, semantic similarity-based metrics, and faithfulness or factuality-based metrics.

N-gram overlap-based metrics

These metrics include **BLEU**, **ROUGE**, and **METEOR**, which measure the quality of generated responses by computing similarity between generated answers and reference answers, with an emphasis on overlap of words and phrases. Let's consider them in detail:

1. **BLEU: Bilingual Evaluation Understudy** or **BLEU** is used to evaluate the n-gram overlap between the generated response and the reference answer, emphasizing precision. It calculates the score through precise **n-gram matches** (i.e., sequences of consecutive n tokens, where n can be 1, 2, 3, 4, etc.).

   The formula for BLEU is as follows:

$$BLEU = BP \times \exp\left(\sum_{n=1}^{N} w_n \log P_n\right)$$

   Figure 9.13: BLEU score: BLEU equals BP times exp of weighted log precision sum

   Here, **BP** is the **Brevity Penalty**, used to prevent the generated response from being too short. If the generated response is shorter than the reference answer, then **BP** is less than 1; otherwise, **BP** equals 1. **Pn** is the n-gram precision. **wn** is the weight for each n-gram, and typically, the values of **w1**, **w2**, **w3**, and **w4** are equal.

   For example, suppose the reference answer is "the cat is on mat", and the generated response is "the cat on mat".

   For **BLEU-1** (1-gram precision), the 1-gram (word) matches include "the", "cat", "on", and "mat"—a total of 4. There are 4 1-grams in the generated response. Therefore, the 1-gram precision is 1.

For **BLEU-2** (2-gram precision), the 2-gram (consecutive two words) matches include "the cat" and "on mat"—a total of 2. There are 3 2-grams in the generated response. Therefore, the 2-gram precision is 2/3, approximately 0.67.

For **BP**, the reference answer contains 5 words, while the generated response contains 4 words. Therefore, a BP less than 1 is applied to lower the score.

In this example, although the generated response is missing the word "is", because it contains most of the words and phrases from the reference answer and is similar in length, the **BLEU** score will still be relatively high.

BLEU is simple and intuitive, and is commonly used to evaluate the quality of tasks with clear answers, such as machine translation. However, its limitation is that it cannot capture semantic similarity.

2. **ROUGE: Recall-Oriented Understudy for Gisting Evaluation**, or **ROUGE**, is used to calculate the overlap of n-grams between generated answers and reference answers, taking into account both precision and recall to provide a relatively balanced evaluation

The formula for **ROUGE** is as follows:

$$ROUGE\text{-}N = \frac{\sum \text{Count of co-occurring } n\text{-grams in the matching } n\text{-grams}}{\sum \text{Total number of } n\text{-grams in the reference(s)}}$$

Figure 9.14: ROUGE-N formula in math notation, showing ngram overlap over total ngrams

Continuing with the previous example, suppose the reference answer is "the cat is on mat" and the generated answer is "the cat on mat".

For **ROUGE-1** (i.e., 1-gram), the matches include "the", "cat", "on", and "mat", totaling 4. There are 5 1-grams in the reference answer. Therefore, **ROUGE-1** is 0.8.

For **ROUGE-2** (i.e., 2-gram), the matches include "the cat" and "on mat", totaling 2. There are 4 2-grams in the reference answer. Therefore, **ROUGE-2** is 0.5.

ROUGE is commonly used to evaluate tasks such as automatic summarization generation, as it can effectively measure whether the generated text retains the key information of the original text. However, its limitation is that it relies too heavily on lexical-level matching and lacks consideration of semantic similarity.

3. **METEOR: Metric for Evaluation of Translation with Explicit Ordering**, or **METEOR**, provides a more detailed assessment of the similarity between generated responses and reference answers by considering factors such as **synonyms**, **stemming**, and **word order**. It not only calculates the harmonic mean of **precision** and **recall** (*F*mean), but also incorporates a **penalty mechanism** to handle word order errors and other mismatches. **METEOR** is able to capture semantic features better than **BLEU** and **ROUGE**.

   The calculation formula for **METEOR** is as follows:

   METEOR = *F*mean × (1 - *P*penalty)

   Here, *F*mean is the harmonic mean of **precision** and **recall**, used to comprehensively measure the degree of match between the generated response and the reference answer. *P*penalty is a penalty term used to penalize **word order errors** and other types of errors.

   Here we still assume the reference answer is "the cat is on mat," and the generated response is "the cat on mat."

   For **precision**, the generated response contains 4 words, all of which are matches, so the precision is 1.

   For **recall**, the reference answer contains 5 words, among which 4 are matches, so the recall is 0.8.

   For the harmonic mean,

$$F_{mean} = \frac{2 \times 1 \times 0.8}{1 + 0.8} = \frac{1.6}{1.8} \approx 0.89$$

Figure 9.15: Mathematical formula for F mean

   As for the **penalty term**, since the generated response is missing the word "is," **METEOR** applies a penalty term *P*penalty. The specific value of this penalty depends on implementation details, but in this example, we can assume it is 0.1.

   Finally, **METEOR** is 0.801.

In this example, **METEOR** is more forgiving than **BLEU-2** and **ROUGE-2** because it allows for missing words in the generated response. In fact, **METEOR** also tolerates minor word order variation and takes into account **synonyms** or **morphological variants**. This makes **METEOR** particularly useful when evaluating tasks that require higher semantic understanding. Especially in translation quality assessment, when the generated translation differs in word order but is semantically close to the reference translation, **METEOR** can still provide a relatively high score.

Alex: I understand that **METEOR** focuses more on **semantic similarity**, but I'm still not quite clear about the key differences between **BLEU** and **ROUGE**.

Lewis: **BLEU** mainly focuses on **precision**, that is, assessing how much of the content generated can be found in the reference text. It does this by calculating the n-gram matches between the generated text and the reference text, emphasizing the proportion of correct matches in the generated output. **BLEU** was originally designed for evaluating **machine translation quality**, measuring translation quality by comparing the n-gram overlaps between the generated translations and the reference translations.

In contrast, **ROUGE** pays more attention to **recall**, that is, considering how much of the reference text's content is covered by the generated text. Although **ROUGE** also involves n-gram matching, its core is to evaluate whether the generated text covers the key information in the reference text. Therefore, **ROUGE** is more commonly used in tasks like **summarization** or **document extraction**.

In the field of **machine translation**, we tend to pursue a high **BLEU** score, as this indicates a higher degree of similarity between the machine translation output and human translation. In addition, because **ROUGE** emphasizes recall, it is more suitable for text generation tasks like **summarization** or **document extraction**. In these scenarios, we hope the generated text can include as much important information from the reference text as possible, rather than strictly matching the wording of the reference text.

Metrics based on semantic similarity

Evaluation methods based on **embeddings** and **semantic similarity** do not rely on lexical matching. Instead, they convert generated responses and reference answers into vectors and use methods such as **cosine similarity** to calculate the semantic similarity between the generated content and the reference answer.

Below, we will review some familiar concepts:

1. **Cosine similarity: Cosine similarity** is used to measure the angular similarity between the embedding of the generated response and that of the reference answer, thus assessing their degree of semantic closeness. The calculation formula is as follows.

$$\text{Cosine Similarity} = \frac{A \cdot B}{||A|| \times ||B||} = \frac{\sum_{i=1}^{n} A_i B_i}{\sqrt{\sum_{i=1}^{n} A_i^2} \times \sqrt{\sum_{i=1}^{n} B_i^2}}$$

Figure 9.16: Mathematical formula for cosine similarity showing the dot product over the product of magnitudes

Although it may not be sufficiently accurate when used alone, the average across multiple instances can provide a rough estimate of the quality of generated answers.

Suppose the embedding of the generated response is `A = [1,0,1]`, and the embedding of the reference answer is `B = [1,1,0]`, then the cosine similarity is

$$\frac{1 \times 1 + 0 \times 1 + 1 \times 0}{\sqrt{1^2 + 0^2 + 1^2} \times \sqrt{1^2 + 1^2 + 0^2}} = \frac{1}{\sqrt{2} \times \sqrt{2}} = 0.5$$

Figure 9.17: A mathematical equation showing a cosine similarity calculation equal to 0.5 using vectors

This indicates that the generated response has a certain degree of similarity to the reference answer.

2. **Euclidean distance: Euclidean distance** is used to measure the straight-line distance between two vectors; the smaller the value, the higher the similarity between them. Its calculation formula is as follows.

$$d = \sqrt{\sum_{i=1}^{n} (A_i - B_i)^2}$$

Figure 9.18: Mathematical formula for Euclidean distance showing the square root of the sum of squared differences

Assuming again that the embedding of the generated answer **A** is =[1,0,1], and the embedding of the reference answer **B** is =[1,1,0], then the Euclidean distance is

$$\sqrt{(1-1)^2+(0-1)^2+(1-0)^2} = \sqrt{0+1+1} = \sqrt{2} \approx 1.41$$

Figure 9.19: Mathematical equation showing the distance formula calculation resulting in the square root of 2 equals about 1.41

This indicates that the similarity between the generated answer and the reference answer is relatively low.

In answer generation tasks, **cosine similarity** is usually considered a more accurate **semantic similarity metric** because it focuses on the directional similarity of vectors, which better reflects **semantic consistency**. However, in recommendation systems, **Euclidean distance** may be more applicable.

Alex: We are already familiar with this knowledge. The takeaway here is that after the **RAG system** generates the final result, we can use the **semantic similarity score** to evaluate the generated answer. A higher score indicates greater similarity between the generated answer and the reference answer.

Metrics based on faithfulness or groundedness

In large model evaluation, **BLEU**, **ROUGE**, **METEOR**, and metrics based on **semantic similarity** are often used to measure the relevance of answers. That is, whether the response generated by the large model is related to the user's query and provides useful information. However, **relevance** is not equivalent to **accuracy**. Even if an answer is semantically aligned with the query, it may still contain hallucination errors or comprehension errors as shown in the following figure:

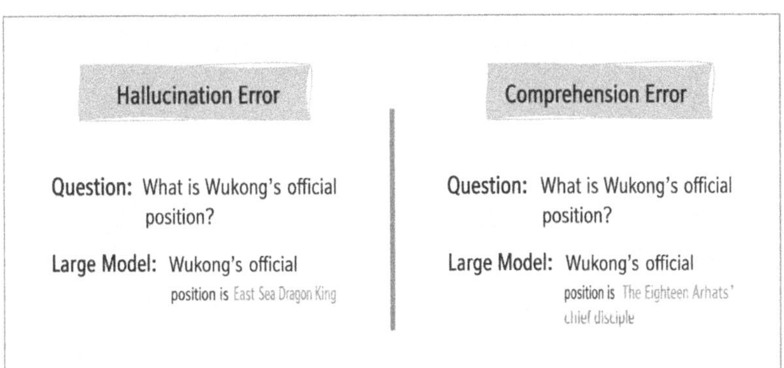

Figure 9.20: A comparison chart showing visual vs comprehension errors about character titles

These kinds of **hallucination errors** are especially dangerous for ordinary users because if users are not familiar with a particular field, they may not be able to identify inaccuracies in the generated response. In contrast, **comprehension errors** caused by obvious logical confusion, although also a type of model failure, are usually easier to detect. **Accuracy-related metrics** are more difficult to quantify, since they often involve answers that appear plausible but are actually incorrect. Therefore, more wisdom and consideration are required in designing specific evaluation rules.

Alex: Indeed, even powerful models like **DeepSeek-R1** can make mistakes in professional fields. Especially when the details in the generated response are seemingly reasonable, it is difficult for non-experts to spot the errors. This may mislead beginners or outsiders who do not study the field in depth, resulting in far-reaching consequences.

Lewis: To address this issue, we have introduced **faithfulness** or **groundedness** as new evaluation criteria. These standards focus on measuring whether the generated response is based on retrieved documents and is accurate and error-free, ensuring that the provided information is not only relevant but also truthful and reliable.

To better quantify **faithfulness**, we can use the following metrics for assessment:

- **Document accuracy and page accuracy:** These metrics are used to measure the accuracy of the documents and specific pages cited by the large model. This requires the large model to clearly annotate its sources when generating answers, in order to reduce the occurrence of fabricated information.
- **Hallucination detection/consistency check:** These metrics aim to determine whether the response generated by the large model is based on the provided context information or whether the factual information given in different queries is consistent. In the evaluation process, a binary assessment (0/1) is adopted. If the generated response cannot be derived from the given documents, even if the answer itself is correct, it is still considered a hallucination.
- **Large model scoring scale**: Use more powerful large models to score the generated responses, for example, using a 0 to 5 point rating scale. The specific scoring criteria can be customized according to business requirements, in order to more flexibly adapt to different application scenarios.
- **Human evaluation**: Domain experts manually check whether the responses generated by the large model are accurate, and verify whether they have reasonably cited the retrieved documents.

The evaluation of **faithfulness** involves a rigorous examination of the logical reasoning ability of the large model's outputs. For instance, even if a generated response is correct, if it cannot be deduced from the provided document, it should still be considered a **hallucination**. Therefore, it is necessary to design special evaluation procedures to handle these issues, including requiring the large model to cite sources in a parsable format, ensuring that the generated answers have clear literature support, and conducting strict context consistency checks to ensure that the large model does not give contradictory answers to different queries.

One way to address the **hallucination** problem is to properly control the amount of information. Although providing more context may help improve evaluation metrics, excessive information may reduce the quality of the large model's responses and increase the likelihood of hallucinations.

Evaluation frameworks for RAG systems

Alex: We don't have to manually implement those **metrics** mentioned earlier, do we?

Lewis: As of now, there is still no universal and widely recognized **RAG framework** that can achieve all the **metrics** introduced above. Therefore, we need to experimentally try out different RAG evaluation frameworks, such as **Retrieval Augmented Generation Assessment Suite (RAGAS)**, **TruLens**, and **DeepEval**. The level of adoption and use cases for these frameworks are quite different. If a specific framework cannot meet your project needs, you may need to combine multiple frameworks, and you may indeed need to manually add your own **evaluation metrics**.

Using RAGAS to evaluate RAG systems

Among the various frameworks for evaluating **RAG systems**, **RAGAS** is currently one of the more popular choices among developers. **RAGAS** provides a set of objective evaluation metrics specifically designed to measure the performance of large model applications, applicable to various scenarios, including **RAG** and **Agentic workflows**, ensuring the quality, accuracy, and consistency of their outputs.

For **RAG systems**, RAGAS evaluation metrics are mainly divided into two categories: **retrieval-related metrics** and **generation-related metrics**.

The main retrieval-related metrics supported by RAGAS are as follows:

- **Context precision**: Measures the relevance of retrieved documents to the query.
- **Context recall**: Evaluates whether the retrieved documents comprehensively cover the information needed to answer the question.

- **Context entity recall**: Focuses on the ability to recall entities (such as people's names, place names, technical terms) during retrieval. This is particularly important for tasks requiring highly accurate entity matching, such as queries in the medical, legal, or financial fields.
- **Noise sensitivity**: Detects the large model's resistance to irrelevant information in the retrieved results.

The main generation-related metrics supported by RAGAS are as follows:

- **Answer relevancy**: Measures whether the generated answer directly and accurately addresses the user's query, avoiding off-topic answers.
- **Faithfulness**: Measures whether the generated answer is based on the retrieved facts, in order to avoid hallucinations. A highly faithful large model ensures its answers are based on verifiable knowledge and does not fabricate content.
- **Multimodal faithfulness**: Applies to multimodal scenarios such as text-image or text-audio, ensuring information consistency across different modalities.
- **Multimodal relevancy**: Measures whether the content output by the model in multimodal tasks meets the user's needs. For example, whether the audio generated by the large model appropriately conveys the emotions described in the text.

The following code example demonstrates how to use **RAGAS** for evaluation. Note that this example uses English data, as during practical operation, it was found that some metrics do not yet support Chinese.

First, import the necessary libraries and configure the relevant settings:

```
import numpy as np
from datasets import Dataset
from ragas.metrics import Faithfulness, AnswerRelevancy
from ragas.llms import LangchainLLMWrapper
from ragas.embeddings import LangchainEmbeddingsWrapper
from langchain_openai import OpenAIEmbeddings
from ragas.embeddings import HuggingfaceEmbeddings
from langchain_deepseek import ChatDeepSeek
from ragas import evaluate
### Prepare the Large Model for Evaluation
llm = LangchainLLMWrapper(ChatDeepSeek(model="deepseek-chat"))
```

When using **RAGAS** for evaluation, a detailed dataset is needed, including **questions, contexts,** and **reference answers**. This evaluation method can provide a more comprehensive analysis of **RAG system performance**, but the preparation workload is relatively large:

```
data = {
    "question": [
        "Who is the main character in Black Myth: Wukong?",
        "What are the special features of the combat system in Black Myth: 
Wukong?",
        "How is the visual quality of Black Myth: Wukong?",
    ],
    "answer": [
        """The main character in Black Myth: Wukong is Sun Wukong, 
based on the Chinese classic 'Journey to the West' but with a new 
interpretation. This version of Sun Wukong is more mature and brooding, 
showing a different personality from the traditional character.""",

        """Black Myth: Wukong's combat system combines Chinese martial 
arts with Soulslike game features, including light and heavy attack 
combinations, technique transformations, and magic systems. Notably, 
Wukong can transform between different weapon forms during combat, such as 
his iconic staff and nunchucks, and use various mystical abilities.""",

        """Black Myth: Wukong is developed using Unreal Engine 5, 
showcasing stunning visual quality. The game's scene modeling, lighting 
effects, and character details are all top-tier, particularly in its 
detailed recreation of traditional Chinese architecture and mythological 
settings.""",
    ],
    "contexts": [
        [
            "Black Myth: Wukong is an action RPG developed by Game 
Science, featuring Sun Wukong as the protagonist based on 'Journey to the 
West' but with innovative interpretations. In the game, Wukong has a more 
composed personality and carries a special mission.",
            "The game is set in a mythological world, telling a new story 
that presents a different take on the source material."
        ],
        [
```

```
            "Combat in Black Myth: Wukong is notable for its fluid martial
arts action inspired by Chinese traditions. In addition to standard
attacks, players can unleash magic powers and perform shape-shifting
transformations that offer new tactics in battle.",
            "Players can wield the protagonist's iconic staff, use weapons
like nunchucks, and access abilities reminiscent of the original legend,
creating a rich and varied fighting system."
        ],
        [
            "Powered by Unreal Engine 5, Black Myth: Wukong offers
extraordinary realism in environments, character models, and animation
quality.",
            "Lighting, physics, and atmospheric effects enhance the
authenticity of ancient Chinese landscapes and fantastical creatures
within the game."
        ]
    ]
}
```

The game's combat system is heavily influenced by **Soulslike games** while incorporating traditional **Chinese martial arts** elements. Players can utilize different **weapon forms**, including the iconic **staff** and other transforming weapons.

During combat, players can unleash various **mystical abilities**, combined with **light and heavy attacks** and **combo systems**, creating a fluid and distinctive combat experience. The game also features a unique **transformation system**.

Black Myth: Wukong demonstrates exceptional visual quality, built with **Unreal Engine 5**, achieving extremely high graphical fidelity. The game's environments and character models are meticulously crafted.

The **lighting effects, material rendering**, and **environmental details** all reach AAA-level standards, perfectly capturing the atmosphere of an **Eastern mythological world**.

Next, you can evaluate whether the generated answers are faithful to the given context, as shown in the following code snippet. Break down the generated answer into simple statements, and then verify whether each statement can be inferred from the context. The **faithfulness metric** requires specifying the **large language model** used for evaluation, but does not require specifying the embedding model.

Refer to https://github.com/PacktPublishing/RAG-from-First-Principles for the complete code:

```
### Evaluate Faithfulness
faithfulness_metric = [Faithfulness(llm=llm)]
print("\nEvaluating faithfulness......")
faithfulness_result = evaluate(dataset, faithfulness_metric)
scores = faithfulness_result['faithfulness']
mean_score = np.mean(scores) if isinstance(scores, (list, np.ndarray))
else scores
print(f"Faithfulness score: {mean_score:.4f}")
```

Expected output:

```
Evaluating faithfulness......Evaluating: 100%|██████████| 3/3
[00:06<00:00,  2.03s/it]
Faithfulness score: 0.6111
```

Next, we will evaluate **answer relevancy,** which uses **embedding models** to calculate semantic similarity and compare open-source embedding models with OpenAI's embedding models (refer to https://github.com/PacktPublishing/RAG-from-First-Principles for the complete code):

```
### Set Up Two Types of Embedding Models
opensource_embedding = LangchainEmbeddingsWrapper(
    HuggingfaceEmbeddings(model_name="sentence-transformers/all-MiniLM-
L6-v2")
)
openai_embedding = LangchainEmbeddingsWrapper(
    OpenAIEmbeddings(model="text-embedding-3-small")
)
### Create Answer Relevancy Evaluation Metric
opensource_relevancy = [
    AnswerRelevancy(llm=llm, embeddings=opensource_embedding)
]
openai_relevancy = [
    AnswerRelevancy(llm=llm, embeddings=openai_embedding)
]
print("\nEvaluating answer relevancy......")
print("\nEvaluating with open-source embedding model:")
```

```
opensource_result = evaluate(dataset, opensource_relevancy)
scores = opensource_result['answer_relevancy']
opensource_mean = (
    np.mean(scores) if isinstance(scores, (list, np.ndarray)) else scores
)
print(f"Relevancy score: {opensource_mean:.4f}")
print("\nEvaluating with OpenAI embedding model:")
openai_result = evaluate(dataset, openai_relevancy)
scores = openai_result['answer_relevancy']
openai_mean = (
    np.mean(scores) if isinstance(scores, (list, np.ndarray)) else scores
)
print(f"Relevancy score: {openai_mean:.4f}")
## Compare the Results of the Two Embedding Models
print("\n=== Embedding Model Comparison ===")
diff = openai_mean - opensource_mean
print(f"Open-source embedding model score: {opensource_mean:.4f}")
print(f"OpenAI embedding model score: {openai_mean:.4f}")
print(
    f"Difference: {diff:.4f} "
    f"({'OpenAI is better' if diff > 0 else 'Open-source embedding model
is better' if diff < 0 else 'Comparable'})"
)
```

Expected output:

```
Evaluating answer relevance......
Using open-source embedding model for evaluation:
Evaluating: 100%|██████████| 3/3 [00:02<00:00,  1.02it/s]
Relevance score: 0.8565
Using OpenAI embedding model for evaluation:
Evaluating: 100%|██████████| 3/3 [00:06<00:00,  2.15s/it]
Relevance score: 0.9426
=== Embedding Model Comparison ===
Open-source embedding model score: 0.8565
OpenAI embedding model score: 0.9426
Difference: 0.0861 (OpenAI is better)
```

The example provided here only demonstrates two representative metrics from the range of evaluation metrics offered by **RAGAS**. In fact, there are many other **metrics** available for evaluation. If you find existing suitable metrics, there is no need to create a new metric system from scratch.

Using TruLens for RAG TRIAD evaluation

TruLens is based on the **RAG TRIAD framework**, focusing on evaluating **RAG systems** from three aspects: contextual relevance, faithfulness, and answer relevance.

TruLens objectively measures the quality and effectiveness of answers generated by large language model applications through **feedback functions**. These functions enable programmatic evaluation of inputs, outputs, and intermediate results, and support scoring using large models or traditional NLP models. The built-in feedback functions include chain-of-thought-based evaluation, faithfulness, contextual relevance, answer relevance, user sentiment, fairness, and bias, as well as assessments of harmful or offensive language. Additionally, TruLens allows users to define custom feedback functions to meet evaluation needs in specific projects or application scenarios.

TruLens supports multiple frameworks, such as **LangChain** and **LlamaIndex** and can monitor evaluation results in real time through a visualization dashboard.

The following code example demonstrates how to use different feedback functions to evaluate the performance of an RAG system (refer to `https://github.com/PacktPublishing/RAG-from-First-Principles` for the complete code):

```
import os
import chromadb
from chromadb.utils.embedding_functions import OpenAIEmbeddingFunction
from openai import OpenAI as OpenAIClient  # Avoid naming conflict with
TruLens's OpenAI class
from trulens.core import TruSession, Feedback, Select
from trulens.apps.app import TruApp, instrument
from trulens.providers.openai import OpenAI as TruLensOpenAI
import numpy as np
### Initialize the Embedding Function
embedding_function = OpenAIEmbeddingFunction(api_key=os.environ.
get("OPENAI_API_KEY"),
model_name="text-embedding-ada-002")
chroma_client = chromadb.Client()
vector_store = chroma_client.get_or_create_collection("Info", embedding_
function=embedding_function)
```

```
### Add Sample Data
vector_store.add("starbucks_info", documents=[
""
Starbucks Corporation is an American multinational chain of coffeehouses
headquartered in Seattle, Washington.
As the world's largest coffeehouse chain, Starbucks is seen to be the main
representation of the United States' second wave of coffee culture.
""
])
class RAG:
    @instrument  # TruLens decorator, used for tracking function calls
    def retrieve(self, query: str):
        """"Retrieve relevant documents""""
        results = vector_store.query(query_texts=[query], n_results=2)
        return results["documents"][0] if results["documents"] else []
    @instrument
    def generate_completion(self, query: str, context: list):
        """"Generate answer""""
        oai_client = OpenAIClient(api_key=os.environ.get("OPENAI_API_
KEY"))
        context_str = "\n".join(context) if context else "No context
available."
        completion = oai_client.chat.completions.create(
            model="gpt-3.5-turbo",
            messages=[{"role": "user", "content": f"Context: {context_
str}\nQuestion: {query}"}]
        ).choices[0].message.content
        return completion
    @instrument
    def query(self, query: str):
        """"Complete RAG query process""""
        context = self.retrieve(query)
        return self.generate_completion(query, context)
### Initialize TruLens Session
session = TruSession(database_redact_keys=True)
session.reset_database()
### Initialize TruLens OpenAI
```

```
provider = TruLensOpenAI(model_engine="gpt-4")
### Define Evaluation Metrics
f_groundedness = Feedback(provider.groundedness_measure_with_cot_reasons,
name="Groundedness") \
    .on(Select.RecordCalls.retrieve.rets).on_output()
f_answer_relevance = Feedback(provider.relevance_with_cot_reasons,
name="Answer Relevance") \
    .on_input().on_output()
f_context_relevance = Feedback(provider.context_relevance_with_cot_
reasons, name="Context Relevance") \
    .on_input().on(Select.RecordCalls.retrieve.rets[:]).aggregate(np.mean)
### Set Up TruApp
rag = RAG()
tru_rag = TruApp(
    rag,
    app_name="RAG",
    app_version="base",
    feedbacks=[f_groundedness, f_answer_relevance, f_context_relevance]
)
### Execute Query and Record
with tru_rag as recording:
    response = rag.query("What wave of coffee culture is Starbucks seen to
represent in the United States?")
    print(f"Response: {response}")
### View Evaluation Result
print(session.get_leaderboard())
```

Expected output:

```
Initialized with db url sqlite:///default.sqlite.
Secret keys will not be included in the database.
In **Groundedness**, input source will be set to __record__.app.retrieve.
rets.
In **Groundedness**, input statement will be set to __record__.main_output
or `Select.RecordOutput`.
In **Answer Relevance**, input prompt will be set to __record__.main_input
or `Select.RecordInput`.
In **Answer Relevance**, input response will be set to __record__.main_
output or `Select.RecordOutput`.
```

```
In **Context Relevance**, input question will be set to __record__.main_
input or `Select.RecordInput`.
In **Context Relevance**, input context will be set to __record__.app.
retrieve.rets[:] .
instrumenting <class '__main__.RAG'> for base <class '__main__.RAG'>
instrumenting retrieve
instrumenting generate_completion
instrumenting query
Response: Starbucks is seen to represent the second wave of coffee culture
in the United States.
app_name, app_version, latency, total_cost
RAG       base         2.397581    0.000147
```

In the example, an evaluation session is created using **TruLens**, with the following evaluation metrics defined:

- `f_groundedness`: Used to assess the accuracy of the answer
- `f_answer_relevance`: Used to assess the relevance of the answer
- `f_context_relevance`: Used to assess the relevance of the retrieved documents

The results show that the system first initializes an **SQLite database** to store evaluation data and sets the input sources for the three evaluation metrics. Evaluation results are saved to the database, but specific results are not shown here. These results can be viewed through the **TruLens dashboard** or exported from the database. The query execution time is approximately 2.4s, and the API call cost is $0.000147.

DeepEval – a powerful open-source large model evaluation framework

Unlike the design philosophies of the two evaluation frameworks introduced earlier, **DeepEval** brings the concept of **testing** from software engineering into the field of **large model evaluation**, supporting the validation of large model performance through **unit tests**. It is an **open-source evaluation framework** specifically designed for large models, providing simple and easy-to-use evaluation, testing, and stress testing tools. **DeepEval** is similar to *Pytest*, but its focus is on providing **unit testing** capabilities for large model outputs, helping developers quickly test and optimize the performance of large model applications using a variety of evaluation metrics, including those built with **RAG** or **fine-tuning**.

Developers can quickly write test cases using declarative syntax to verify key properties such as **answer accuracy**, **safety**, or **response latency** of large models for specific scenarios. **DeepEval** is deeply integrated with **CI/CD** (Continuous Integration/Continuous Deployment) processes, supporting automated **regression testing** to ensure that core performance indicators do not degrade during model iteration. For **industry assistant applications** that require frequent knowledge base updates, **DeepEval** can effectively maintain system stability, making it particularly suitable for agile development teams to build quality guardrails and ensure model quality and performance after each iteration.

DeepEval provides dedicated evaluation tools for RAG systems, aiming to help developers thoroughly assess the effectiveness of **retrievers** and **generators** to ensure the accuracy and relevance of large model outputs:

- **Retrieval evaluation**: Assesses the effectiveness of the retriever using metrics such as context precision, context recall, and context relevance. These metrics help developers ensure that the retrieved information is highly relevant to the query, reasonably ordered, and not excessively redundant.
- **Generation evaluation**: Evaluates the generator's performance through metrics like answer relevance and faithfulness, ensuring that the information output by the large model is accurate, highly relevant, and avoids hallucinations.
- **End-to-end RAG evaluation**: **DeepEval** supports combined evaluation of retrieval and generation, enabling developers to comprehensively assess the overall RAG pipeline performance.
- **Custom evaluation metrics**: Developers can create custom evaluation metrics by inheriting **DeepEval's base metric classes** and seamlessly integrating them into the **DeepEval ecosystem**.

DeepEval is highly flexible: you can execute test files on the **command line interface**, or directly use the `evaluate` function in local Python scripts to utilize these **metrics**. In addition, learners can also choose to run evaluation tasks in the cloud, with **Confident AI** providing the infrastructure to execute large-scale evaluations for free.

The following **RAG evaluation example** demonstrates how to use a Pytest-like approach, leveraging the evaluate function to batch evaluate an entire dataset (refer to `https://github.com/PacktPublishing/RAG-from-First-Principles` for the complete code):

```
from deepeval.metrics import ContextualPrecisionMetric,
AnswerRelevancyMetric
```

```
from deepeval.test_case import LLMTestCase
### Define the Test Case
test_case = LLMTestCase(
input="What if these shoes don't fit?",
actual_output="We offer a 30-day no-questions-asked full refund service.",
expected_output="Customers can return the shoes within 30 days for a full refund.",
retrieval_context=["All customers are eligible for a 30-day no-questions-asked full refund service."]
)
### Define Evaluation Metrics
contextual_precision = ContextualPrecisionMetric()
answer_relevancy = AnswerRelevancyMetric()
### Run Evaluation
contextual_precision.measure(test_case)
answer_relevancy.measure(test_case)
print("Contextual Precision Score: ", contextual_precision.score)
print("Answer Relevancy Score: ", answer_relevancy.score)
```

Expected output:

```
Contextual Precision Score: 1.0
Answer Relevancy Score: 0.0
```

In the above example, both the **contextual precision** and **answer relevance** showed high levels of performance. However, the **answer relevance** score in the output failed to reflect the actual performance, which may be related to the limitations of this framework's support for the Chinese language. If tested with English documents, it is expected that more accurate evaluations would be obtained.

DeepEval not only provides powerful evaluation tools for large models but also features excellent hyperparameter management capabilities, enabling developers to record key **hyperparameters** for each test, such as **text chunk size, retrieved top-K values, embedding models used**, and more. This ability ensures that large model evaluations can be conducted efficiently and reliably during both development and production processes, helping to promptly identify and resolve potential issues, thereby improving the stability and security of large model applications.

DeepEval can seamlessly integrate into any **CI/CD environment**, providing automated testing support for large model applications to ensure these models continue to run stably in production environments. When combined with **Confident AI**, it can deliver continuous evaluation throughout the full lifecycle of large models. Developers can use **DeepEval** to record evaluation results, analyze passing or failing metrics, optimize hyperparameters, debug model outputs, and achieve real-time evaluation and dataset enhancement in production environments, thus rapidly optimizing RAG processes.

Phoenix – interactive model diagnostics and analysis platform

Phoenix, developed by **Arize**, features the use of visual analytical techniques to provide **interactive diagnostic capabilities** for large models. Its core functions include automatic detection of **hallucinations** in generated answers, identification of **knowledge blind spots**, and analysis of input prompts. Phoenix's built-in **semantic search** allows developers to quickly locate failure cases, while **multi-dimensional clustering analysis** helps reveal potential systemic biases. This tool is particularly effective when debugging complex dialog systems, enabling engineers to trace the root causes of errors through a visual interface; for example, discovering the model's misunderstanding of specific domain terms or identifying question patterns likely to trigger incorrect answers.

Phoenix also evaluates **RAG systems** from both retrieval and response aspects. With its visual interface, Phoenix can monitor RAG process inputs and outputs in real time, supports multimodal data and cross-framework operations (such as **LlamaIndex**, **LangChain**), provides a visual analysis interface, and focuses on tracking long-term performance trends.

The frameworks introduced earlier cover the full spectrum of needs, from basic performance evaluation (**RAGAS**), security detection (**DeepEval**), to long-term monitoring (**Phoenix**). For further expansion, you can combine **Prometheus** for operational monitoring or use **LlamaIndex Evaluator** to optimize the RAG system under specific frameworks.

Summary

This chapter analyzed the key points in evaluating **RAG systems**. Among these, the focus of **retriever evaluation** is on the accuracy of retrieving relevant documents, while the evaluation of the **generator** is more complex and must be considered from multiple dimensions.

For a comprehensive evaluation, we need to integrate both quantitative and qualitative metrics, and also take **manual evaluation** as an indispensable supplementary method. By applying a diverse set of metrics, you can gain a comprehensive understanding of the performance of the **RAG system** and identify specific areas in need of improvement.

The following table summarizes the various evaluation frameworks we learned in the chapter:

Evaluation framework	Core advantages	Applicable scenarios
RAGAS	Reference-free evaluation, automated test set generation	Rapid verification of basic RAG system performance
TruLens	Triplet evaluation, visual monitoring	Comprehensive evaluation compatible with multiple frameworks
DeepEval	Security detection, CI/CD integration	Security and compliance evaluation for enterprise-level applications
Phoenix	Long-term trend analysis, multimodal support	Observability needs in complex scenarios

Table 9.1: Comparing RAG evaluation frameworks

Lewis's view remains that there is still no existing "one-size-fits-all" standard and specification for evaluating **RAG systems**. The essence of **RAG system evaluation** depends on the specific task objectives you want to achieve, which determines the relevant evaluation data you need to prepare, as well as the evaluation standards and frameworks you choose. If you cannot find a suitable existing framework, it may be necessary to build the required evaluation system yourself.

10

Complex RAG Paradigms

Alex: Lewis, I've noticed that as **RAG systems** develop to deeper levels, they are no longer just a "simple retrieval + generation" model. New retrieval strategies and paradigms are continuously emerging.

Lewis: That's right. **RAG systems** are no longer limited to traditional keyword or vector retrieval and generation. They are now attempting to combine retrieval with **reasoning, contextual understanding, knowledge graphs, cross-modal information processing**, and **adaptive optimization**, forming a series of **advanced retrieval strategies and paradigms**, also known as **complex RAG paradigms.**

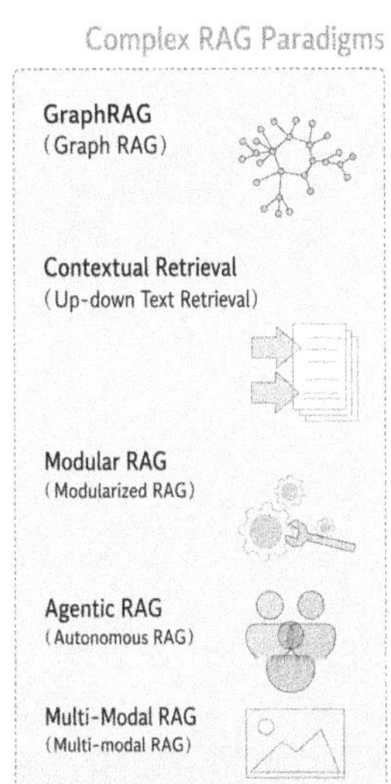

Figure 10.1: Listing the complex RAG paradigms

An overview of complex RAG paradigms

Alex: Can you give me an overview of some of the more innovative **complex RAG paradigms**?

Lewis: Sure. However, due to space limitations in this *course*, I'll introduce several typical **complex RAG paradigms** in a concise manner. For more details, you'll need to consult relevant technology websites on your own. In addition, these new paradigms are in a phase of rapid development. While writing this *course*, many technologies are still evolving.

Therefore, I recommend keeping up with the latest research progress and delving deeper by reading cutting-edge literature. As time goes by, these innovative approaches will be tested in practice and gradually form more mature and reliable technical systems.

GraphRAG integration of RAG and knowledge graphs

Graph-based Retrieval-Augmented Generation (**GraphRAG**), enhances the retrieval capabilities of large models by incorporating **knowledge graphs (KG)**. Its goal is to address the issues traditional **RAG systems** face with complex queries, **multi-hop reasoning**, and global information integration. The core idea of GraphRAG is to convert unstructured text into a structured knowledge graph and utilize **graph database algorithms** such as **associative retrieval** and **community detection** to improve the accuracy and interpretability of generated responses.

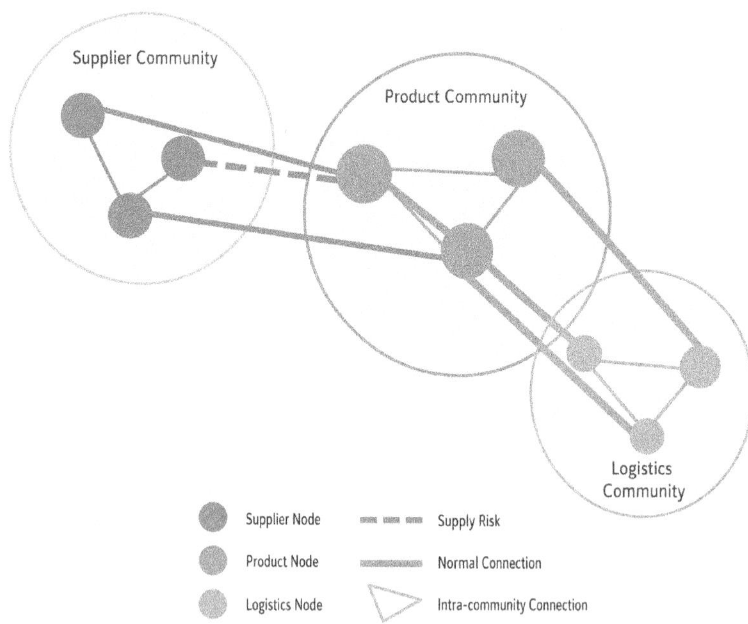

Figure 10.2: Interconnected supplier, product, and logistics communities showing supply risks

Microsoft's open-source **GraphRAG** project demonstrates how to achieve semantic connections across documents by building a knowledge graph, thereby significantly improving the effectiveness of RAG systems in handling knowledge bases. Unlike viewing knowledge as merely a collection of independent documents, GraphRAG generates a knowledge graph from the knowledge base, linking **entities** and their **relationships**. During retrieval, the system takes into account not only the textual information of the nodes (i.e., entities) themselves but also searches along graph edges for related entities to obtain higher-level context. This approach makes retrieval results more relevant and logical.

The implementation of GraphRAG is divided into two main phases: the **indexing phase** and the **querying phase**. The characteristics of the indexing phase are as follows:

- **Text segmentation and entity extraction**: Documents are segmented into paragraph or sentence units, and a large model is used to extract **entities**, **relationships**, and key assertions (such as people, places, events) to construct the initial knowledge graph.
- **Hierarchical clustering and community summarization**: The **Leiden algorithm** is employed for hierarchical clustering of the graph, forming tightly associated community structures, and community summaries are generated bottom-up. For example, in an academic paper repository, mathematics and physics disciplines might form independent communities, each generating a summary of its core topics.

The characteristics of the querying phase are as follows:

- **Global search**: For queries involving the entire dataset (such as "AI research trends in the past 5 years"), multiple rounds of information aggregation are performed through community summaries to generate consolidated responses
- **Local search**: Focused on specific entities (such as "New features of Microsoft's Cosmos DB"), relevant entities are retrieved from a **vector database**, and precise answers are generated in combination with community reports

The advantages and disadvantages of **GraphRAG** are both very apparent. While it can greatly expand the coverage of retrieval and reveal the chains of relationships between current retrieval content and underlying associated nodes, it also consumes a large amount of computing resources and may introduce excessive irrelevant contextual information during the generation process. To address these issues, some optimization approaches have already been proposed in the industry.

LazyGraphRAG, launched shortly after by Microsoft, significantly reduces computational costs by simplifying the index construction process. **LazyGraphRAG** no longer relies on large models to extract entity relationships, but instead uses **NLP noun phrases** and co-occurrence relationships to build a lightweight graph, with indexing costs only 0.1% of that of traditional GraphRAG. During querying, LazyGraphRAG dynamically invokes large models for relevance evaluation and combines **best-first search** and **breadth-first search** strategies to achieve answer quality comparable to the full GraphRAG, but with significantly reduced query costs.

OG-RAG introduces domain **ontologies**, mapping documents into a **hypergraph structure** and using **greedy algorithms** to select the hyperedges covering the most relevant nodes, thereby generating compact contexts. For example, in the agriculture domain, defining entity relationships such as "crop-soil" can improve query precision in specific fields.

HyBGRAG combines **text retrieval (vector search)** and **graph retrieval (entity relationship extraction)**, and optimizes retrieval strategies through **router** and **reflection modules.** If the initial retrieval results are not accurate enough, the **large model reviewer** provides feedback and adjusts the selection of retrieval modules to improve the reliability of the results.

Through the deep integration of **structured knowledge graphs** and **large models**, GraphRAG is reshaping the paradigm of **information retrieval** and **generation.** The evolution of technology is continuously balancing **efficiency** and **quality**, and industry applications have already penetrated fields such as **healthcare** and **finance.** In the future, as **multimodal expansion** and **adaptive frameworks** mature, GraphRAG is expected to become the core engine of **AI cognitive capabilities**, driving the development of more intelligent and trustworthy generative applications.

Contextual retrieval: breaking through the contextual challenges of traditional RAG

The **contextual retrieval** method was proposed by **Anthropic** to address the **semantic isolation** issue caused by text chunking in traditional RAG systems. This approach enhances retrieval effectiveness by adding specific explanatory context to each text chunk before embedding, thereby improving retrieval accuracy and the quality of generated content.

In contextual retrieval, the retriever considers not only the semantics of your query but also incorporates contextual factors such as **conversation history**, **user preferences**, and **task objectives.** For example, when you require background information from previous rounds of Q&A in a continuous conversation, such as asking **What was the company's revenue growth in Q2 of 2025**, if the chunk of information only contains "revenue growth 3%" without the company name and time, it cannot accurately match your query needs.

Contextual retrieval automatically includes such information in the retrieval scope through the following methods, thus providing documents that better align with the current context:

- **Context embedding**: Before chunking, use a large model to generate a contextual description of 50–100 tokens for each text chunk. For example, expand "revenue growth 3%" to "This chunk is from the company's Q2 2025 financial report. Last quarter's revenue was $314 million, with a 3% growth this quarter."
- **Context BM25**: After merging the original text with the contextual description, build the **BM25** index to enhance the ability for precise terminology matching.

According to **Anthropic**'s experiments, combining **semantic vector search** with **BM25** through a **hybrid retrieval strategy** reduces the retrieval failure rate of the top 20 relevant chunks by 49%. If **re-ranking** is further added, the retrieval failure rate can be additionally reduced by 67%. At the same time, with **prompt caching** technology, contextual retrieval can load documents into the cache at once, thereby reducing redundant token consumption from repeated large model calls.

When conducting contextual retrieval, there may be challenges posed by **dynamic updates**, which can be optimally addressed using **incremental graph construction** or a **sliding window strategy**.

Modular RAG: transitioning from fixed processes to flexible architectures

As application demands continue to grow, the complexity of traditional **RAG systems** is also increasing, which limits their flexibility and scalability. For this reason, Lewis has meticulously deconstructed **RAG components** in this course and provided optimization directions for each component.

Dr. Yunfan Gao and others from Tongji University proposed the **Modular RAG** framework in their paper *Modular RAG: Transforming RAG Systems into Lego-like Reconfigurable Frameworks*, which splits complex **RAG systems** into independent **modules (components)** to form a highly reconfigurable architecture. Through this **modular design**, **RAG systems** can be flexibly assembled and adjusted like Lego blocks according to specific needs.

This design surpasses the traditional linear **"retrieve-generate" process** by introducing **routing**, **scheduling**, and **fusion mechanisms**. It supports more complex operational modes, such as **conditional branching** and **loop processing**. The paper presents several common **RAG patterns**, such as sequential, conditional branching, multi-branch, and loop types, and analyzes the implementation details of each.

A major challenge faced by **Modular RAG** is the high complexity of coordination among components. To address this, **agent collaboration mechanisms** are usually introduced. For example, the division of labor among multiple intelligent agents, or the adoption of adaptive decision models to optimize interactions among components. The **self-correction loop** in **Corrective RAG** can automatically adjust the retrieval and generation processes based on feedback, thus improving the accuracy and efficiency of the system.

Agentic RAG or agent-driven RAG systems

The transition from **RAG** to **Agentic RAG** is an important trend, marking a shift from passive response to **active participation** in information retrieval and decision-making processes. **Agentic RAG** is not only able to passively respond to user queries, but also acts as an "intelligent agent" that can proactively formulate retrieval plans, select information sources, question results, and iteratively optimize to improve output quality. As a result, the **RAG system** has evolved from a simple tool into an "intelligent information interaction body" with strategic thinking and decision-making capabilities, able to proactively provide users with high-quality information and solutions.

Agentic RAG introduces autonomous **agents** to achieve **dynamic decision-making** and **task planning**. Its core patterns mainly include the following four types:

- **Reflection mode**: The agent optimizes retrieval strategies by iteratively evaluating its own decisions and output quality. For example, in medical diagnosis, the agent adjusts the retrieval scope based on patient feedback to improve diagnostic accuracy.
- **Planning mode**: Complex queries are decomposed into a series of subtasks for multi-step reasoning. For example, a financial analysis agent can plan a workflow of **"data retrieval → trend analysis → risk assessment"** to generate investment recommendations.
- **Tool utilization mode**: Integrating external tools (such as APIs, databases, etc.) to extend its own capabilities. For example, a legal agent can call **contract databases** and **compliance rule repositories** to generate legal opinions.
- **Multi-agent collaboration mode**: Multiple specialized agents collaborate and divide responsibilities to complete complex tasks together. For example, in a customer service system, **FAQ retrieval agents**, **ticket processing agents**, and **sentiment analysis agents** can work in tandem to improve response efficiency and service quality.

CRAG, **Self-RAG**, and **RRR**, introduced earlier, are all important improvements to traditional RAG systems and can also be seen as a step toward agentic RAG. The following designs reflect the characteristics of agentic RAG:

- Scoring the relevance of retrieved documents
- Re-optimizing queries when necessary
- Supplementing information using a web search

When the documents initially retrieved are not sufficiently relevant or comprehensive, **agentic RAG** can dynamically adjust retrieval strategies, such as switching between single-step or multi-step retrieval according to the complexity of the query, thus significantly enhancing the system's ability to answer complex questions.

Multimodal RAG

When information is not limited to text but also includes images, audio, video, and other types of modal data, **multimodal retrieval-augmented generation** (**MMRAG** or **Multimodal RAG**) is needed to handle it. These systems can extract feature vectors from images for retrieval, such as selecting appropriate segments from videos or extracting keyword information from audio, and fuse these results with text-based retrieval to provide more comprehensive knowledge support.

Multimodal RAG expands the semantic understanding boundary of traditional **RAG systems** by integrating text, image, audio, and other multimodal data. Its technical architecture is as follows:

- **Multimodal encoder**: Uses models such as *CLIP* (Contrastive Language-Image Pretraining) to align cross-modal semantics, for example, associating the text "red sports car" with the corresponding image.
- **Dynamic retrieval strategy**: Selects the priority modality to process based on the type of query. For instance, in visual question answering scenarios, images are retrieved first, supplemented by text descriptions.
- **Cross-modal fusion**: Uses attention mechanisms to integrate information from different sources, for example, considering both imaging and textual content in medical report analysis.

Representative frameworks include Alibaba's *OmniSearch* and *HyBGRAG*. These frameworks support hybrid retrieval of text, tables, and images, helping to reduce hallucinations by large models and enhancing complex reasoning abilities through the combination of image retrieval and multimodal data.

Typical application scenarios of **multimodal RAG** are as follows:

- **Medical image analysis**: Combines CT images and medical record texts to generate diagnostic suggestions, such as tumor localization and staging analysis
- **Industrial quality inspection**: Integrates product images with defect databases to detect abnormalities on production lines in real time
- **Education**: Enables retrieval of multimodal teaching materials, such as physics experiment videos combined with explanatory texts to promote interactive learning
- **Retail recommendation**: Analyzes user reviews (text), product images (visual), and purchase records (structured data) to generate personalized recommendations

In the future, **multimodal RAG** has huge development potential. Developers can use lightweight multimodal models to reduce the computing power required for environmental perception, thus enabling efficient operation on consumer-grade hardware. In addition, by introducing dynamic routing mechanisms, optimal modality combinations can be automatically selected according to task requirements, such as prioritizing speech input and outputting in text.

A highly promising direction is the deep integration of **agentic RAG** and **multimodal RAG**. For example, in the field of autonomous driving, **multimodal agents** can be used to integrate road condition images, sensor data, and traffic rule databases in real time, achieving dynamic path planning. Similarly, developing dedicated vertical **MMRAG system frameworks** for specific industries such as healthcare, manufacturing, and others also shows great potential.

Summary

Beyond the new advances listed in this chapter, new paradigms and methods continue to emerge in the **RAG** field. Below is a brief list of some of these, which may provide some inspiration to you:

- **Turing-Complete RAG (TC-RAG)**: Aims to make the retrieval process programmable, even approaching Turing completeness. By embedding operators and programming logic into the retrieval process, RAG systems can dynamically compose query and data processing steps, thus completing complex reasoning tasks.
- **Iterative retrieval** (such as `ITER`, `CRAG`, `Self-RAG`, `RRR`, etc.): The retrieval module is called multiple times in a single query, each time using the previous retrieval results and generator feedback to refine the query strategy. This gradually improves retrieval quality, so the final documents found are closer to user expectations.

- **Adaptive retrieval** (methods such as FLARE): Dynamically adjusts retrieval strategies based on system state, user feedback, and context changes. Through online learning and dynamic optimization, RAG systems can continuously improve over time, constantly enhancing retrieval accuracy and usability.
- **Information retrieval Chain-of-Thought** (**IRCoT**): Introduces the chain-of-thought concept into the retrieval stage. Not only returns the result documents, but it can also present the retrieval path and intermediate reasoning process, helping users and higher-level generation modules better understand the ins and outs of retrieval strategies, reducing blind spots and misleading results.
- **PlanRAG**: Incorporates explicit planning logic in the retrieval stage, formulating retrieval strategy "plans," such as first querying knowledge in a specific domain and then expanding to related upstream and downstream knowledge points. This makes the retrieval results more organized and allows the generator to use resources more efficiently.
- **T-RAG**: Introduces task decomposition and role division in the retrieval process, splitting complex tasks into sub-tasks, each handled by different specialized retrievers. The results are then aggregated, providing multidimensional information input for the generator.
- **AutoRAG**: Attempts to automate and optimize the RAG process by automatically selecting the best retrieval strategies and parameters, as well as continuously tuning the retrieval and generation modules at different stages, achieving closed-loop optimization and reducing manual intervention.
- **Retrieval-augmented fine-tuning** (**RAFT**): Introduces retrieved information into the fine-tuning process of large models. During model training, knowledge provided by the retriever is used for reinforcement learning or supervised fine-tuning, so that the model naturally possesses a "knowledge embedding" feature during inference, improving the accuracy and practicality of answers.

Anna: These complex retrieval strategies and paradigms make **RAG** systems not simply about extracting information from an ocean of content, but endow them with layered thinking, flexible adaptation, and multimodal fusion capabilities. The future **RAG** will be more like an all-purpose information broker, able to automatically screen, analyze, and integrate valuable information for users.

Lewis: Exactly. The introduction of these complex strategies upgrades **RAG** from the traditional single retrieval mode to a multidimensional, multi-strategy framework for knowledge acquisition and utilization. Together with **AI Agent**, **MCP**, and other large-model application development technologies, it paves the way for achieving higher-level intelligent interaction.

Subscribe for a free eBook

11

Unlock Your Exclusive Benefits

Your copy of this book includes the following exclusive benefits:

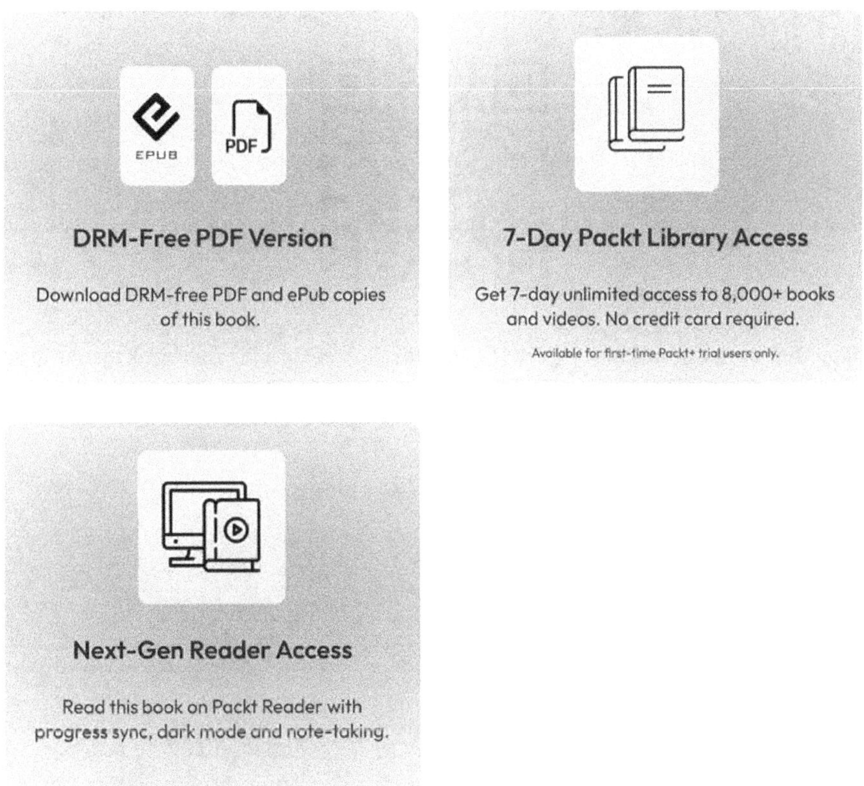

Follow the guide below to unlock them. The process takes only a few minutes and needs to be completed once.

Unlock this Book's Free Benefits in 3 Easy Steps

Step 1

Keep your purchase invoice ready for *Step 3*. If you have a physical copy, scan it using your phone and save it as a PDF, JPG, or PNG.

For more help on finding your invoice, visit `https://www.packtpub.com/en-us/unlock?step=1`.

Note: If you bought this book directly from Packt, no invoice is required. After *Step 2*, you can access your exclusive content right away.

Step 2

Scan the QR code or go to `packtpub.com/unlock`.

On the page that opens (similar to *Figure 11.1* on desktop), search for this book by name and select the correct edition.

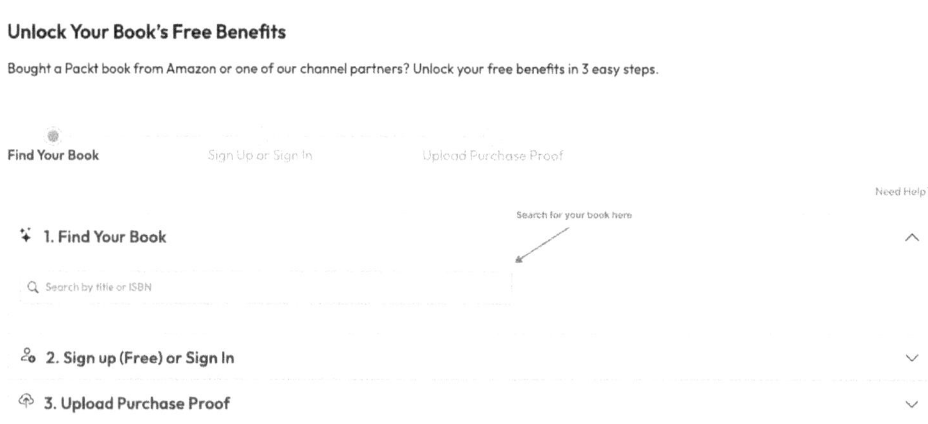

Figure 11.1: Packt unlock landing page on desktop

Step 3

After selecting your book, sign in to your Packt account or create one for free. Then upload your invoice (PDF, PNG, or JPG, up to 10 MB). Follow the on-screen instructions to finish the process.

Need Help

If you get stuck and need help, visit `https://www.packtpub.com/unlock-benefits/help` for a detailed FAQ on how to find your invoices and more. This QR code will take you to the help page.

Note: If you are still facing issues, reach out to `customercare@packt.com`.

packtpub.com

Subscribe to our online digital library for full access to over 7,000 books and videos, as well as industry leading tools to help you plan your personal development and advance your career. For more information, please visit our website.

Why subscribe?

- Spend less time learning and more time coding with practical eBooks and Videos from over 4,000 industry professionals
- Improve your learning with Skill Plans built especially for you
- Get a free eBook or video every month
- Fully searchable for easy access to vital information
- Copy and paste, print, and bookmark content

At `www.packtpub.com`, you can also read a collection of free technical articles, sign up for a range of free newsletters, and receive exclusive discounts and offers on Packt books and eBooks.

Other Books You May Enjoy

If you enjoyed this book, you may be interested in these other books by Packt:

RAG-Driven Generative AI - Second Edition

Denis Rothman

ISBN: 978-1-80742-494-7

- Bring intelligence directly to the data within Oracle Database 23ai
- Defeat hallucinations and data poisoning with DualRAG, synchronizing vector semantics with structured SQL
- Build MAS-RAG pipelines with Planner, Agent Registry, and MCP-standardized sovereign agents
- Engineer an inference-time router using hybrid adaptive RAG to switch between reasoning, retrieval, and human feedback
- Fuse vector similarity, Oracle Spatial, and SQL Property Graph traversal into a converged hyper-query
- Multimodal video RAG with version-controlled schema registry and semantic vector search over visual assets

Building AI Agents with LLMs, RAG, and Knowledge Graphs

Salvatore Raieli, Gabriele Iuculano

ISBN: 978-1-83508-038-2

- Learn how LLMs work, their structure, uses, and limits, and design RAG pipelines to link them to external data
- Build and query knowledge graphs for structured context and factual grounding
- Develop AI agents that plan, reason, and use tools to complete tasks
- Integrate LLMs with external APIs and databases to incorporate live data
- Apply techniques to minimize hallucinations and ensure accurate outputs
- Orchestrate multiple agents to solve complex, multi-step problems
- Optimize prompts, memory, and context handling for long-running tasks
- Deploy and monitor AI agents in production environments

Packt is searching for authors like you

If you're interested in becoming an author for Packt, please visit `authors.packt.com` and apply today. We have worked with thousands of developers and tech professionals, just like you, to help them share their insight with the global tech community. You can make a general application, apply for a specific hot topic that we are recruiting an author for, or submit your own idea.

Share your thoughts

Now you've finished *RAG from First Principles*, we'd love to hear your thoughts! Scan the QR code below to go straight to the Amazon review page for this book and share your feedback or leave a review on the site that you purchased it from.

https://packt.link/r/1835888674

Your review is important to us and the tech community and will help us make sure we're delivering excellent quality content.

Index

D

J

K

L

N

O

P

Q

R

S

www.ingramcontent.com/pod-product-compliance
Lightning Source LLC
LaVergne TN
LVHW060016210926
848481LV00013B/3722
9781835888667